7

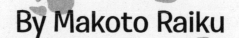

By Makoto Raiku

Translated and adapted by Stephen Paul

Lettered by Kiyoko Shiromasa

KC
KODANSHA
COMICS

I think we're at the turning point of a new era. I can feel many things around me making huge changes as I draw my manga.

Makoto Raiku

7

ANIMAL LAND

Makoto Raik

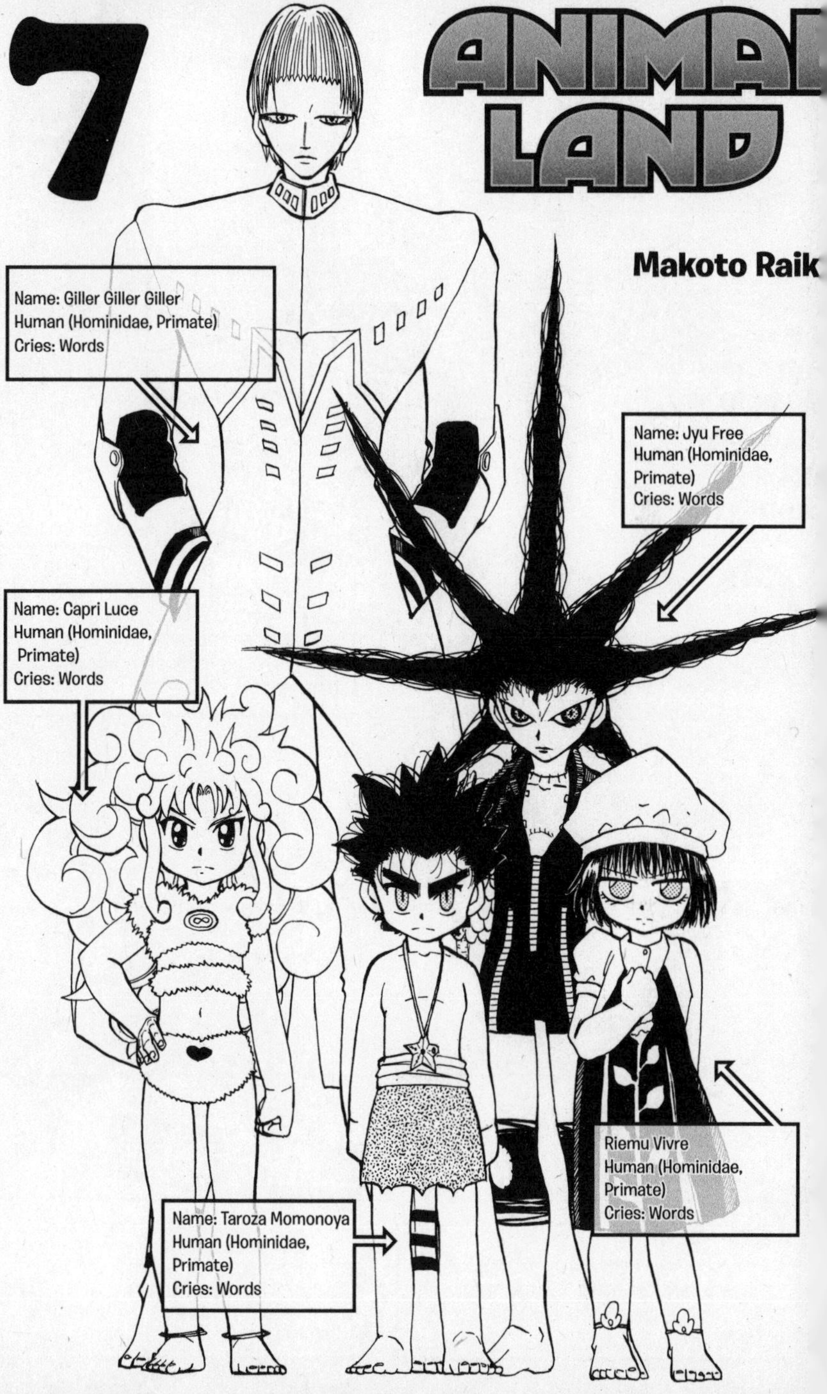
Name: Giller Giller Giller
Human (Hominidae, Primate)
Cries: Words
Name: Jyu Free
Human (Hominidae, Primate)
Cries: Words
Name: Capri Luce
Human (Hominidae, Primate)
Cries: Words
Riemu Vivre
Human (Hominidae, Primate)
Cries: Words
Name: Taroza Momonoya
Human (Hominidae, Primate)
Cries: Words

ANIMAL LAND
Character Profiles

Taroza

A human boy whose cries (speech) enable him to communicate with all different species of animal. Raised from a baby by Monoko. He lives in a village with a variety of herbivores, and hopes to someday bring carnivores into the group.

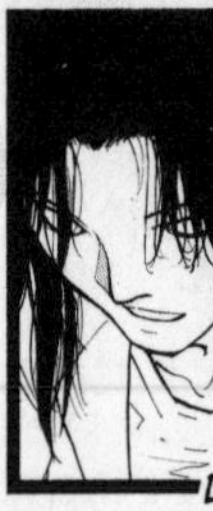
Did his birth mother abandon her own baby?

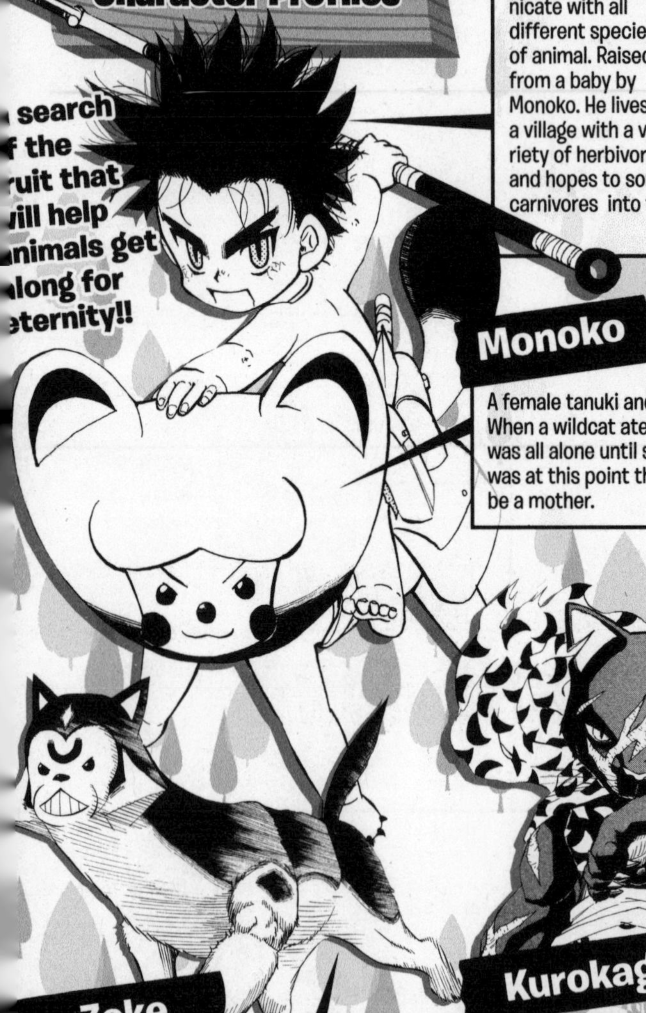
search f the ruit that vill help nimals get long for eternity!!

Monoko

A female tanuki and Taroza's mother. When a wildcat ate her parents, she was all alone until she met Taroza. It was at this point that she decided to be a mother.

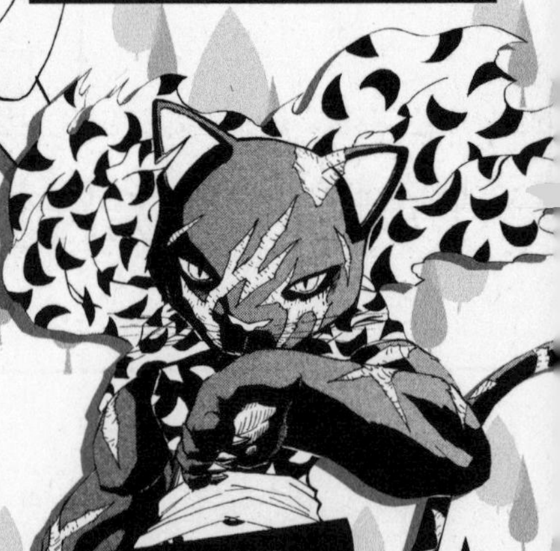

Zeke

A wolf pup whose family was attacked and killed by a bear. He now lives in the tanuki village and considers Taroza and Monoko part of his family.

Kurokagi

A large wildcat with misgivings about the "survival of the fittest" laws of the world. When Taroza's words save his life, he makes it his duty to protect the boy. Even now, he is a valuable warrior protecting Taroza's village.

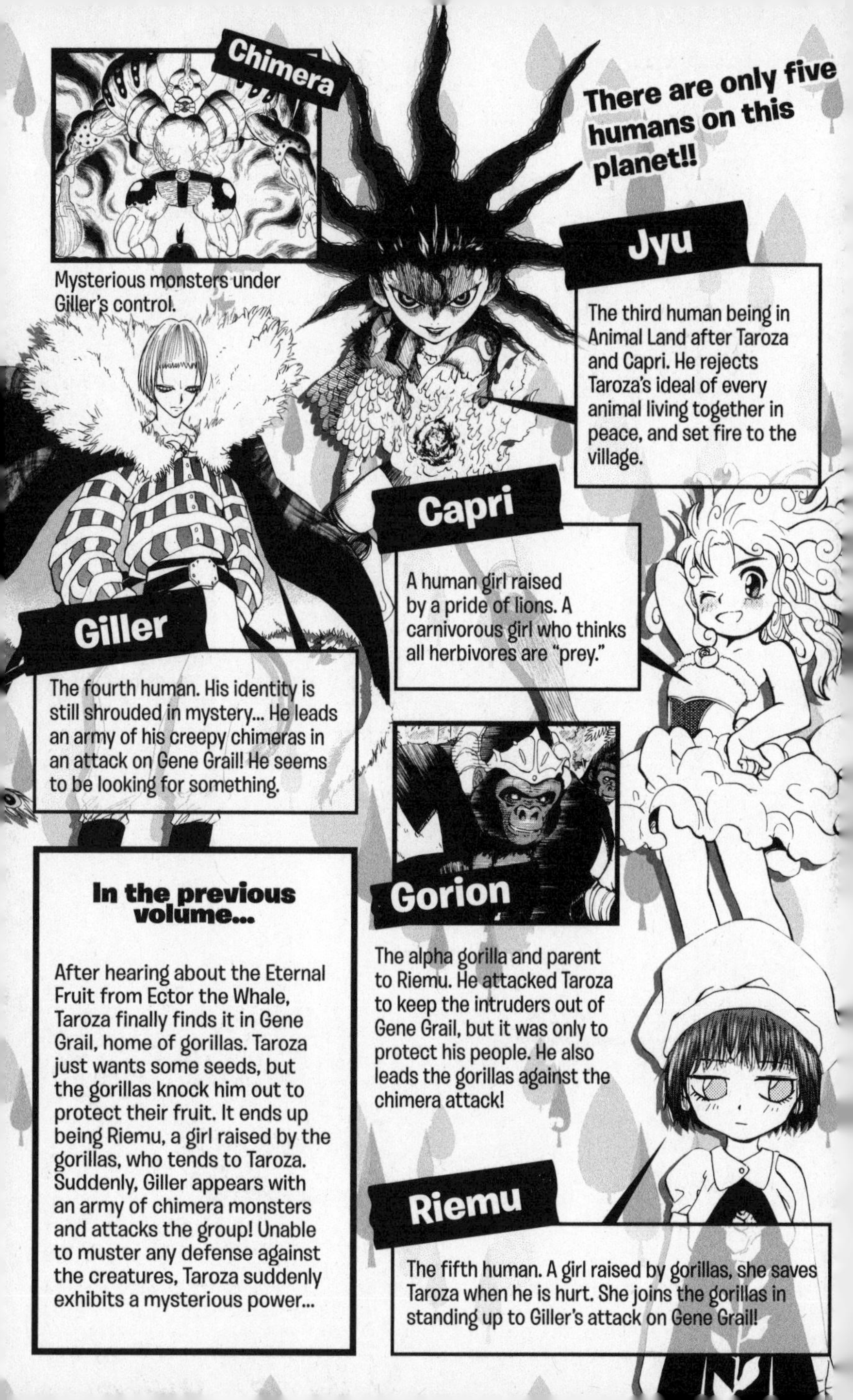
Chimera
Mysterious monsters under Giller's control.
There are only five humans on this planet!!
Jyu
The third human being in Animal Land after Taroza and Capri. He rejects Taroza's ideal of every animal living together in peace, and set fire to the village.
Capri
A human girl raised by a pride of lions. A carnivorous girl who thinks all herbivores are "prey."
Giller
The fourth human. His identity is still shrouded in mystery... He leads an army of his creepy chimeras in an attack on Gene Grail! He seems to be looking for something.
Gorion
The alpha gorilla and parent to Riemu. He attacked Taroza to keep the intruders out of Gene Grail, but it was only to protect his people. He also leads the gorillas against the chimera attack!
Riemu
The fifth human. A girl raised by gorillas, she saves Taroza when he is hurt. She joins the gorillas in standing up to Giller's attack on Gene Grail!

In the previous volume...

After hearing about the Eternal Fruit from Ector the Whale, Taroza finally finds it in Gene Grail, home of gorillas. Taroza just wants some seeds, but the gorillas knock him out to protect their fruit. It ends up being Riemu, a girl raised by the gorillas, who tends to Taroza. Suddenly, Giller appears with an army of chimera monsters and attacks the group! Unable to muster any defense against the creatures, Taroza suddenly exhibits a mysterious power...

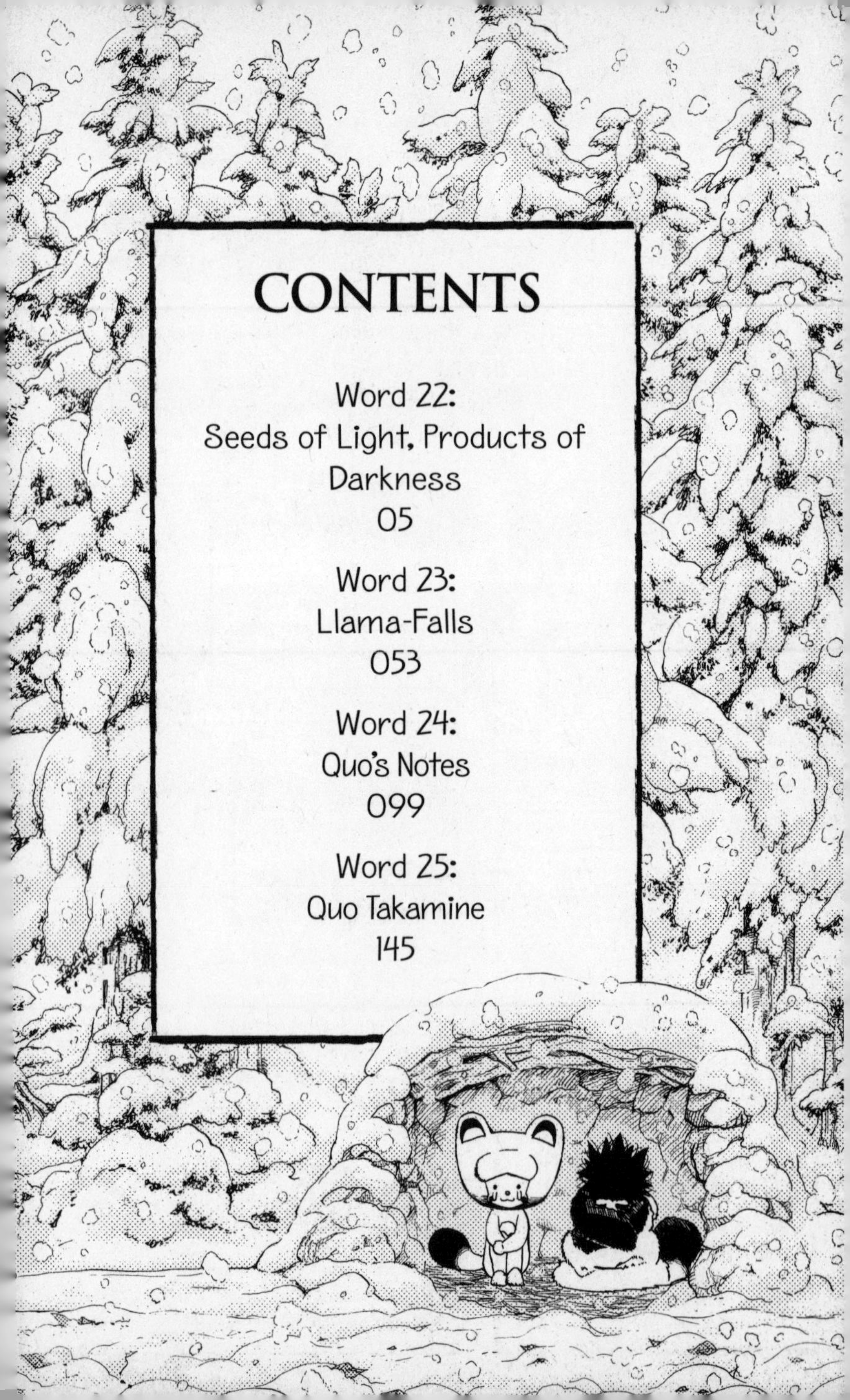

CONTENTS

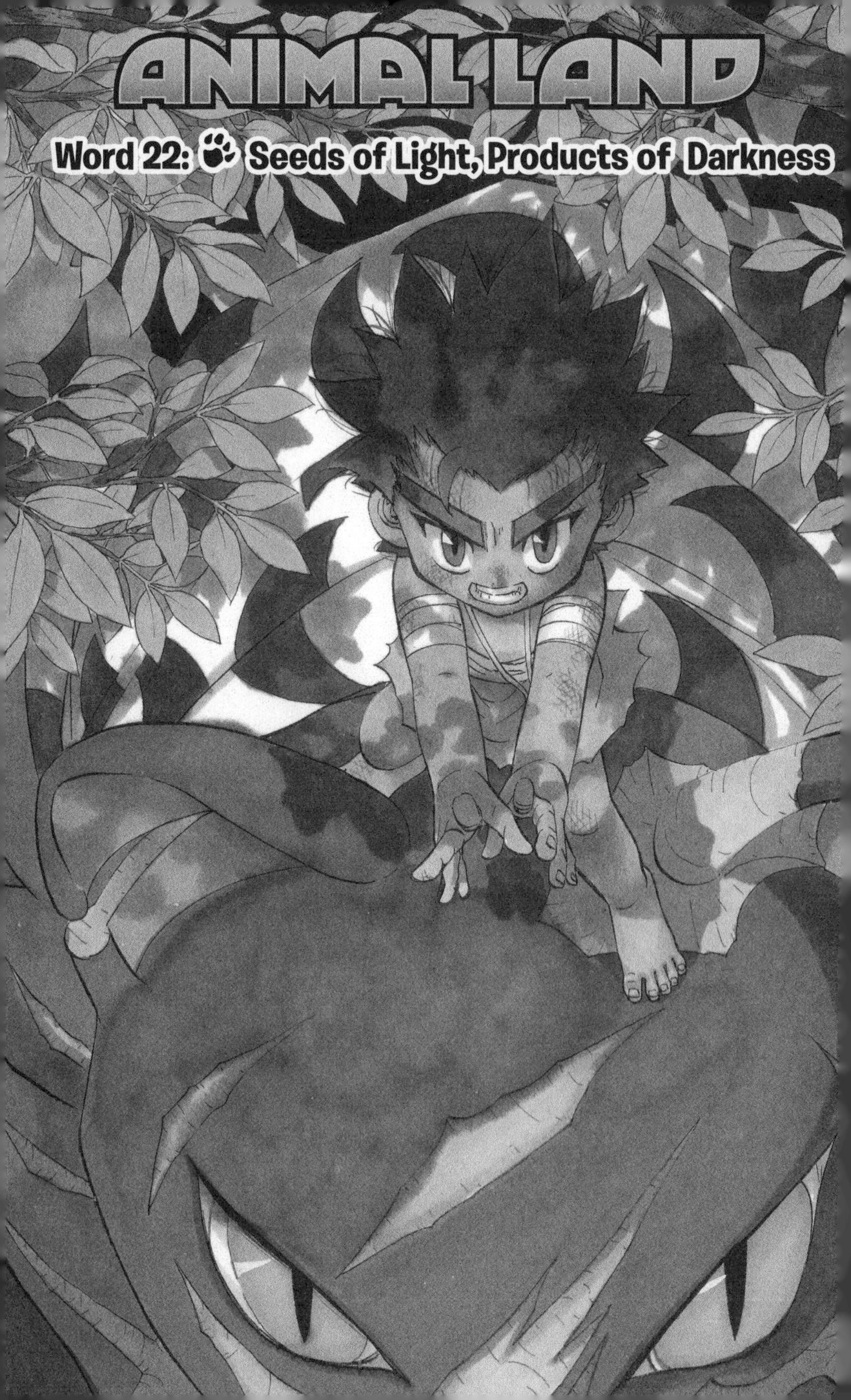
ANIMAL LAND
Word 22: Seeds of Light, Products of Darkness

ANIMAL LAND

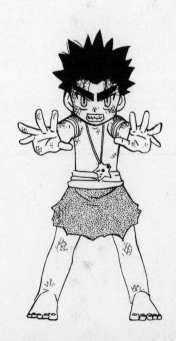

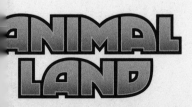

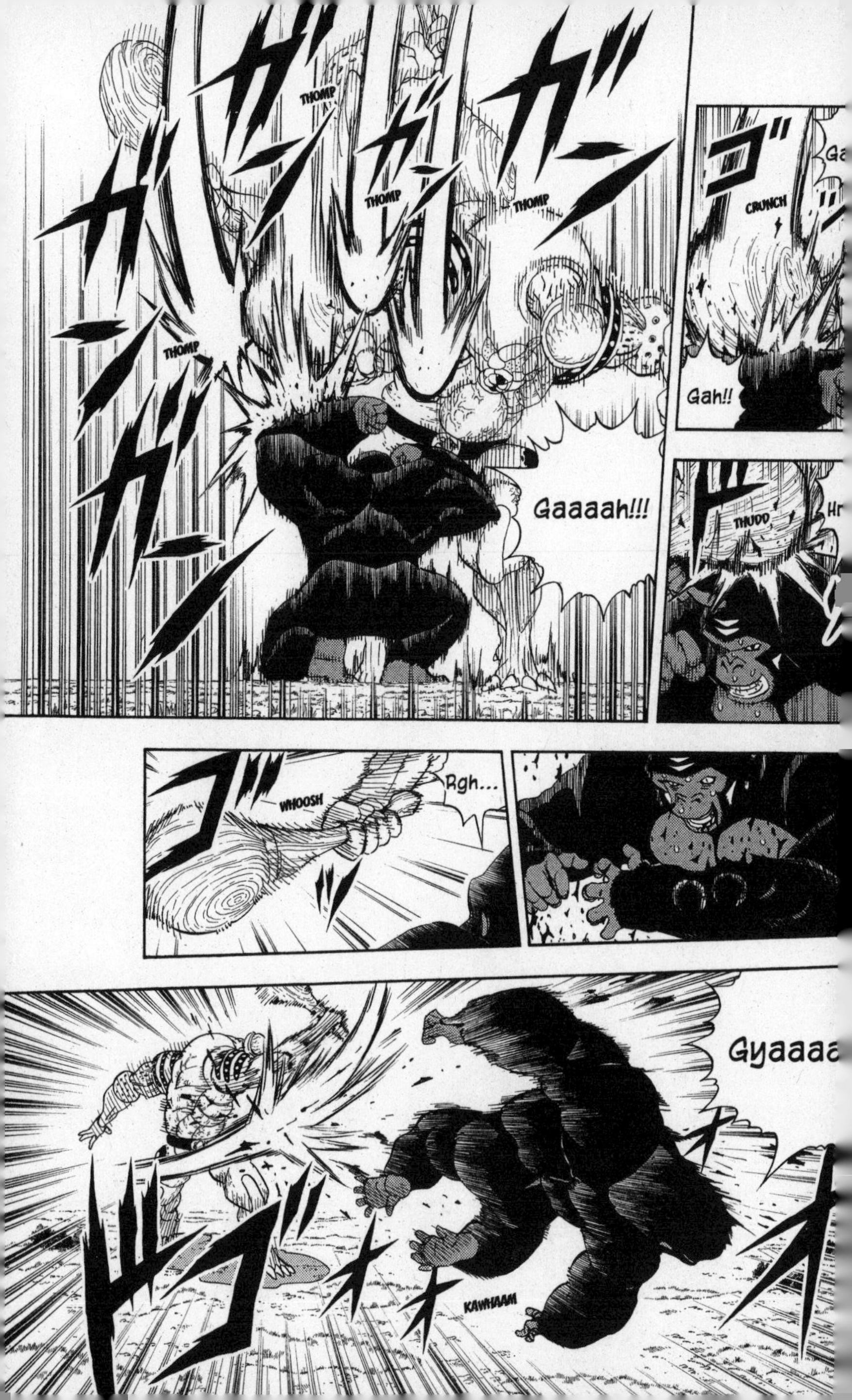
CRUNCH
Gah!!
THUDD
THOMP
THOMP
THOMP
THOMP
Gaaaah!!!
WHOOSH
Rgh...
Gyaaaa
KAWHAAM

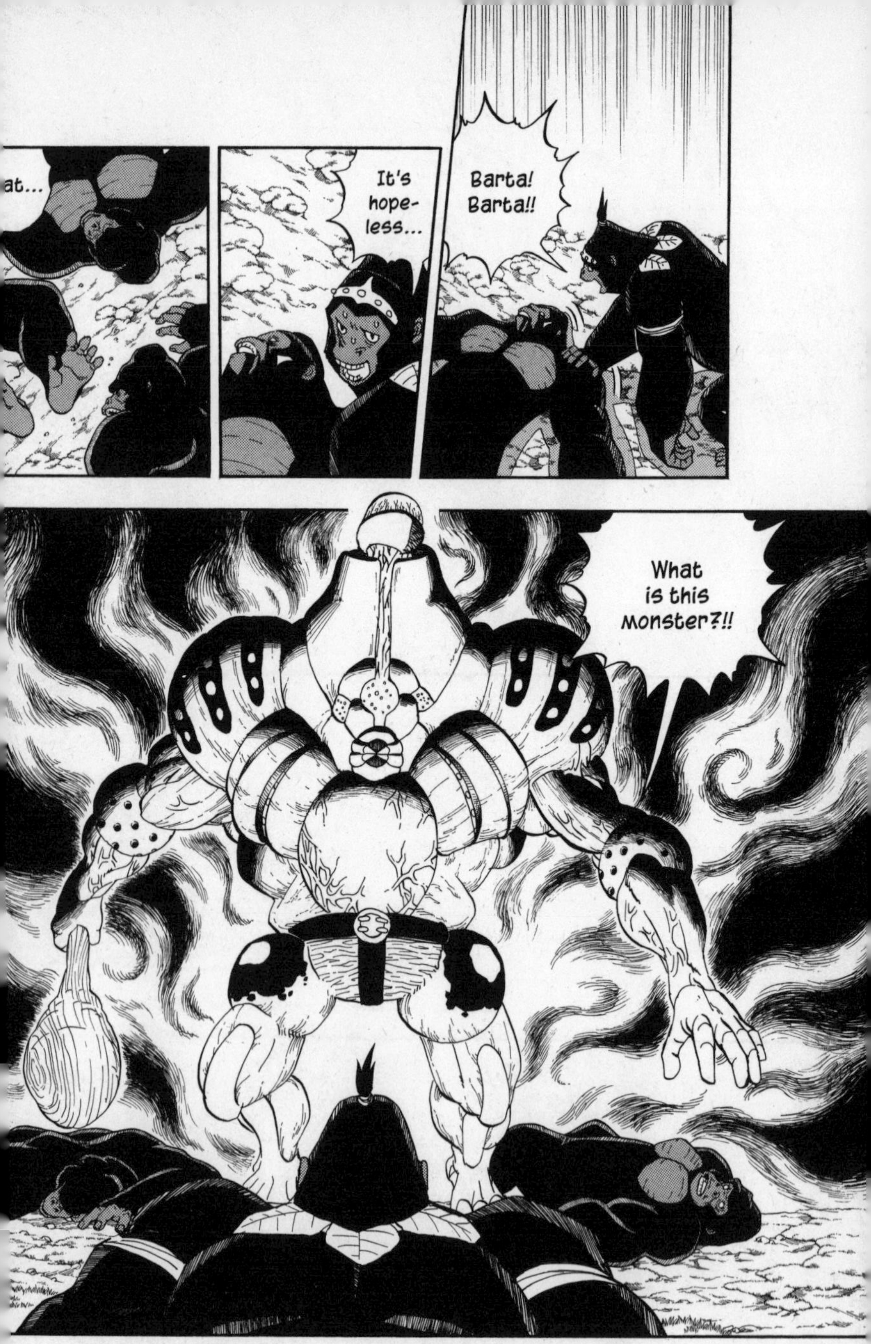
Barta! Barta!!
It's hope-less...
at...
What is this monster?!!

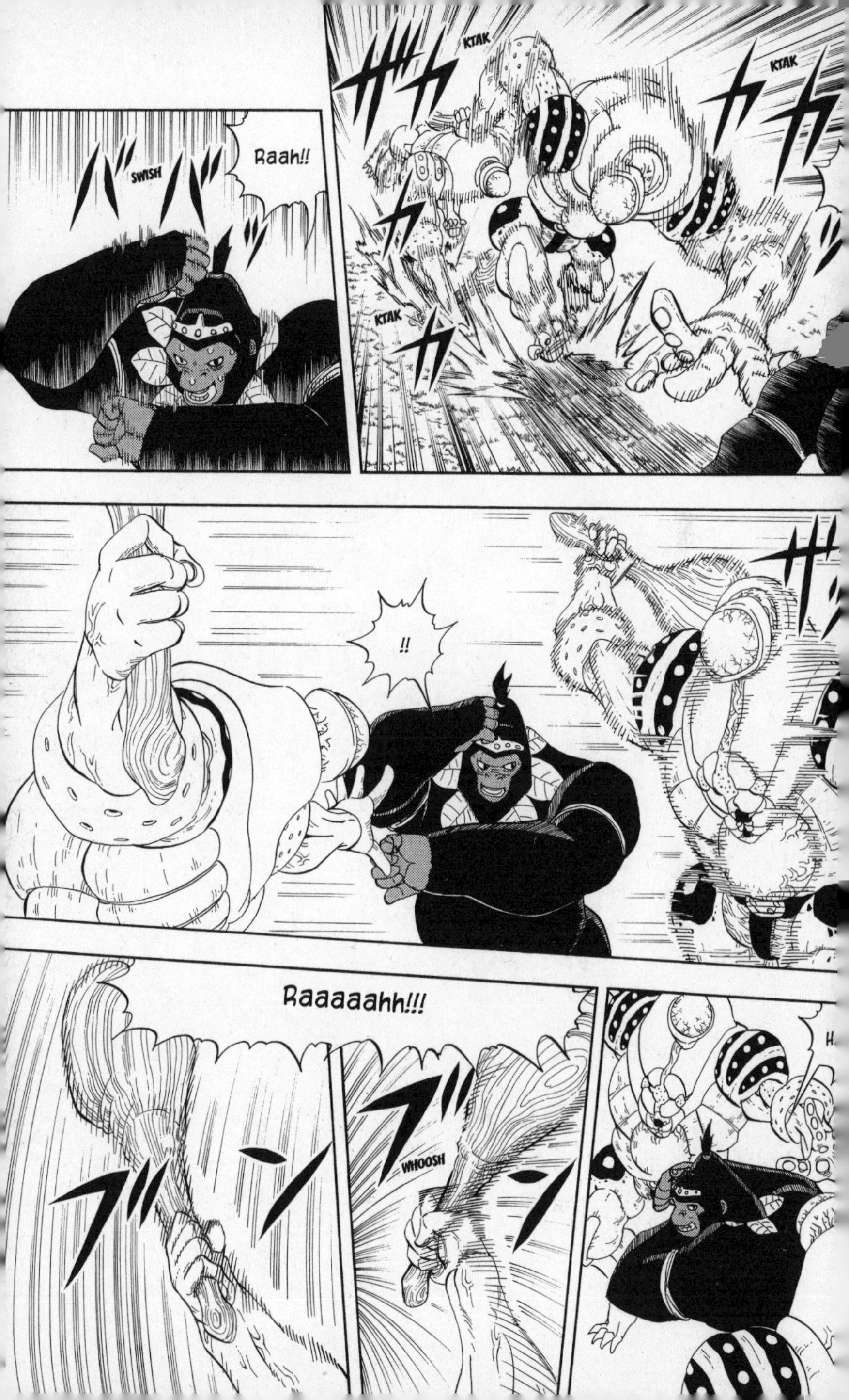
KTAK
KTAK
KTAK
SWISH
Raah!!
!!
WHOOSH
Raaaaaahh!!!

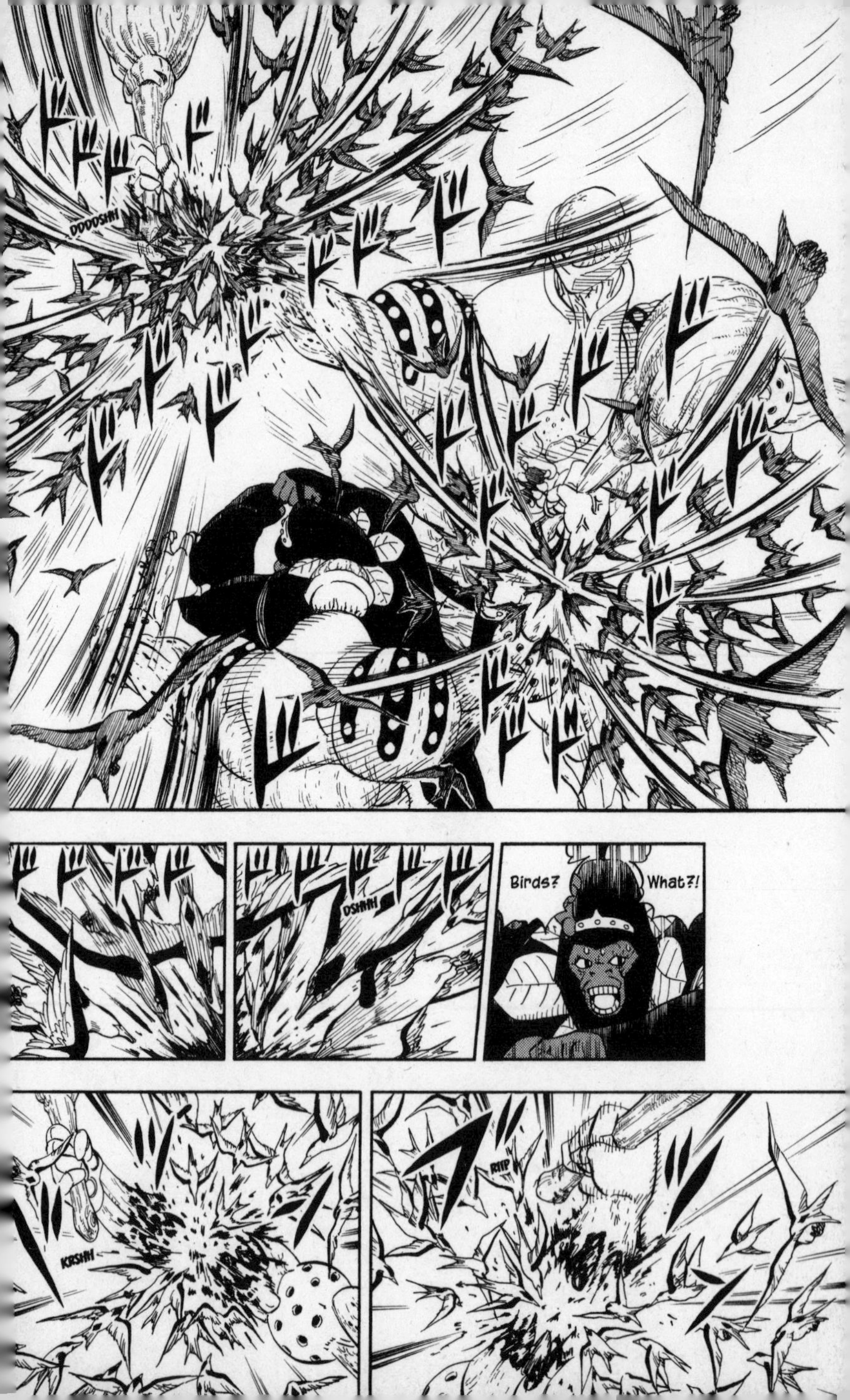
DOOOSHH
What?!
Birds?
DSHHH
RIIP
KRSHH

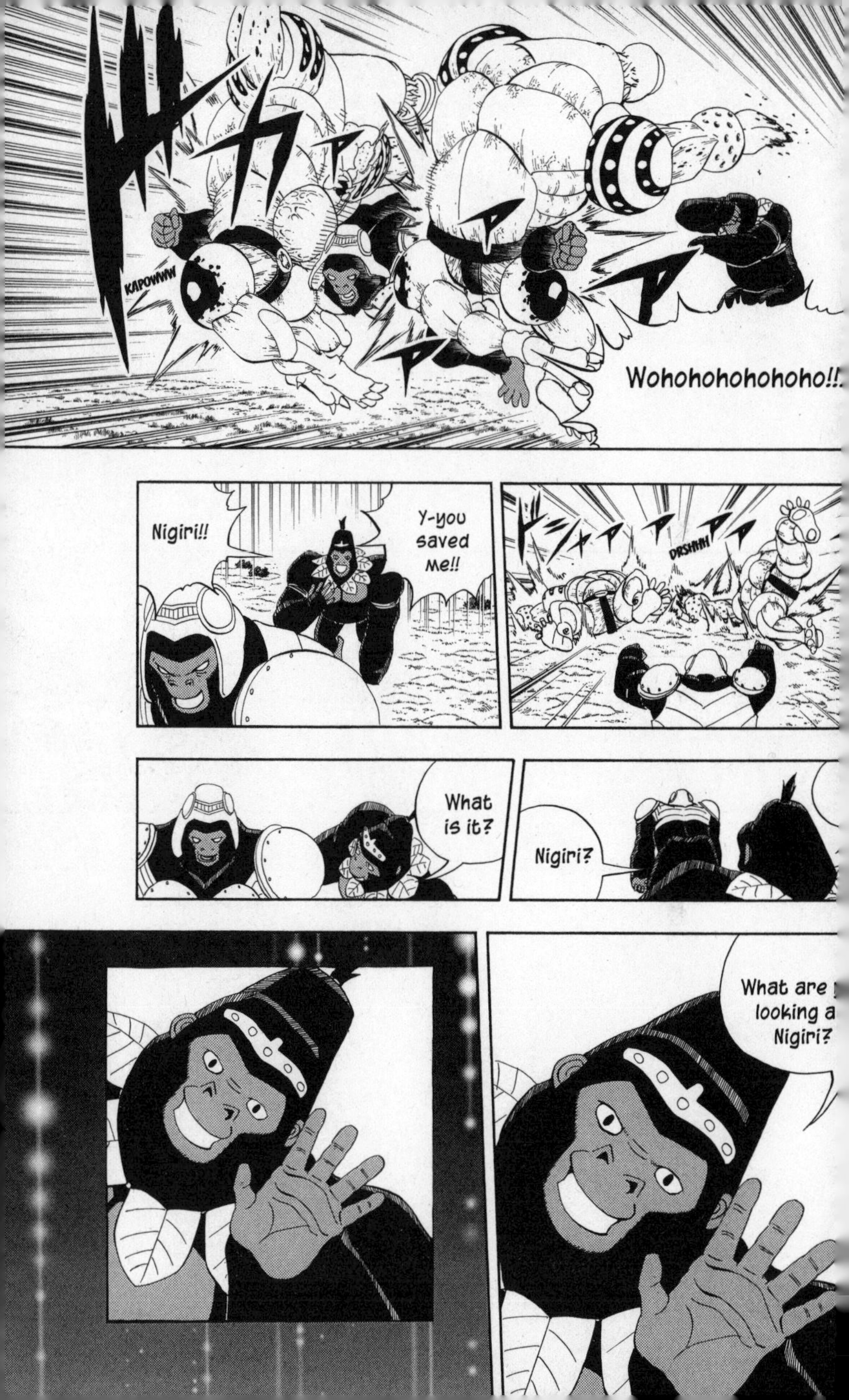
Wohohohohohoho!!
KAPOWWW
DRSHHH
Y-you saved me!!
Nigiri!!
Nigiri?
What is it?
What are
looking a
Nigiri?

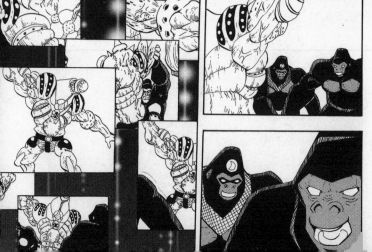

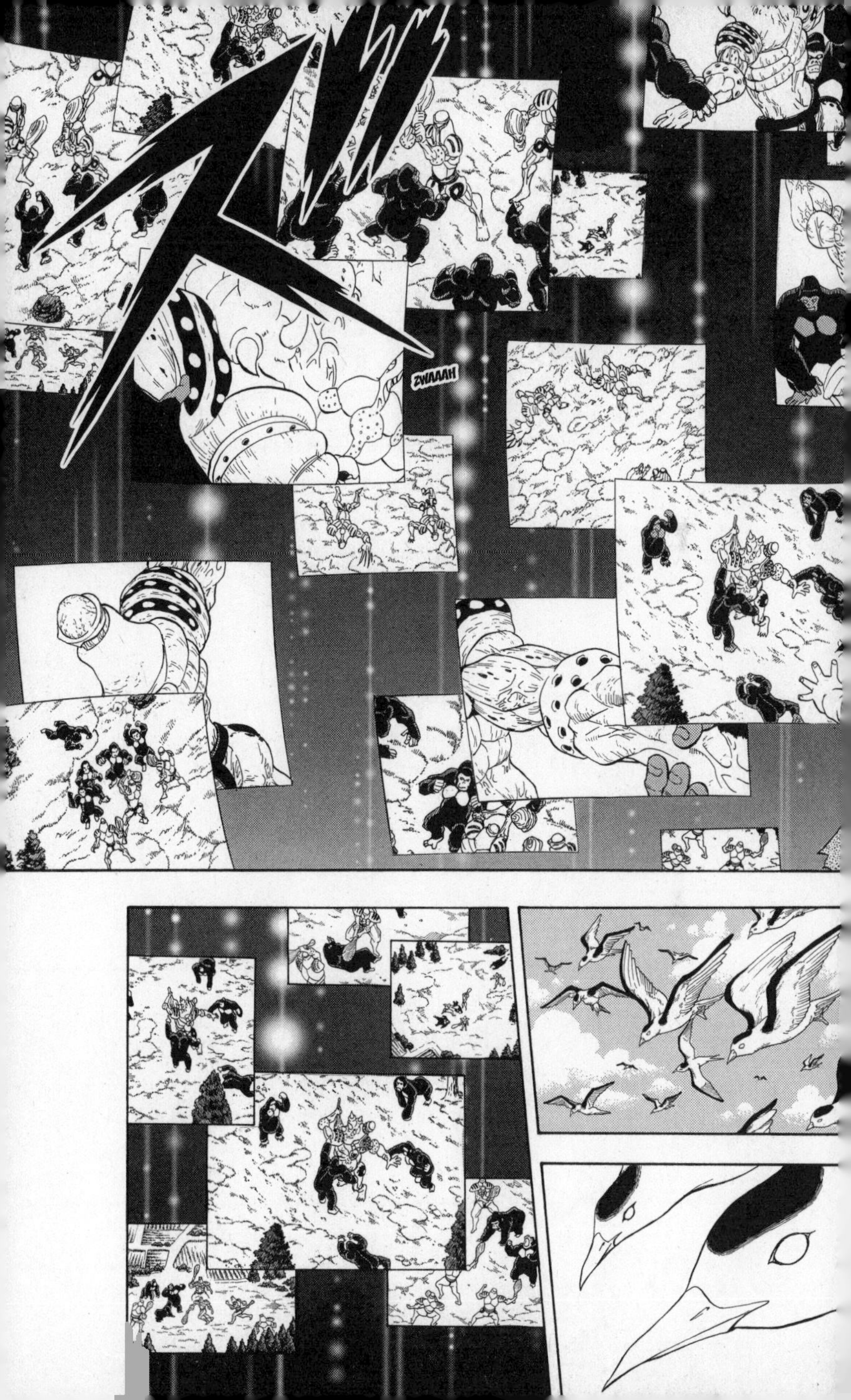
ZWAAAH

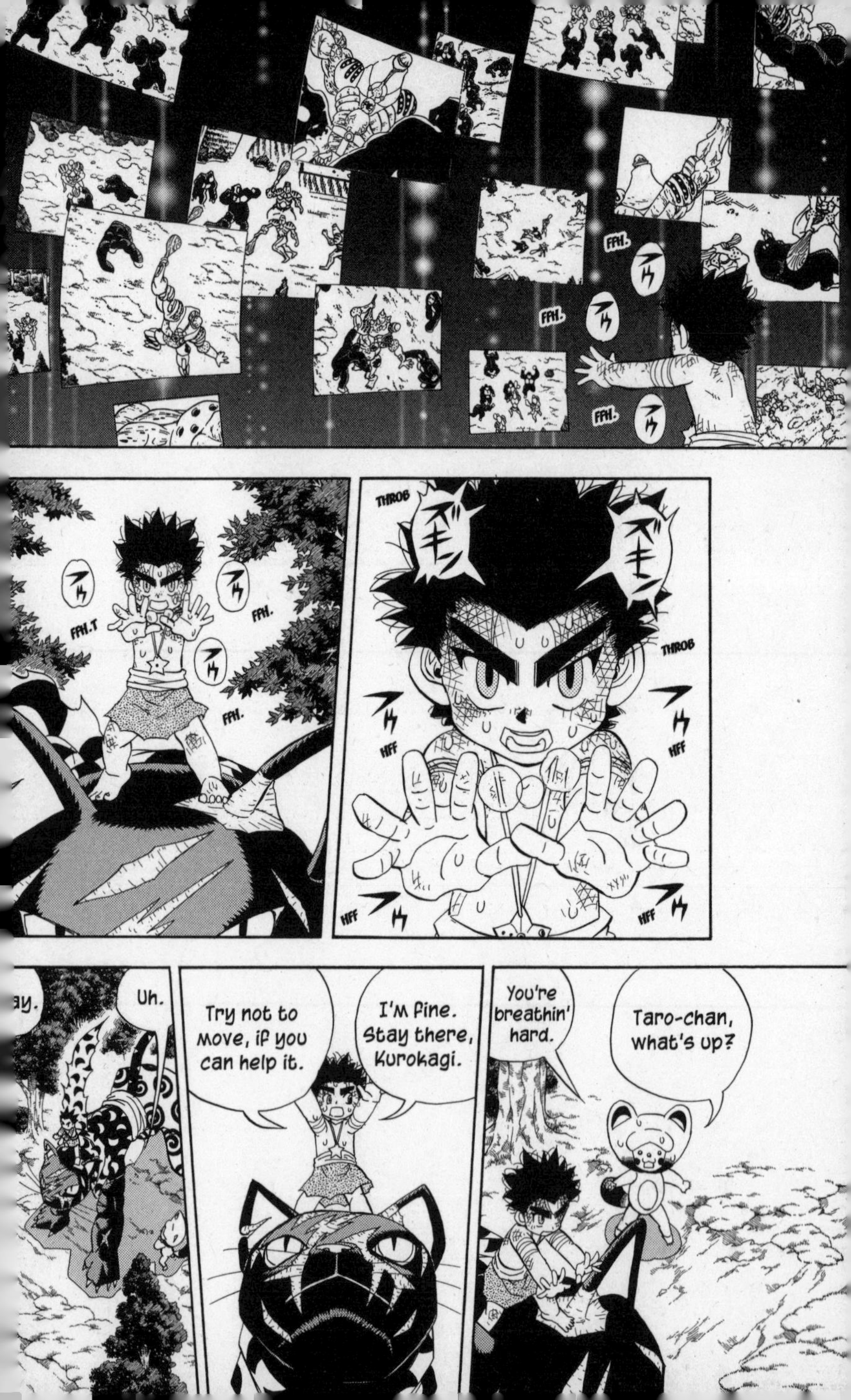
FFH.
FFH.
FFH.
THROB
THROB
HFF
HFF
HFF
HFF
FFH.
FFH.T
FFH.
Taro-chan, what's up?
You're breathin' hard.
I'm fine. Stay there, Kurokagi.
Try not to move, if you can help it.
Uh.
ay.

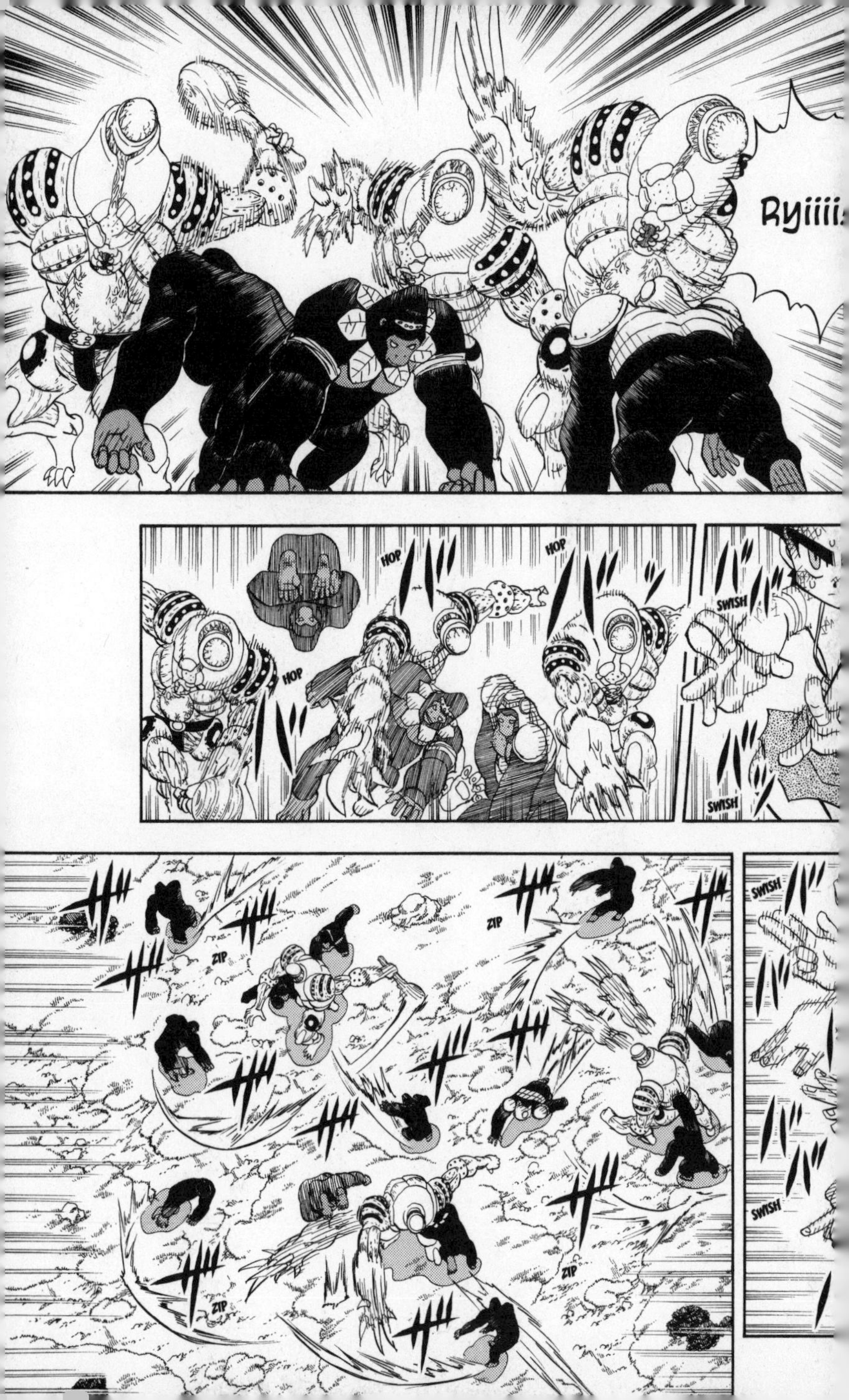
Ryiiii
SWISH
SWISH
HOP
HOP
HOP
SWISH
SWISH
ZIP
ZIP
ZIP
ZIP

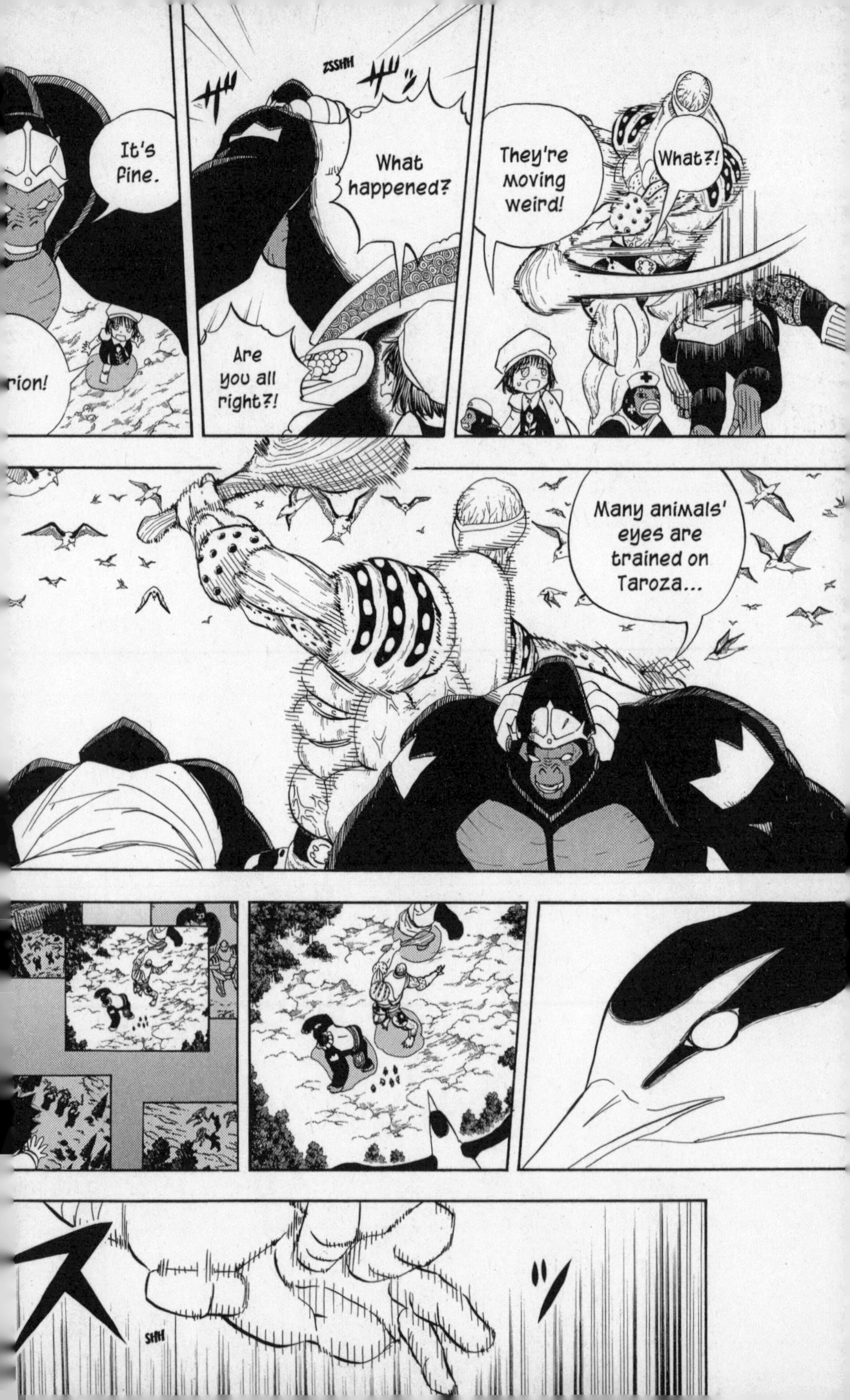
What?!
They're moving weird!
ZSSHH
What happened?
Are you all right?!
It's fine.
rion!
Many animals' eyes are trained on Taroza...
SHH

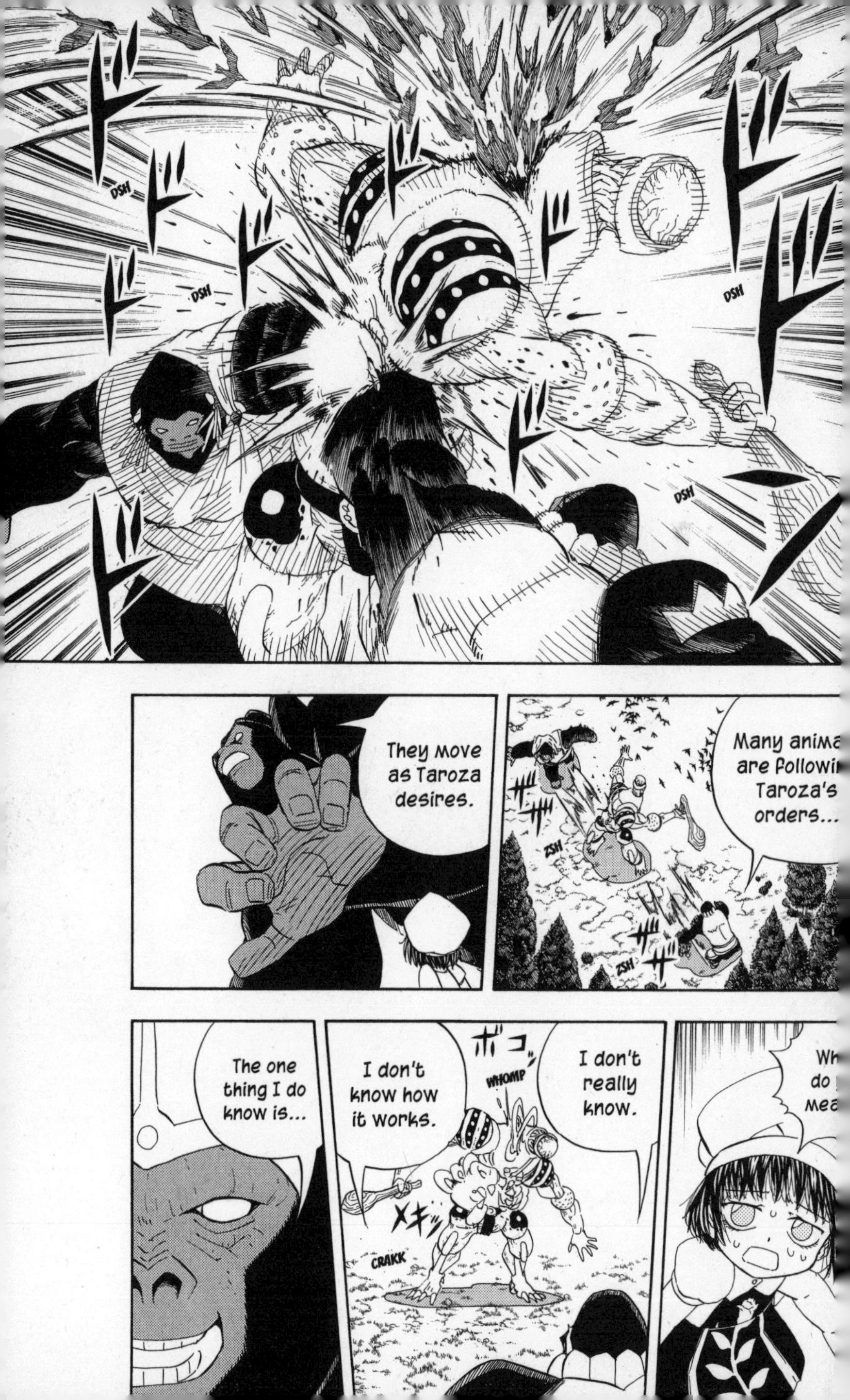
ドド
ドド
ドド
DSH
DSH
DSH
DSH
Many anima are followi Taroza's orders...
ZSH
ZSH
They move as Taroza desires.
Wh do mea
I don't really know.
ボコッ
WHOMP
I don't know how it works.
メキッ
CRAKK
The one thing I do know is...

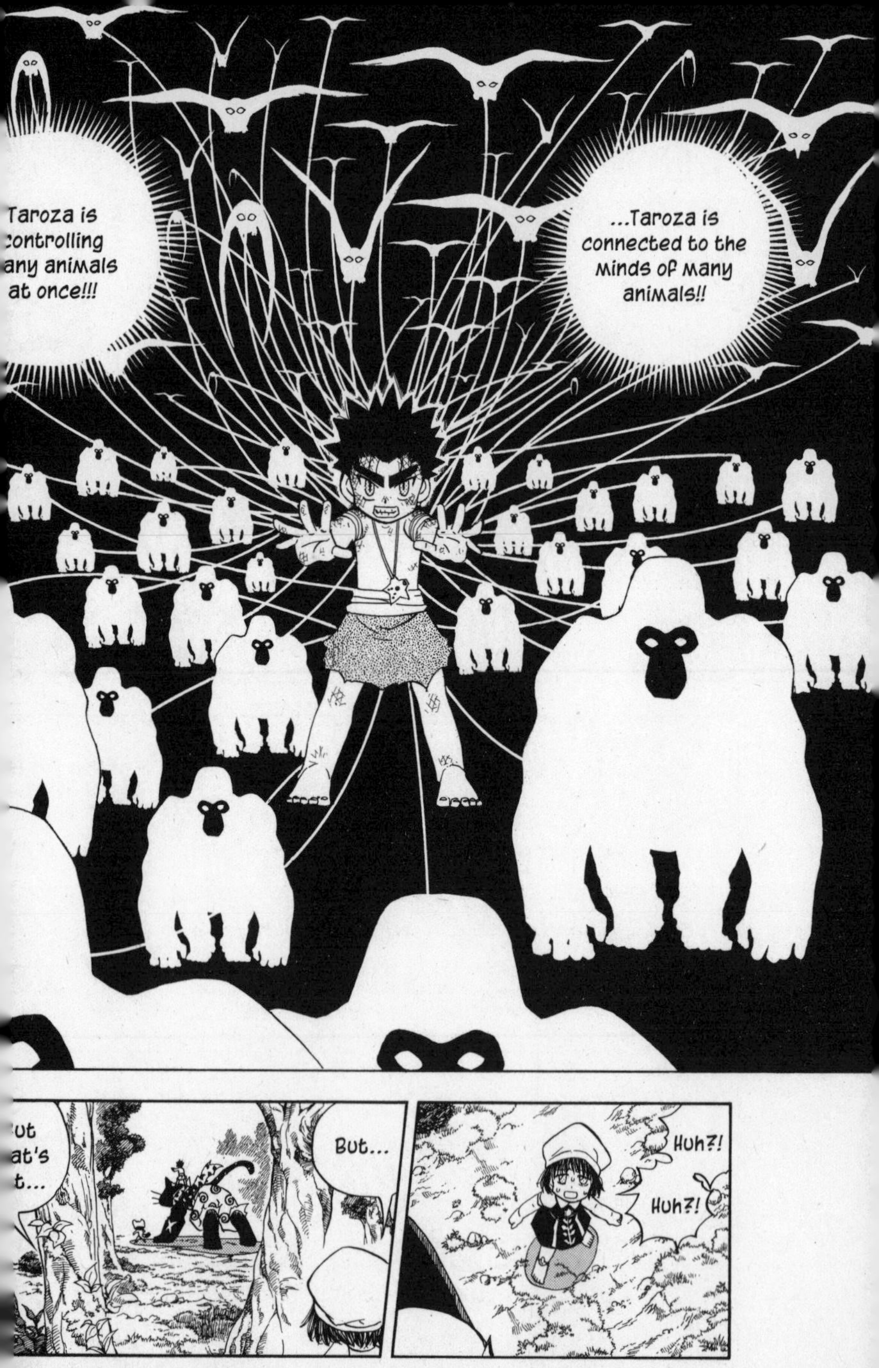
...Taroza is connected to the minds of many animals!!
Taroza is controlling any animals at once!!!
Huh?!
Huh?!
But...

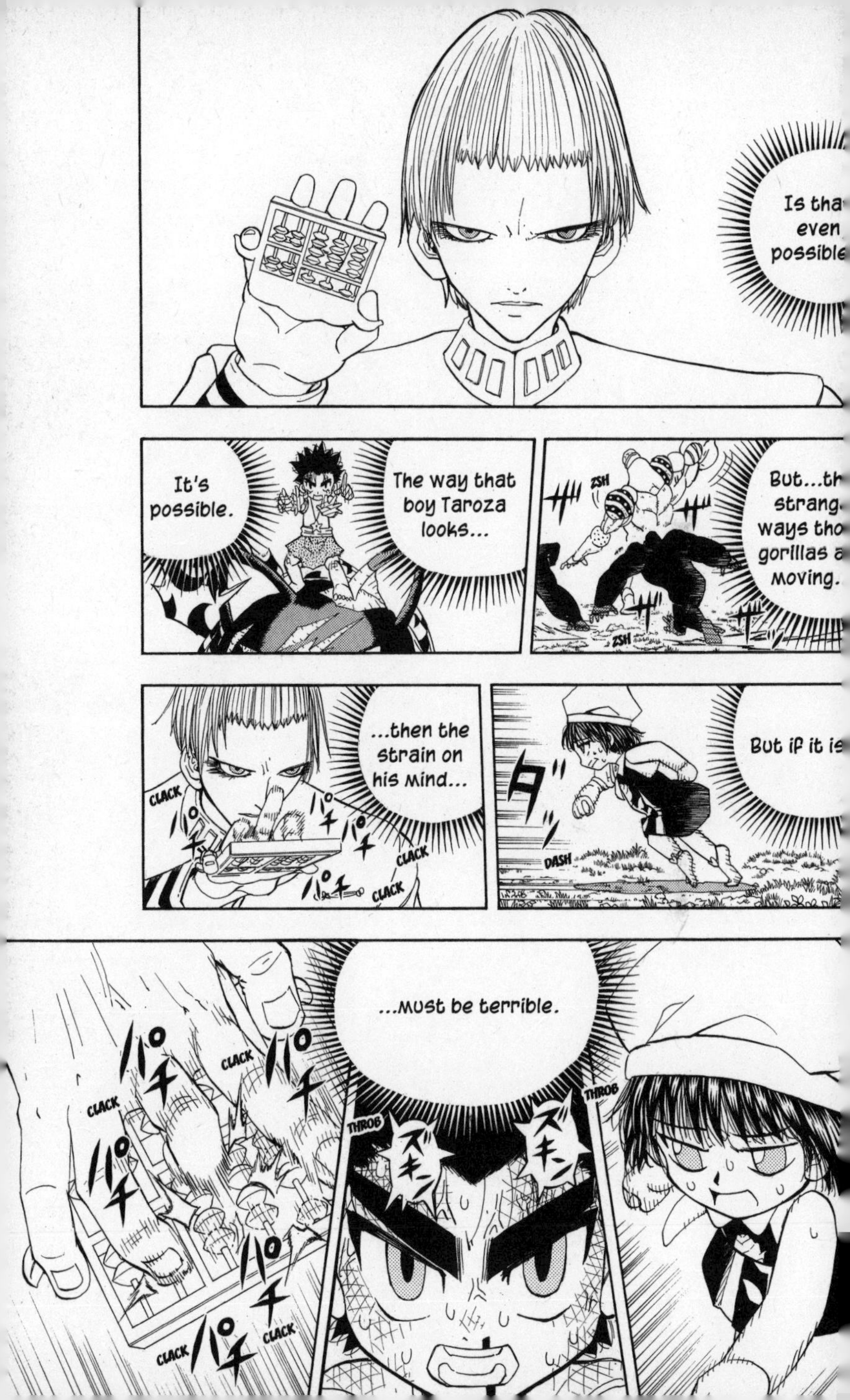

Is tha
even
possible
But...th
strang
ways tho
gorillas a
moving.
ZSH
ZSH
The way that boy Taroza looks...
It's possible.
But if it is
DASH
...then the strain on his mind...
CLACK
CLACK
CLACK
...must be terrible.
THROB
THROB
CLACK
CLACK
CLACK
CLACK

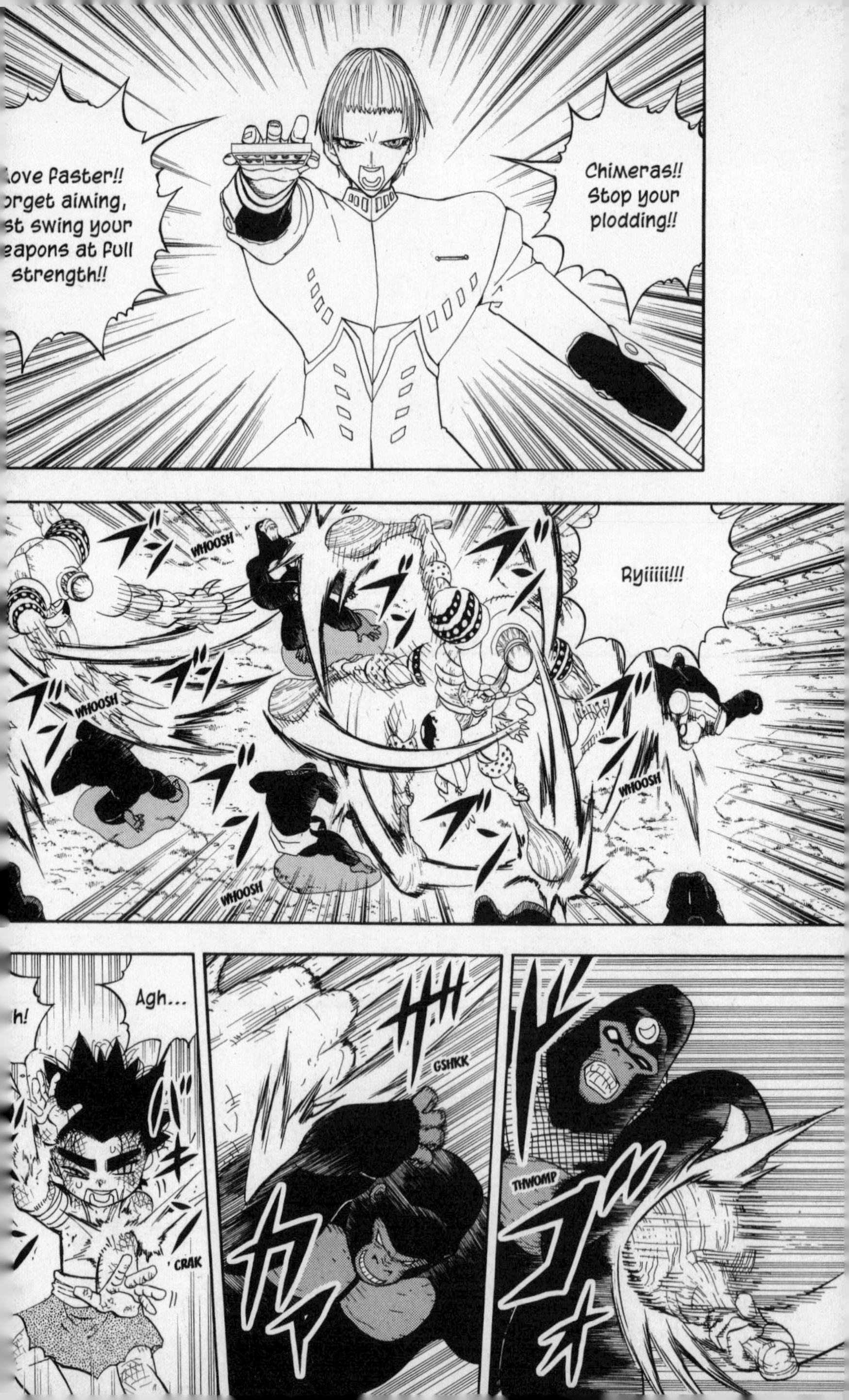
Chimeras!! Stop your plodding!!
ove faster!! orget aiming, st swing your eapons at full strength!!
Ryiiiii!!!
WHOOSH
WHOOSH
WHOOSH
WHOOSH
THWOMP
GSHKK
Agh...
h!
CRAK

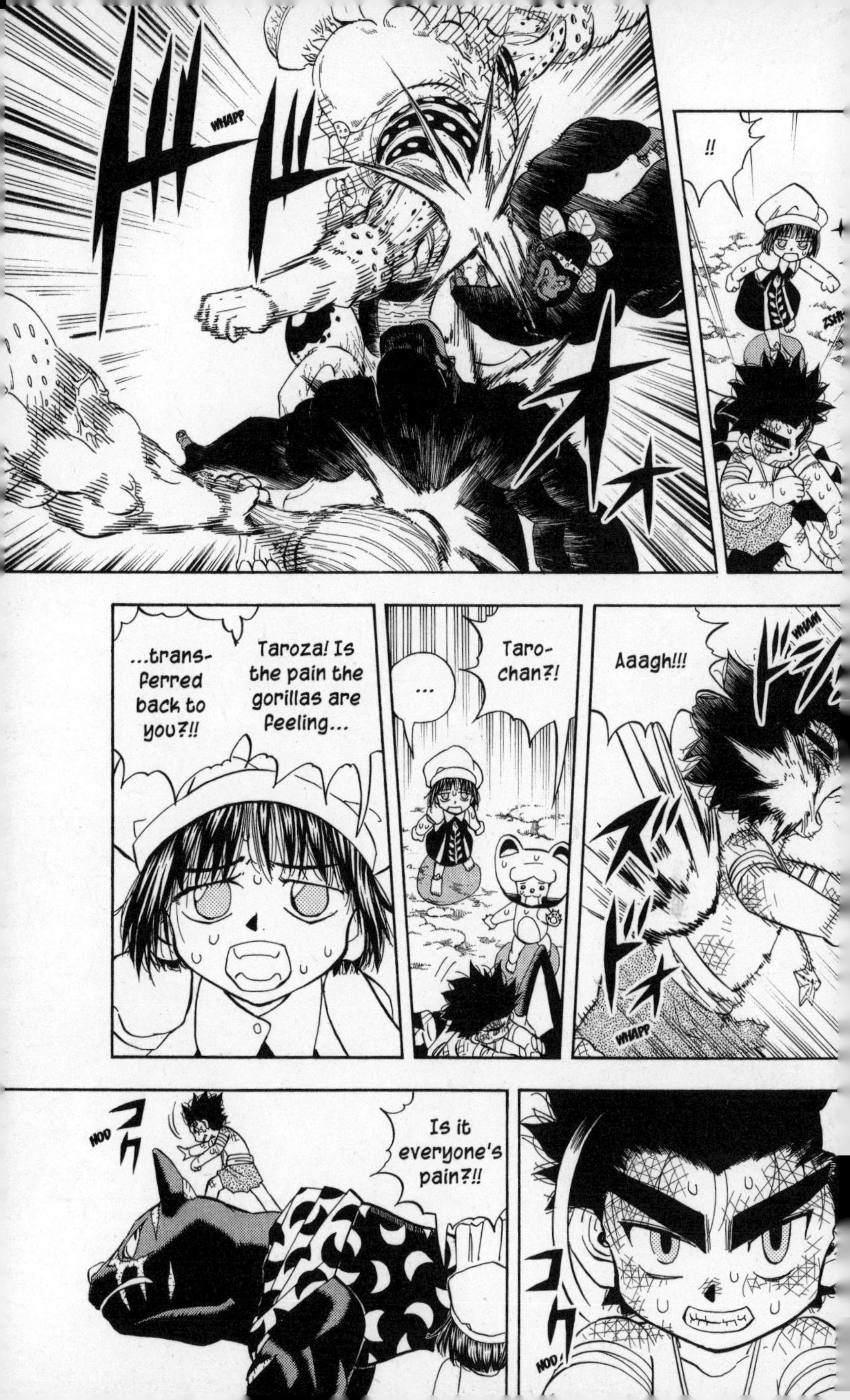
!!
ZSHH
WHAPP
WHAM
Aaagh!!!
WHAPP
Taro-chan?!
...
Taroza! Is the pain the gorillas are feeling...
...trans-ferred back to you?!!
NOD
Is it everyone's pain?!!
NOD

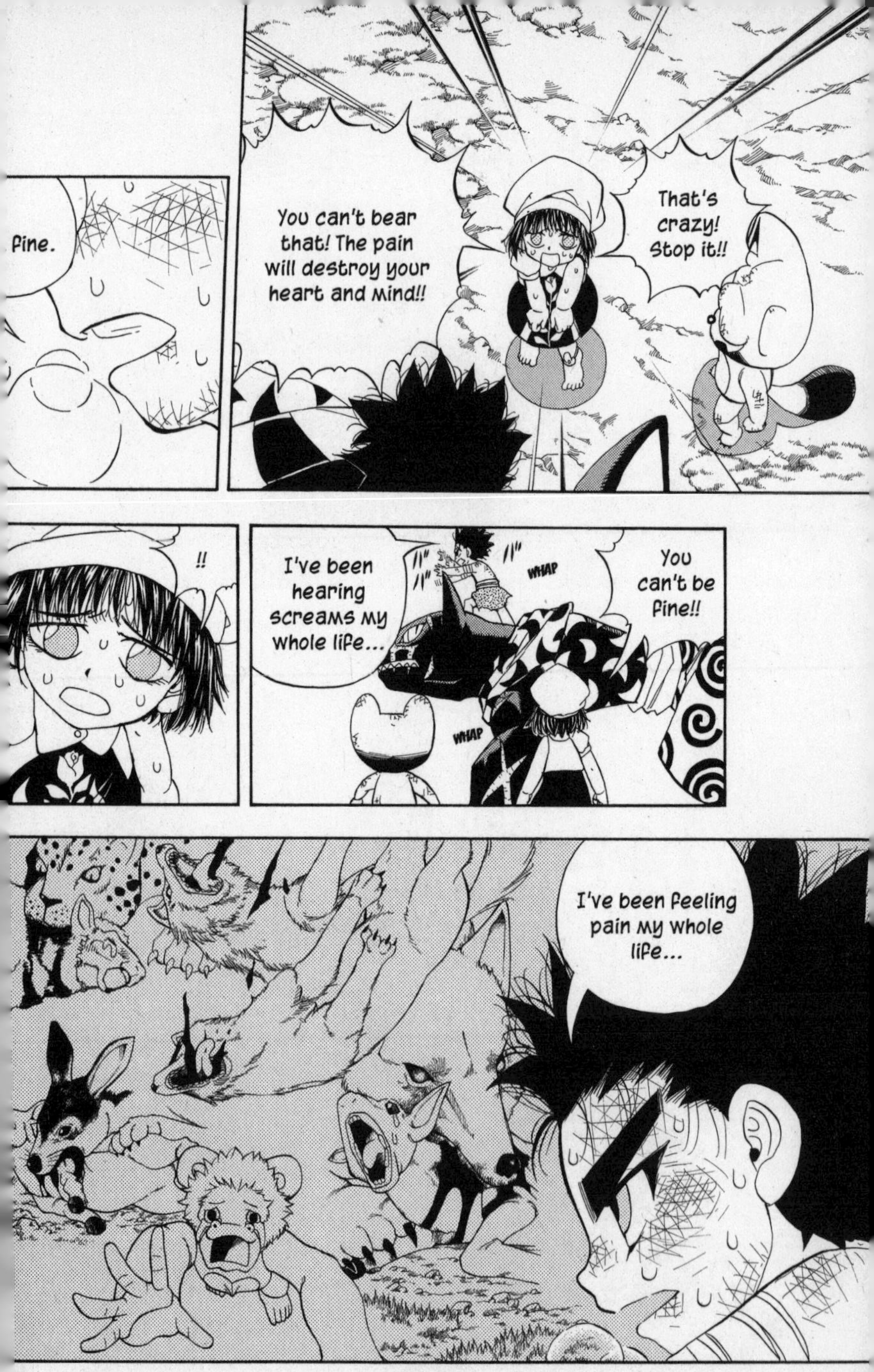
That's crazy! Stop it!!
You can't bear that! The pain will destroy your heart and mind!!
fine.
You can't be fine!!
WHAP
I've been hearing screams my whole life...
WHAP
!!
I've been feeling pain my whole life...

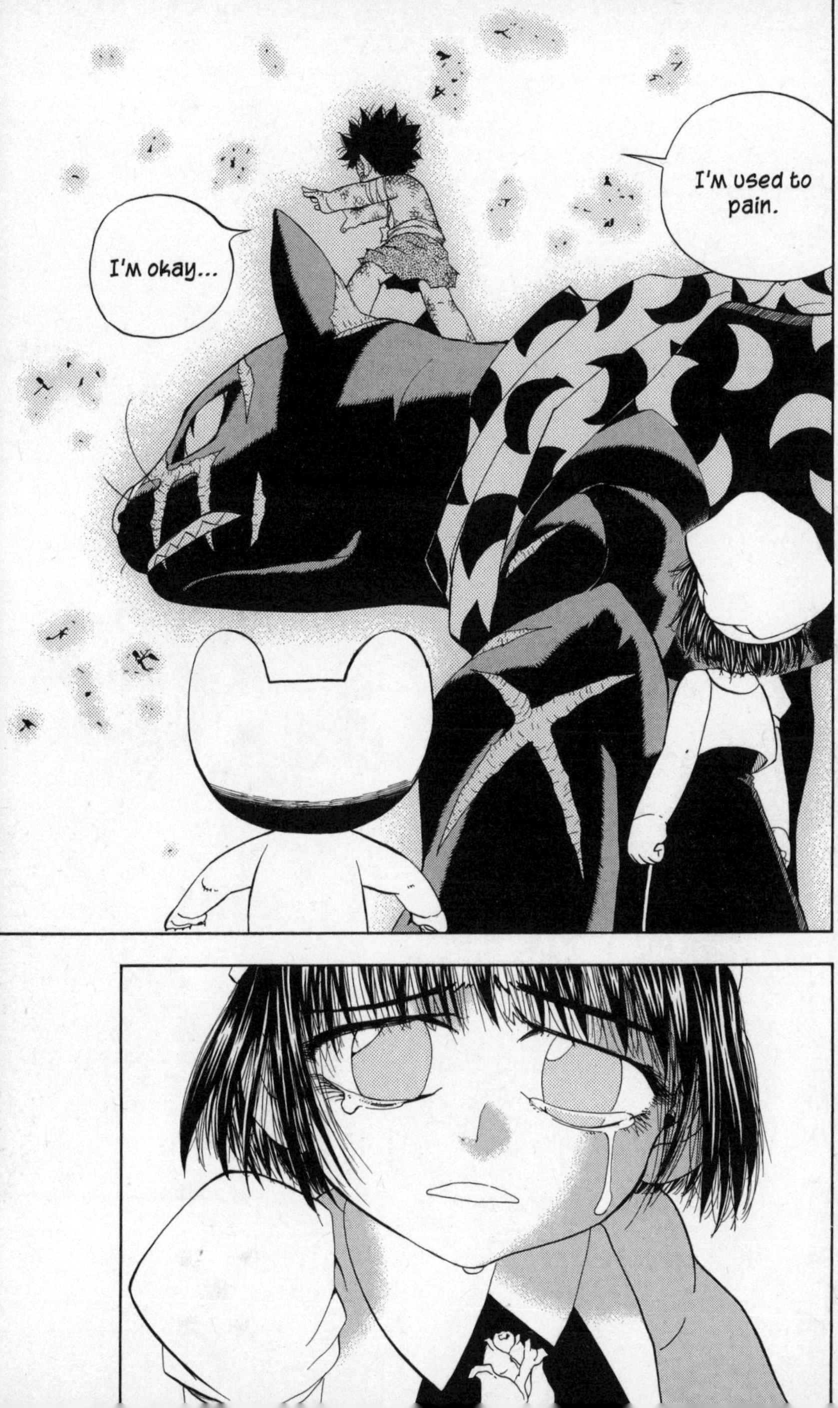
I'm used to pain.
I'm okay...

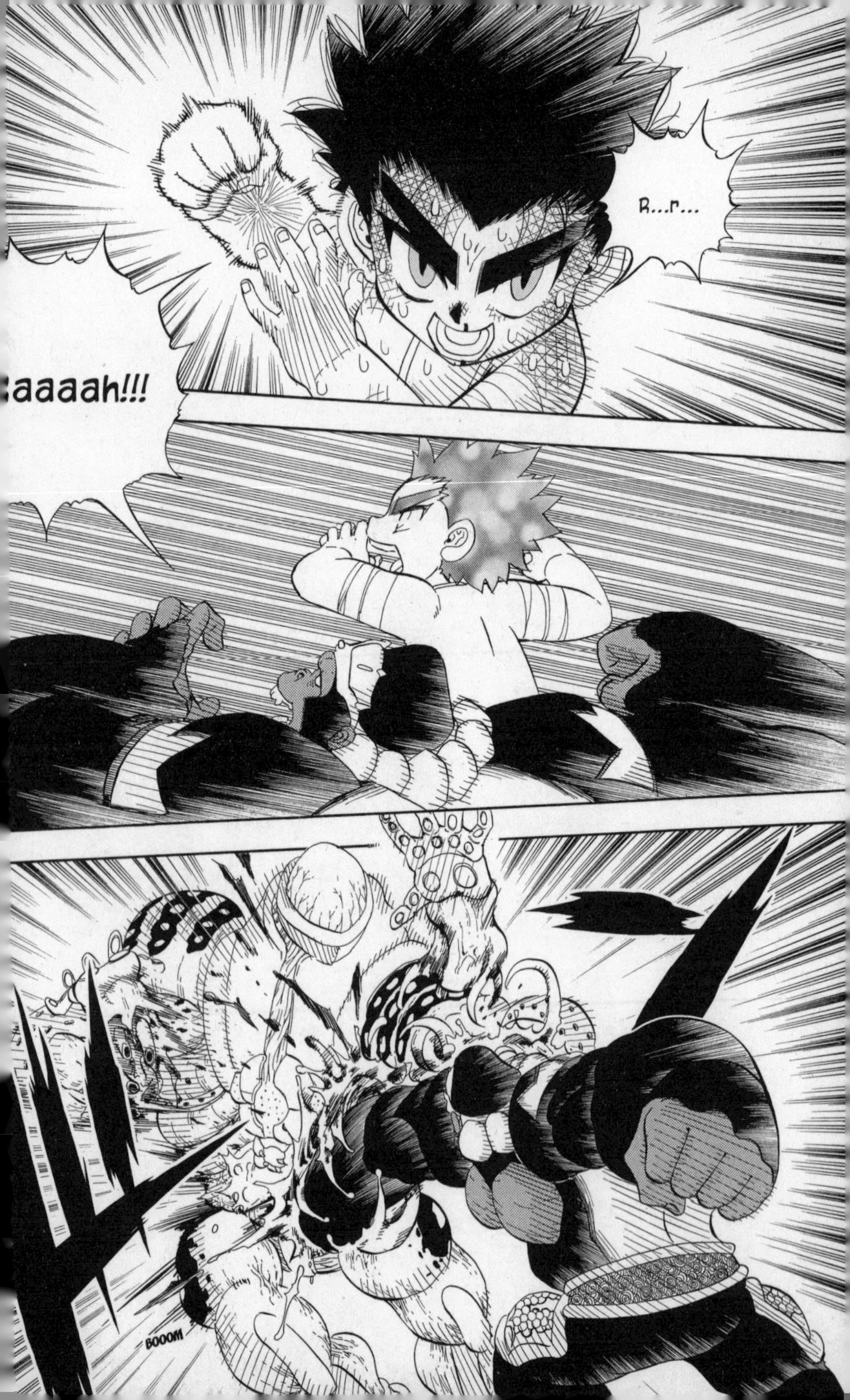
R...r...
aaaah!!!
BOOOM

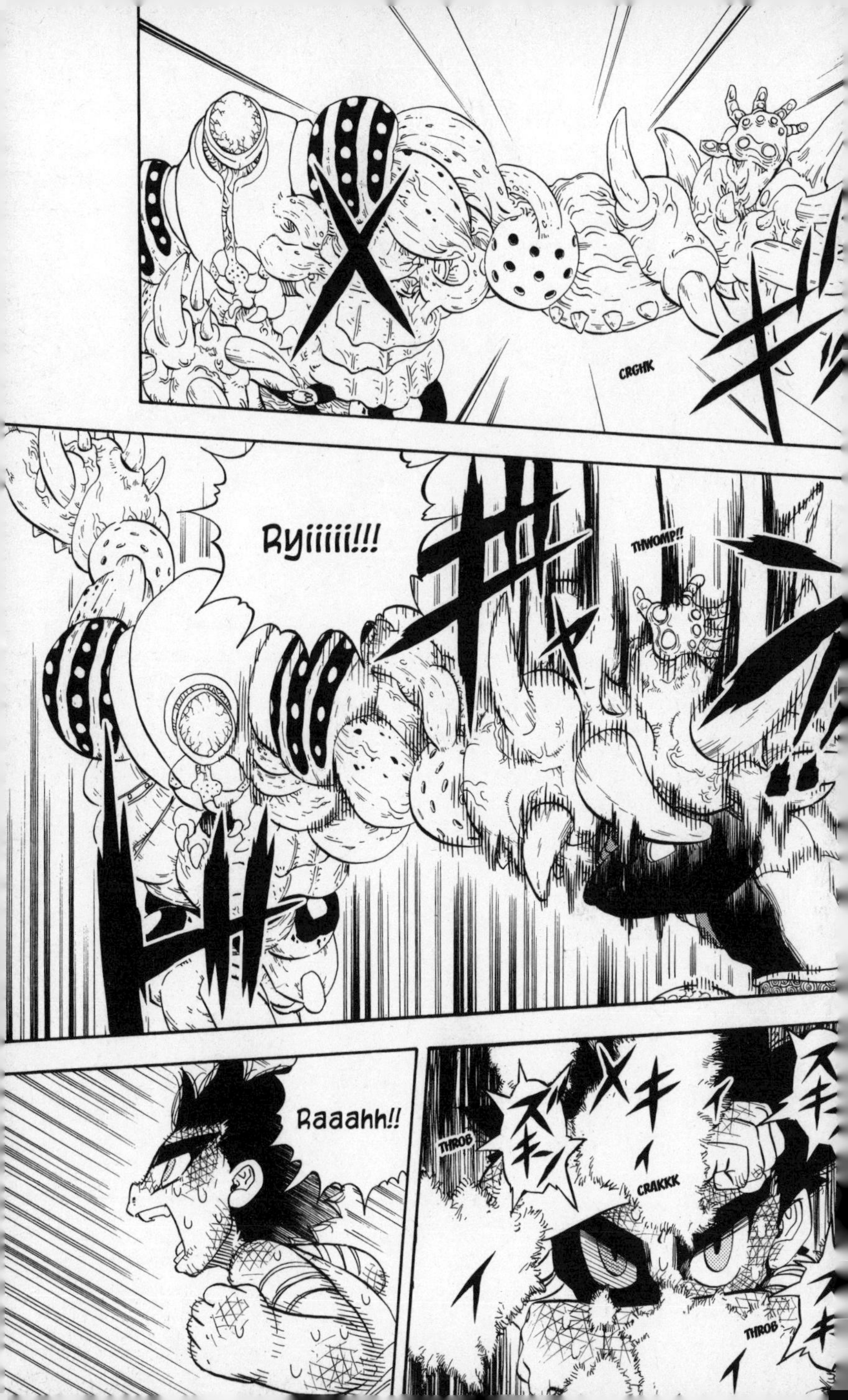
CRGHK
THWOMP!!
Ryiiiiii!!!
THROB
CRAKKK
THROB
Raaahh!!

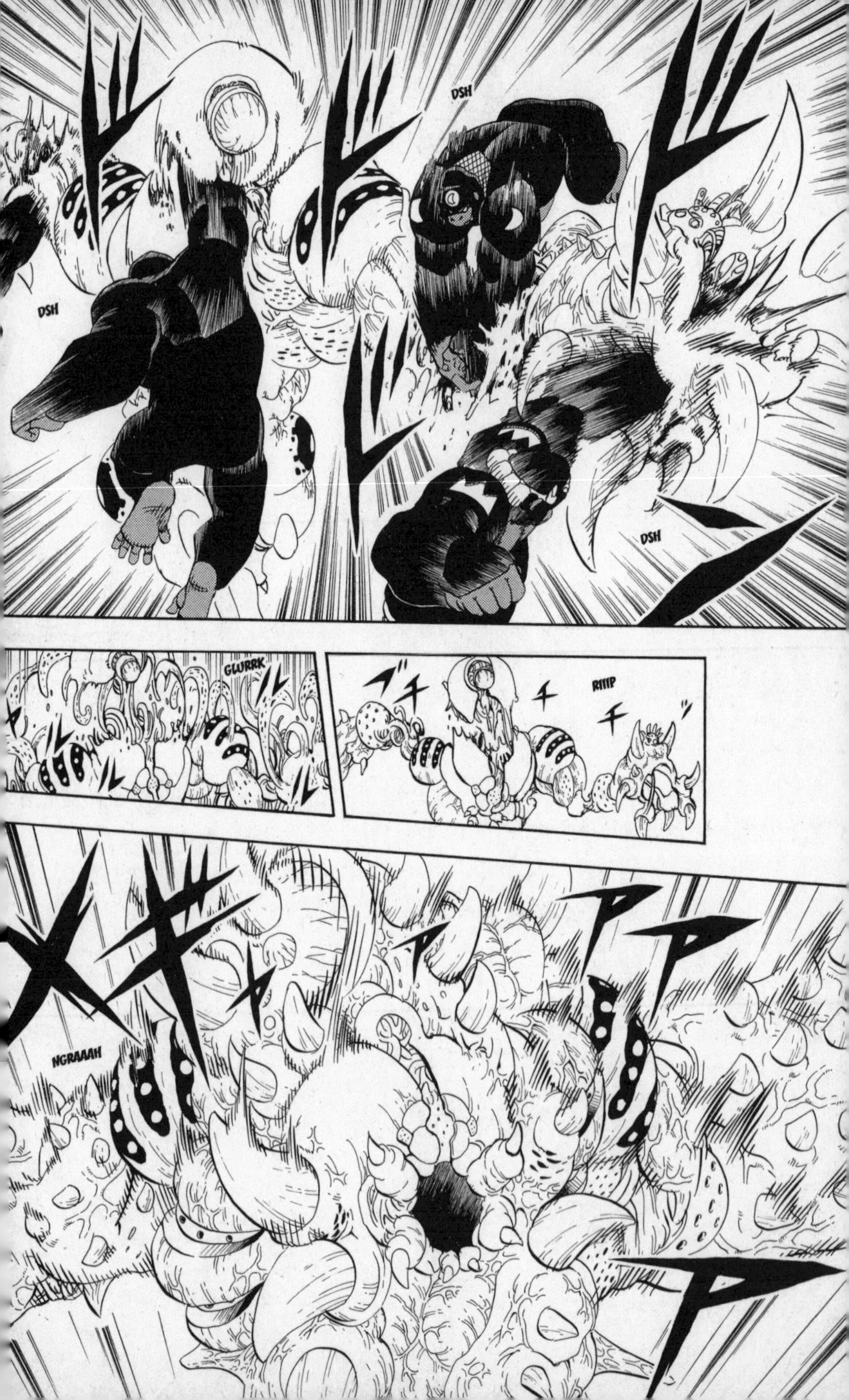
DSH
DSH
DSH
RIIP
GLURRK
NGRAAAH

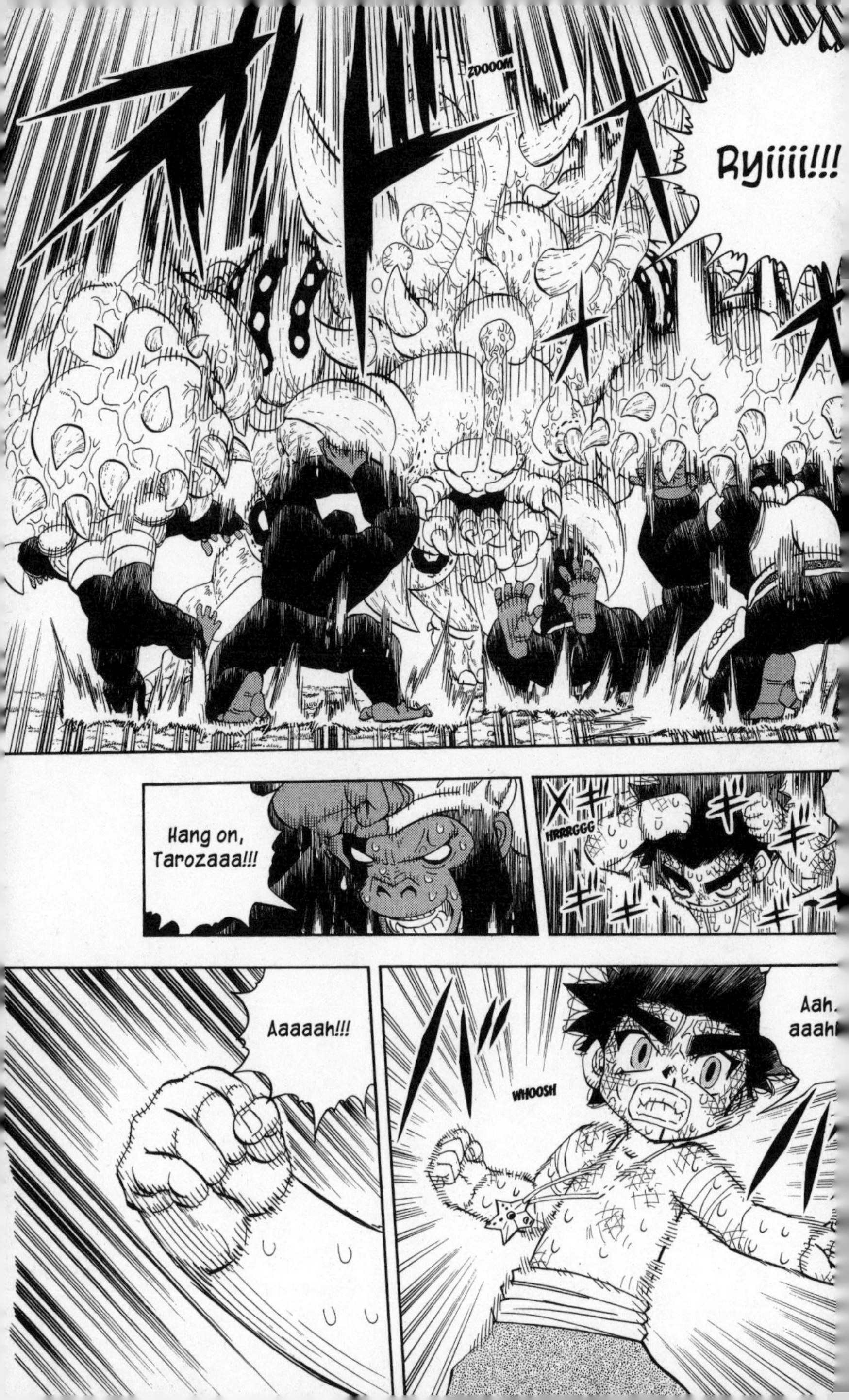
ZOOOM
Ryiiii!!!
HRRRGGG
Hang on, Tarozaaa!!!
Aah.
aaah
WHOOSH
Aaaaah!!!

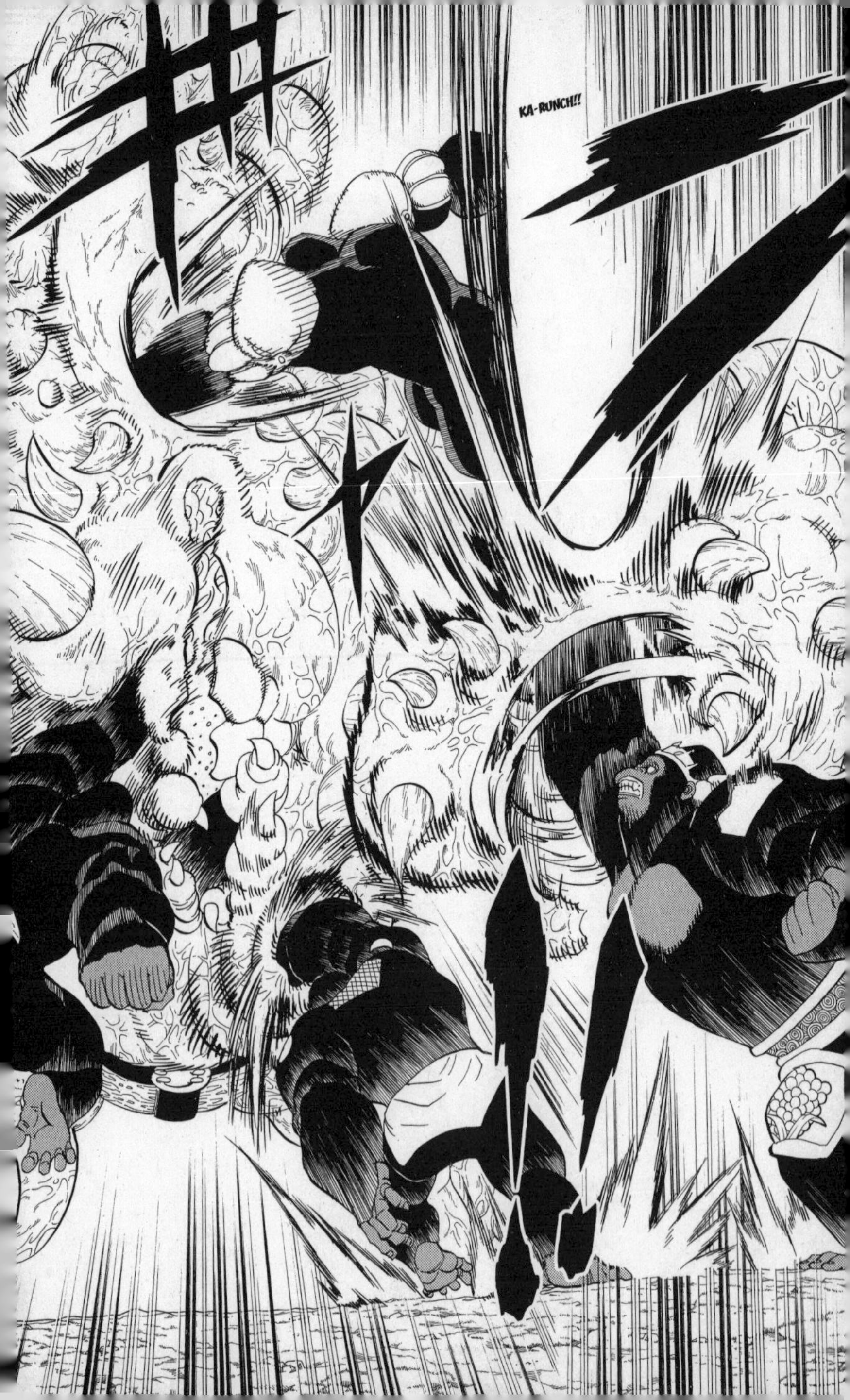
KA-RUNCH!!

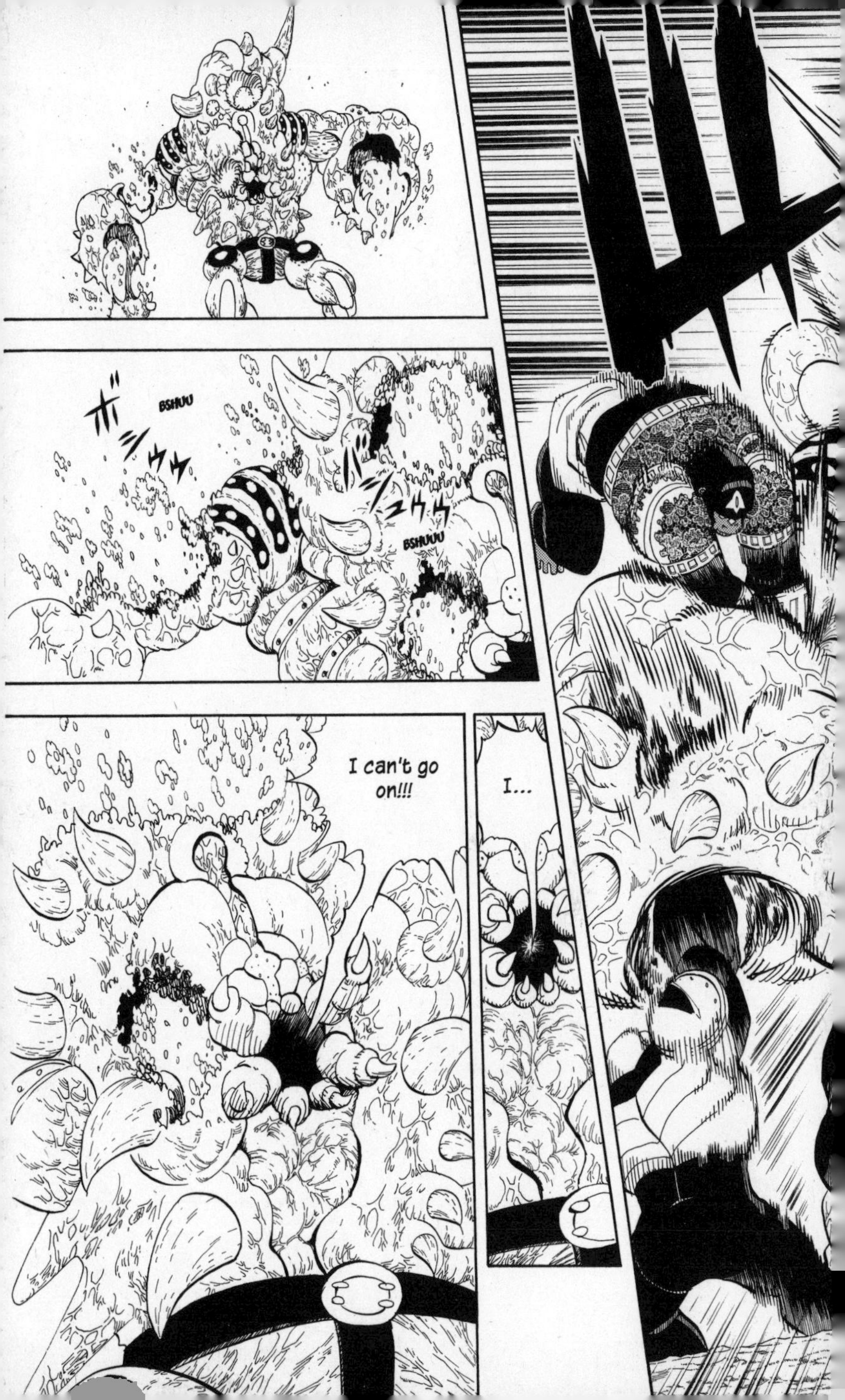
BSHUUU
BSHUU
I...
I can't go
on!!!

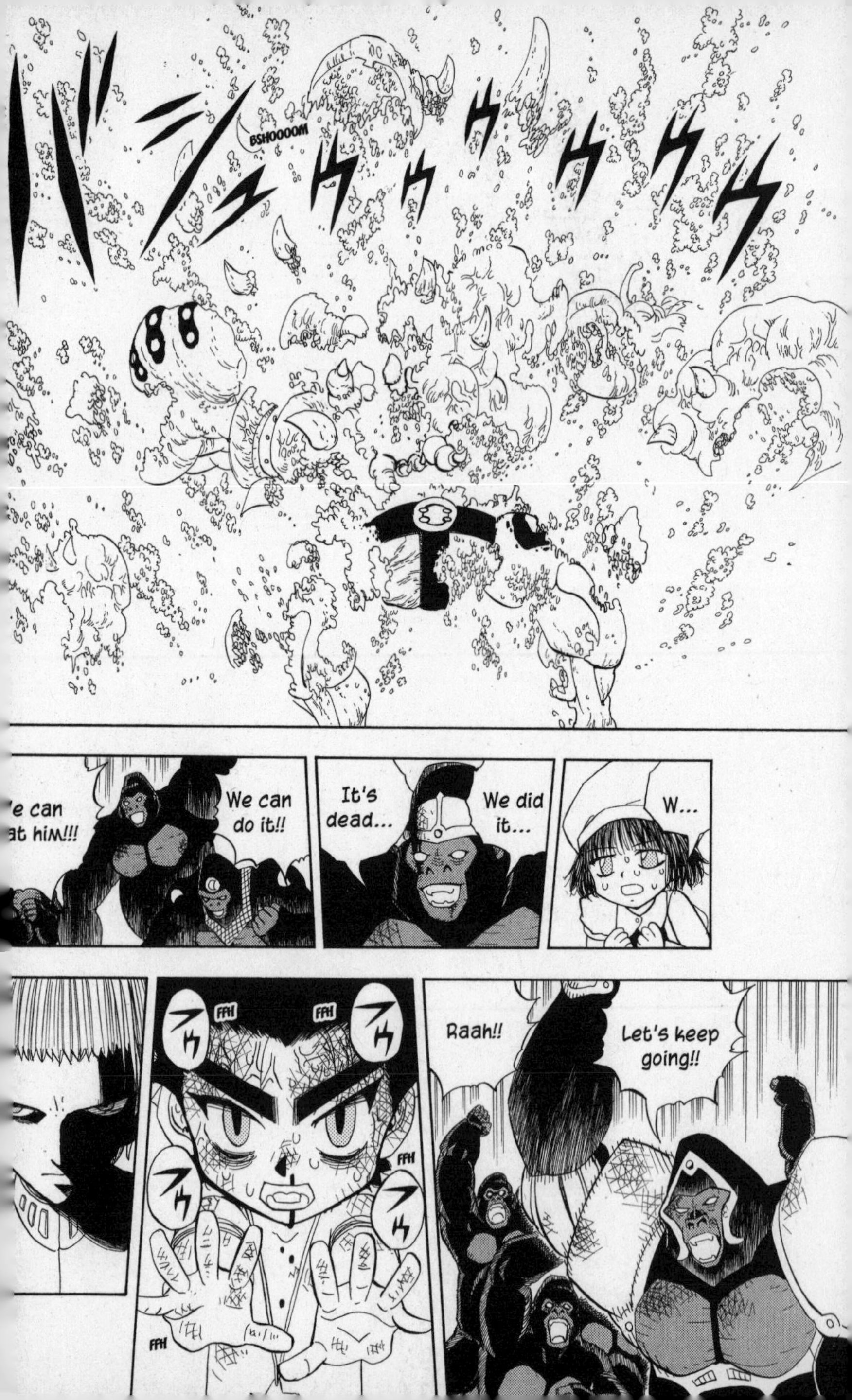
BSHOOOOM
W...
We did it...
It's dead...
We can do it!!
e can
at him!!!
Let's keep going!!
Raah!!
FFH
FFH
FFH
FFH

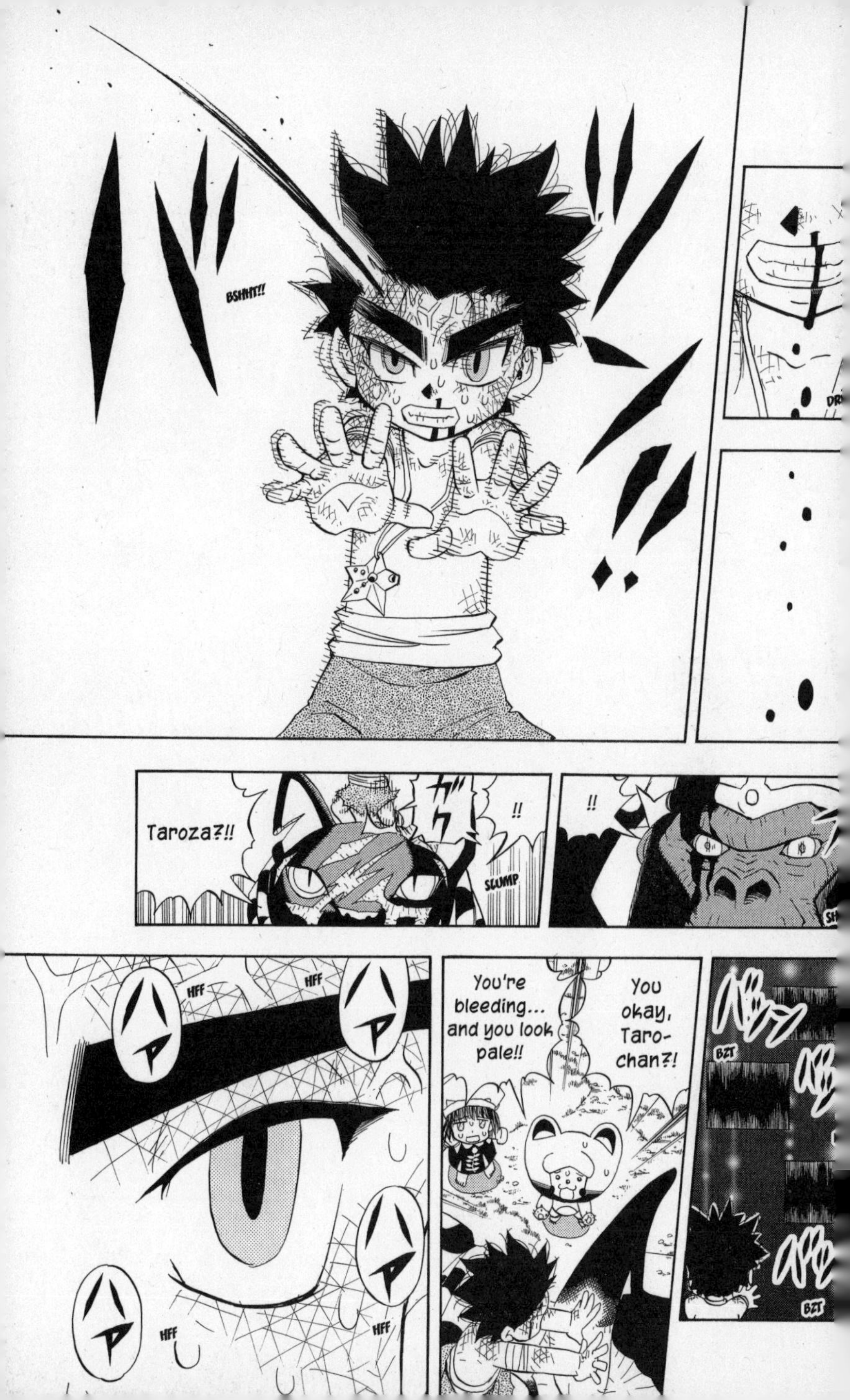

BSHHT!!
!!
!!
Taroza?!!
SLUMP
BZT
BZT
You okay, Taro-chan?!
You're bleeding... and you look pale!!
HFF
HFF
HFF
HFF

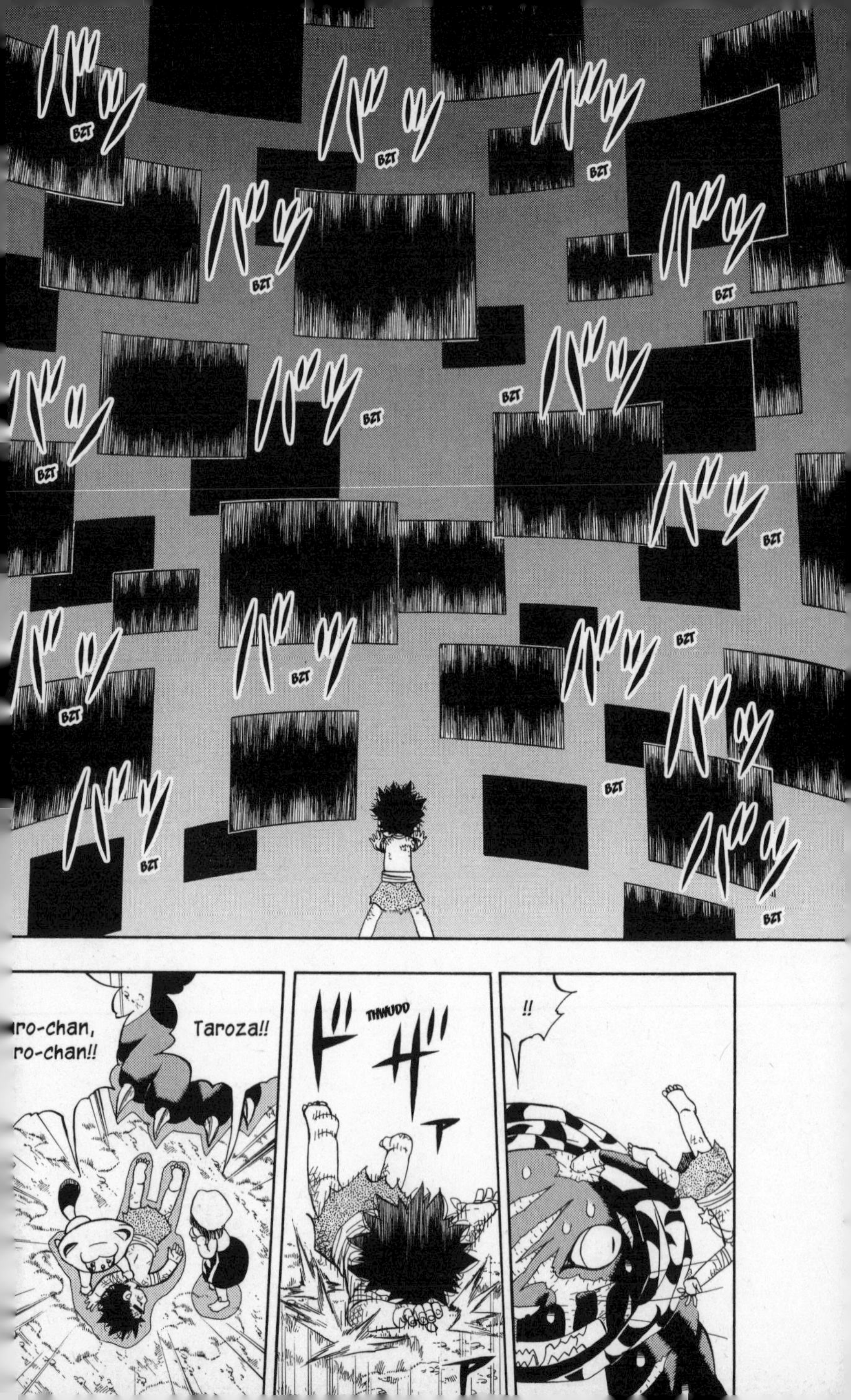
BZT
BZT
BZT
BZT
BZT
BZT
BZT
BZT
BZT
BZT
BZT
BZT
BZT
BZT
BZT
!!
THWUDD
Taroza!!
ro-chan,
ro-chan!!

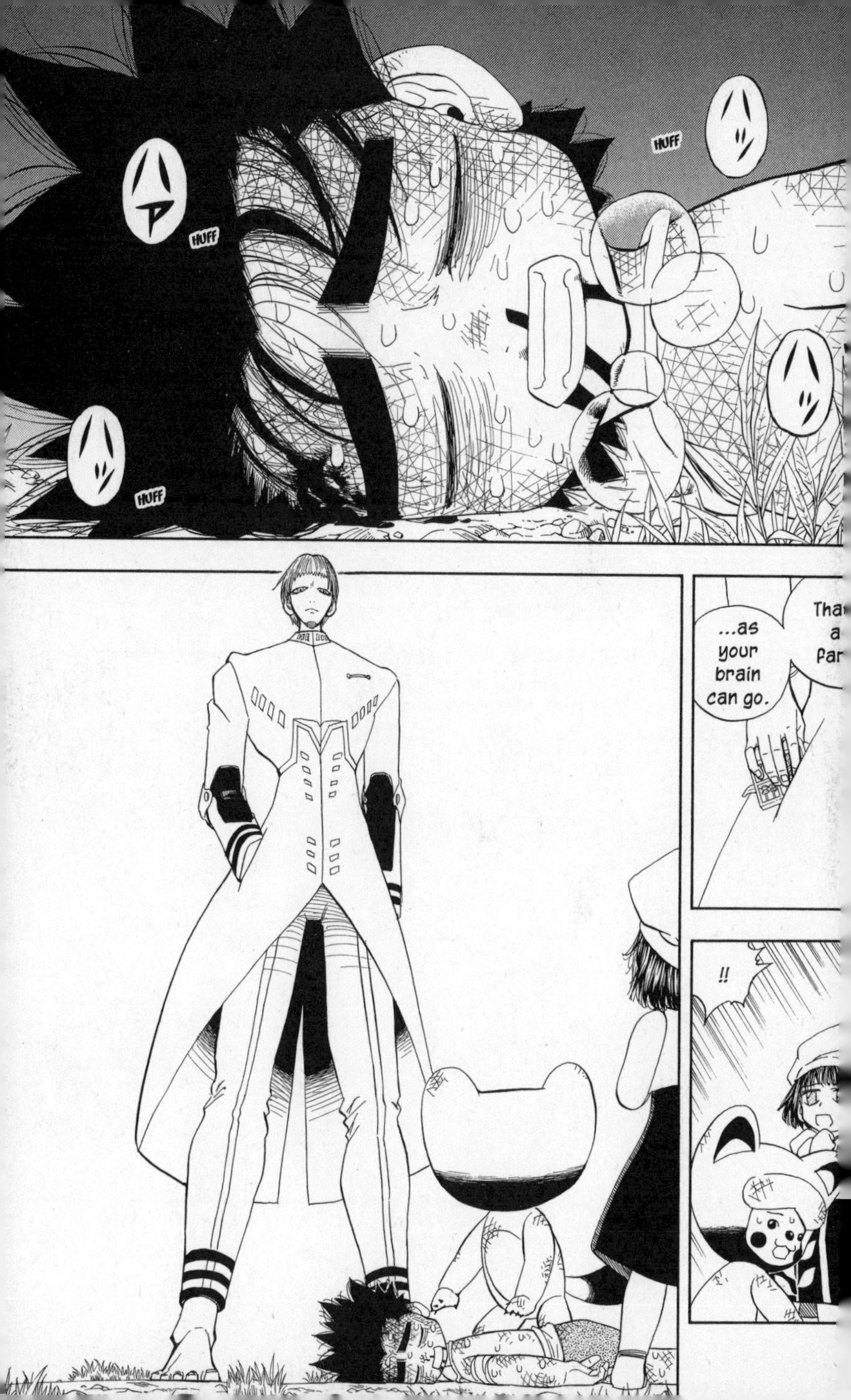

HUFF
HUFF
HUFF
Tha a far
...as your brain can go.
!!

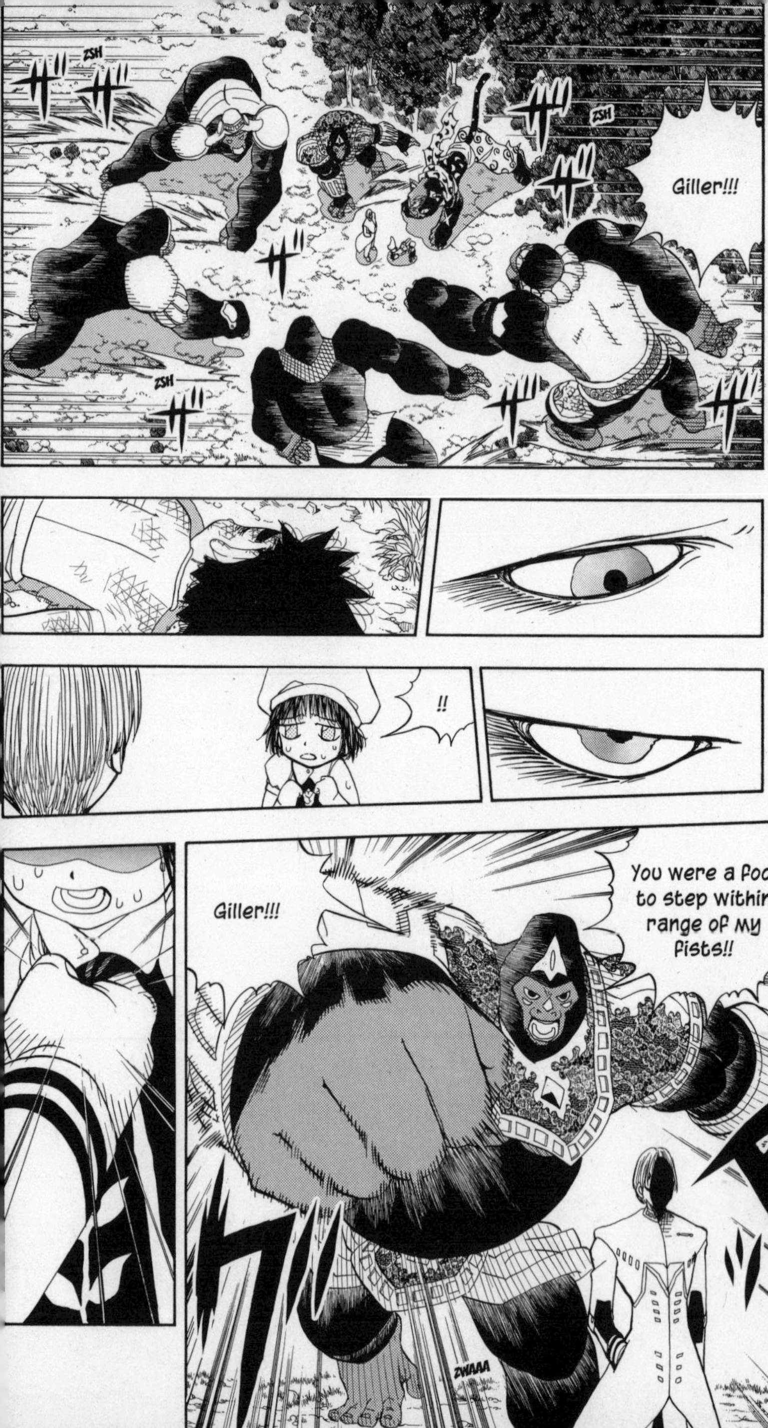
ZSH
Giller!!!
ZSH
ZSH
!!
You were a fool to step within range of my fists!!
Giller!!!
ZWAAA

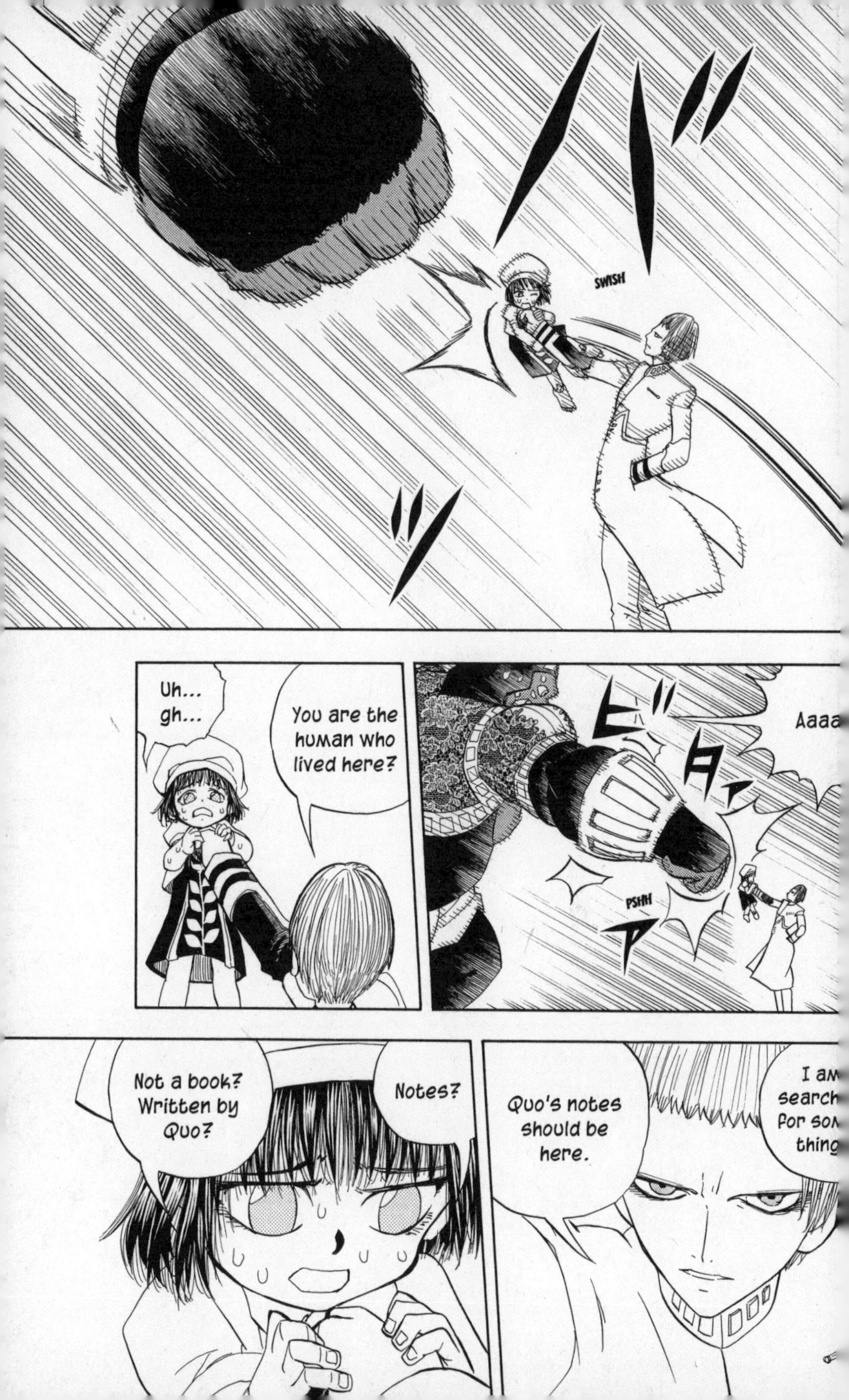

SWISH
Aaaa
PSHH
You are the human who lived here?
Uh... gh...
I am search for som thing
Quo's notes should be here.
Notes?
Not a book? Written by Quo?

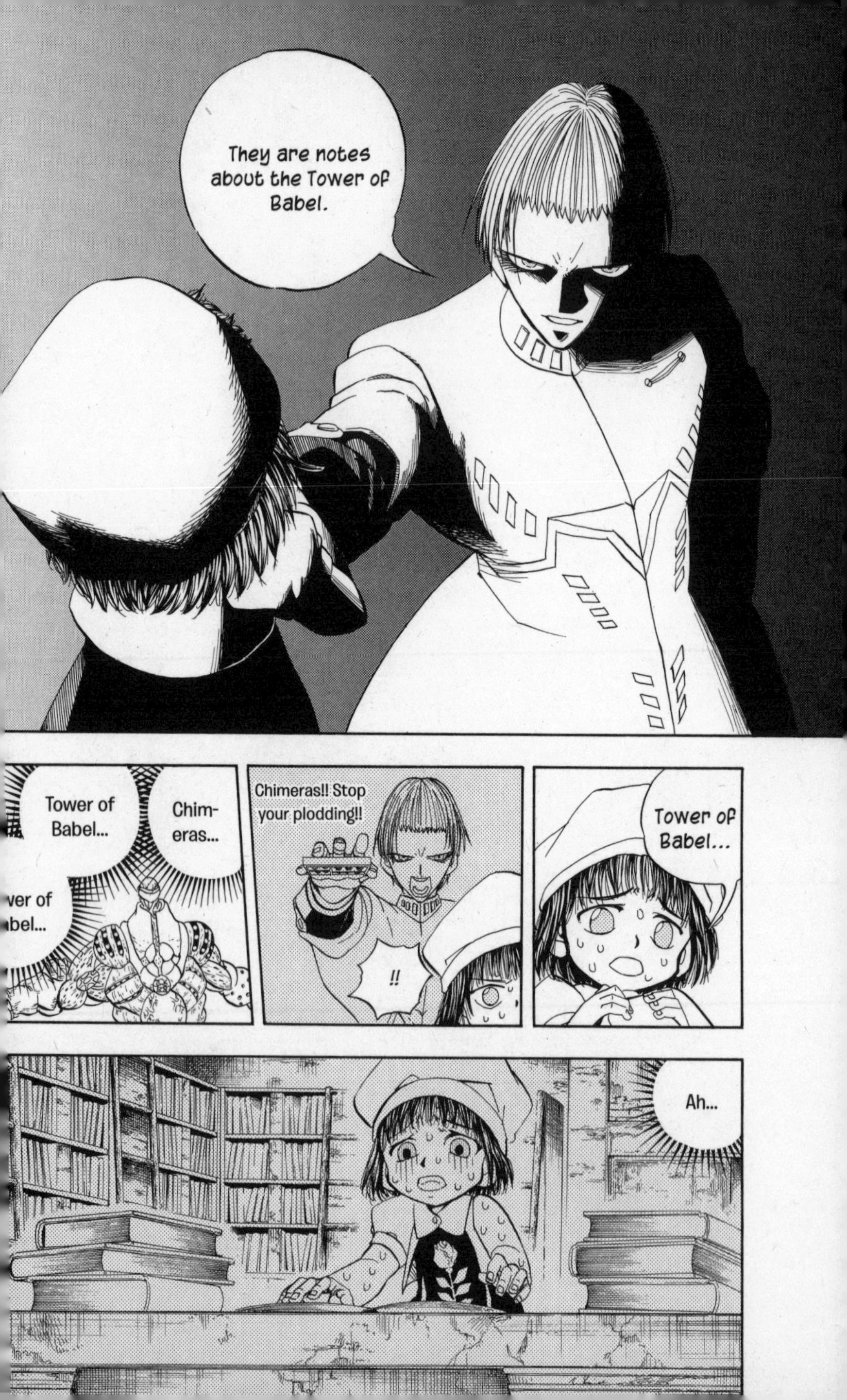
They are notes about the Tower of Babel.
Tower of Babel...
Chimeras!! Stop your plodding!!
!!
Chim- eras...
Tower of Babel...
ver of
bel...
Ah...

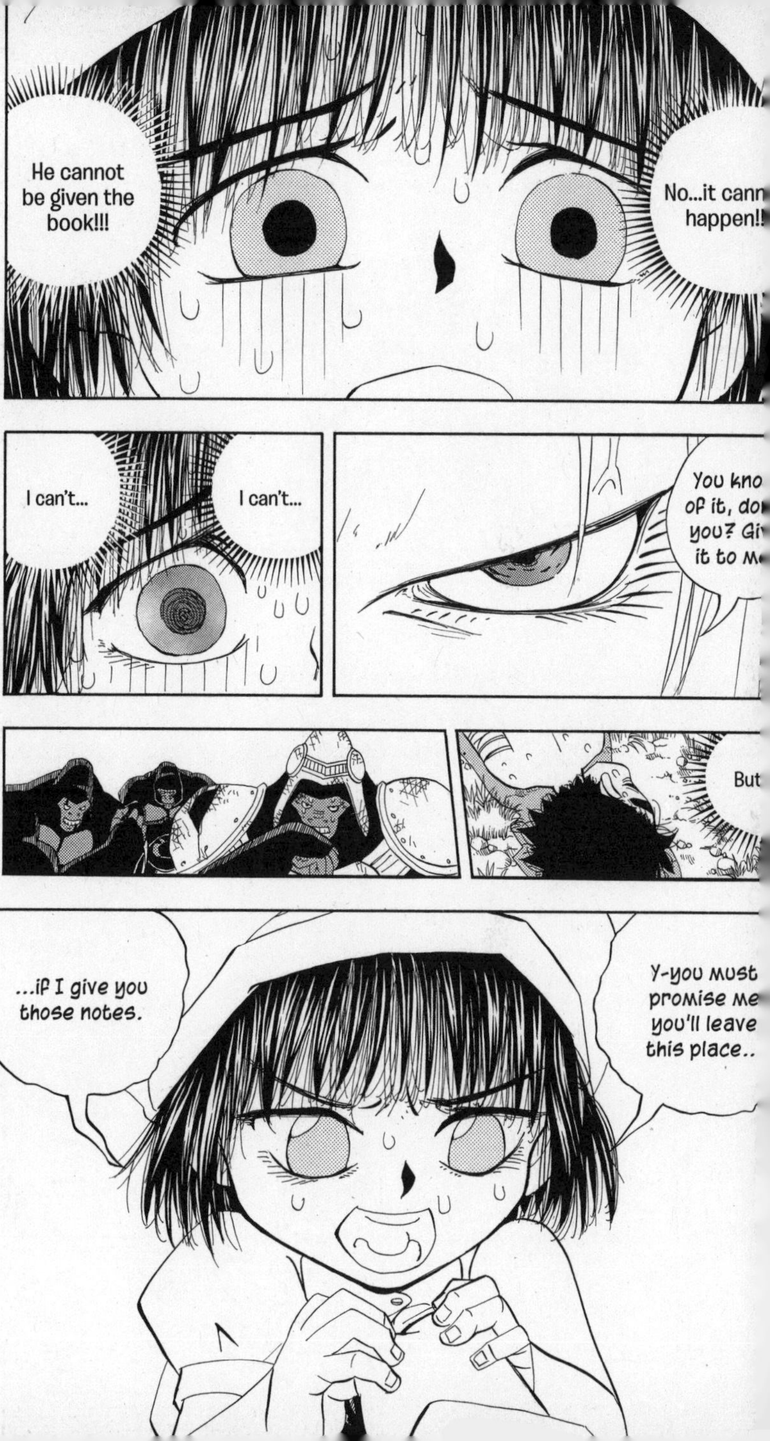
No...it cann happen!!
He cannot be given the book!!!
You kno of it, do you? Gi it to M
I can't...
I can't...
But
Y-you must promise me you'll leave this place..
...if I give you those notes.

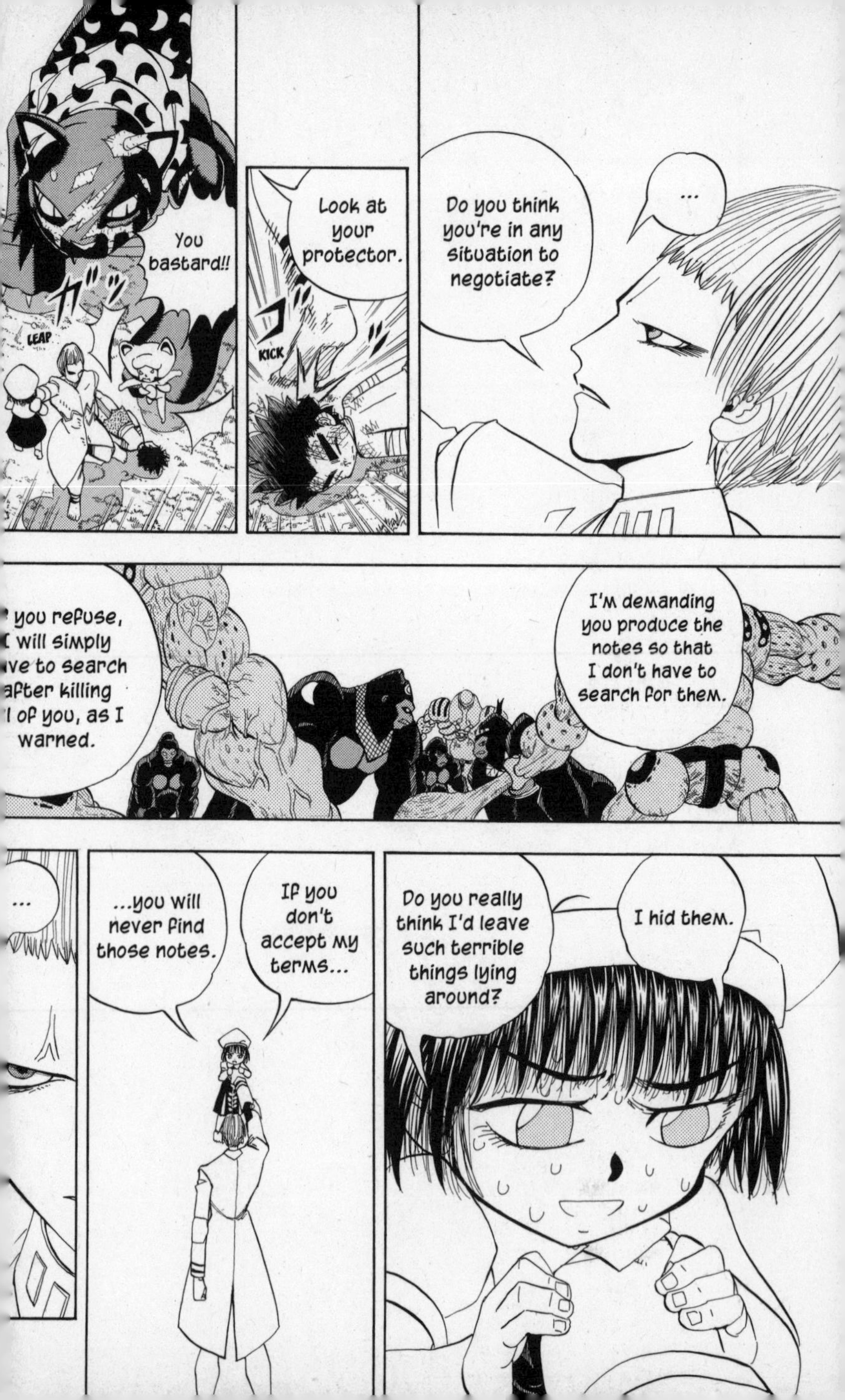
...
Do you think you're in any situation to negotiate?
Look at your protector.
KICK
You bastard!!
LEAP
I'm demanding you produce the notes so that I don't have to search for them.
you refuse, will simply ve to search after killing l of you, as I warned.
I hid them.
Do you really think I'd leave such terrible things lying around?
If you don't accept my terms...
...you will never find those notes.
...

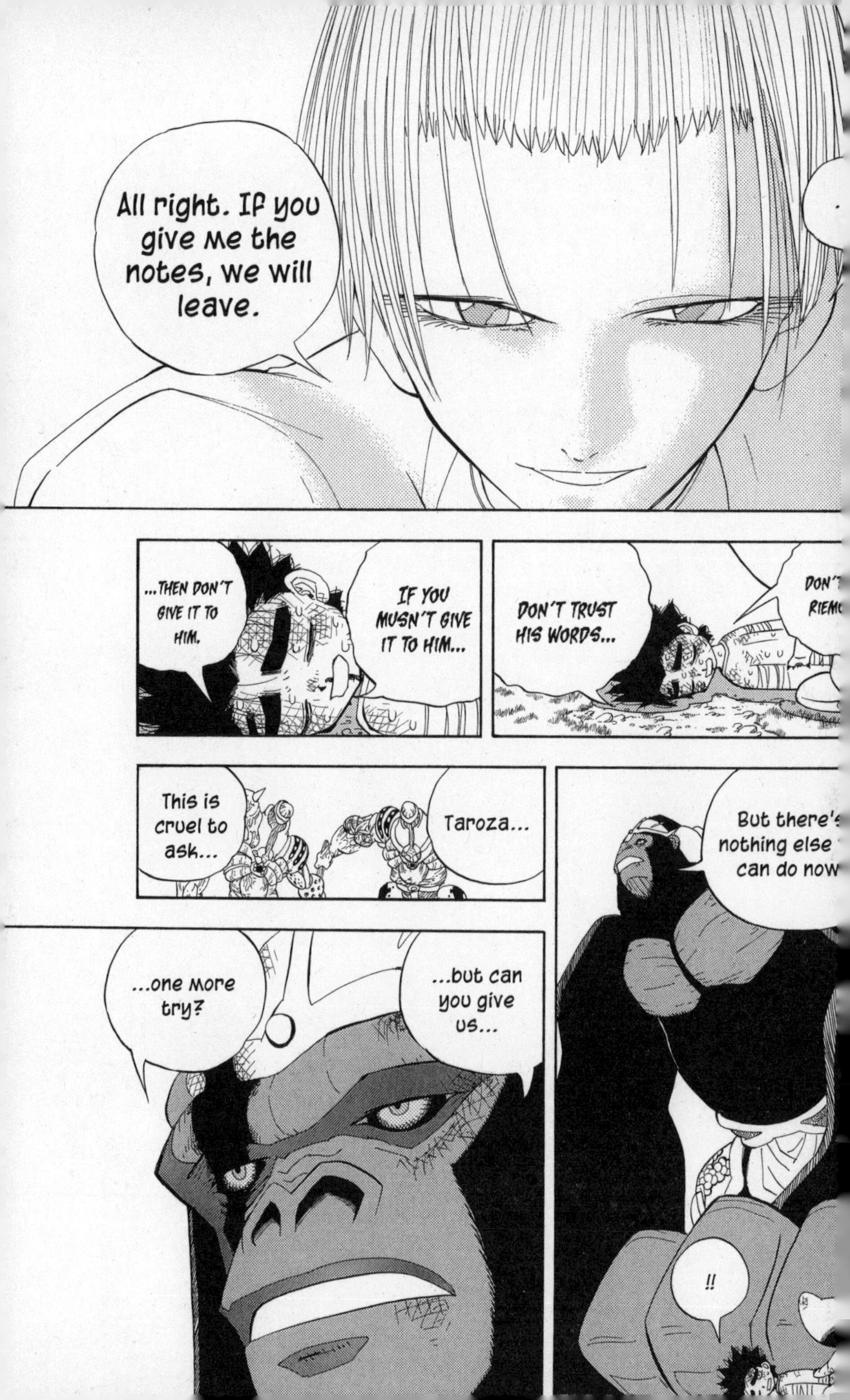
All right. If you give me the notes, we will leave.
DON'T TRUST HIS WORDS...
IF YOU MUSN'T GIVE IT TO HIM...
...THEN DON'T GIVE IT TO HIM.
But there's nothing else can do now
!!
Taroza...
This is cruel to ask...
...but can you give us...
...one more try?

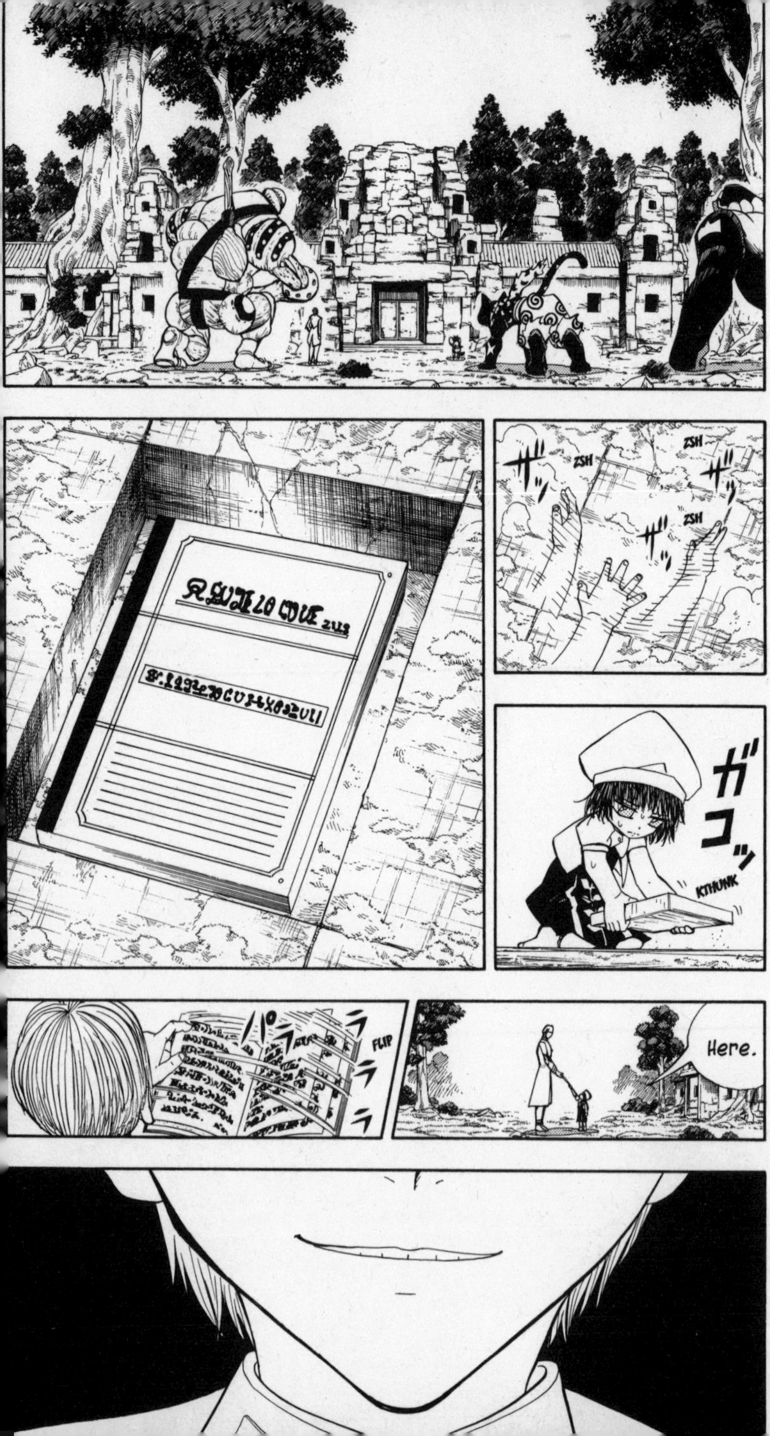

ザッ
ZSH
ザッ
ZSH
ザッ
ZSH
ガコッ
KTHUNK
Here.
パラ
FLIP

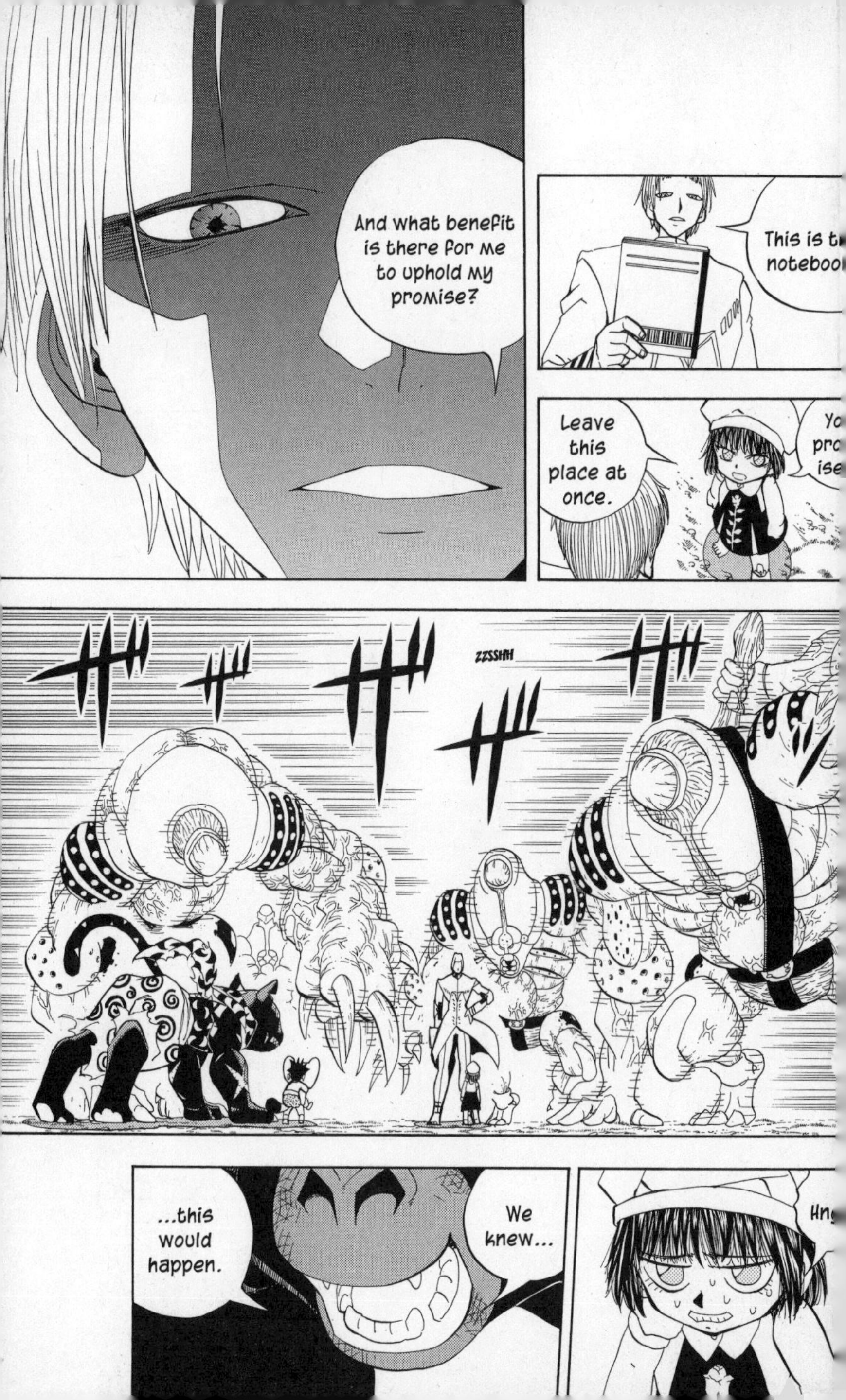

This is t noteboo
Yo pro ise
Leave this place at once.
And what benefit is there for me to uphold my promise?
ZZSSHH
Hn
We knew...
...this would happen.

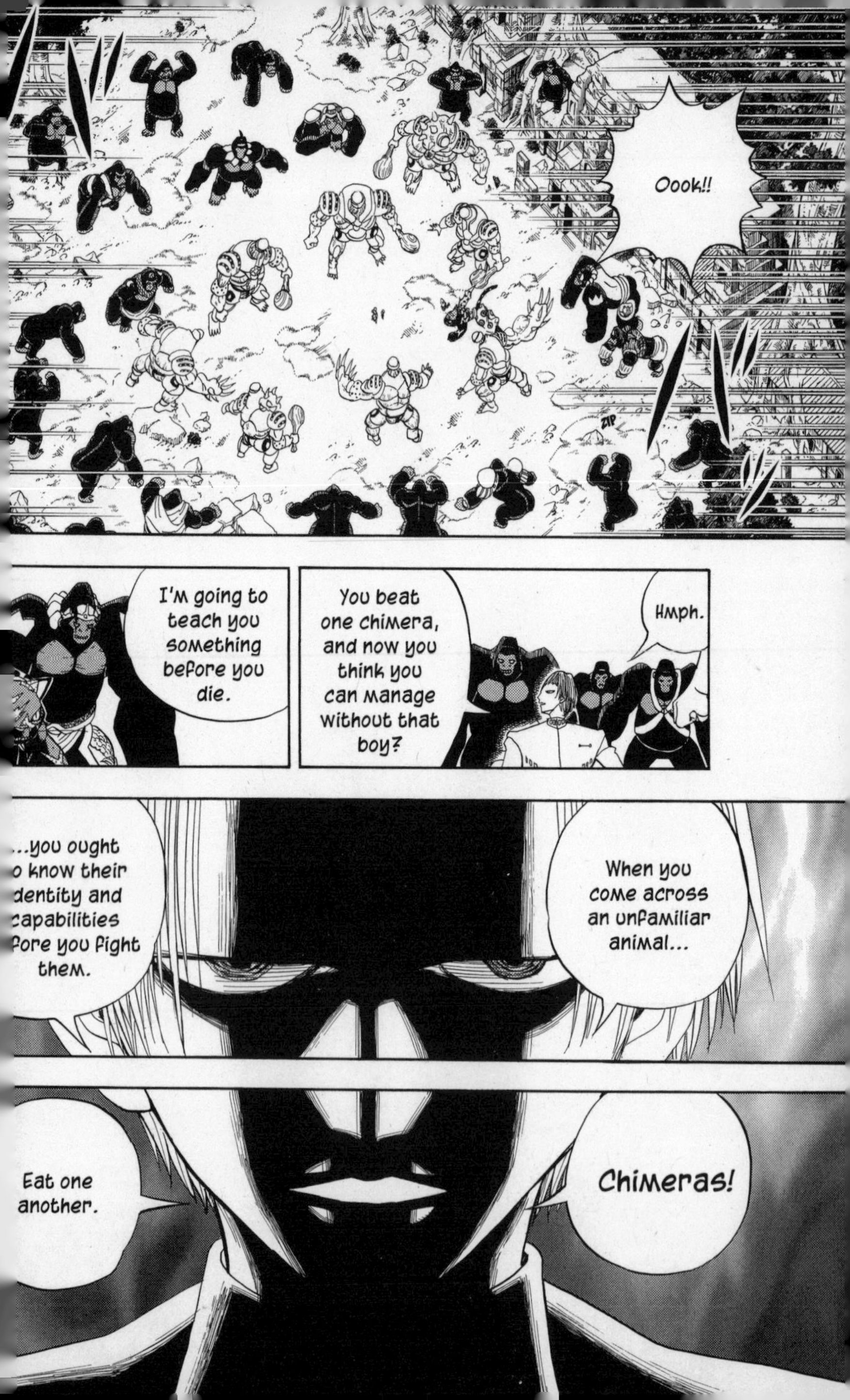

Oook!!
ZIP
Hmph.
You beat one chimera, and now you think you can manage without that boy?
I'm going to teach you something before you die.
When you come across an unfamiliar animal...
...you ought o know their dentity and capabilities fore you fight them.
Chimeras!
Eat one another.

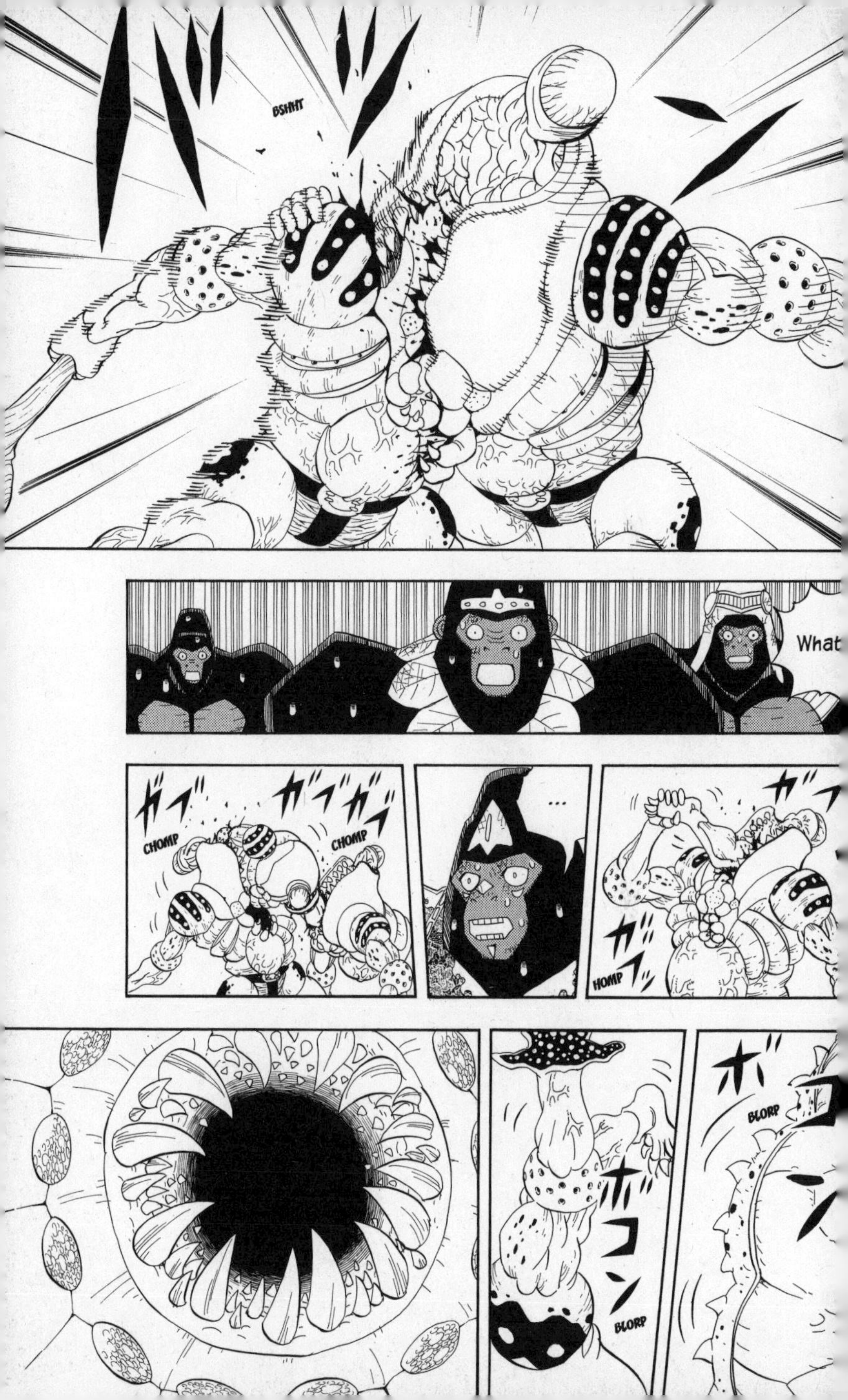

BSHHT
What
ガブ
HOMP
...
ガブ
CHOMP
ガブガブ
CHOMP
ボ
BLORP
ボコン
BLORP

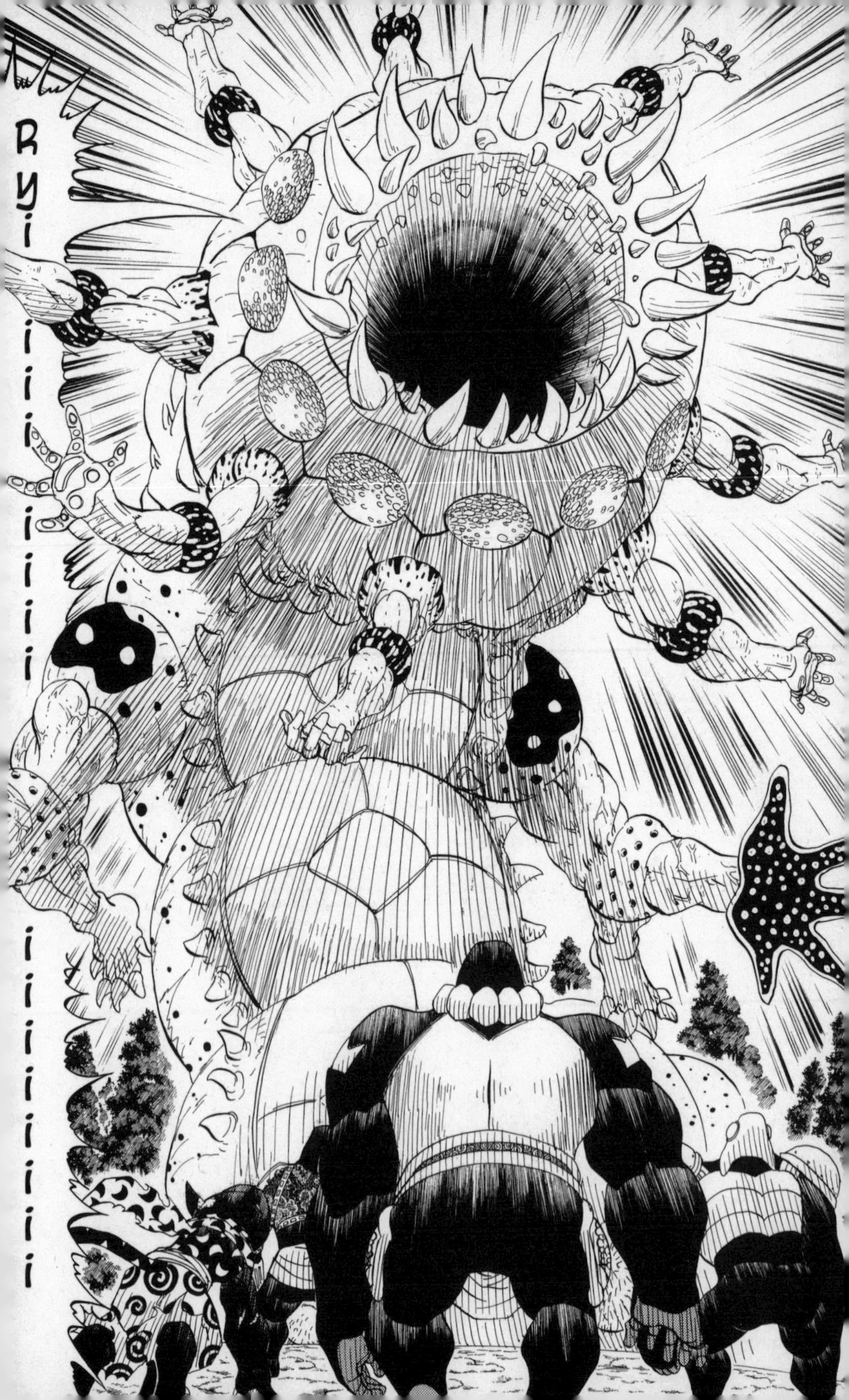
Ryiiiiiiiiiiiiii

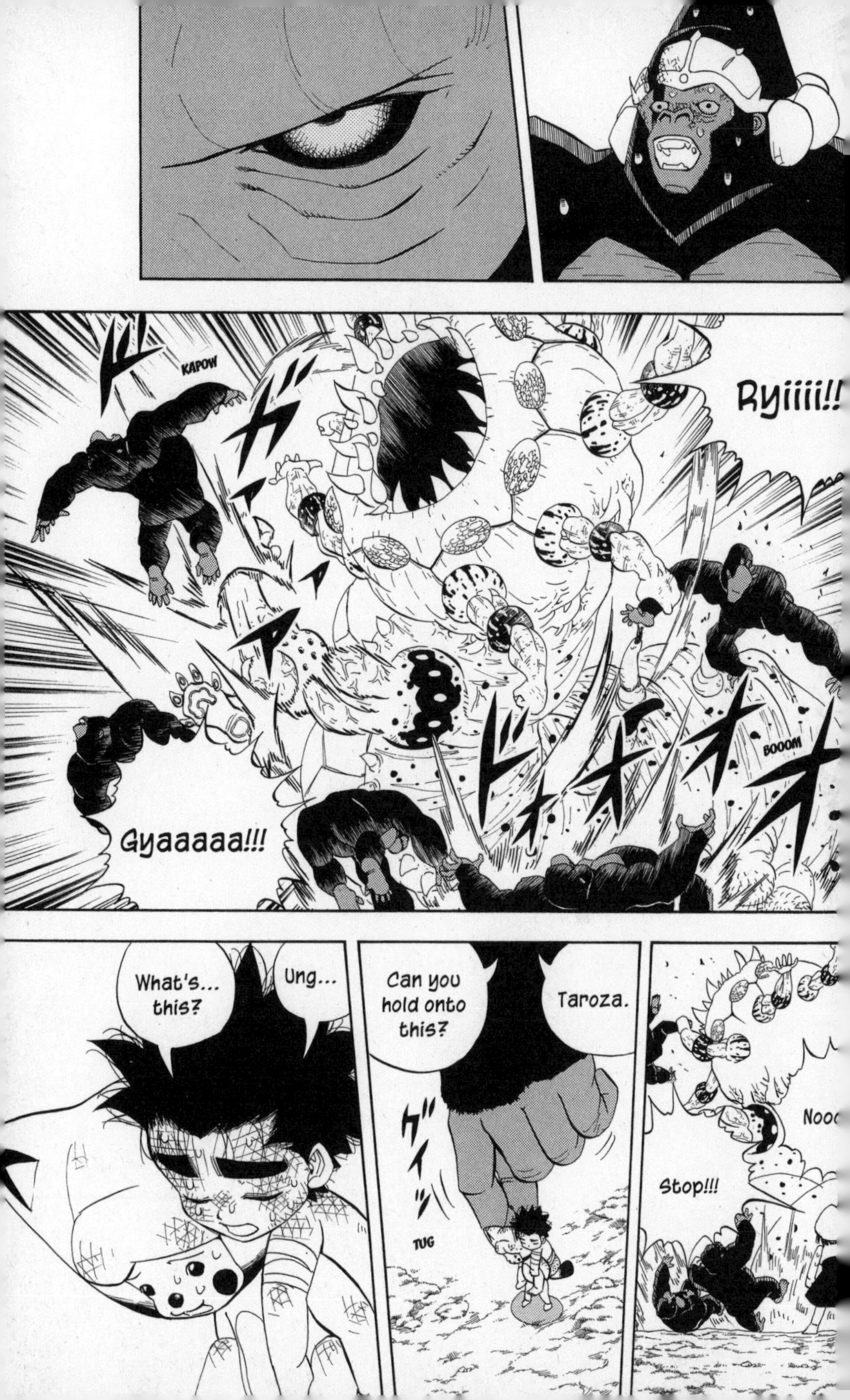

Ryiiii!!
KAPOW
BOOOM
Gyaaaaa!!!
Noo
Stop!!!
Taroza.
Can you hold onto this?
TUG
Ung...
What's... this?

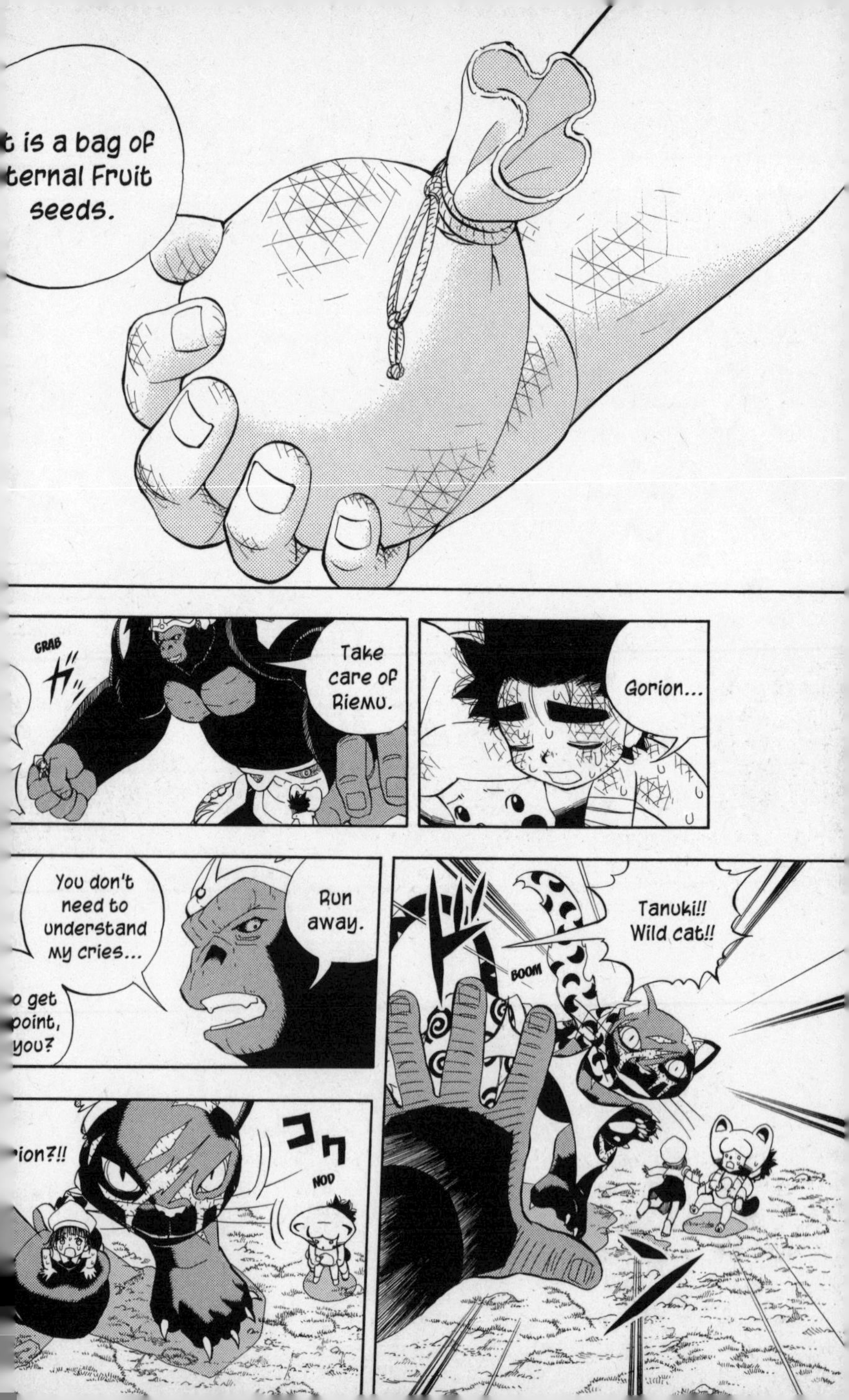
t is a bag of ternal Fruit seeds.
Gorion...
Take care of Riemu.
GRAB
Tanuki!! Wild cat!!
BOOM
Run away.
You don't need to understand my cries...
o get point, you?
rion?!!
NOD

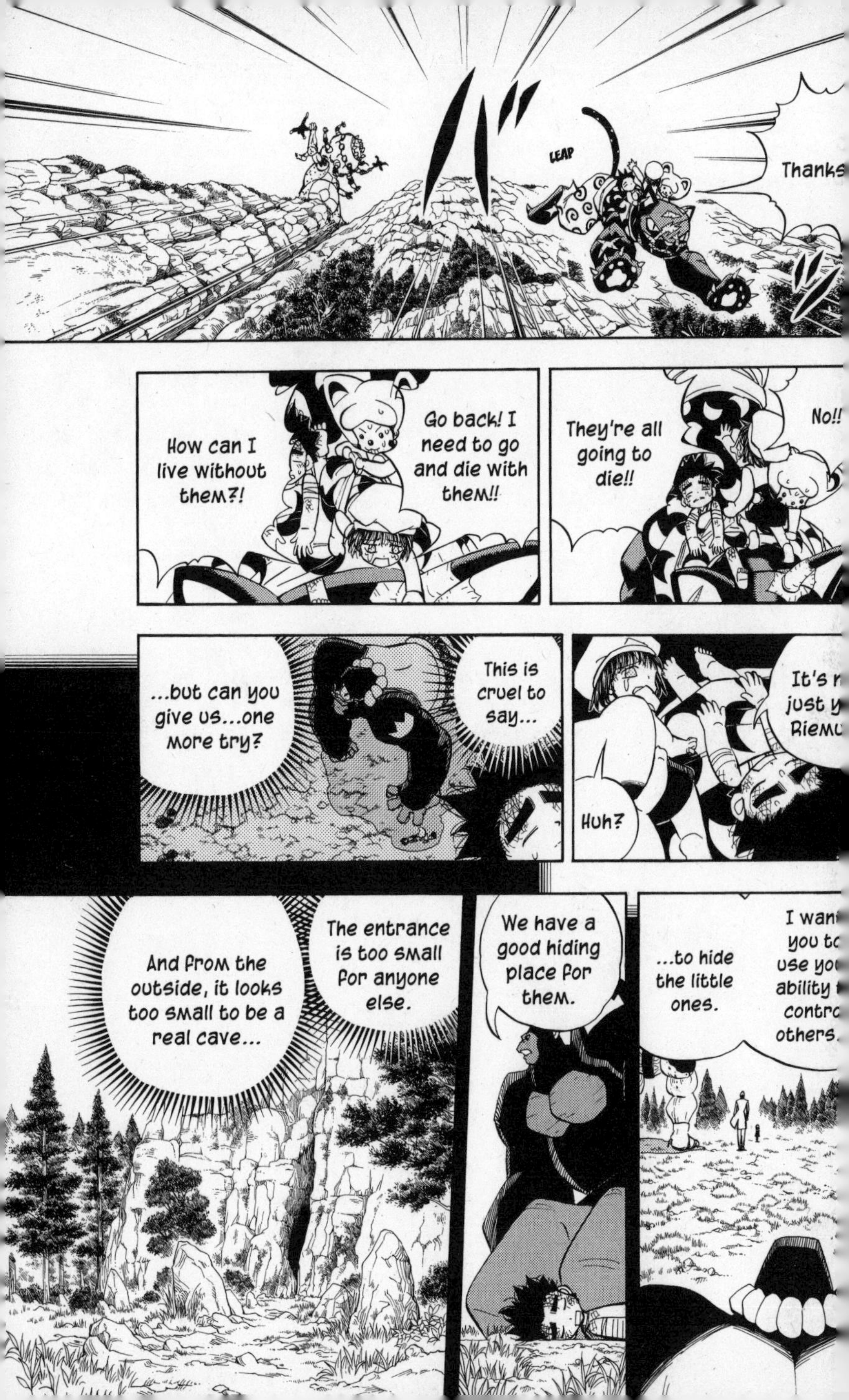
Thanks
LEAP
No!!
They're all going to die!!
Go back! I need to go and die with them!!
How can I live without them?!
It's just Riemu
Huh?
This is cruel to say...
...but can you give us...one more try?
I wan you to use you ability contro others.
...to hide the little ones.
We have a good hiding place for them.
The entrance is too small for anyone else.
And from the outside, it looks too small to be a real cave...

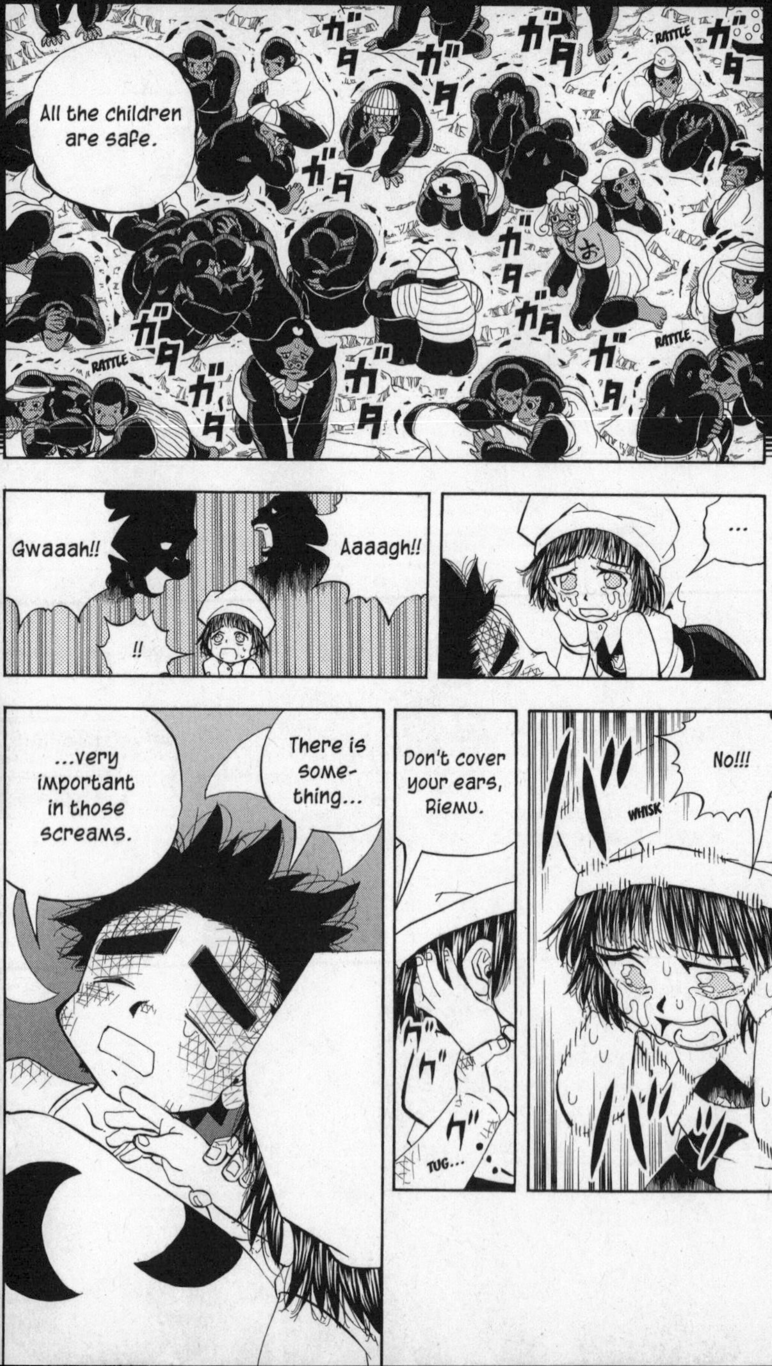

RATTLE
ガタ
All the children are safe.
ガタ
RATTLE
ガタ
...
Aaaagh!!
Gwaaah!!
!!
No!!!
WHISK
Don't cover your ears, Riemu.
TUG...
There is some-thing...
...very important in those screams.

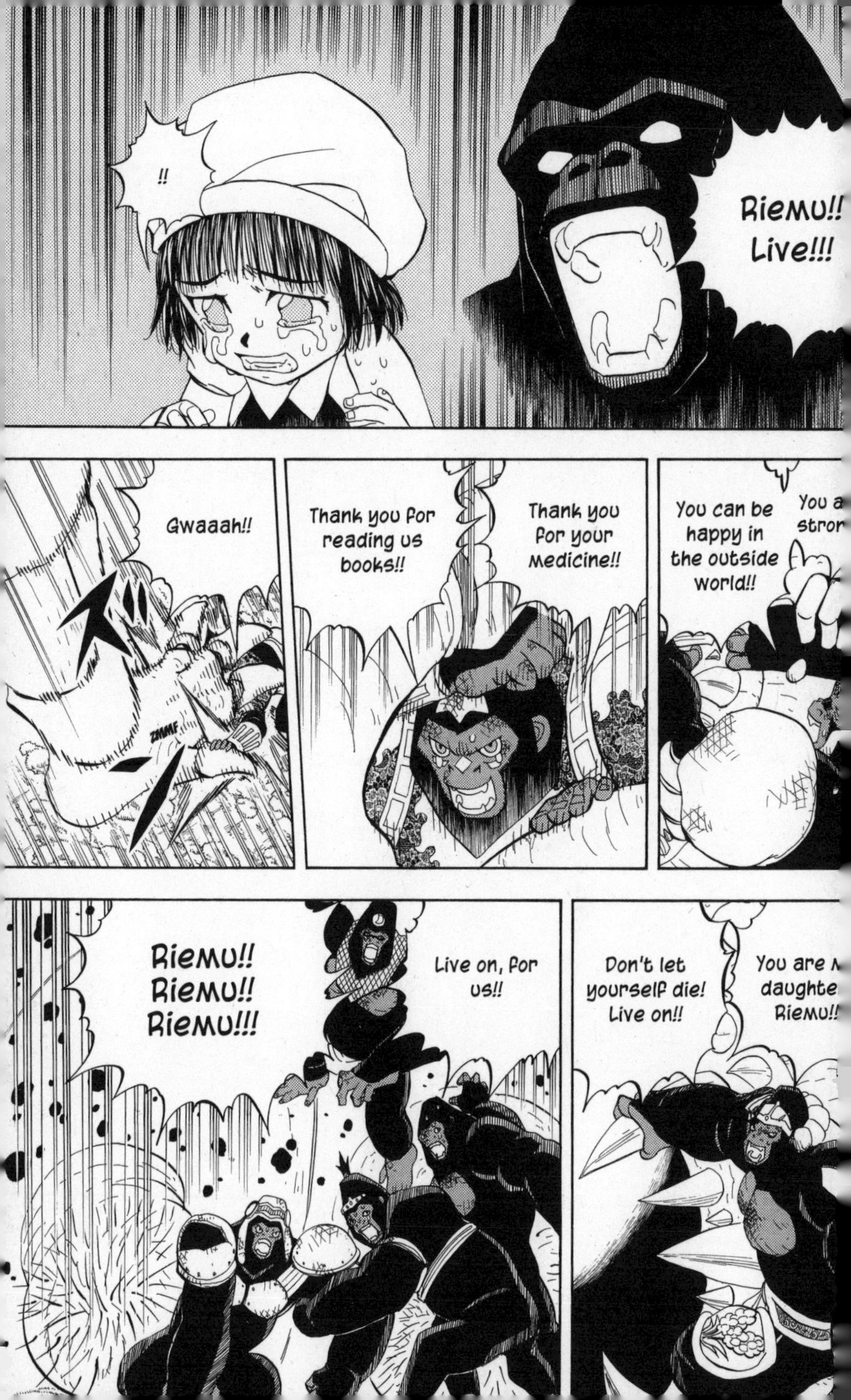
Riemu!! Live!!!
!!
You a
stron
You can be happy in the outside world!!
Thank you for your medicine!!
Thank you for reading us books!!
Gwaaah!!
ZMMF
You are m
daughte
Riemu!!
Don't let yourself die! Live on!!
Live on, for us!!
Riemu!! Riemu!! Riemu!!!

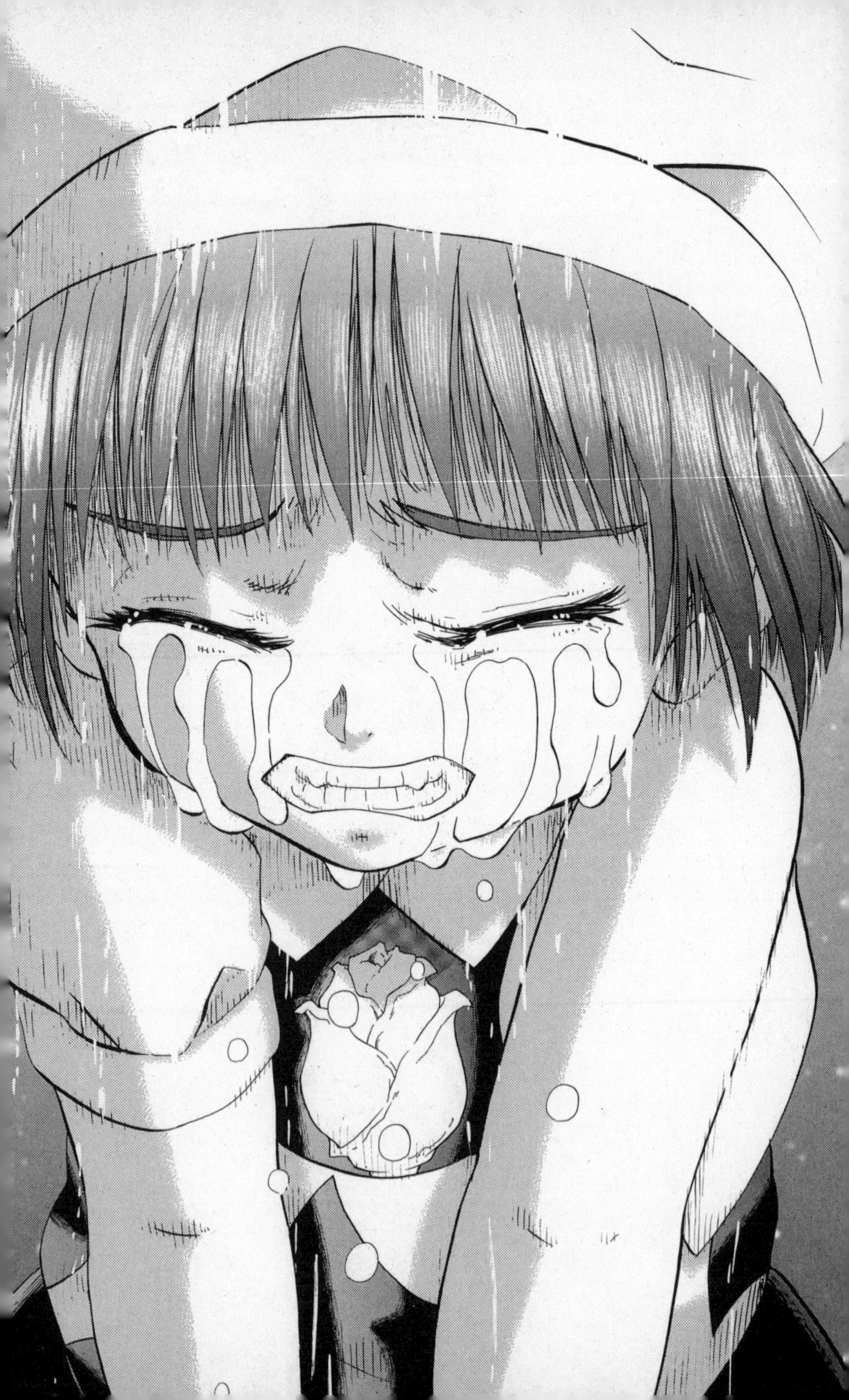

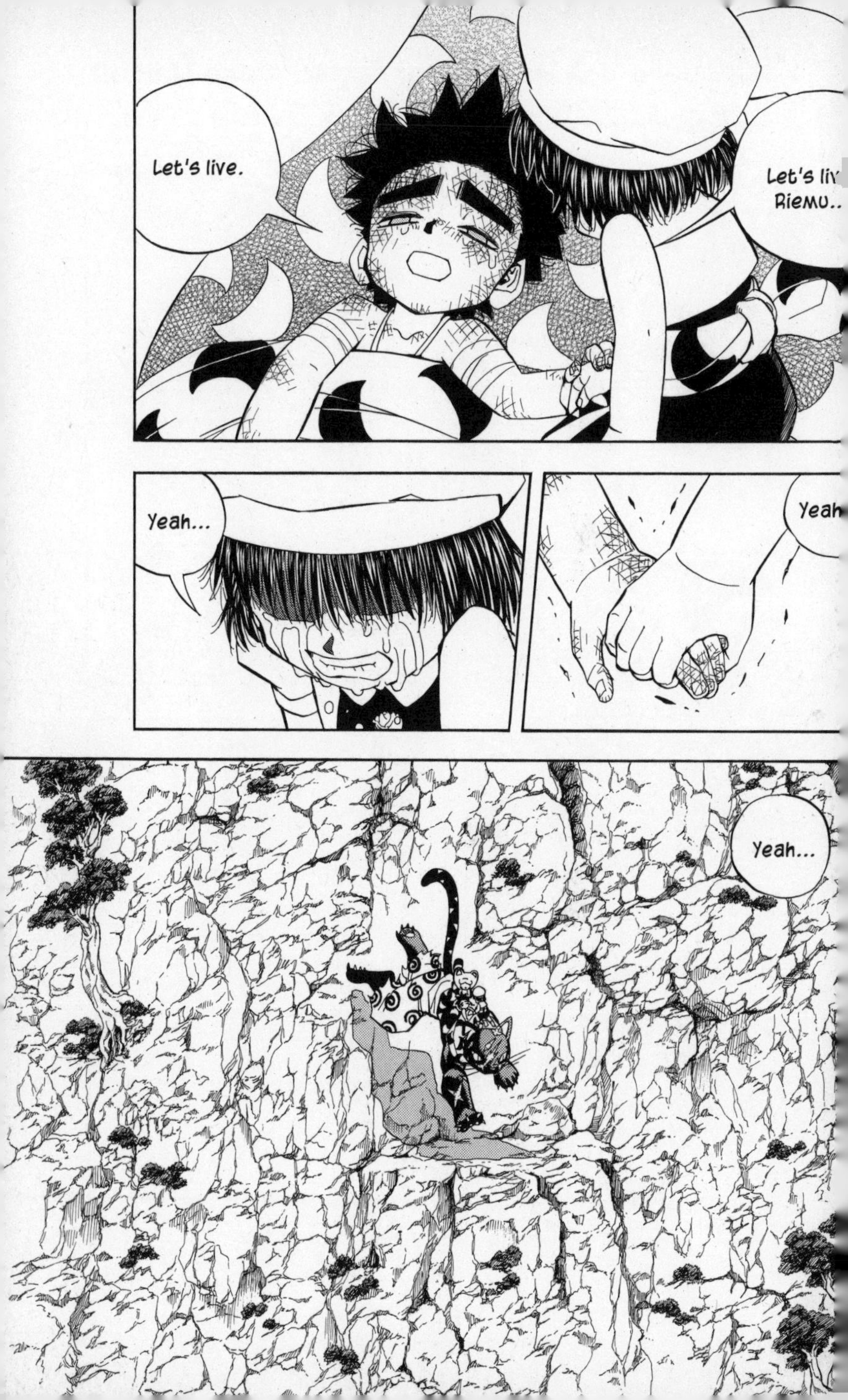
Let's liv
Riemu..
Let's live.
Yeah
Yeah...
Yeah...

Bonus Page 1: Crane Master Style!! Akiko Llama!!

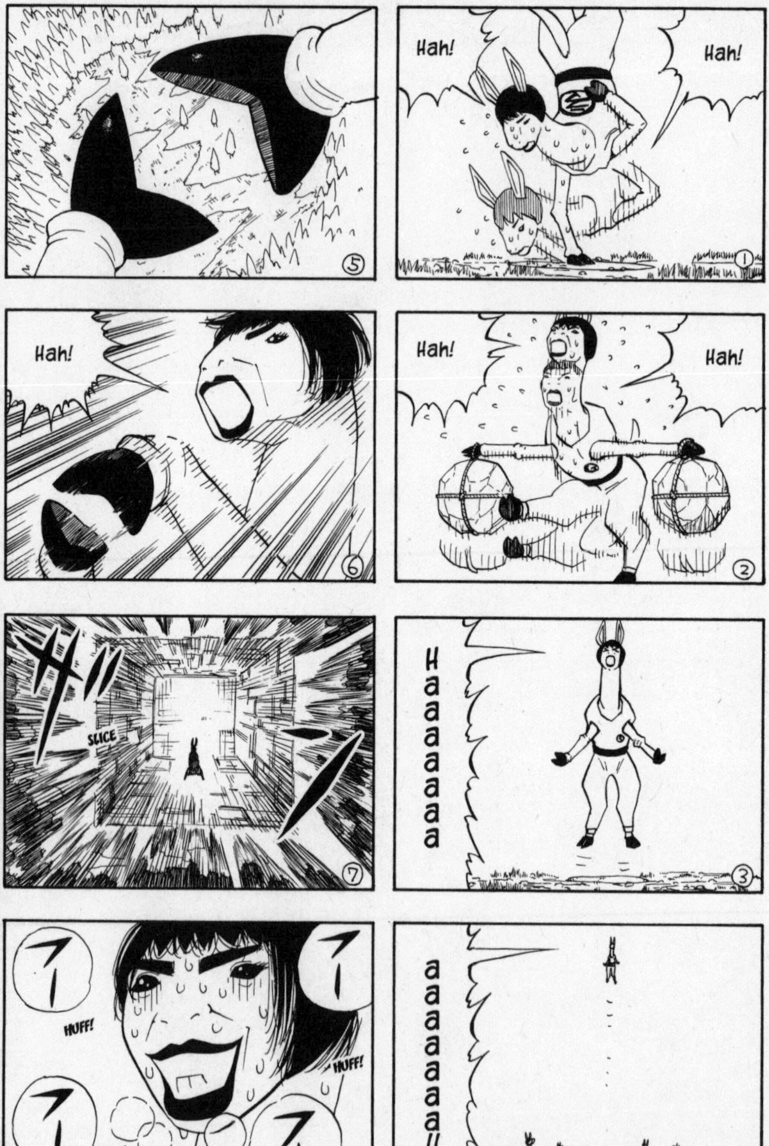
Hah!
Hah!
Hah!
Hah!
Haaaaaaa
aaaaaaa!!
Hah!
SLICE
HUFF!
HUFF!
HUFF!
HUFF!

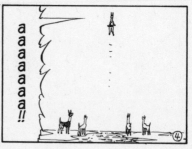

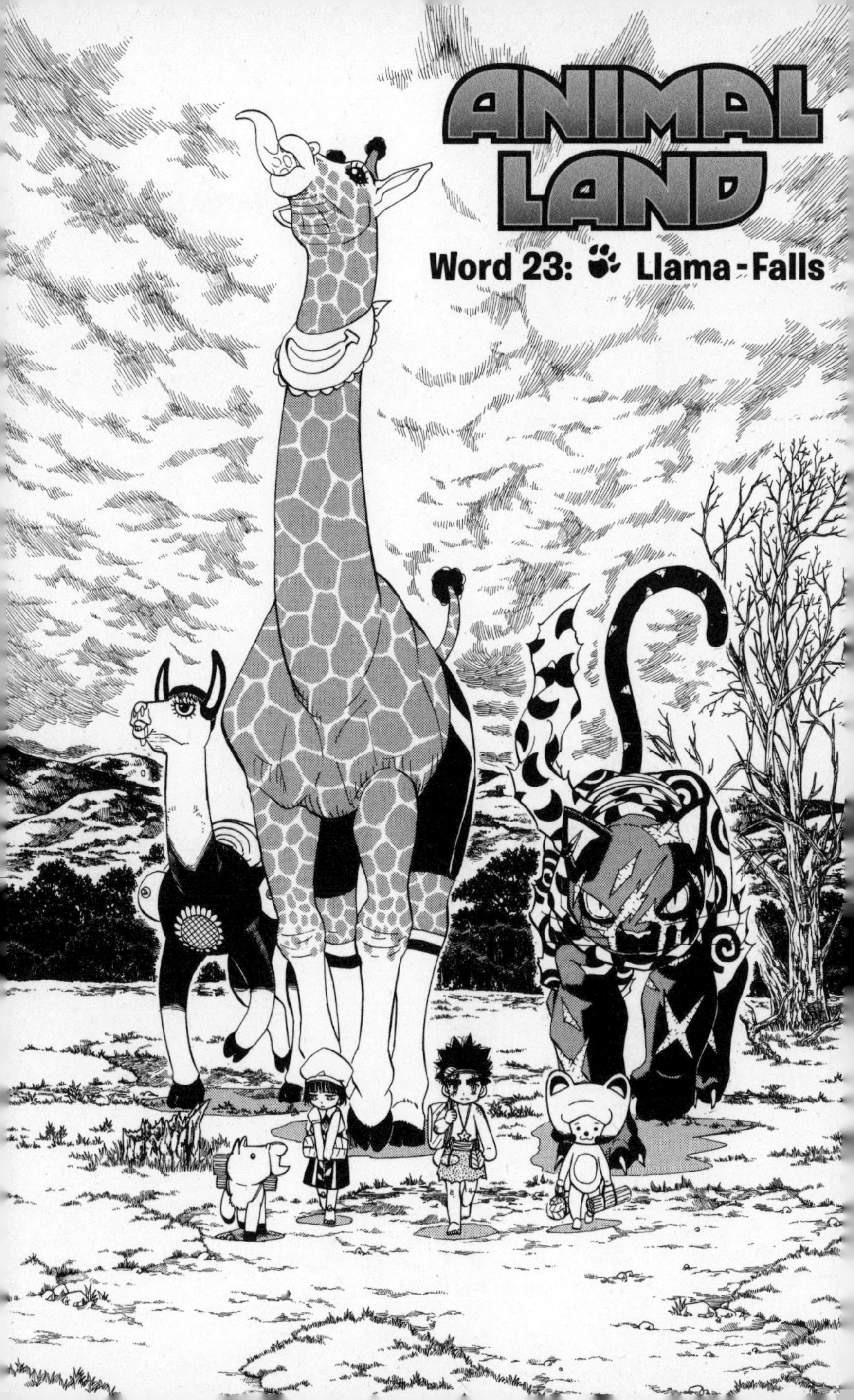
ANIMAL LAND
Word 23: Llama-Falls

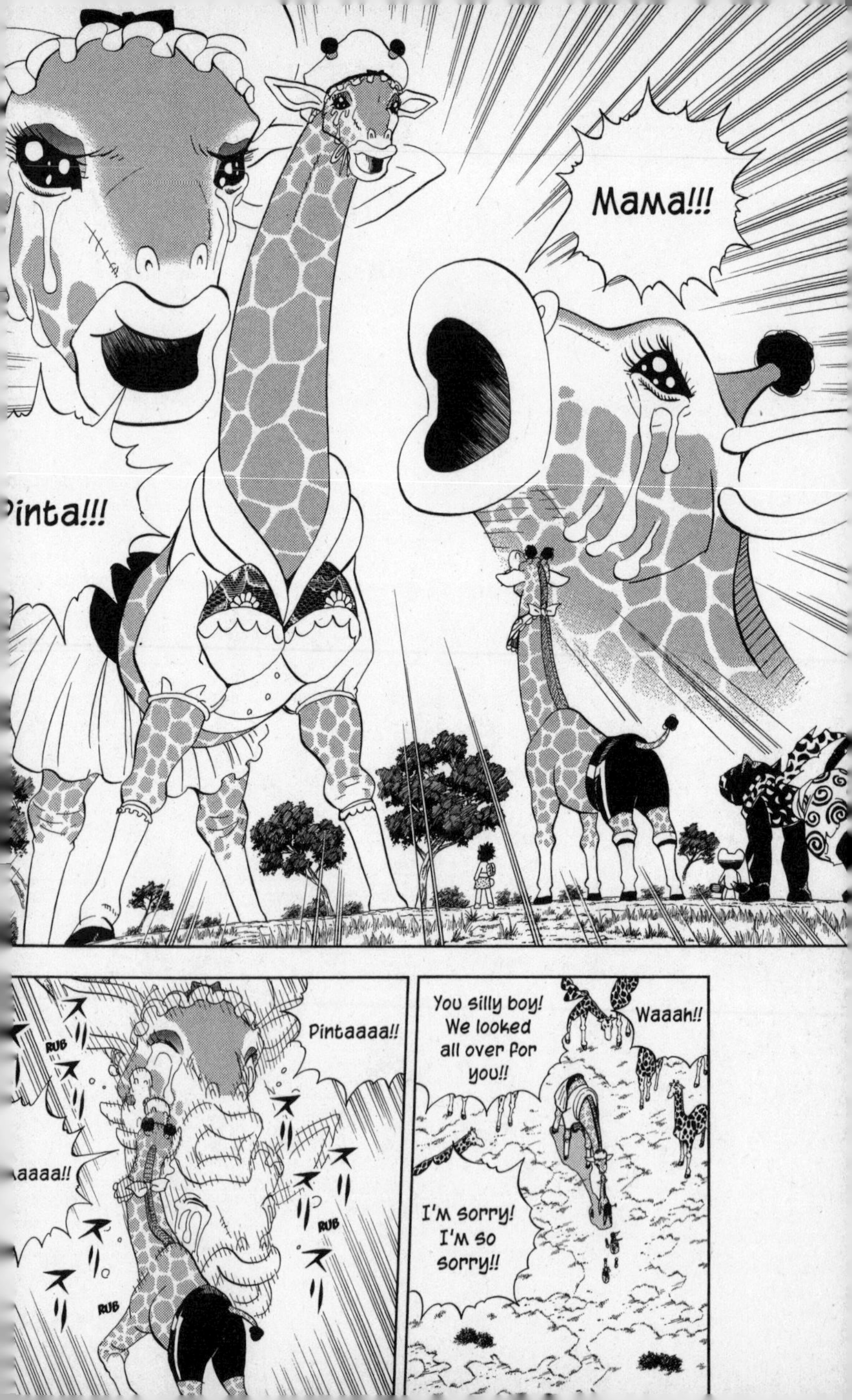
Mama!!!
Pinta!!!
Waaah!!
You silly boy! We looked all over for you!!
I'm sorry! I'm so sorry!!
Pintaaaa!!
RUB
RUB
RUB
aaaa!!

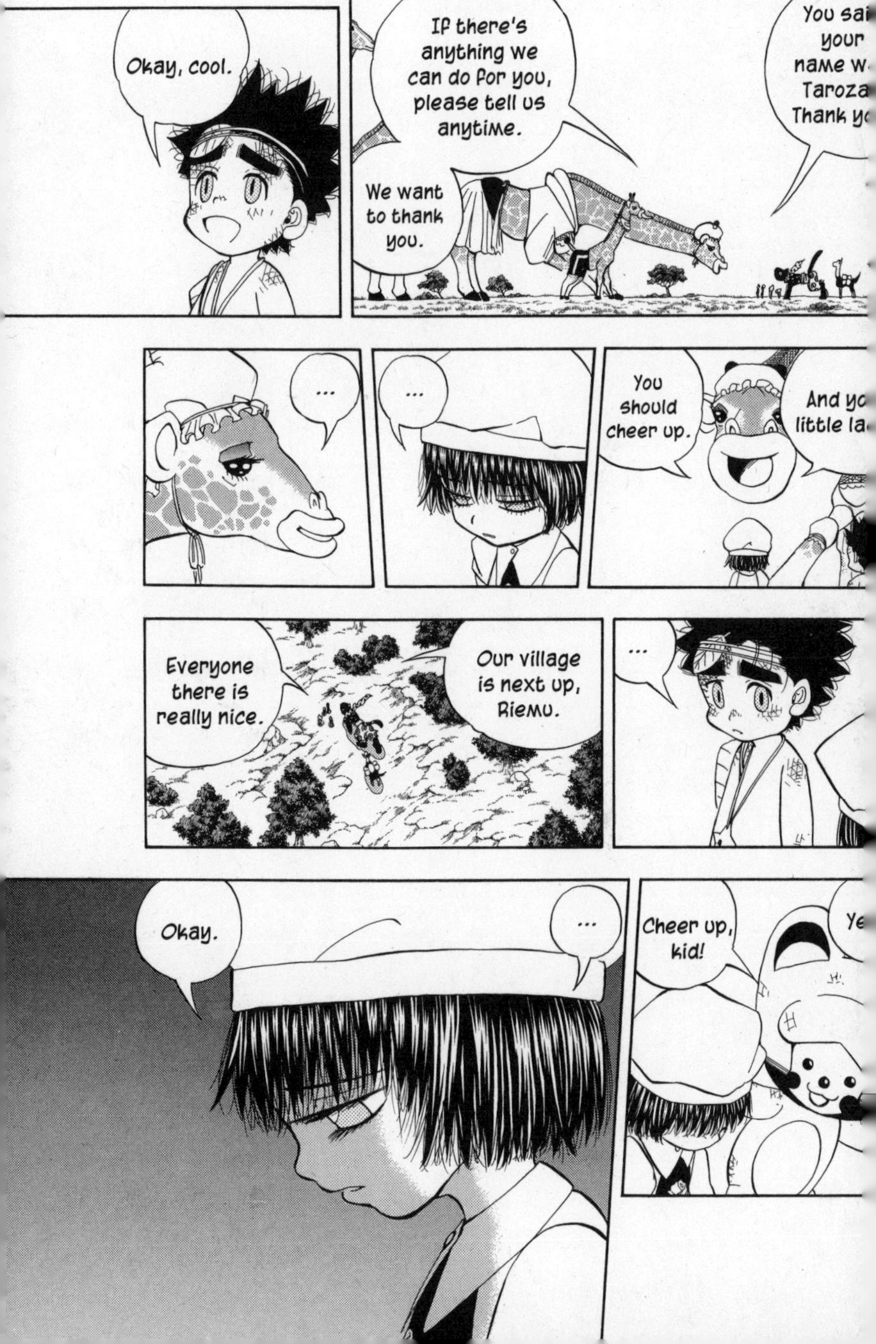
You sai your name w Taroza Thank yo
If there's anything we can do for you, please tell us anytime.
We want to thank you.
Okay, cool.
And yo little la
You should cheer up.
...
...
...
Our village is next up, Riemu.
Everyone there is really nice.
Ye
Cheer up, kid!
...
Okay.

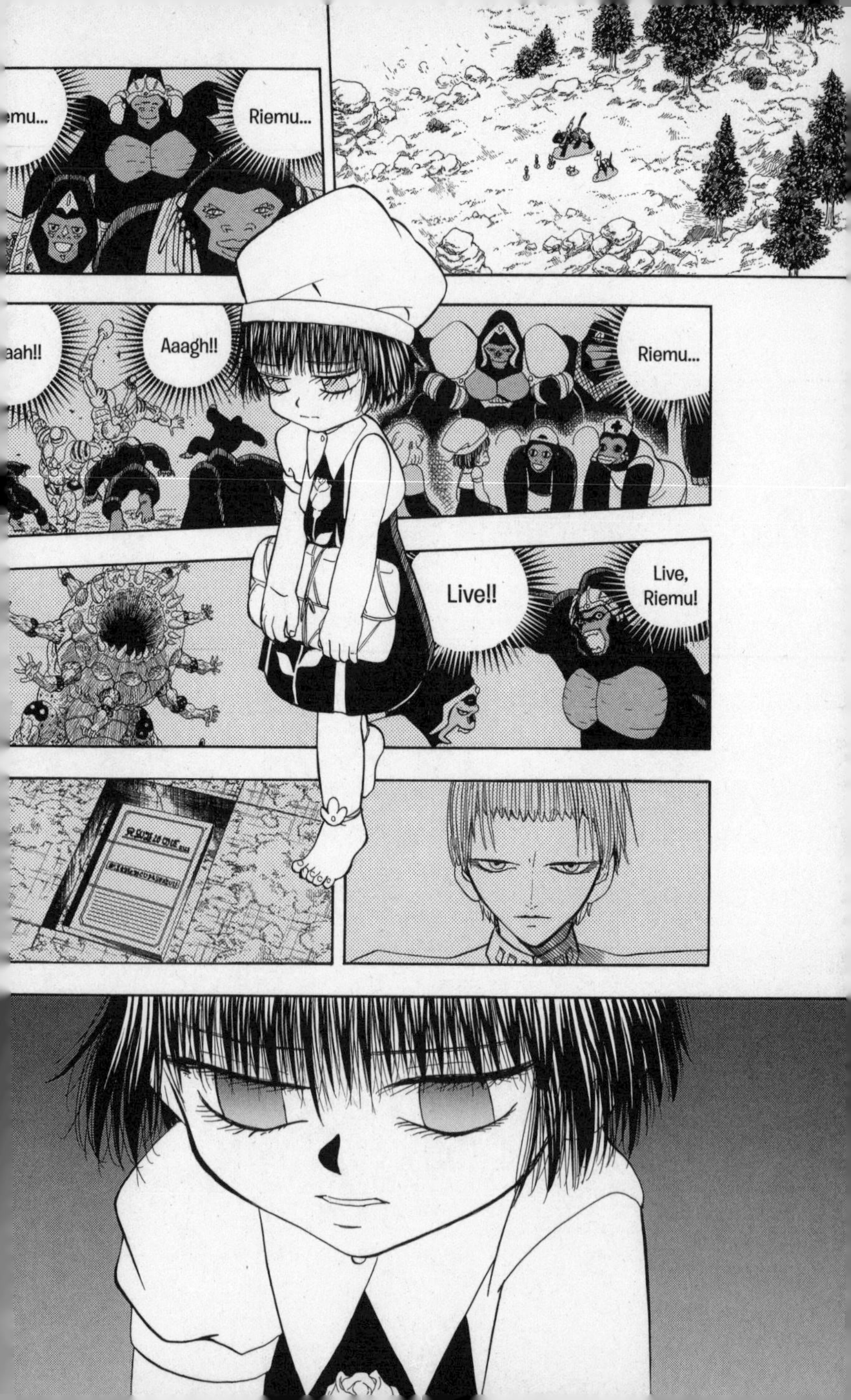
Riemu...
emu...
Riemu...
Aaagh!!
aah!!
Live, Riemu!
Live!!

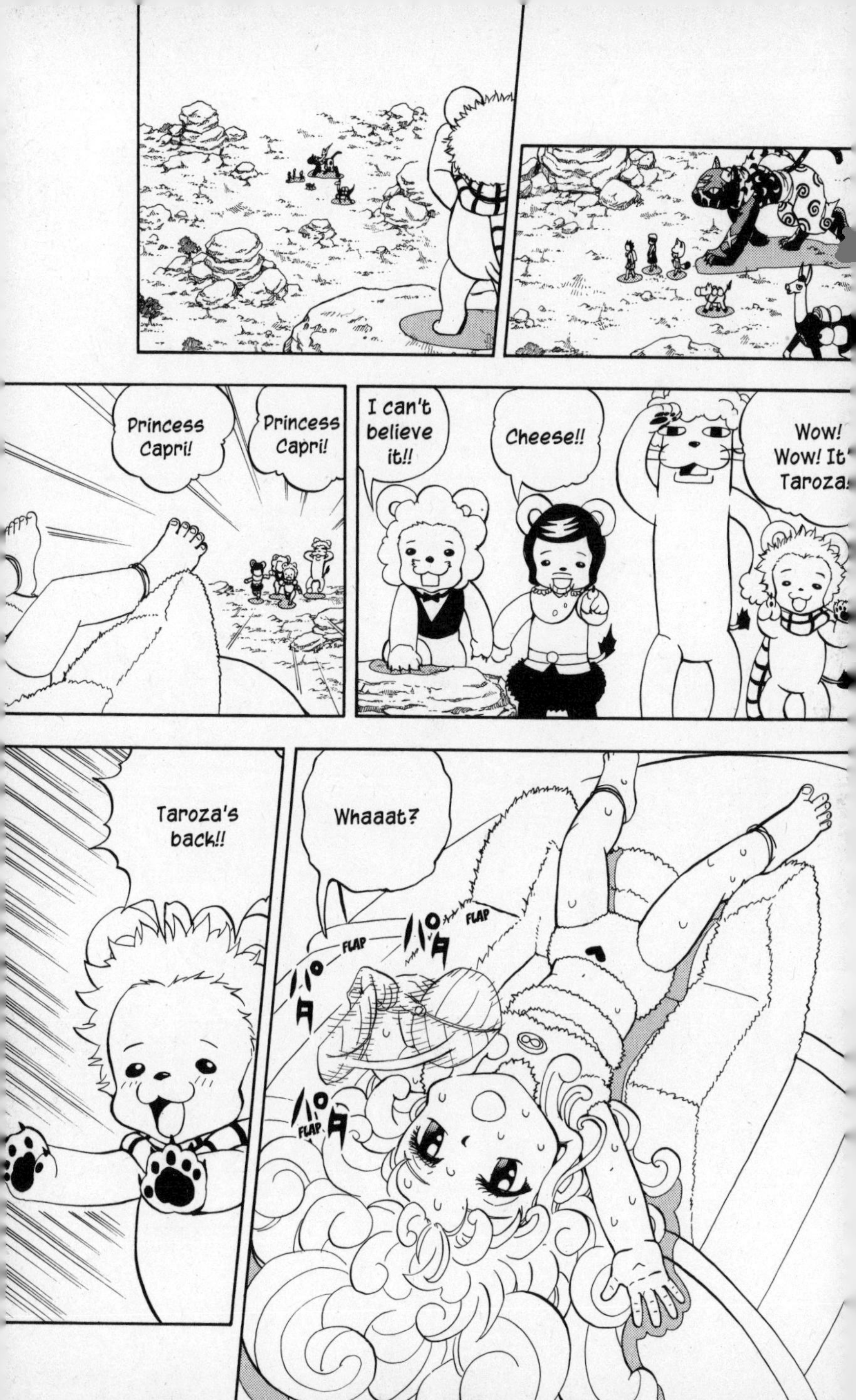
Wow! Wow! It' Taroza!
Cheese!!
I can't believe it!!
Princess Capri!
Princess Capri!
FLAP
FLAP
Whaaat?
FLAP
Taroza's back!!

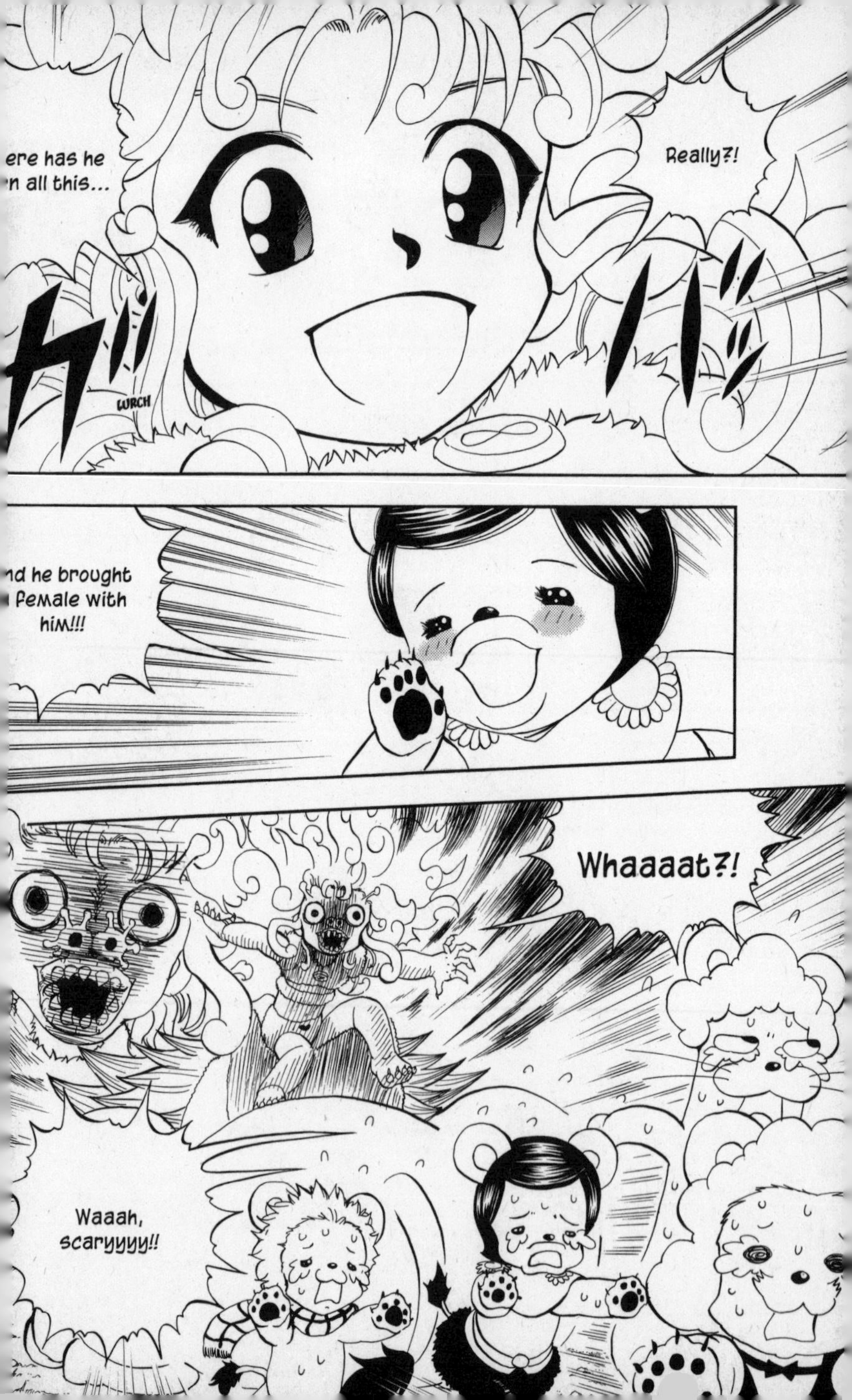
Really?!
ere has he
n all this...
LURCH
nd he brought
female with
him!!!
Whaaaat?!
Waaah,
scaryyyy!!

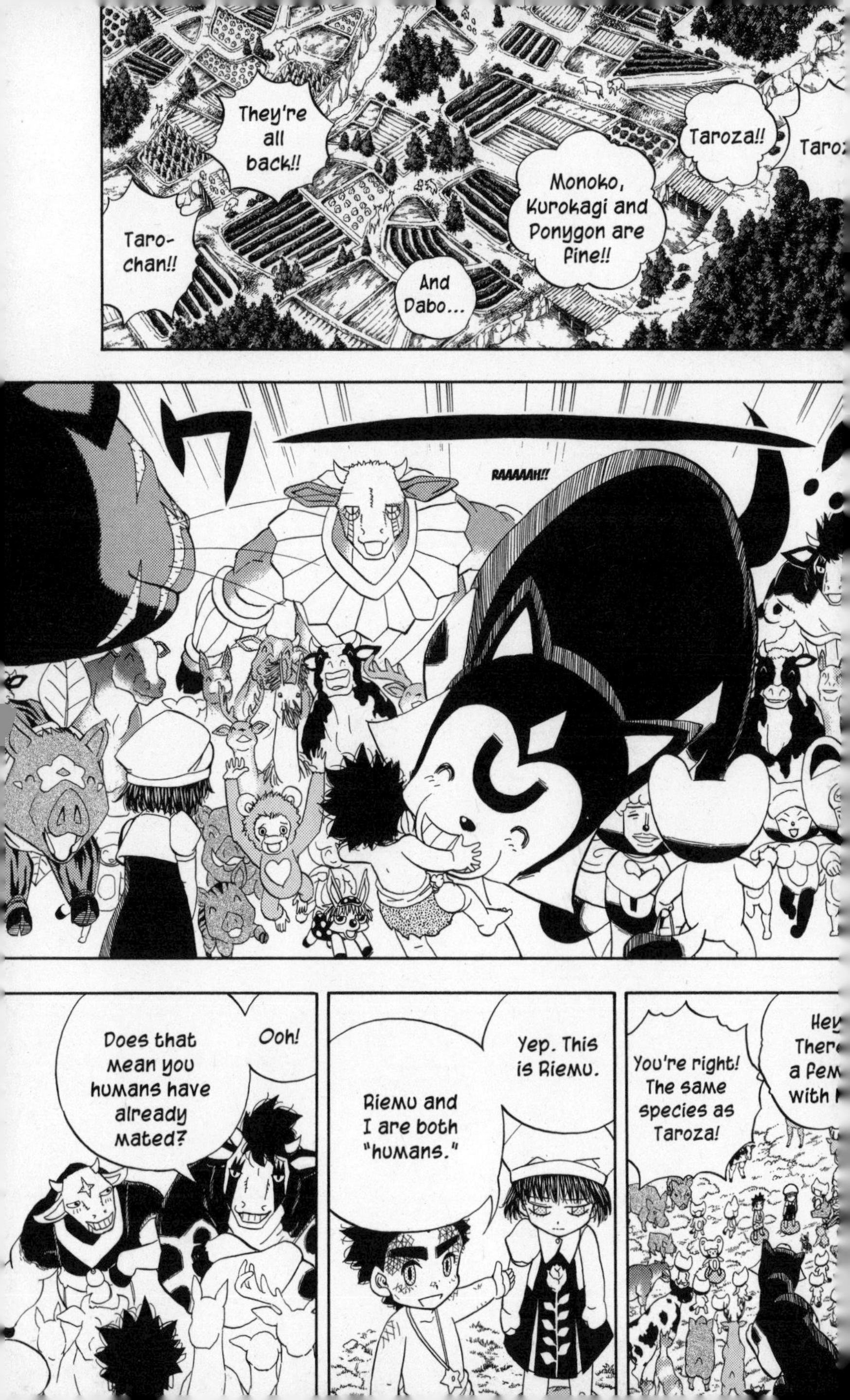
Taroza!!
Monoko, Kurokagi and Ponygon are fine!!
And Dabo...
They're all back!!
Taro-chan!!
RAAAAAH!!
You're right! The same species as Taroza!
Yep. This is Riemu.
Riemu and I are both "humans."
Ooh!
Does that mean you humans have already mated?

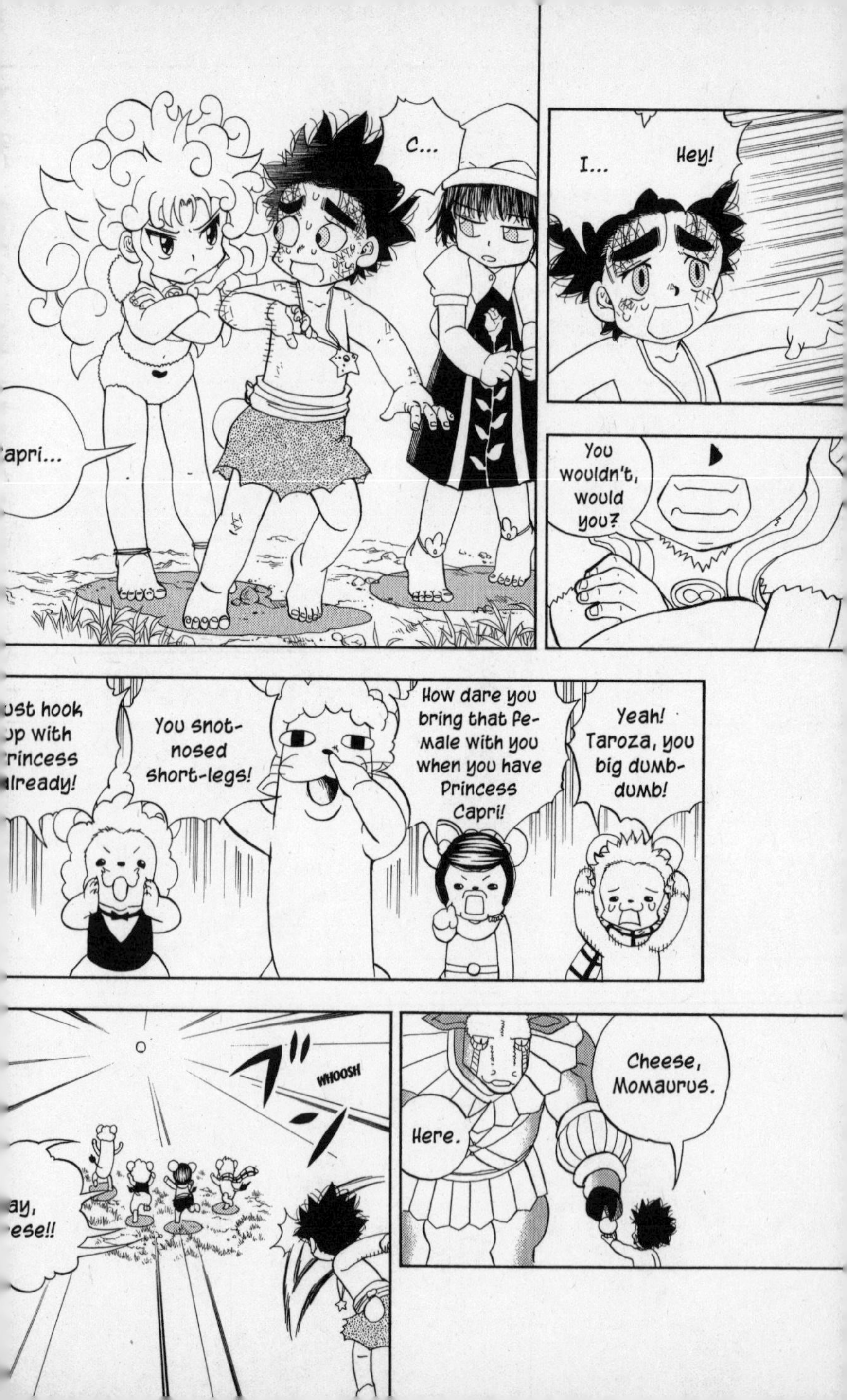
Hey!
I...
You wouldn't, would you?
C...
apri...
Yeah! Taroza, you big dumb-dumb!
How dare you bring that fe-male with you when you have Princess Capri!
You snot-nosed short-legs!
ust hook up with rincess already!
Cheese, Momaurus.
Here.
WHOOSH
ay, ese!!

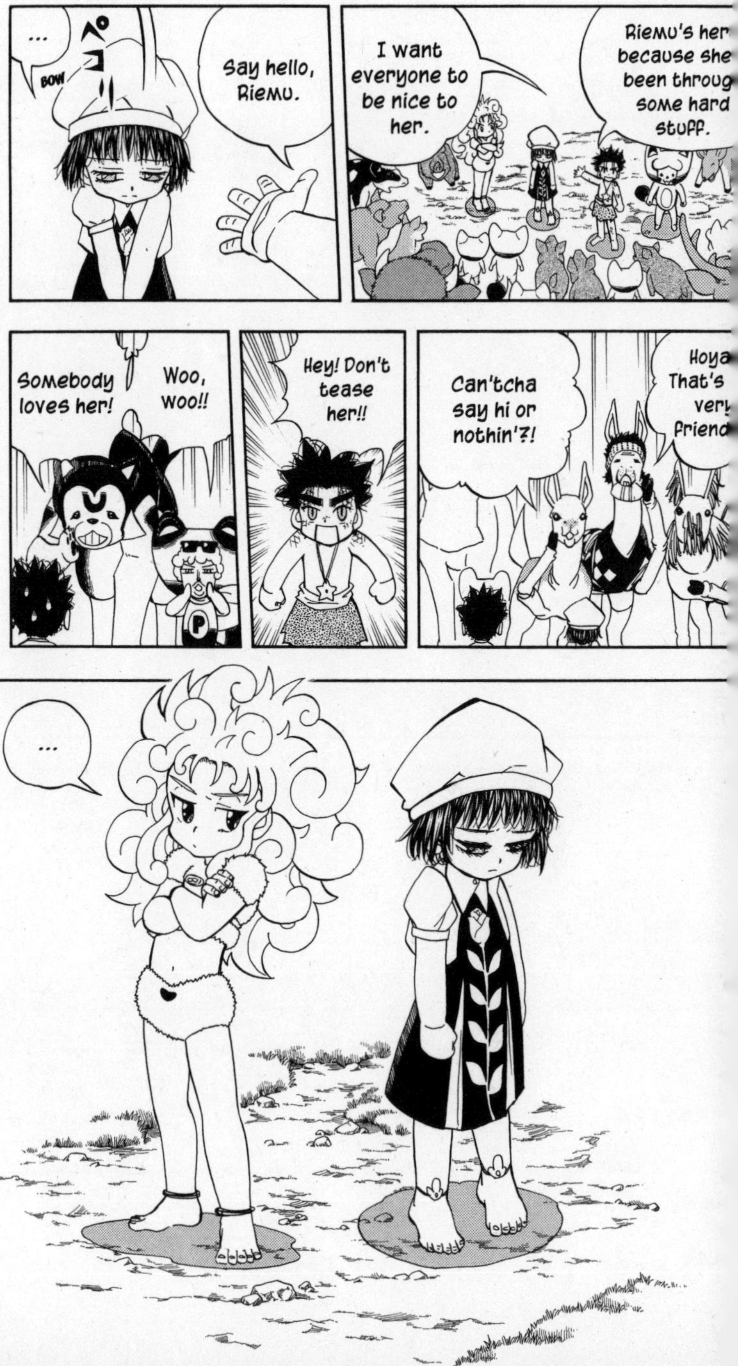
Riemu's her because she been throug some hard stuff.
I want everyone to be nice to her.
Say hello, Riemu.
ペコ
BOW
...
Hoya That's very friend
Can'tcha say hi or nothin'?!
Hey! Don't tease her!!
Woo, woo!!
Somebody loves her!
...

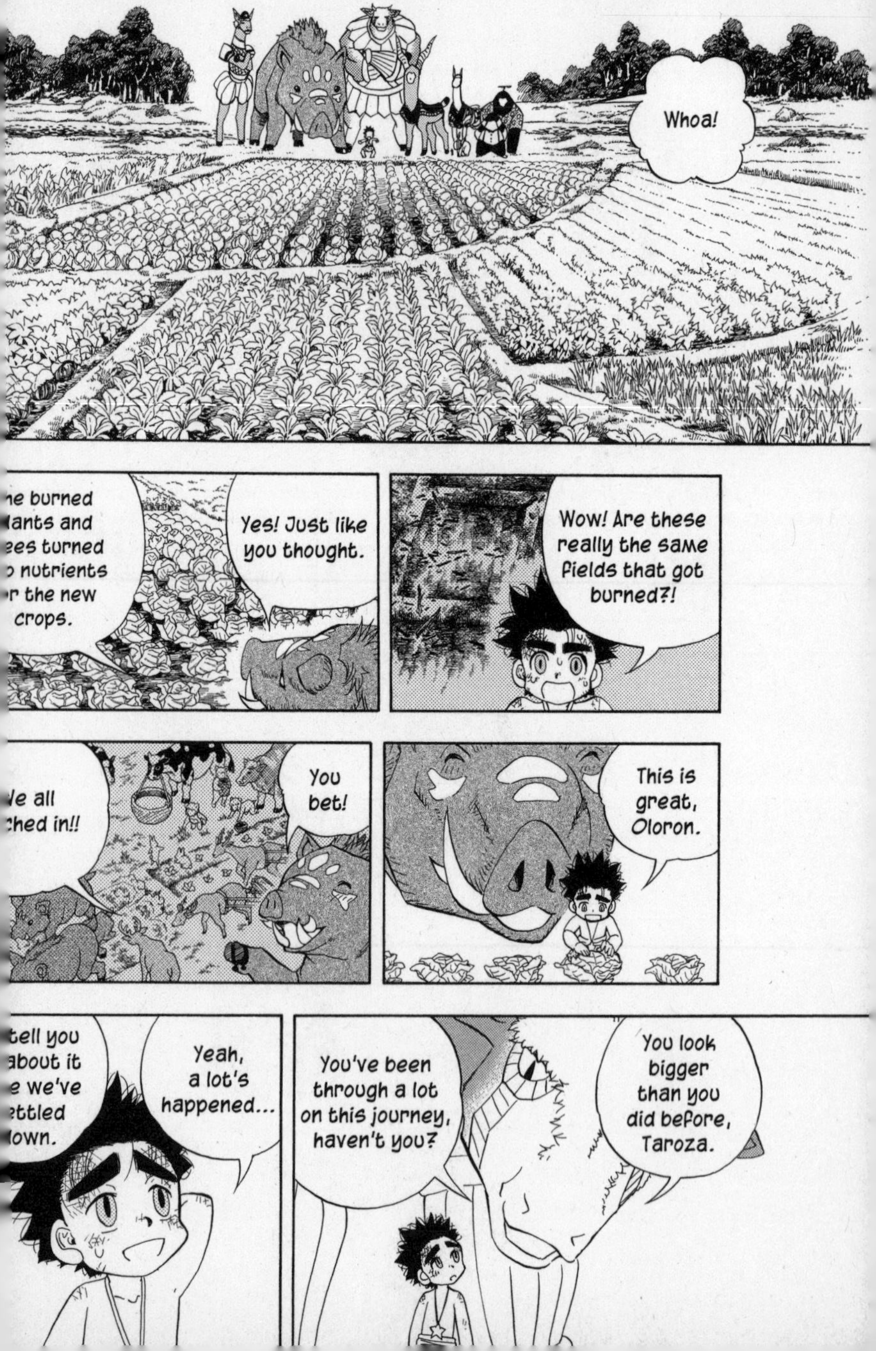
Whoa!
Wow! Are these really the same fields that got burned?!
Yes! Just like you thought.
ne burned lants and ees turned o nutrients r the new crops.
This is great, Oloron.
You bet!
e all hed in!!
You look bigger than you did before, Taroza.
You've been through a lot on this journey, haven't you?
Yeah, a lot's happened...
tell you about it e we've ettled own.

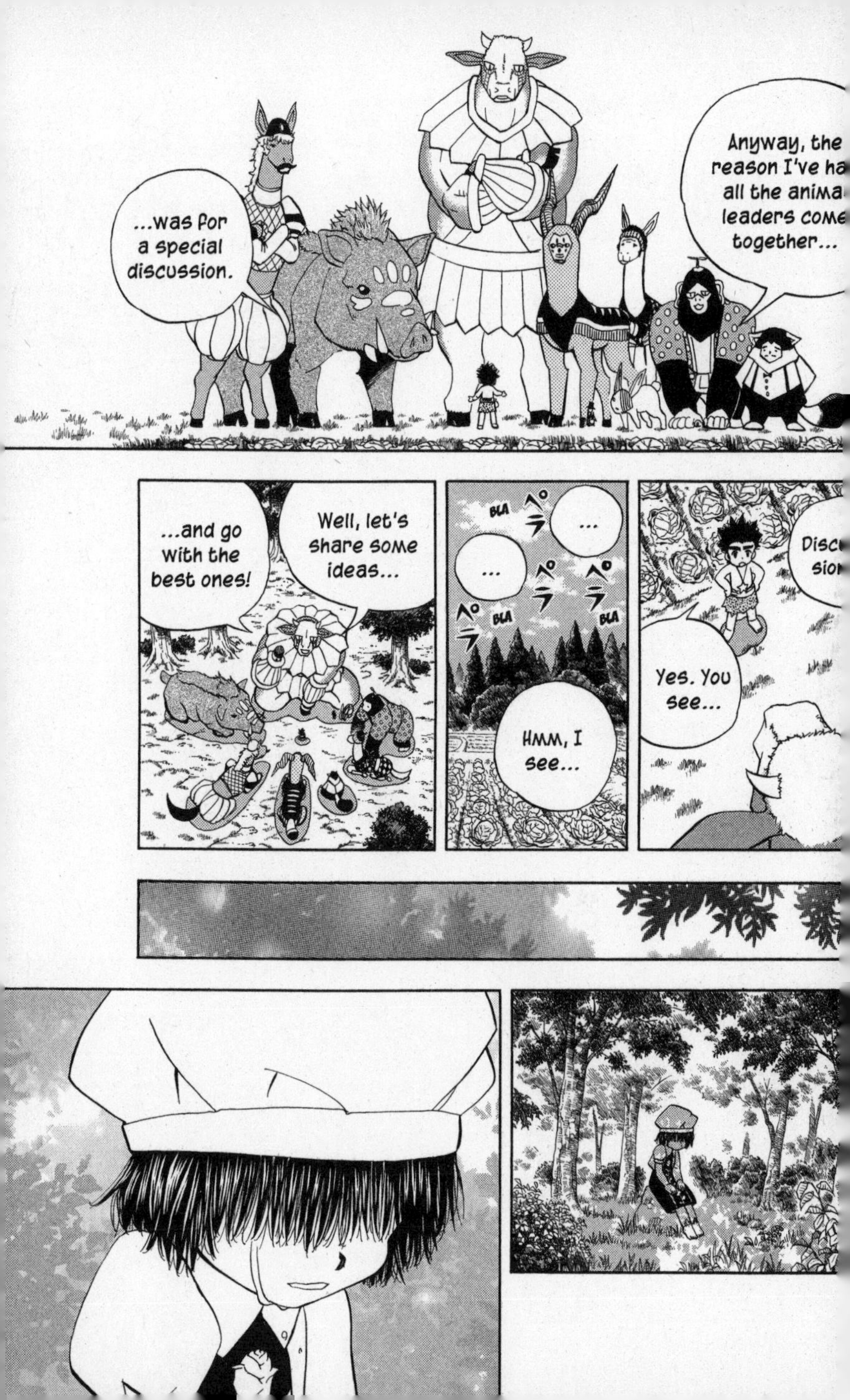
Anyway, the reason I've ha all the anima leaders come together...
...was for a special discussion.
Disc sion
Yes. You see...
BLA
...
...
BLA
BLA
HMM, I see...
Well, let's share some ideas...
...and go with the best ones!

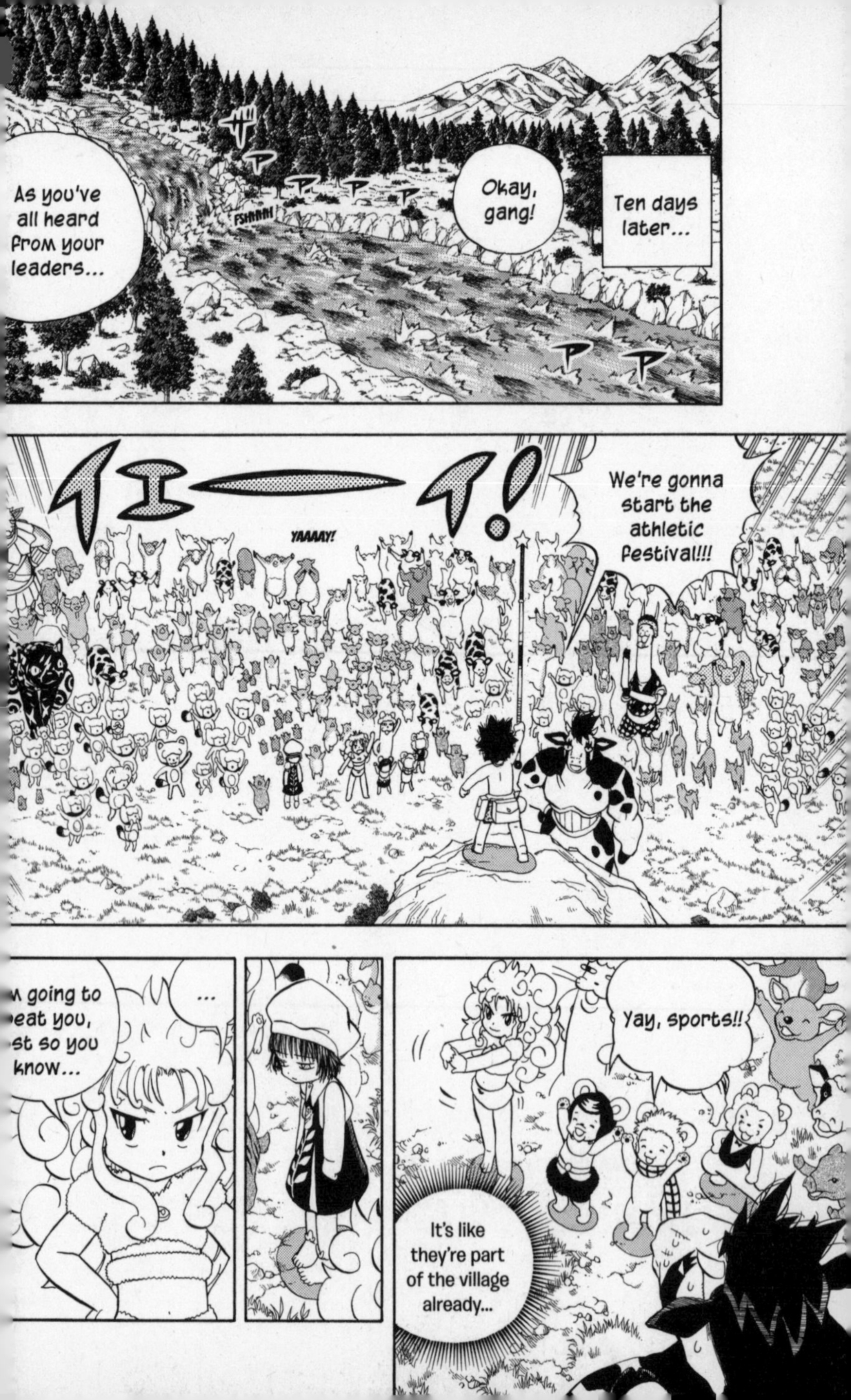
Ten days later...
Okay, gang!
FSHHHHH
As you've all heard from your leaders...
We're gonna start the athletic festival!!!
イエーーーイ!
YAAAAY!
Yay, sports!!
It's like they're part of the village already...
...
m going to eat you, st so you know...

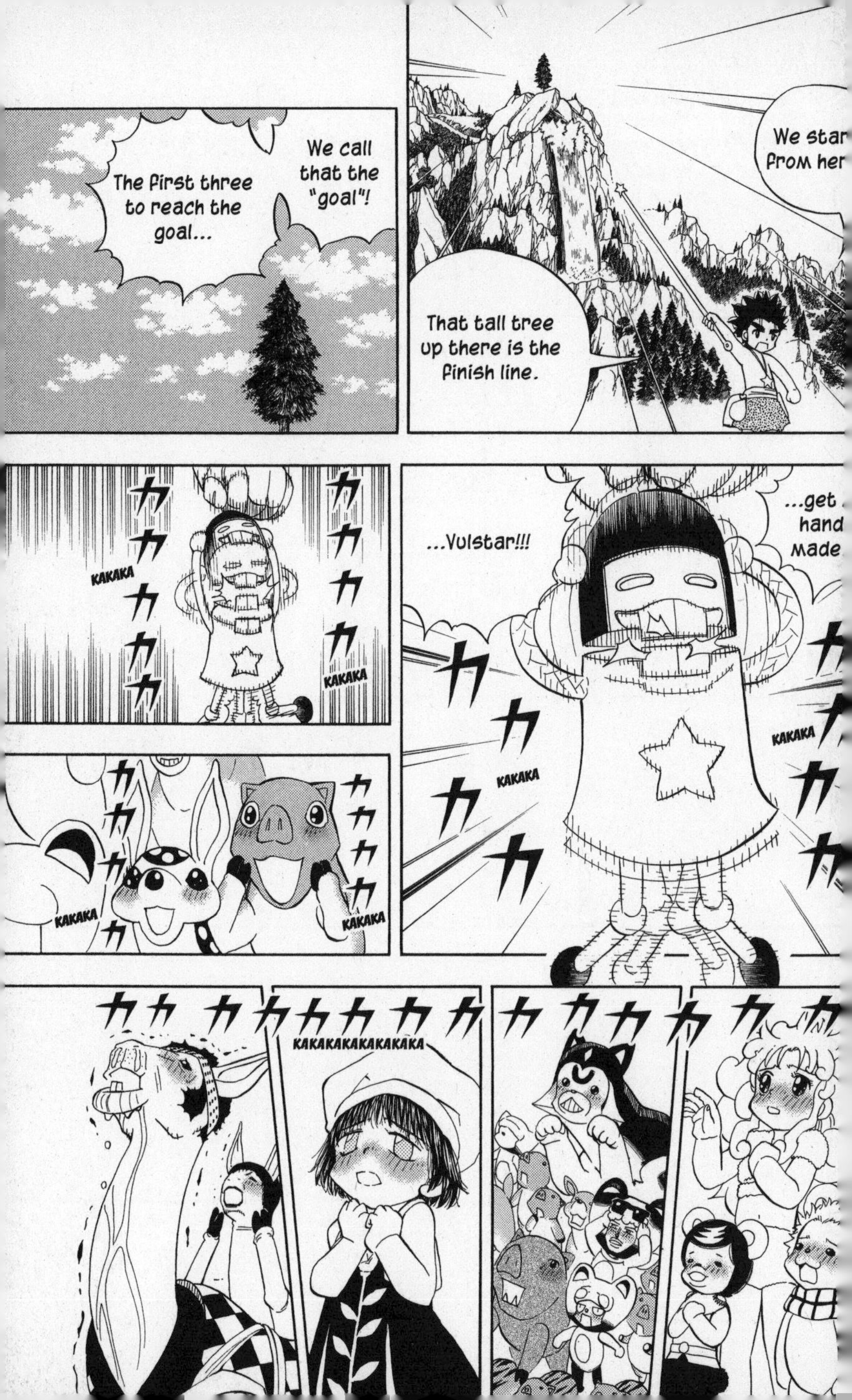
We star
from her
That tall tree up there is the finish line.
We call that the "goal"!
The first three to reach the goal...
...get
hand
made
...Vulstar!!!
KAKAKA
KAKAKA
KAKAKA
KAKAKA
KAKAKA
KAKAKA
KAKAKAKAKAKAKAKA

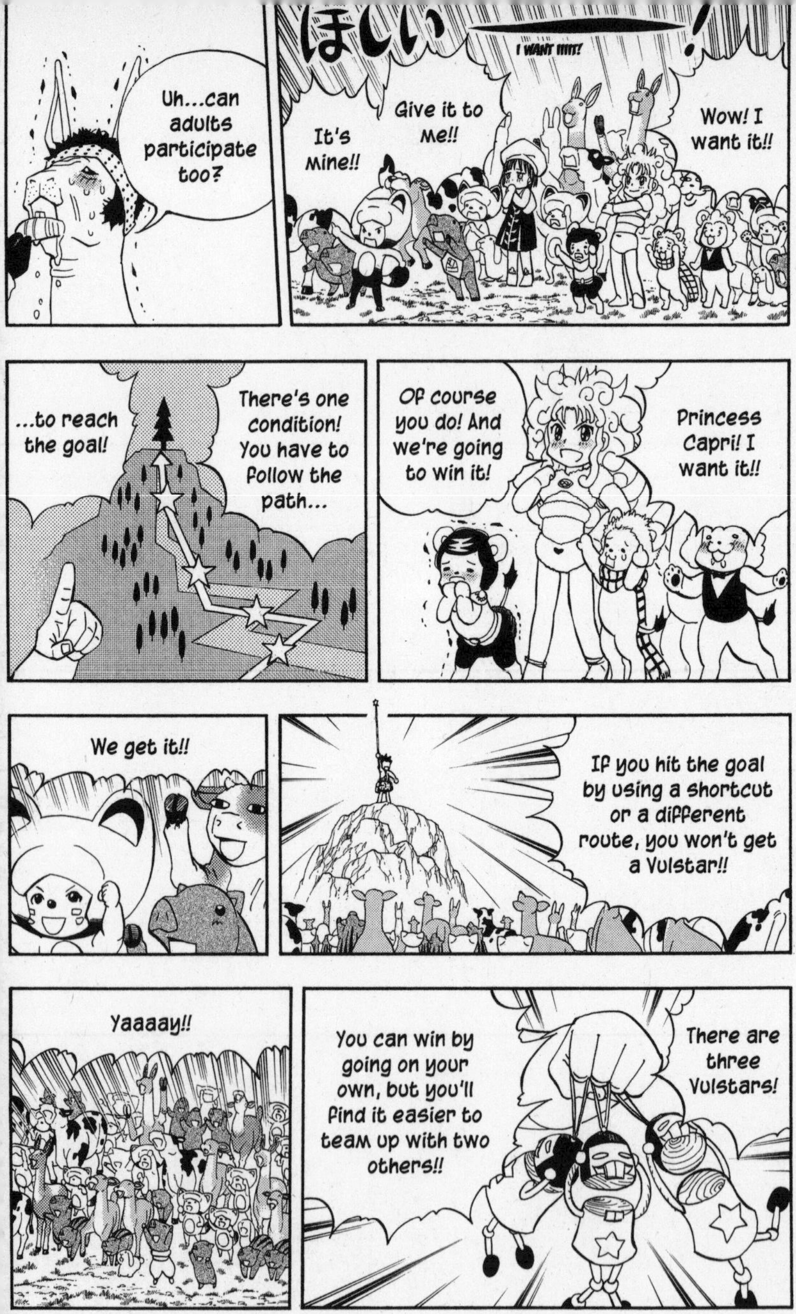
ほしい—!
I WANT IIIIT!
Wow! I want it!!
Give it to me!!
It's mine!!
Uh...can adults participate too?
Princess Capri! I want it!!
Of course you do! And we're going to win it!
There's one condition! You have to follow the path...
...to reach the goal!
If you hit the goal by using a shortcut or a different route, you won't get a Vulstar!!
We get it!!
There are three Vulstars!
You can win by going on your own, but you'll find it easier to team up with two others!!
Yaaaay!!

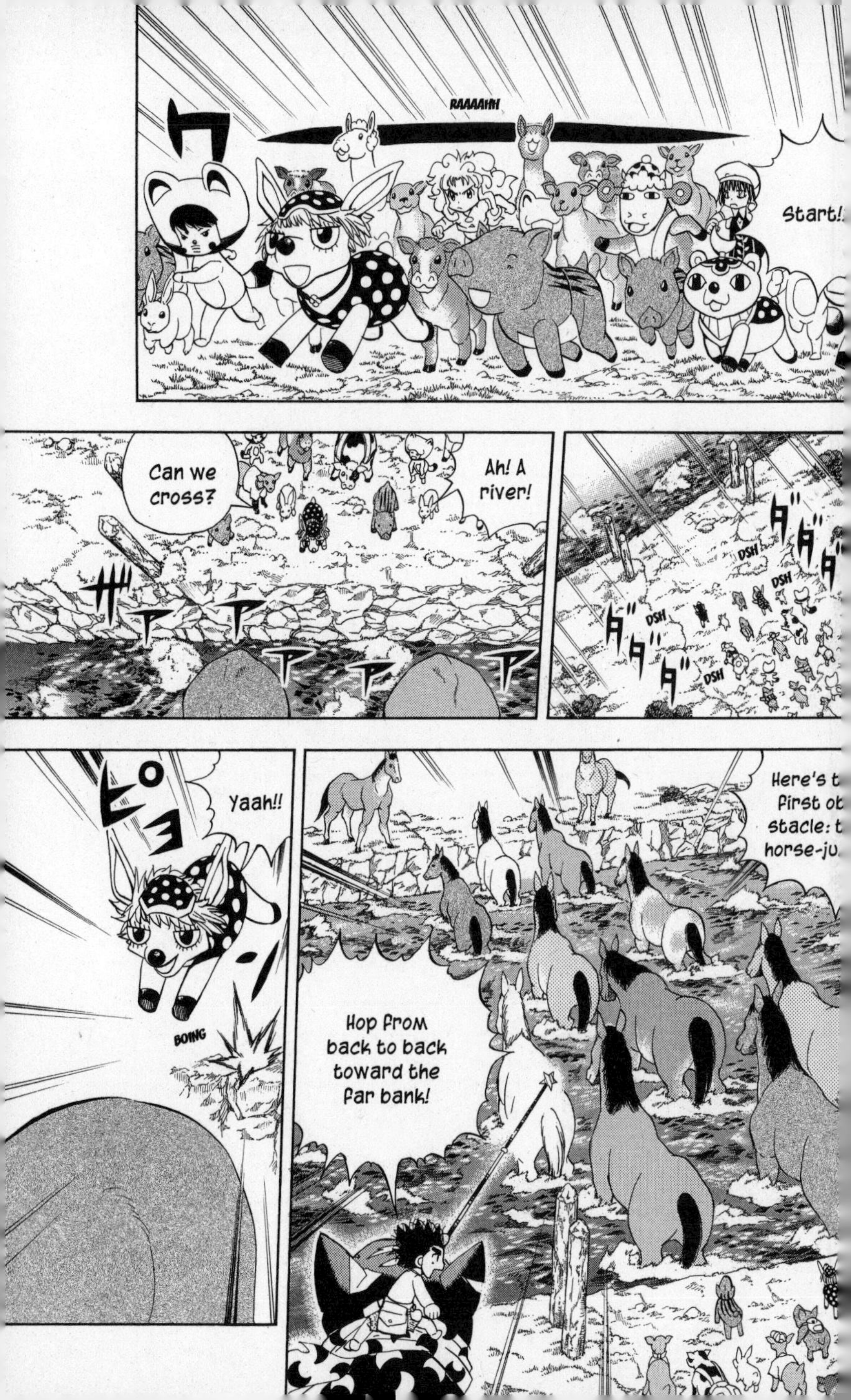
RAAAAHH
Start!
DSH
DSH
DSH
DSH
Ah! A river!
Can we cross?
Here's t first ob stacle: t horse-ju
Hop from back to back toward the far bank!
Yaah!!
BOING

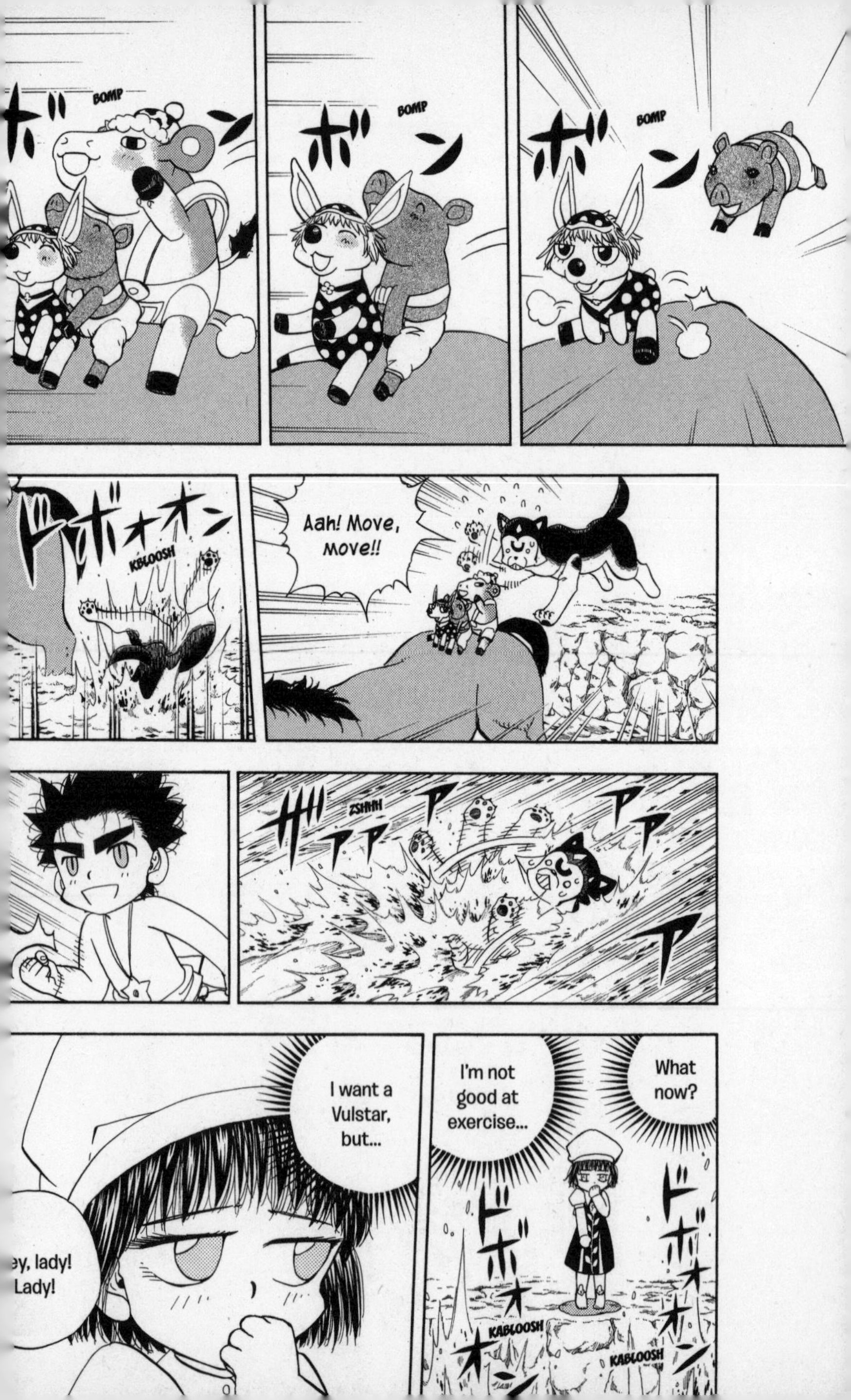
BOMP
BOMP
BOMP
Aah! Move, move!!
KBLOOSH
ZSHHH
What now?
I'm not good at exercise...
KABLOOSH
KABLOOSH
I want a Vulstar, but...
ey, lady! Lady!

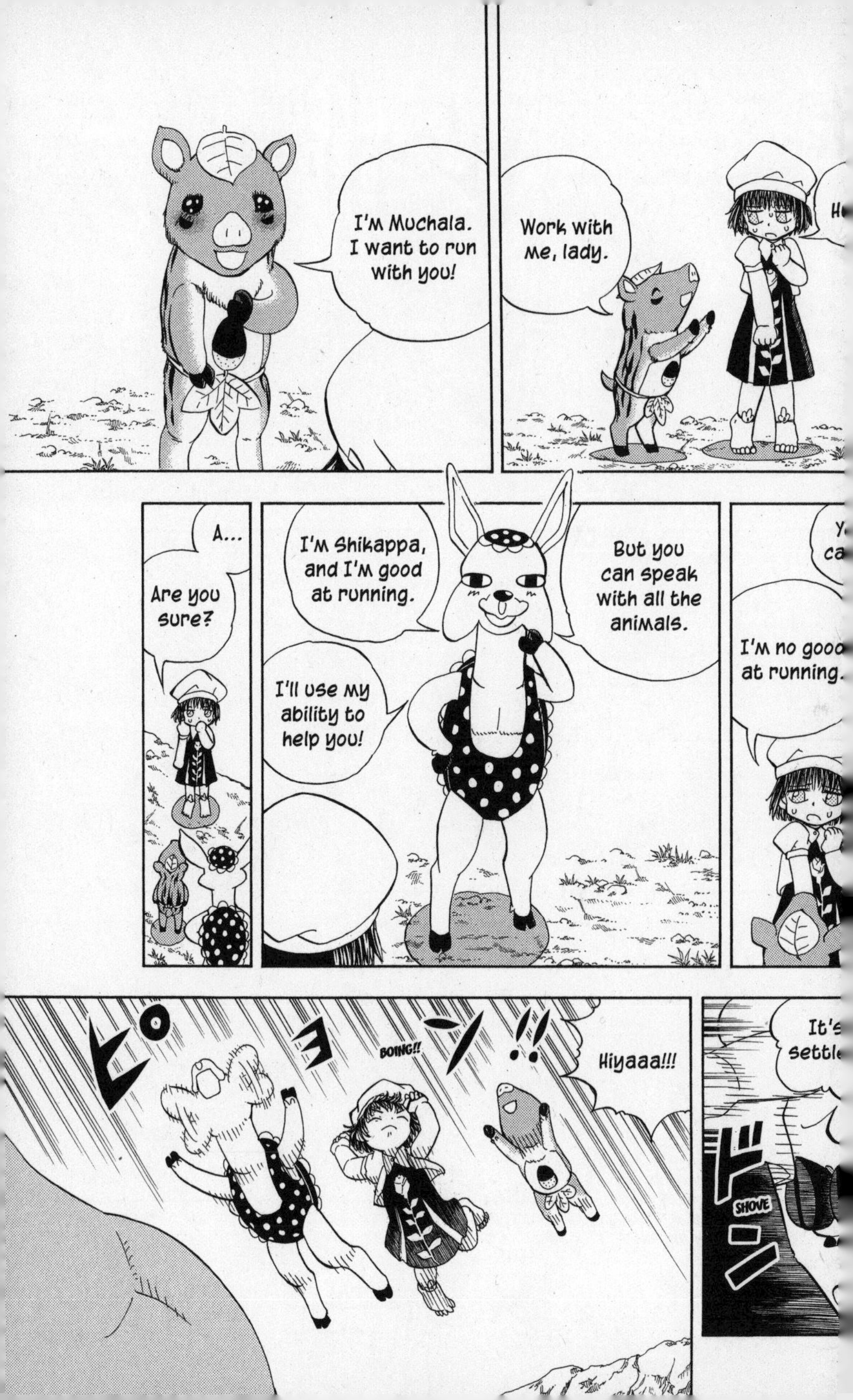

Work with me, lady.
I'm Muchala. I want to run with you!
I'm no good at running.
But you can speak with all the animals.
I'm Shikappa, and I'm good at running.
I'll use my ability to help you!
A...
Are you sure?
SHOVE
Hiyaaa!!!
BOING!!

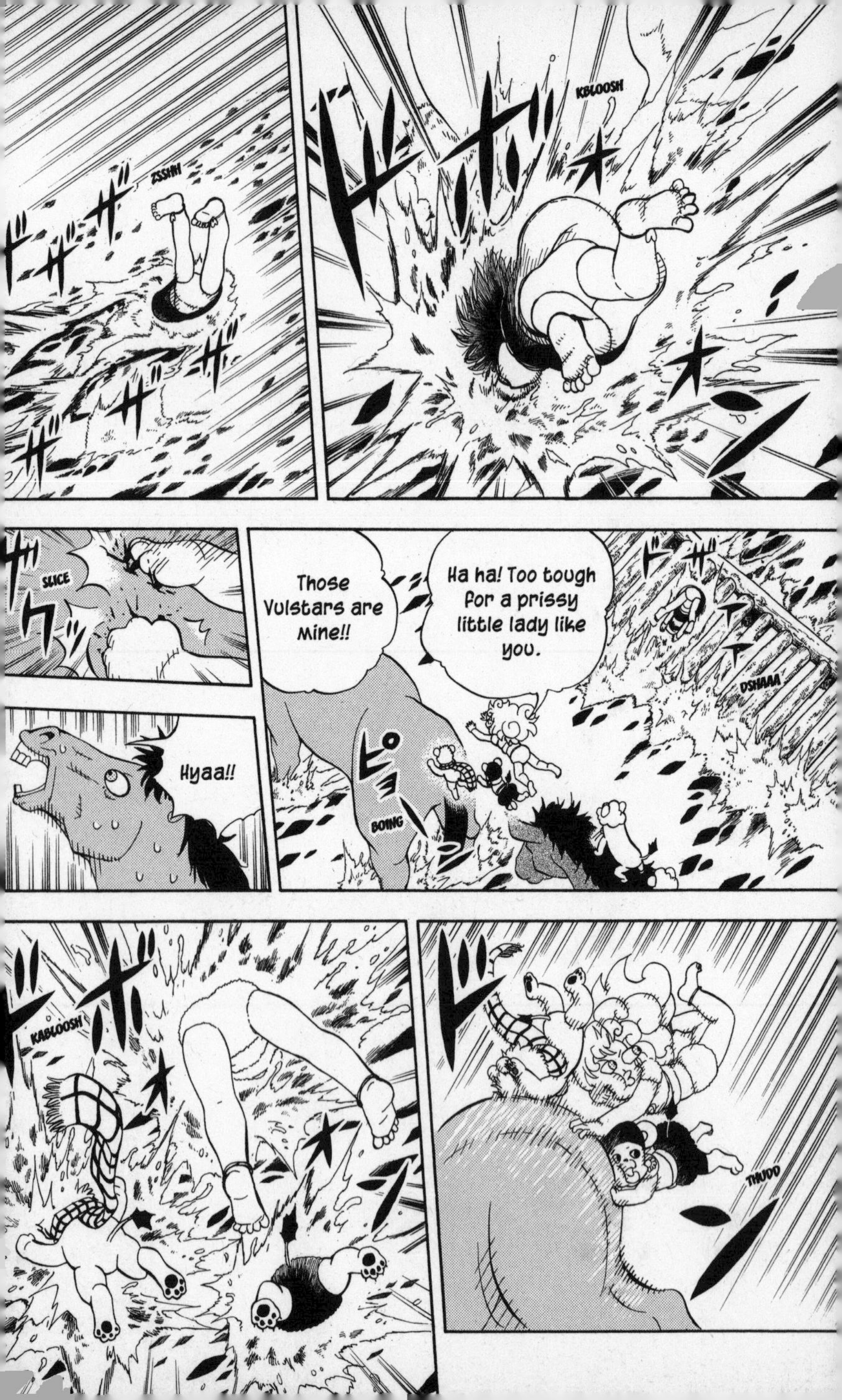

KBLOOSH
ZSSHH
Ha ha! Too tough for a prissy little lady like you.
Those Vulstars are Mine!!
DSHAAA
BOING
SLICE
Hyaa!!
THUDD
KABLOOSH

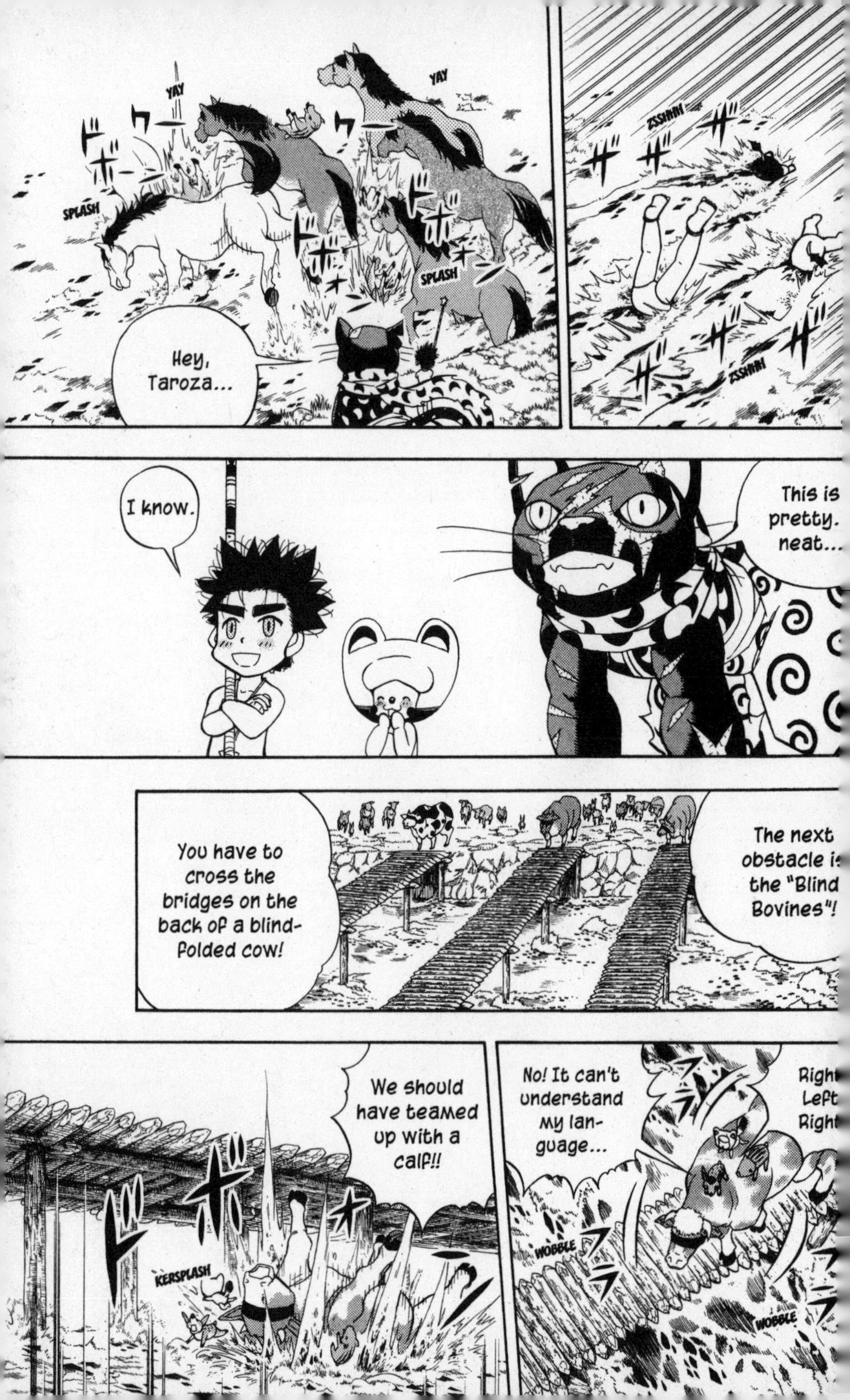
ZSSHHH
ZSSHHH
YAY
YAY
SPLASH
SPLASH
Hey, Taroza...
This is pretty. neat...
I know.
The next obstacle is the "Blind Bovines"!
You have to cross the bridges on the back of a blind-folded cow!
Righ Left Righ
No! It can't understand my language...
WOBBLE
WOBBLE
We should have teamed up with a calf!!
KERSPLASH

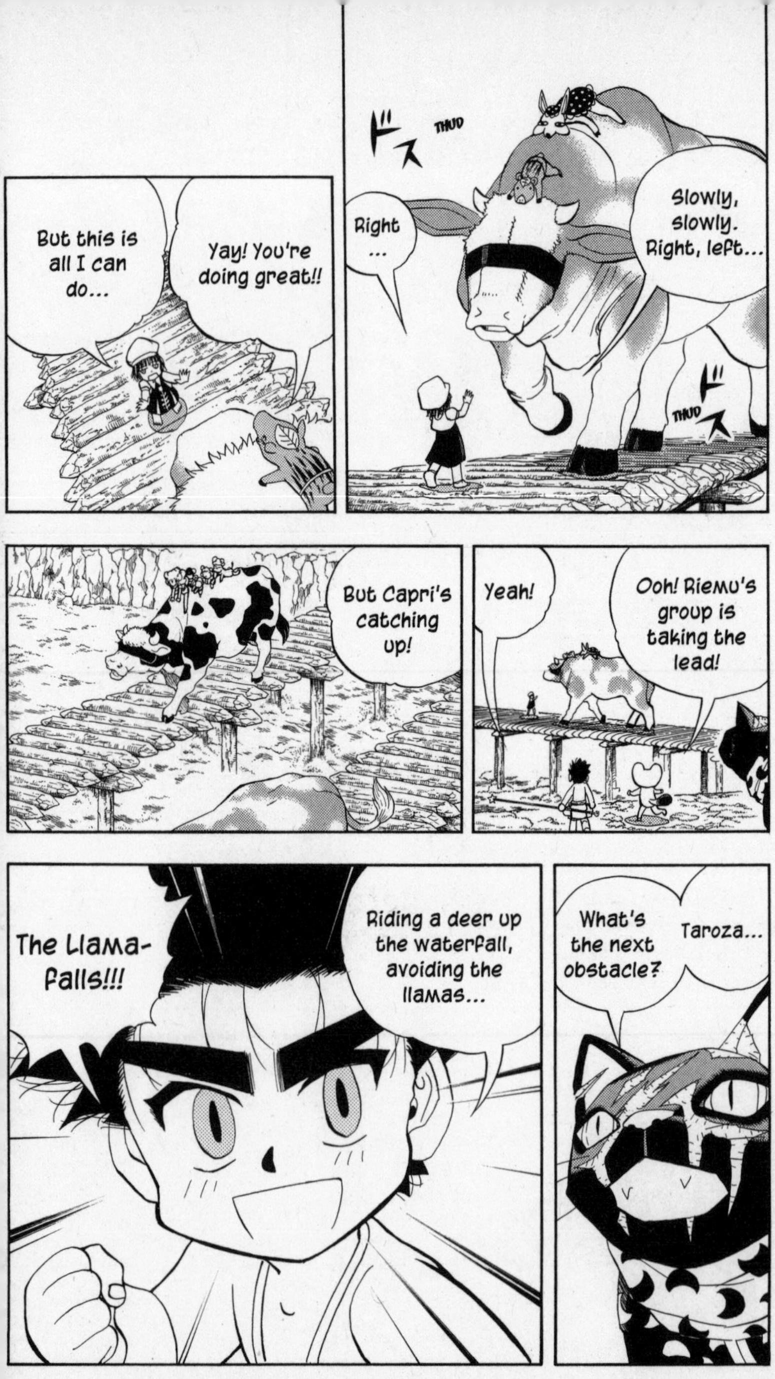
ドス THUD
Slowly, slowly. Right, left...
Right ...
ドス THUD
Yay! You're doing great!!
But this is all I can do...
Ooh! Riemu's group is taking the lead!
Yeah!
But Capri's catching up!
Taroza...
What's the next obstacle?
Riding a deer up the waterfall, avoiding the llamas...
The Llama-falls!!!

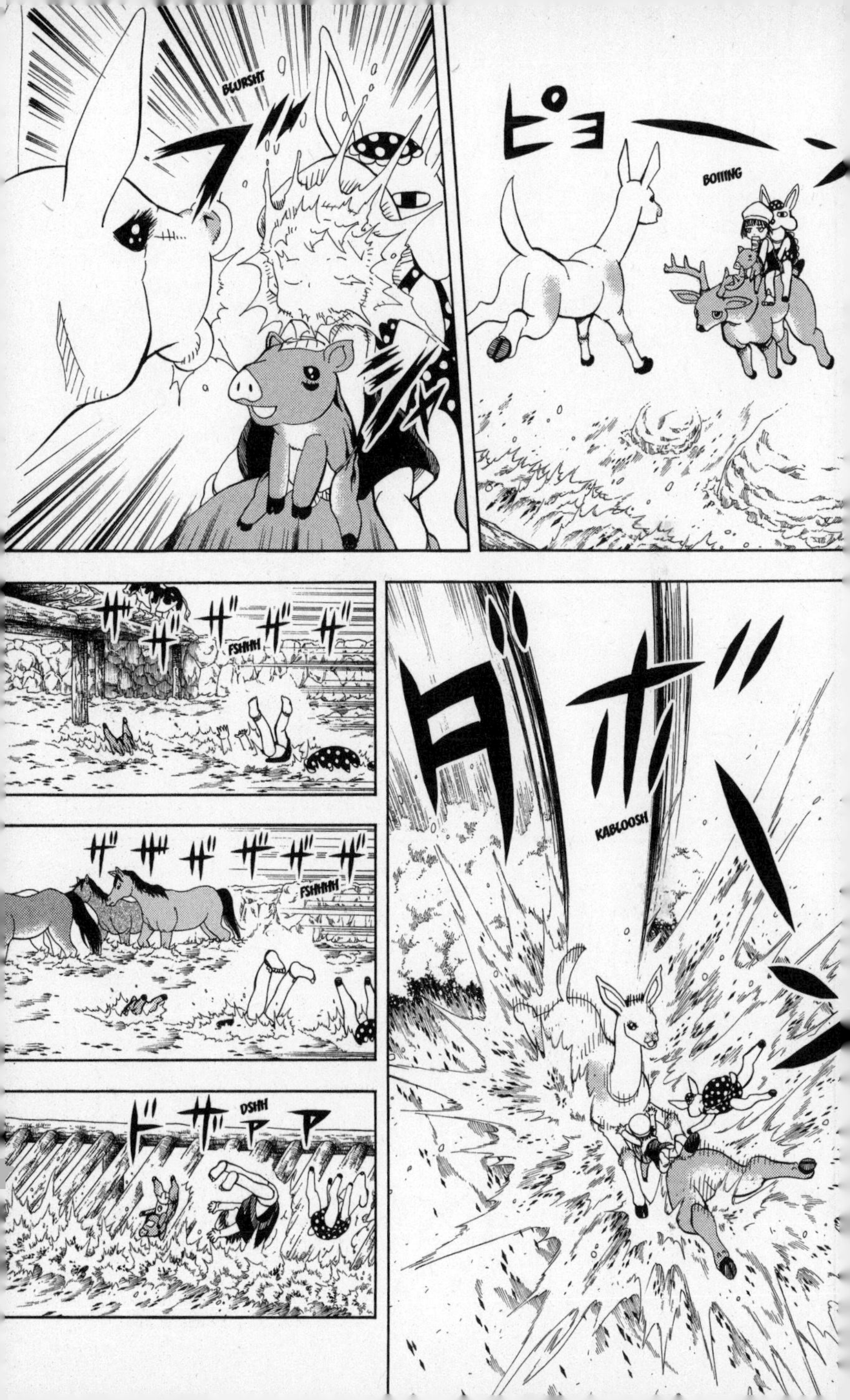
BOIIING
BLURSHT
KABLOOSH
FSHHH
FSHHHH
DSHH

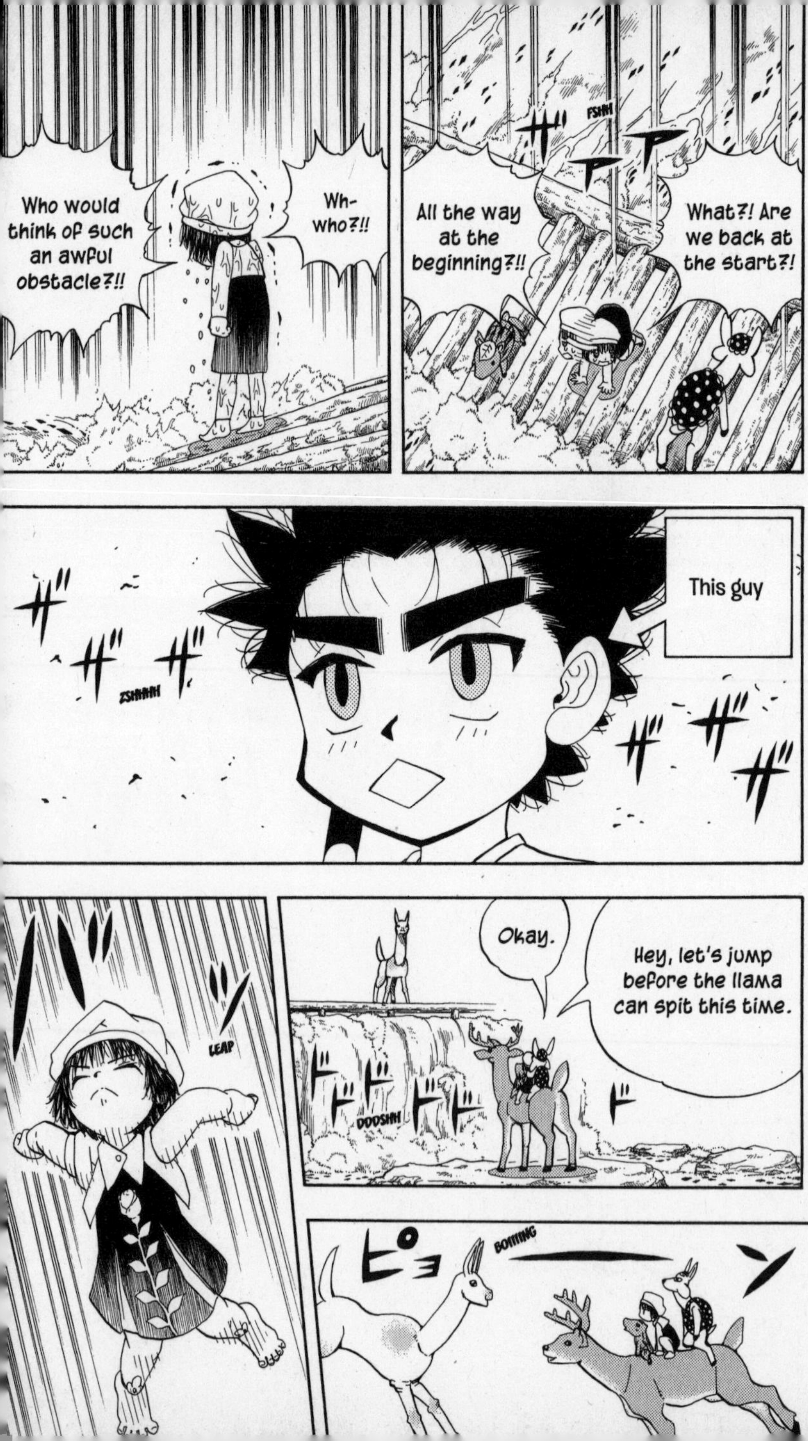
FSHH
What?! Are we back at the start?!
All the way at the beginning?!!
Wh-who?!!
Who would think of such an awful obstacle?!!
This guy
ZSHHHH
Hey, let's jump before the llama can spit this time.
Okay.
DOOSHH
BOIIING
LEAP

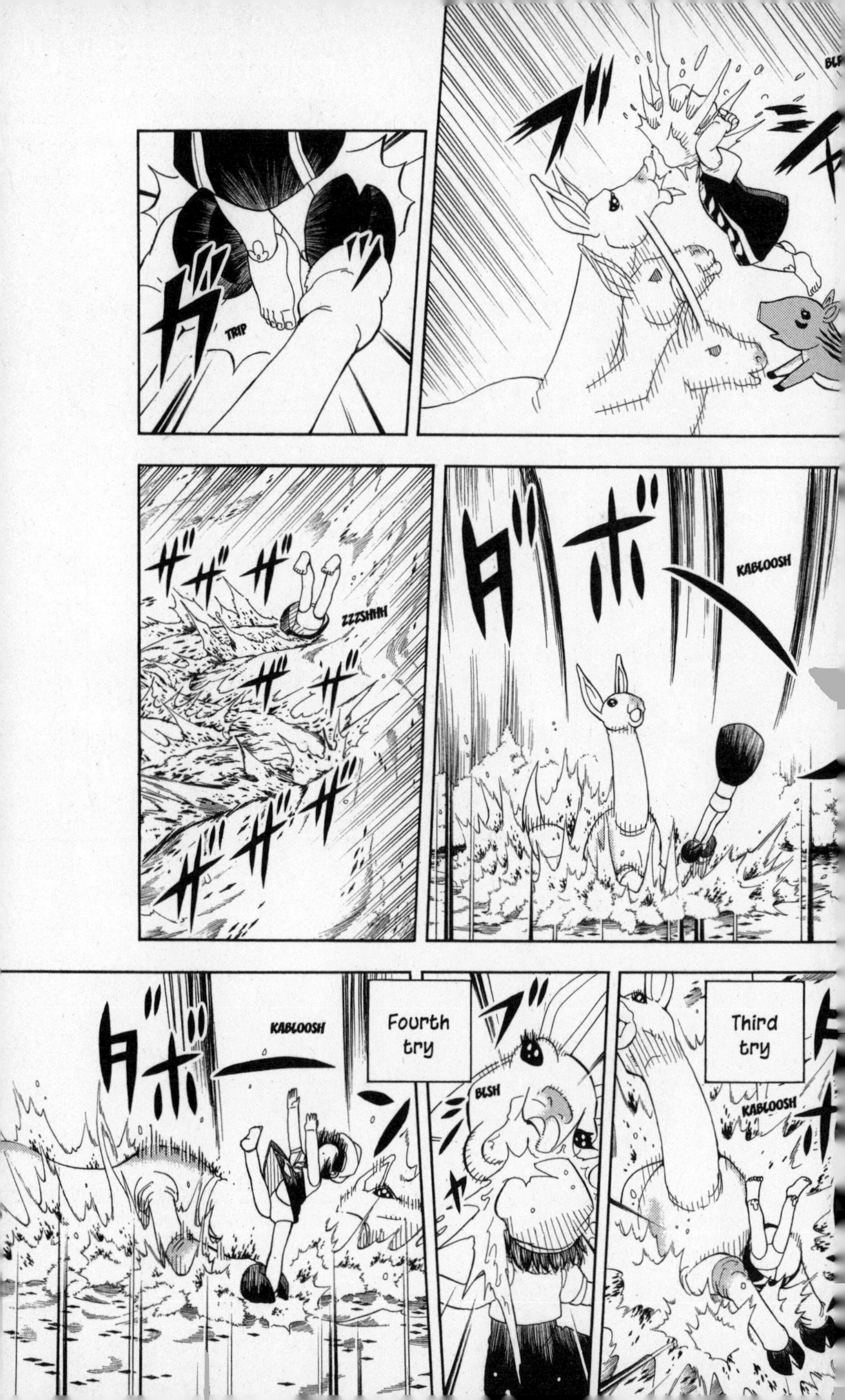
TRIP
KABLOOSH
ZZZSHHH
Third try
KABLOOSH
Fourth try
BLSH
KABLOOSH

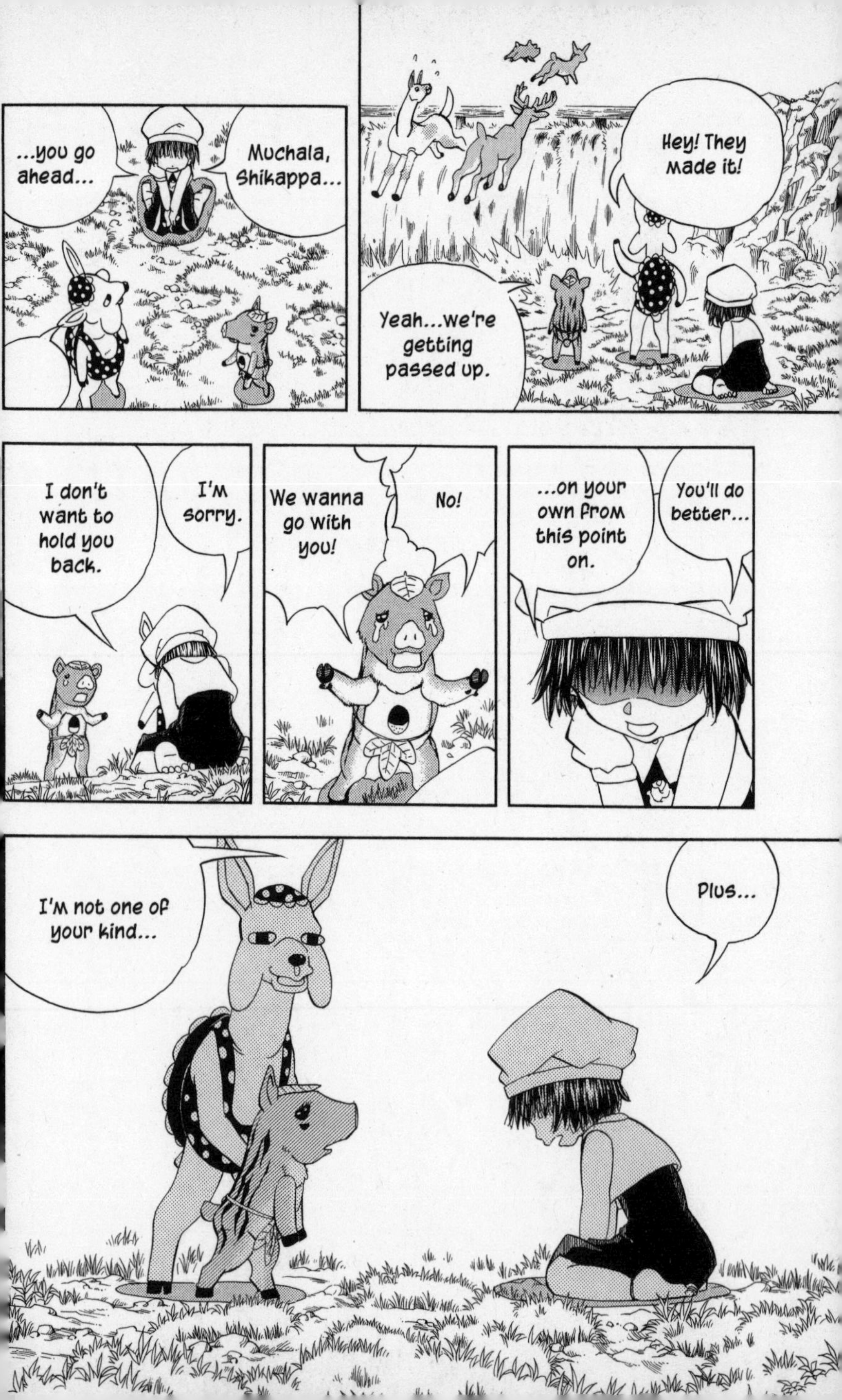
Hey! They made it!
Yeah...we're getting passed up.
Muchala, Shikappa...
...you go ahead...
You'll do better...
...on your own from this point on.
No!
We wanna go with you!
I'm sorry.
I don't want to hold you back.
Plus...
I'm not one of your kind...

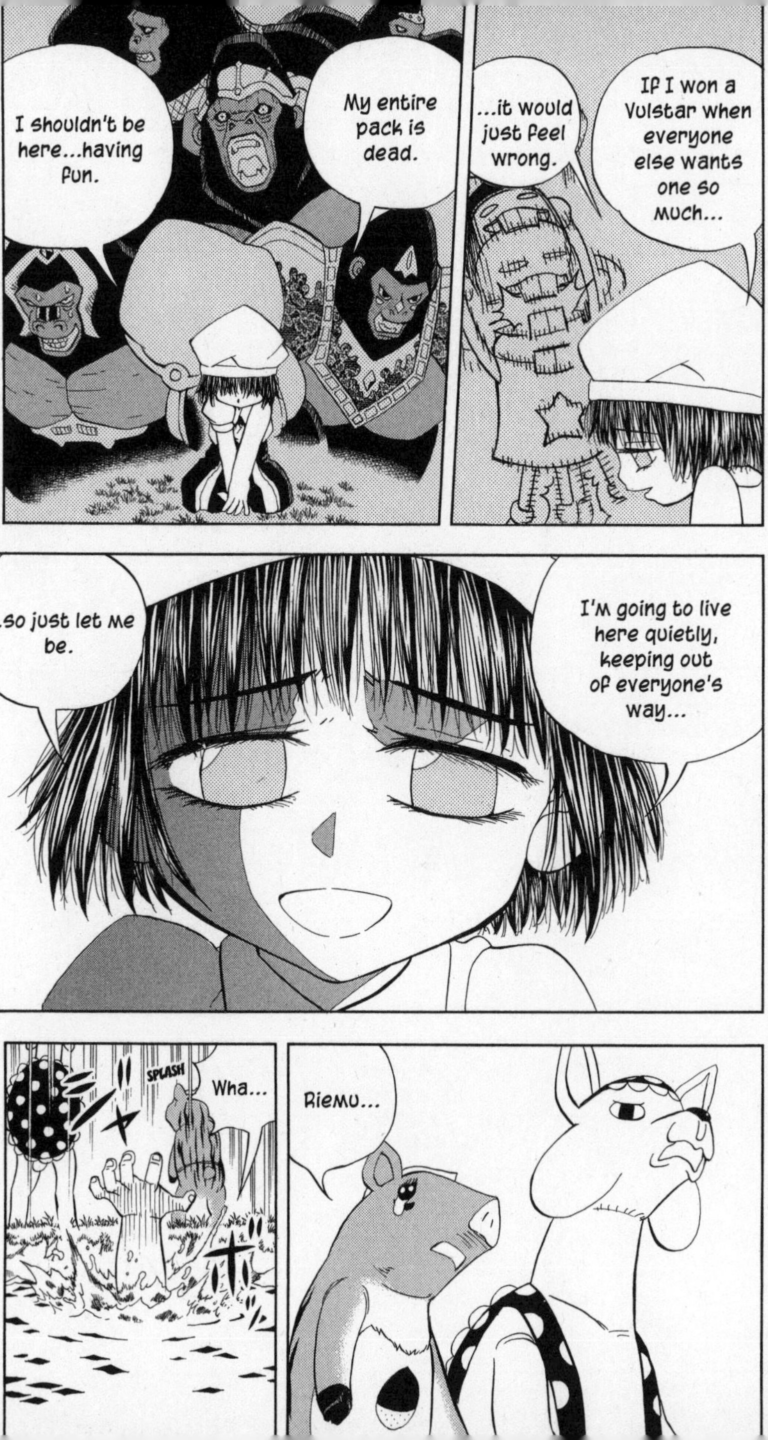
If I won a Vulstar when everyone else wants one so much...
...it would just feel wrong.
My entire pack is dead.
I shouldn't be here...having fun.
I'm going to live here quietly, keeping out of everyone's way...
...so just let me be.
Riemu...
Wha...
SPLASH

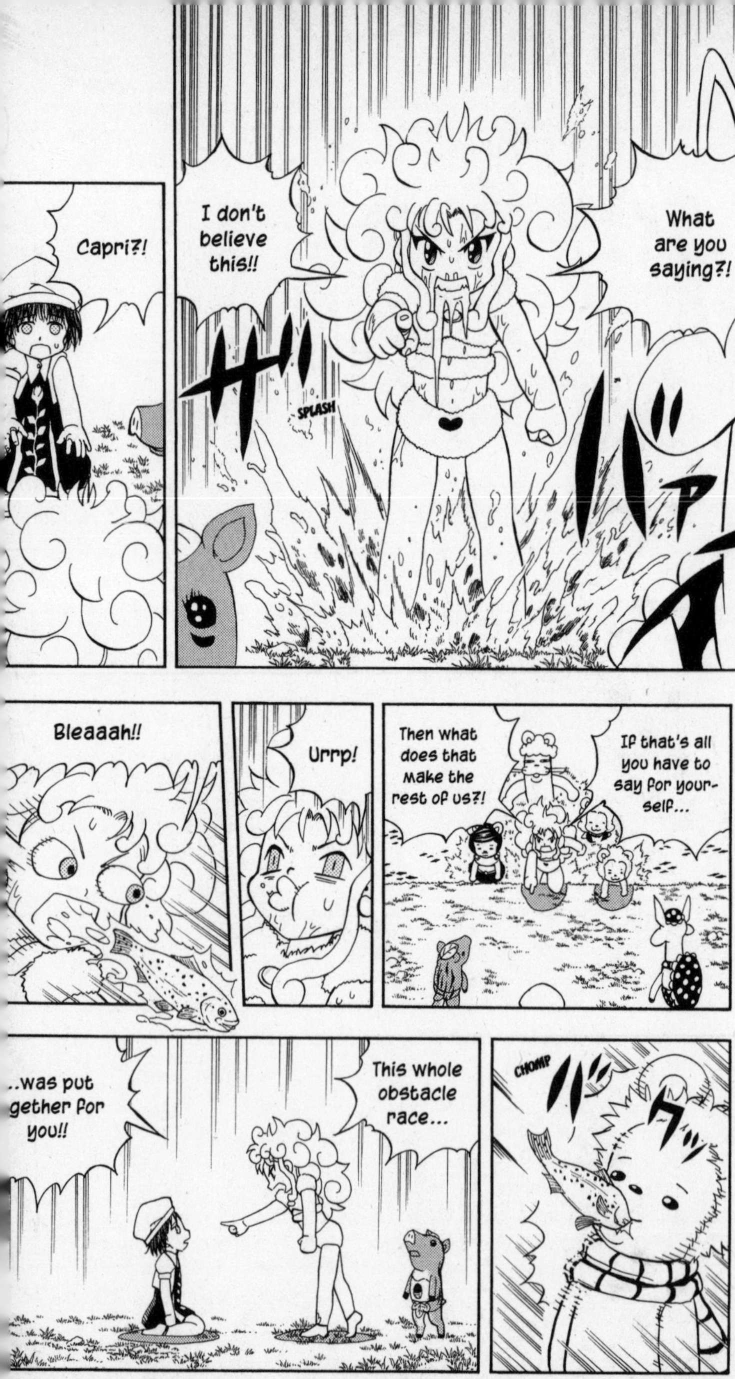
What are you saying?!
I don't believe this!!
SPLASH
Capri?!
If that's all you have to say for your-self...
Then what does that make the rest of us?!
Urrp!
Bleaaah!!
CHOMP
This whole obstacle race...
..was put gether for you!!

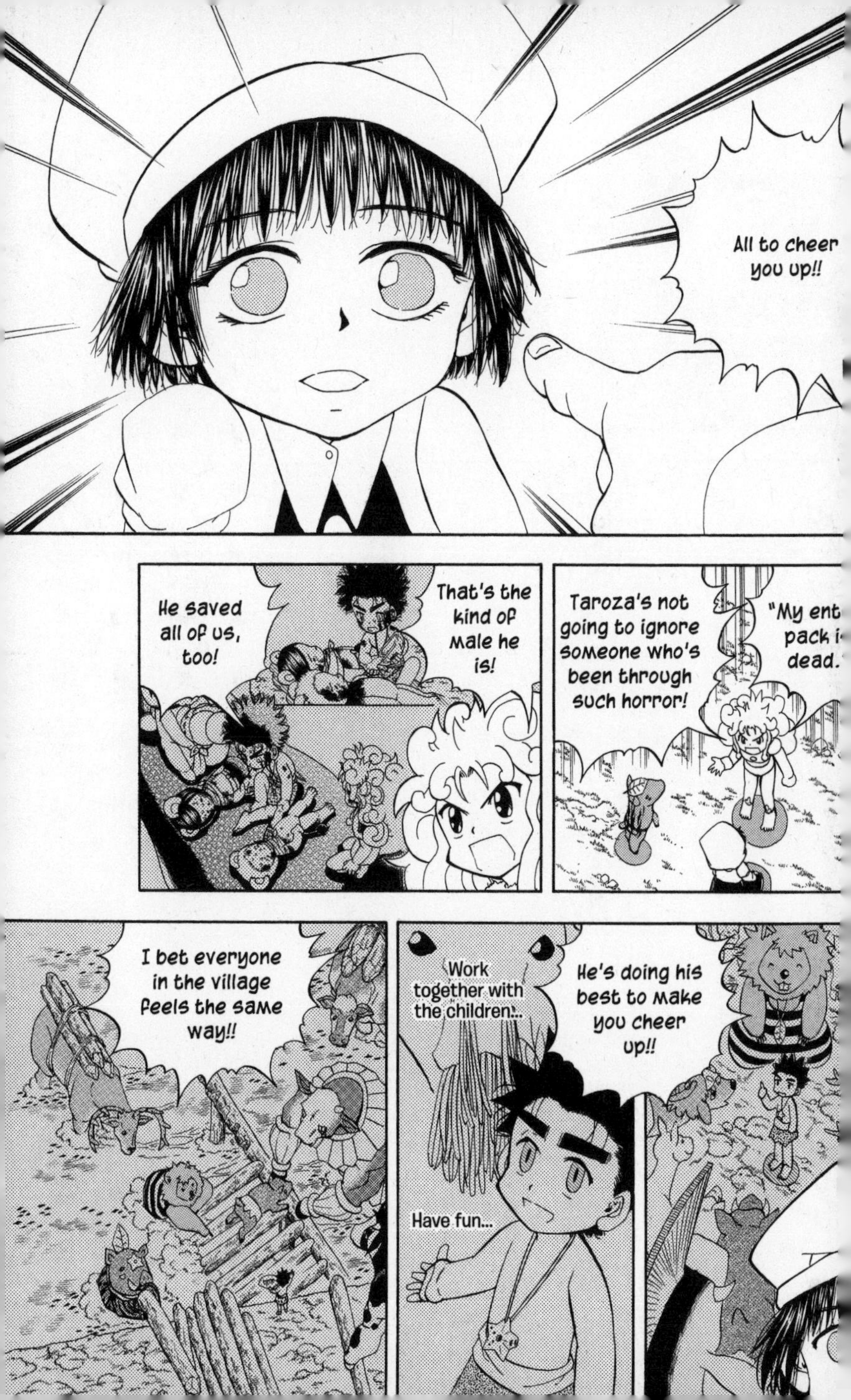
All to cheer you up!!
"My ent pack i dead.
Taroza's not going to ignore someone who's been through such horror!
That's the kind of male he is!
He saved all of us, too!
He's doing his best to make you cheer up!!
Work together with the children...
Have fun...
I bet everyone in the village feels the same way!!

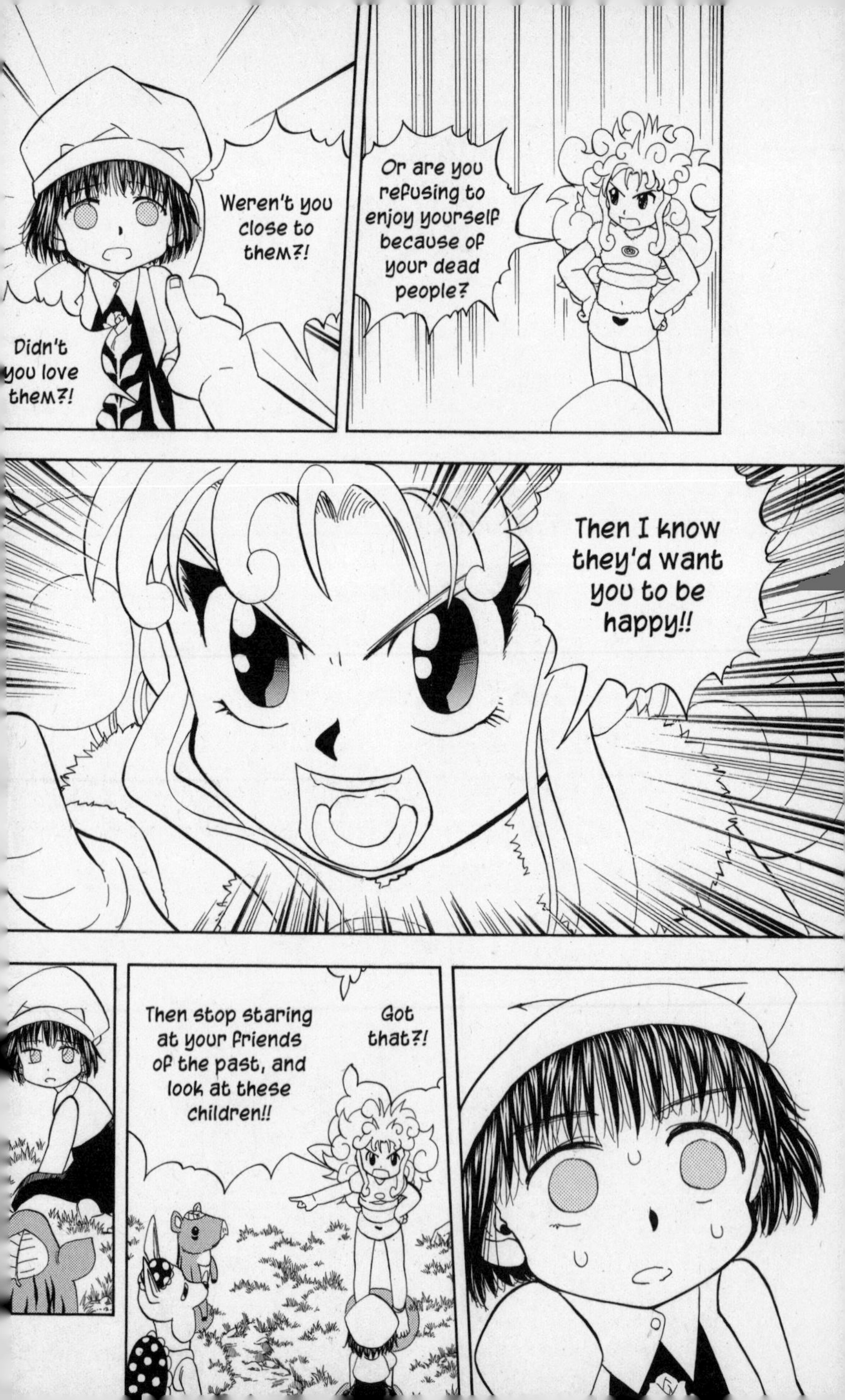
Or are you refusing to enjoy yourself because of your dead people?
Weren't you close to them?!
Didn't you love them?!
Then I know they'd want you to be happy!!
Got that?!
Then stop staring at your friends of the past, and look at these children!!

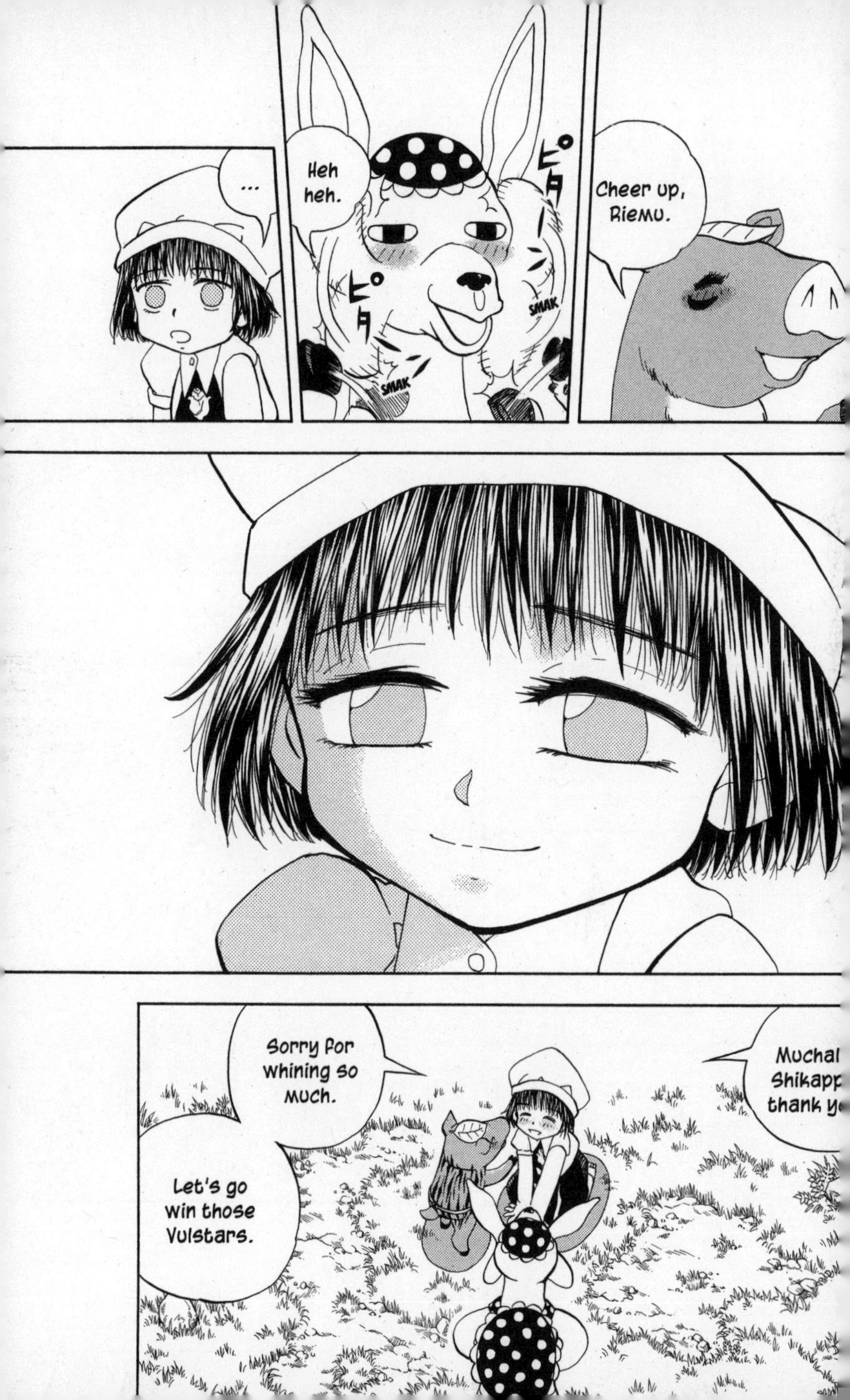

Cheer up, Riemu.
Heh heh.
ピタ
ピタ
SMAK
SMAK
...
Muchal
Shikapp
thank y
Sorry for whining so much.
Let's go win those Vulstars.

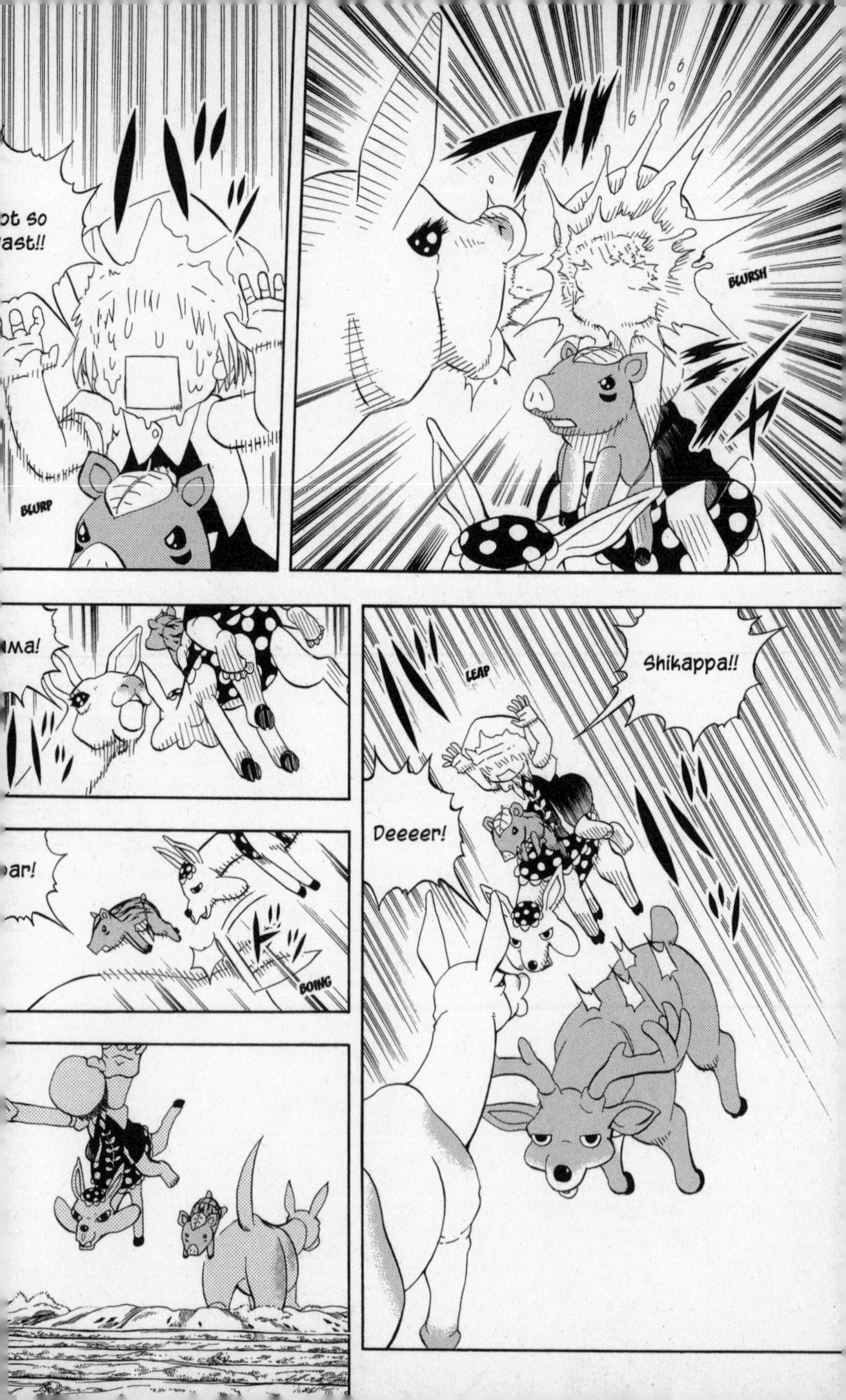
BLURSH
ot so
ast!!
BLURP
Shikappa!!
LEAP
Deeeer!
ma!
ar!
BOING

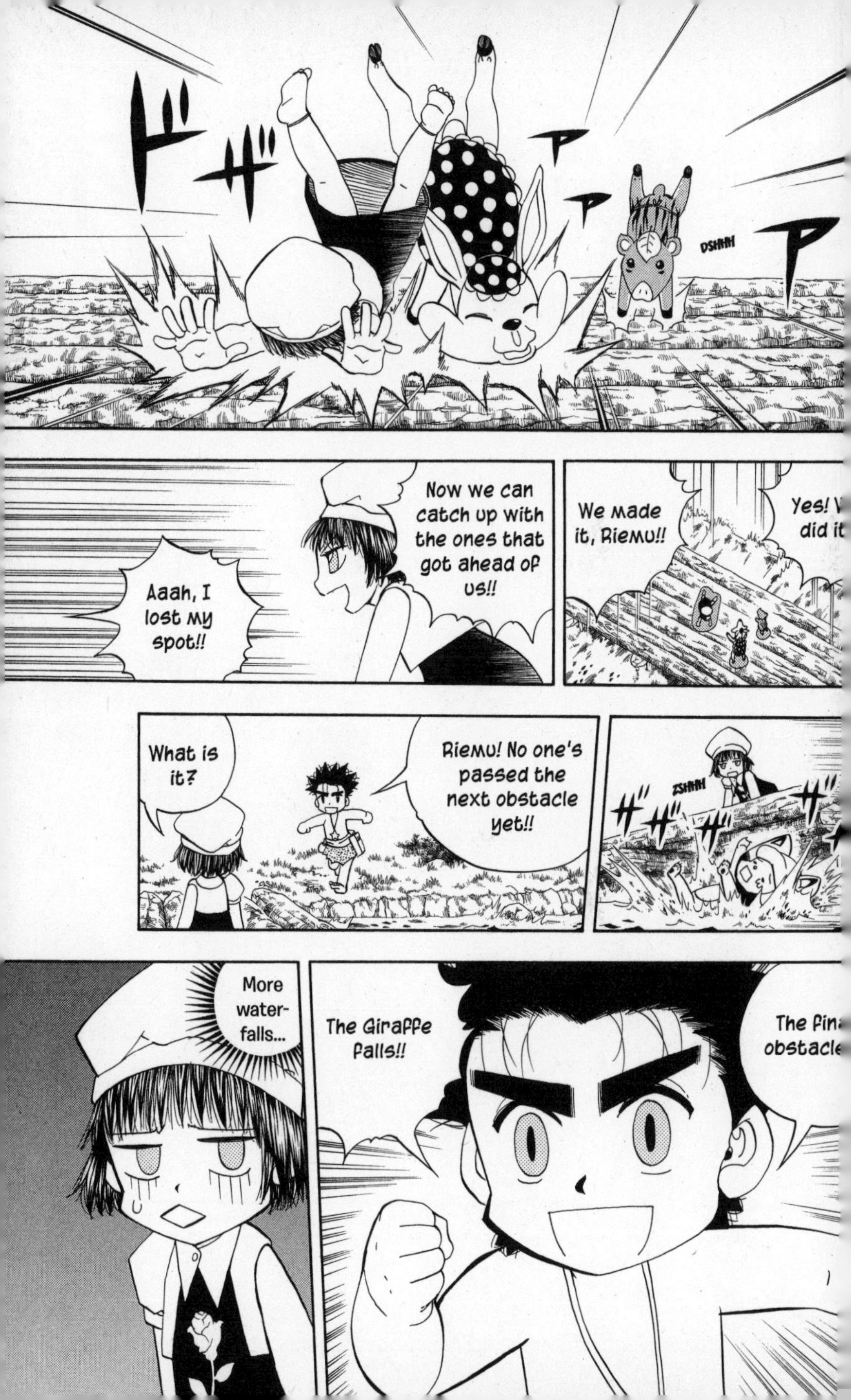
DSHHH
We made it, Riemu!!
Yes!
did it
Now we can catch up with the ones that got ahead of us!!
Aaah, I lost my spot!!
ZSHHH
Riemu! No one's passed the next obstacle yet!!
What is it?
The fina obstacle
The Giraffe falls!!
More water-falls...

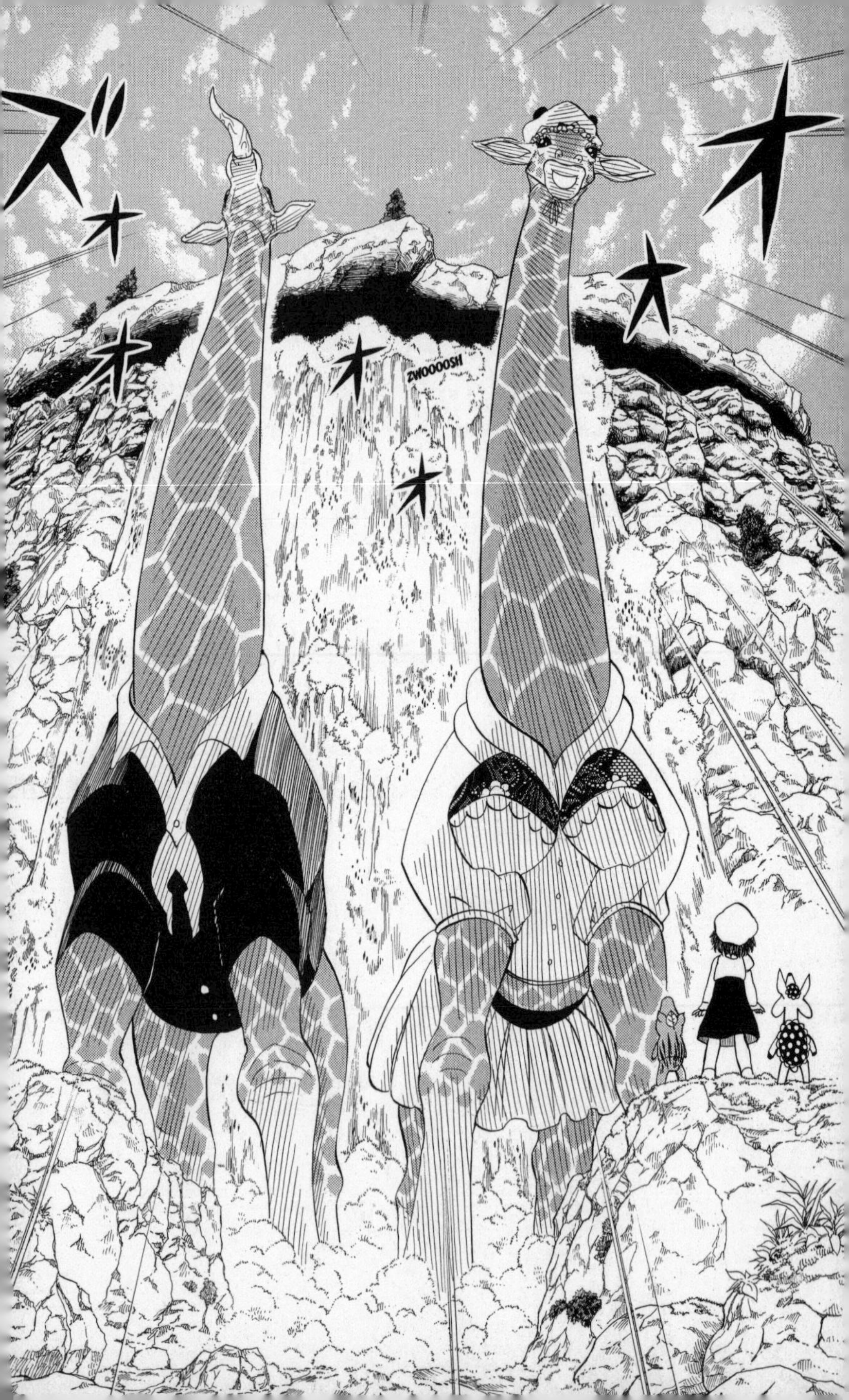
ZWOOOOSH

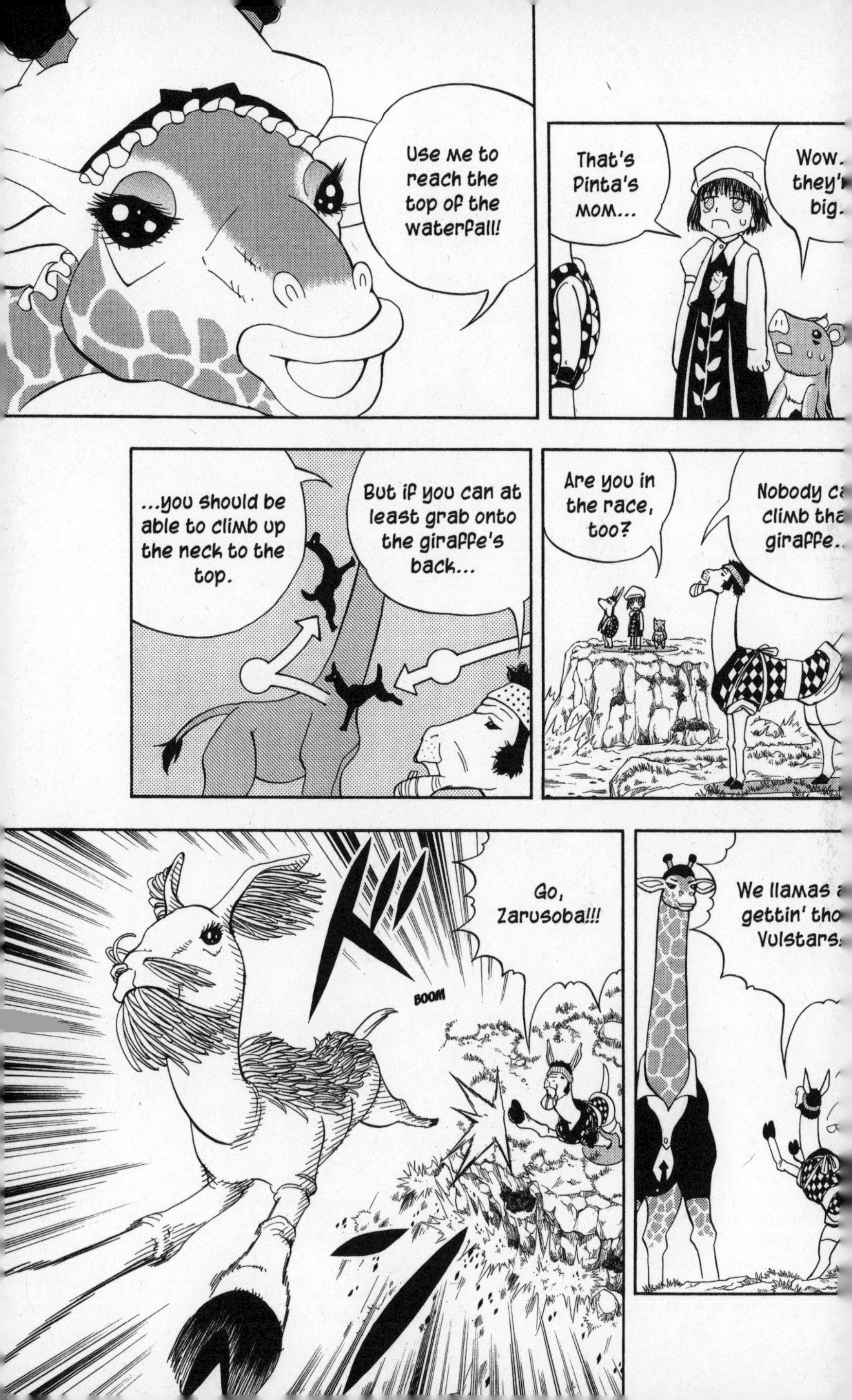
Wow. they' big.
That's Pinta's MOM...
Use me to reach the top of the waterfall!
Nobody c climb tha giraffe..
Are you in the race, too?
But if you can at least grab onto the giraffe's back...
...you should be able to climb up the neck to the top.
We llamas gettin' tho Vulstars.
Go, Zarusoba!!!
BOOM

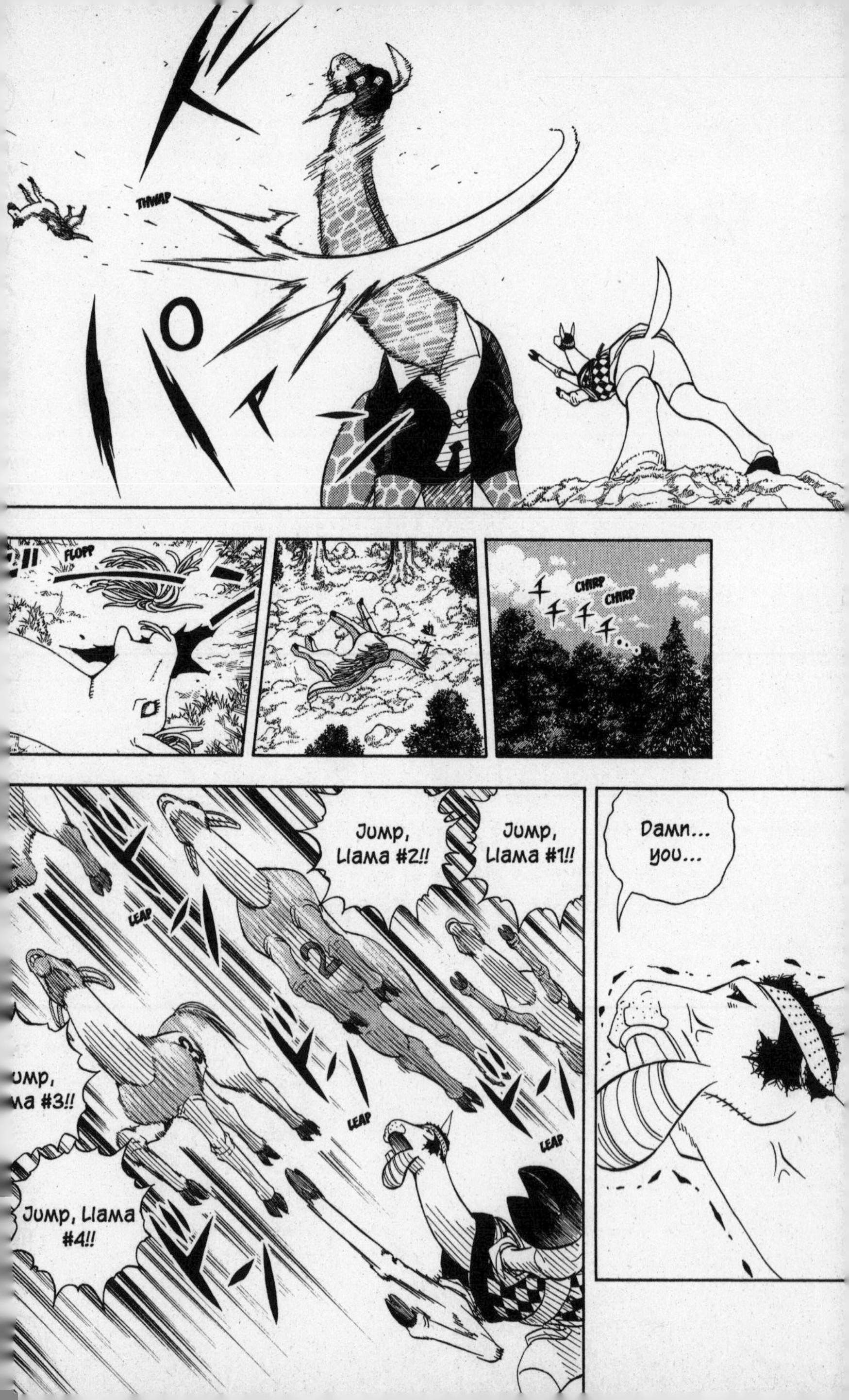
THWAP
CHIRP
CHIRP
FLOPP
Damn... you...
Jump, Llama #1!!
Jump, Llama #2!!
LEAP
LEAP
LEAP
ump, ma #3!!
Jump, Llama #4!!

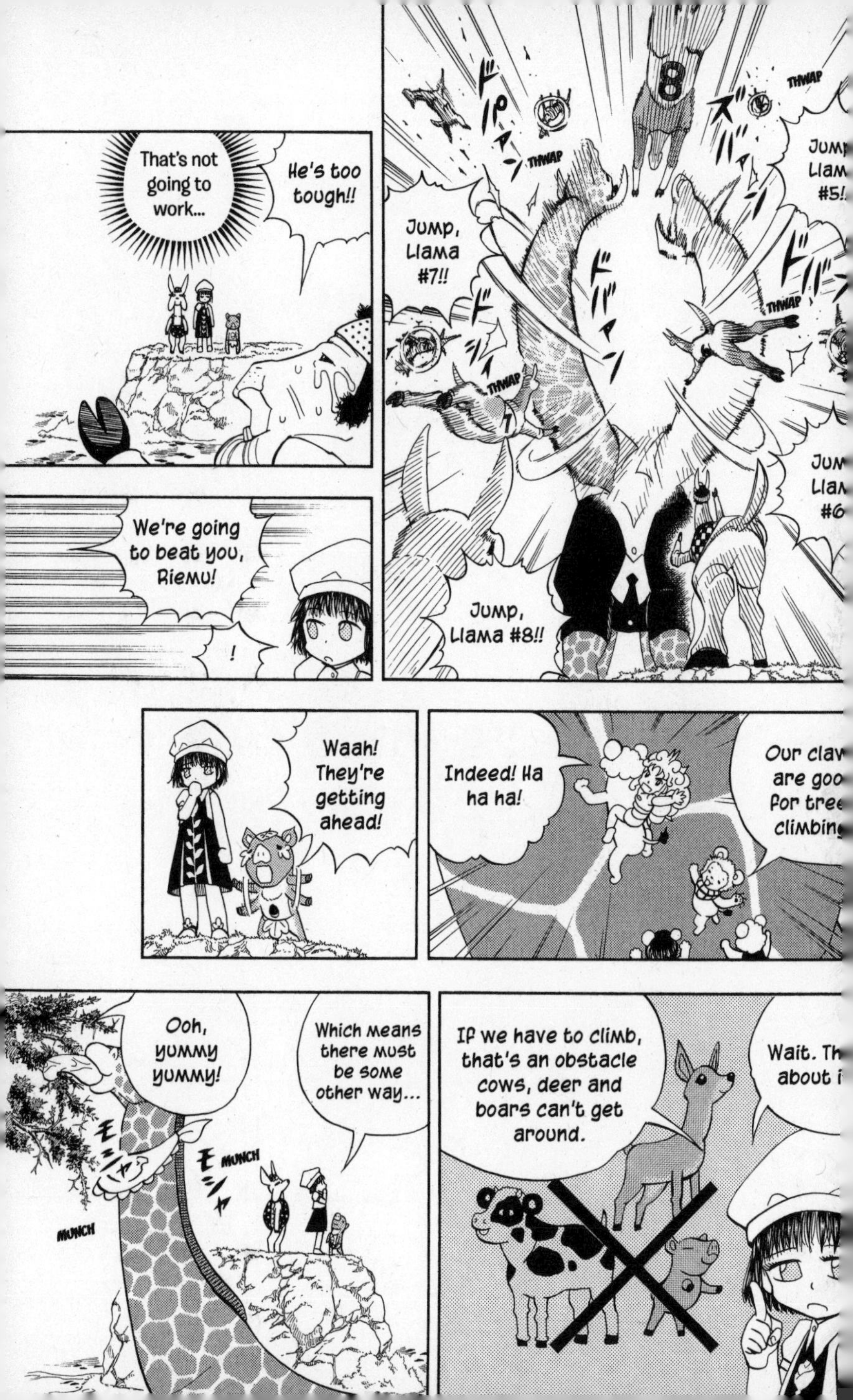
THWAP
Jum Llam #5!
THWAP
Jum Llam #6
Jump, Llama #7!!
THWAP
THWAP
Jump, Llama #8!!
He's too tough!!
That's not going to work...
We're going to beat you, Riemu!
!
Our clav are goo for tree climbin
Indeed! Ha ha ha!
Waah! They're getting ahead!
Wait. Th about i
If we have to climb, that's an obstacle cows, deer and boars can't get around.
Which means there must be some other way...
Ooh, yummy yummy!
MUNCH
MUNCH

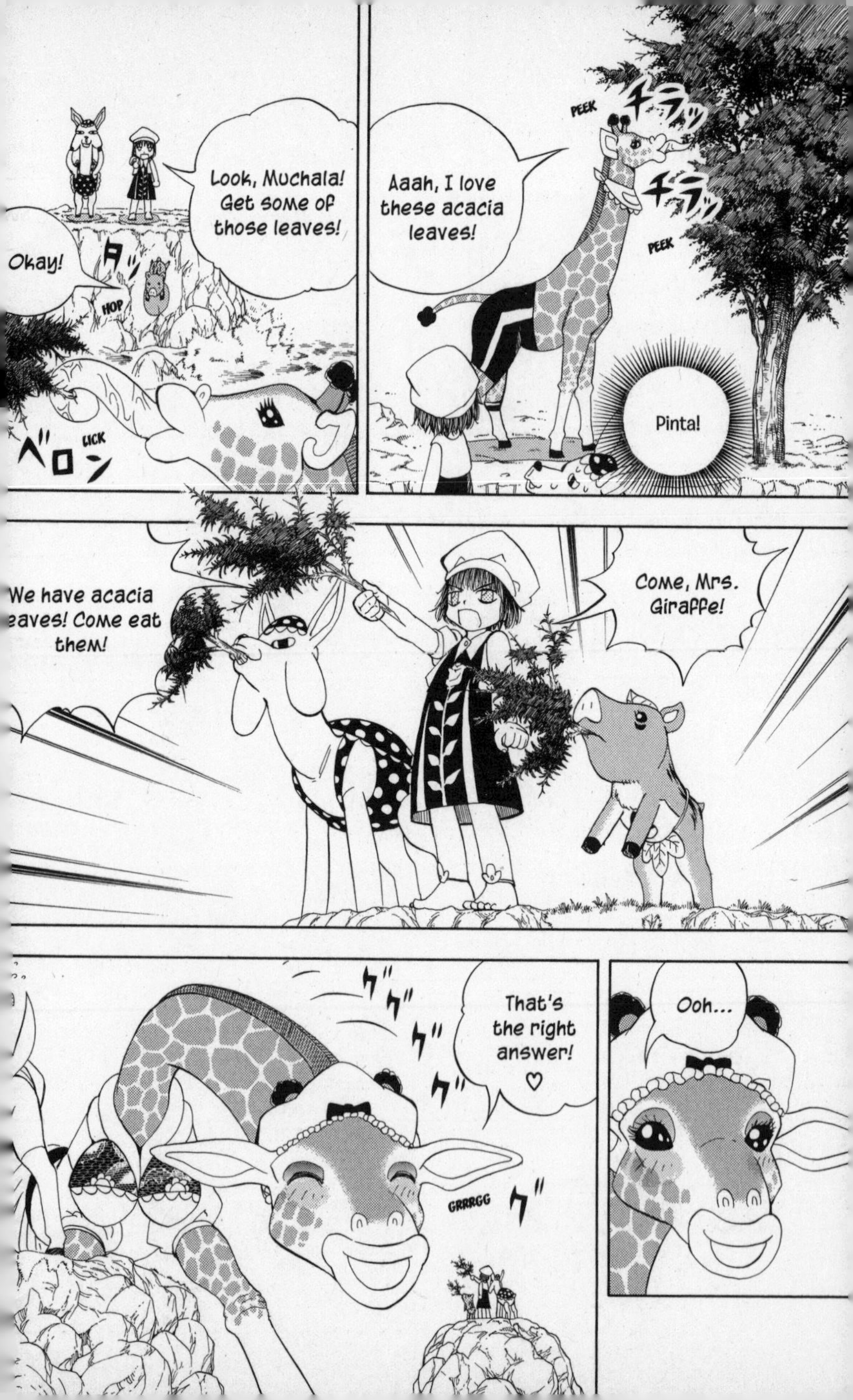
PEEK
Aaah, I love these acacia leaves!
PEEK
Pinta!
Look, Muchala! Get some of those leaves!
Okay!
HOP
LICK
Come, Mrs. Giraffe!
We have acacia
eaves! Come eat them!
Ooh...
That's the right answer! ♡
GRRRGG

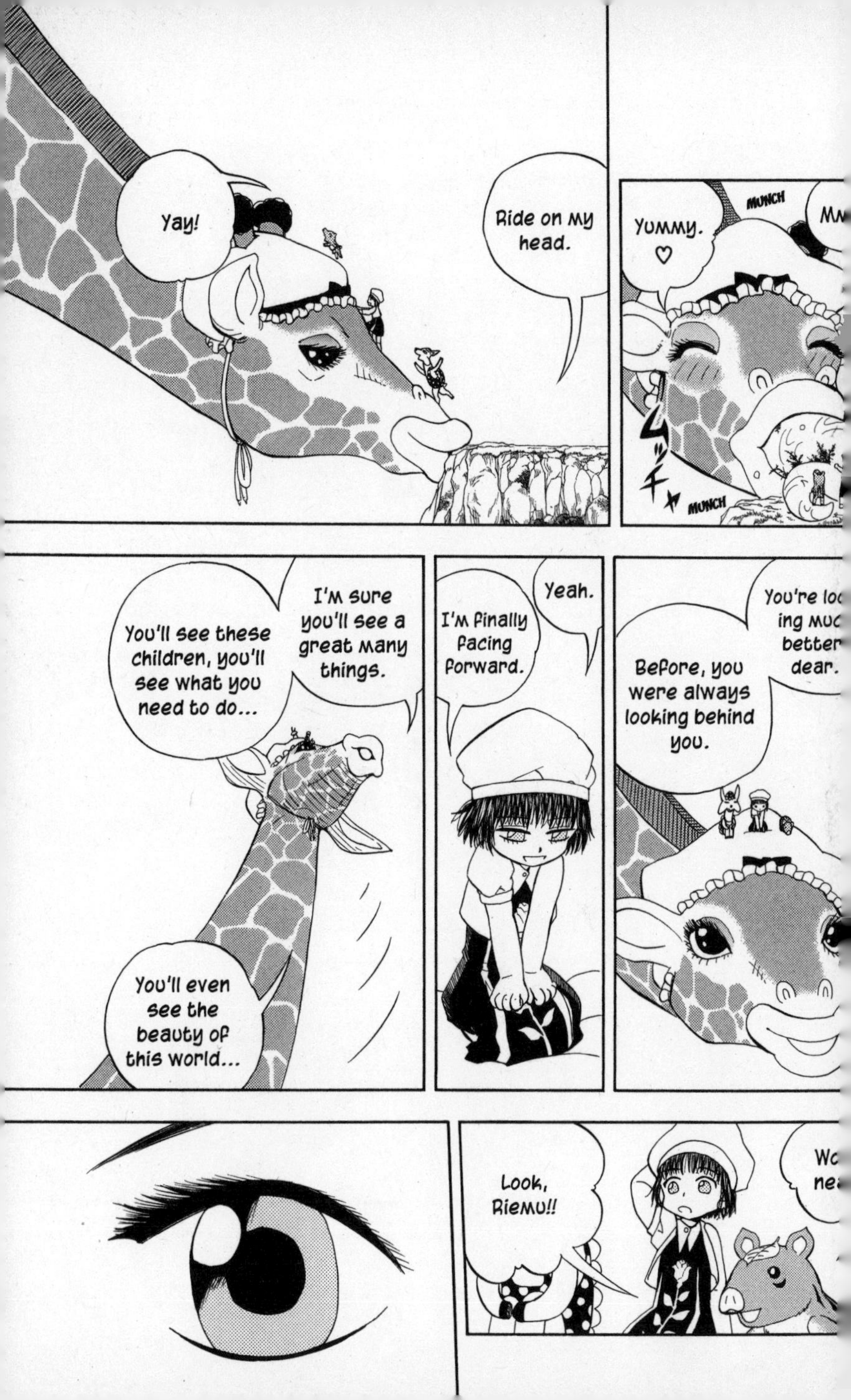
Yummy. ♡
MUNCH
MUNCH
Ride on my head.
Yay!
You're loo ing muc better dear.
Before, you were always looking behind you.
Yeah.
I'm finally facing forward.
I'm sure you'll see a great many things.
You'll see these children, you'll see what you need to do...
You'll even see the beauty of this world...
Look, Riemu!!

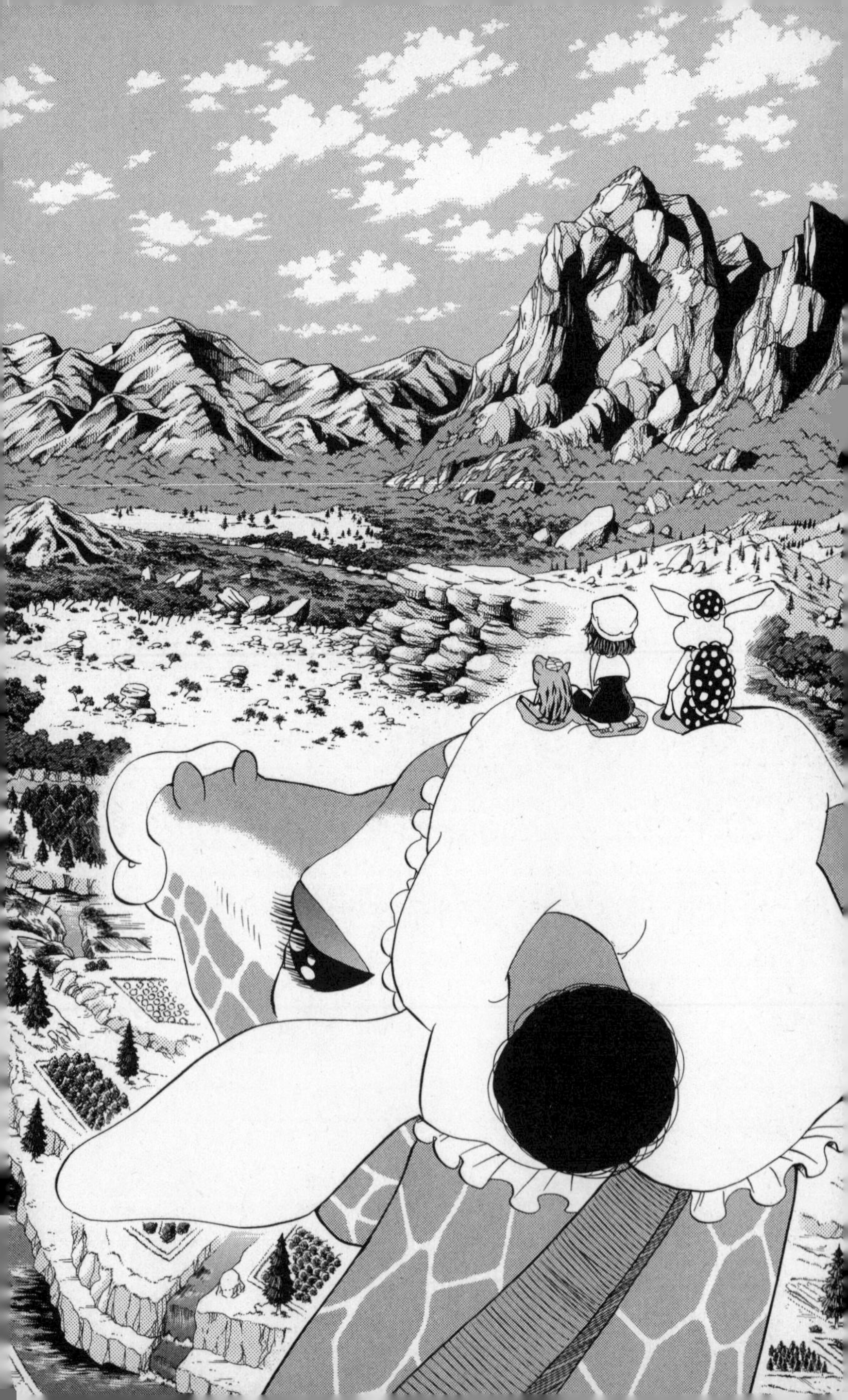

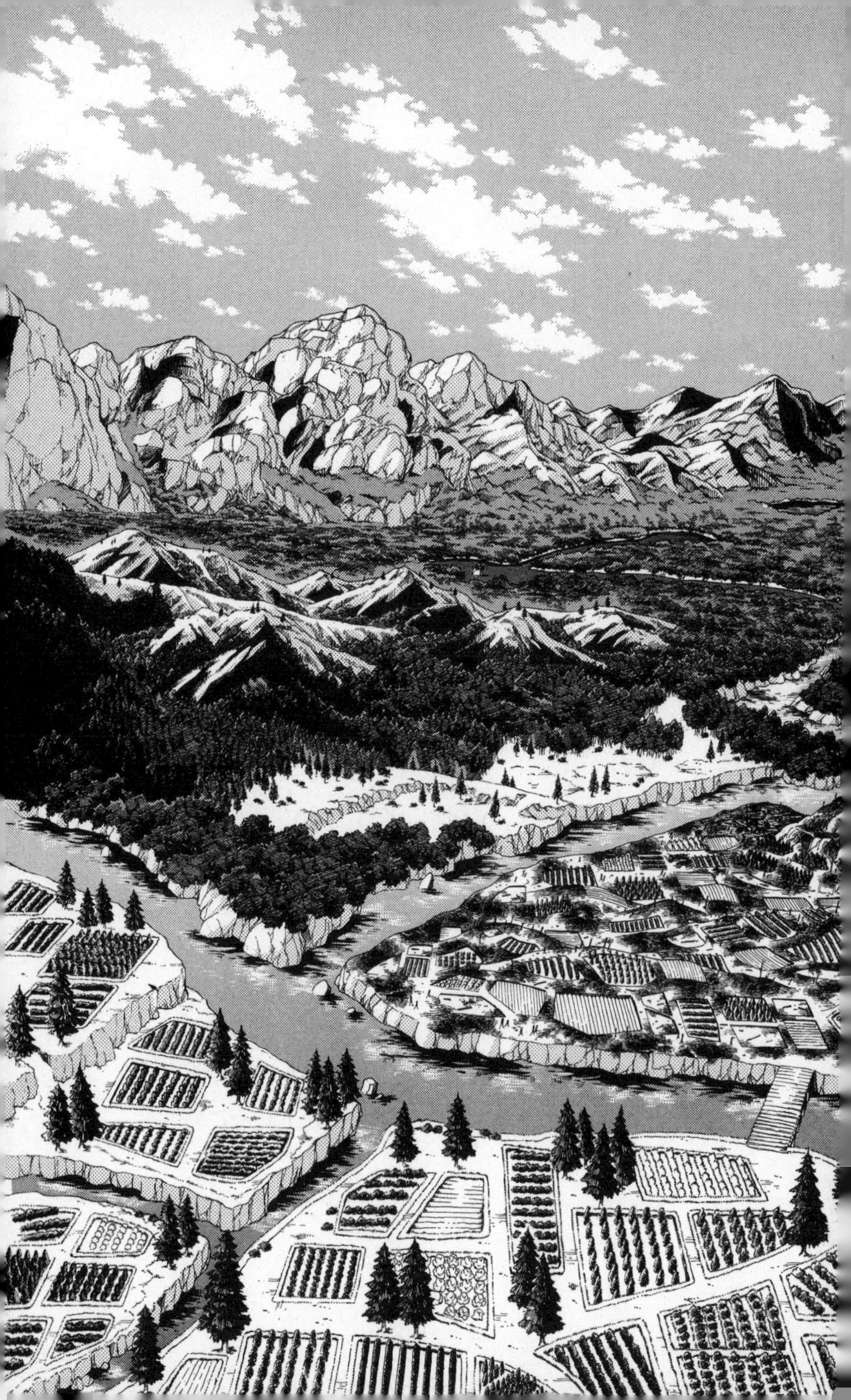

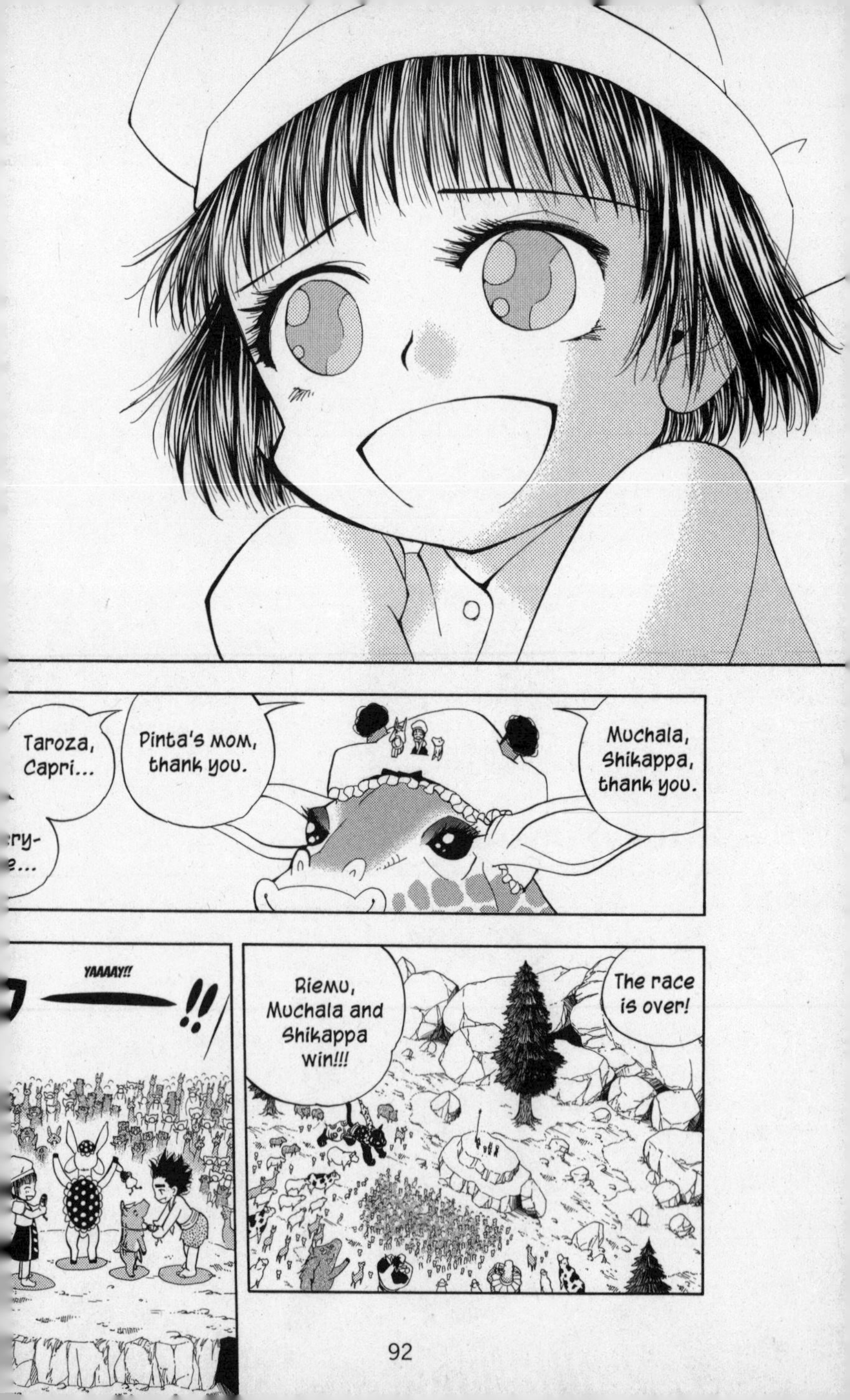
Muchala, Shikappa, thank you.
Pinta's MOM, thank you.
Taroza, Capri...
The race is over!
Riemu, Muchala and Shikappa win!!!
YAAAAY!!

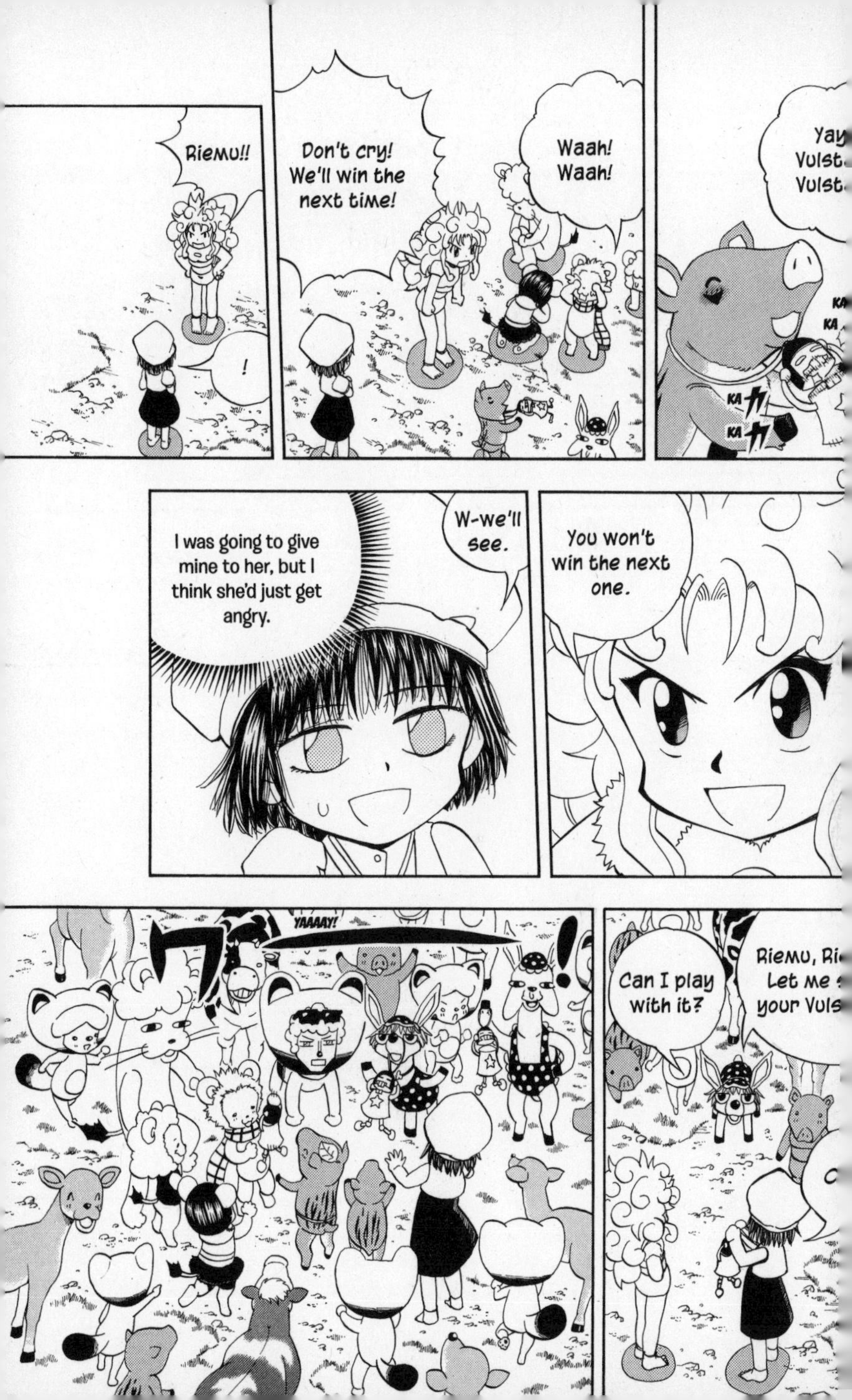

Yay
Vulst
Vulst
KA KA
KA カ KA カ
Waah! Waah!
Don't cry! We'll win the next time!
Riemu!!
!
You won't win the next one.
W-we'll see.
I was going to give mine to her, but I think she'd just get angry.
Riemu, Ri
Let me
your Vuls
Can I play with it?
YAAAAY!
!

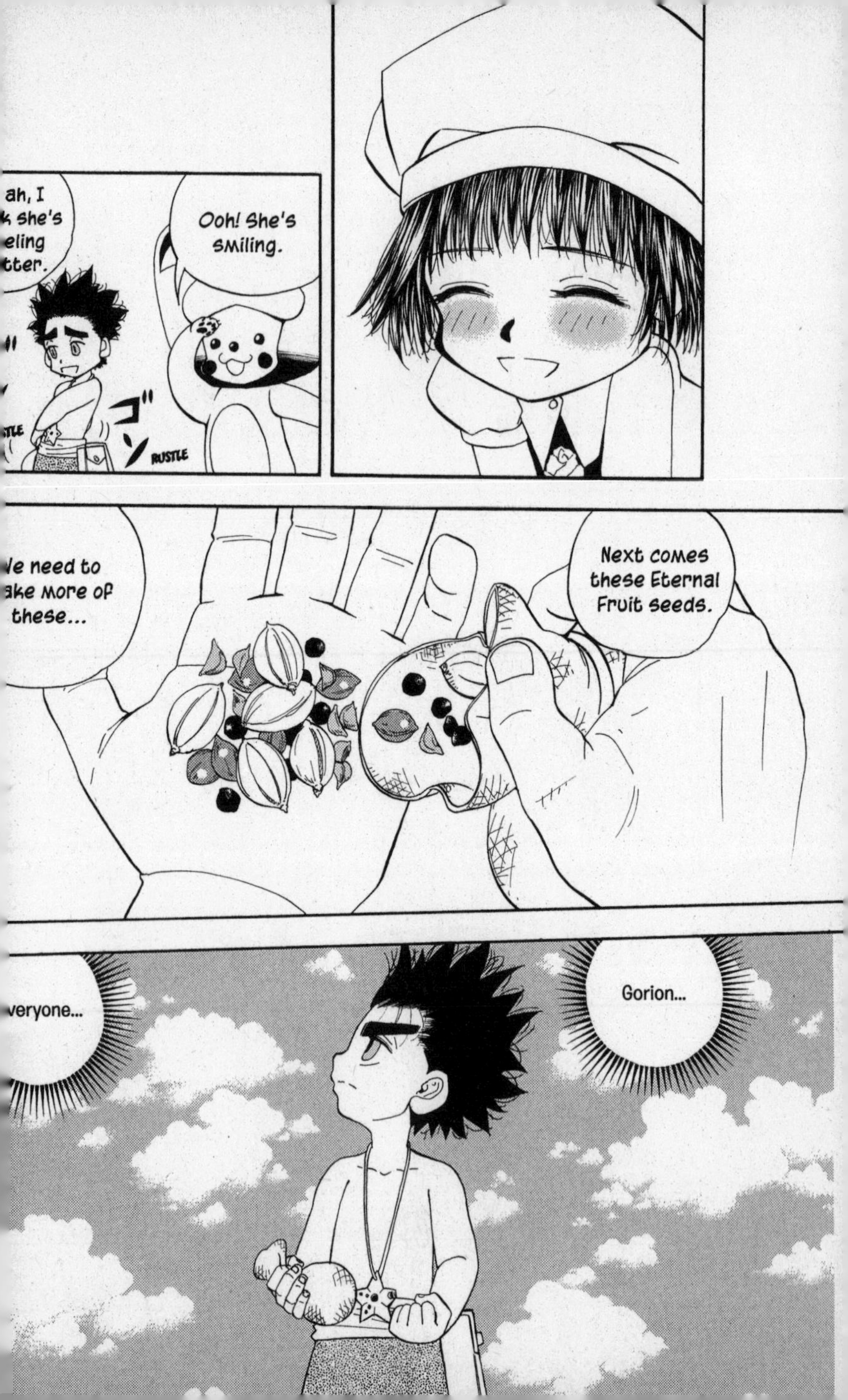
Ooh! She's smiling.
ah, I
k she's
eling
tter.
ゴソ
RUSTLE
STLE
Next comes these Eternal Fruit seeds.
Ve need to
ake more of
these...
Gorion...
veryone...

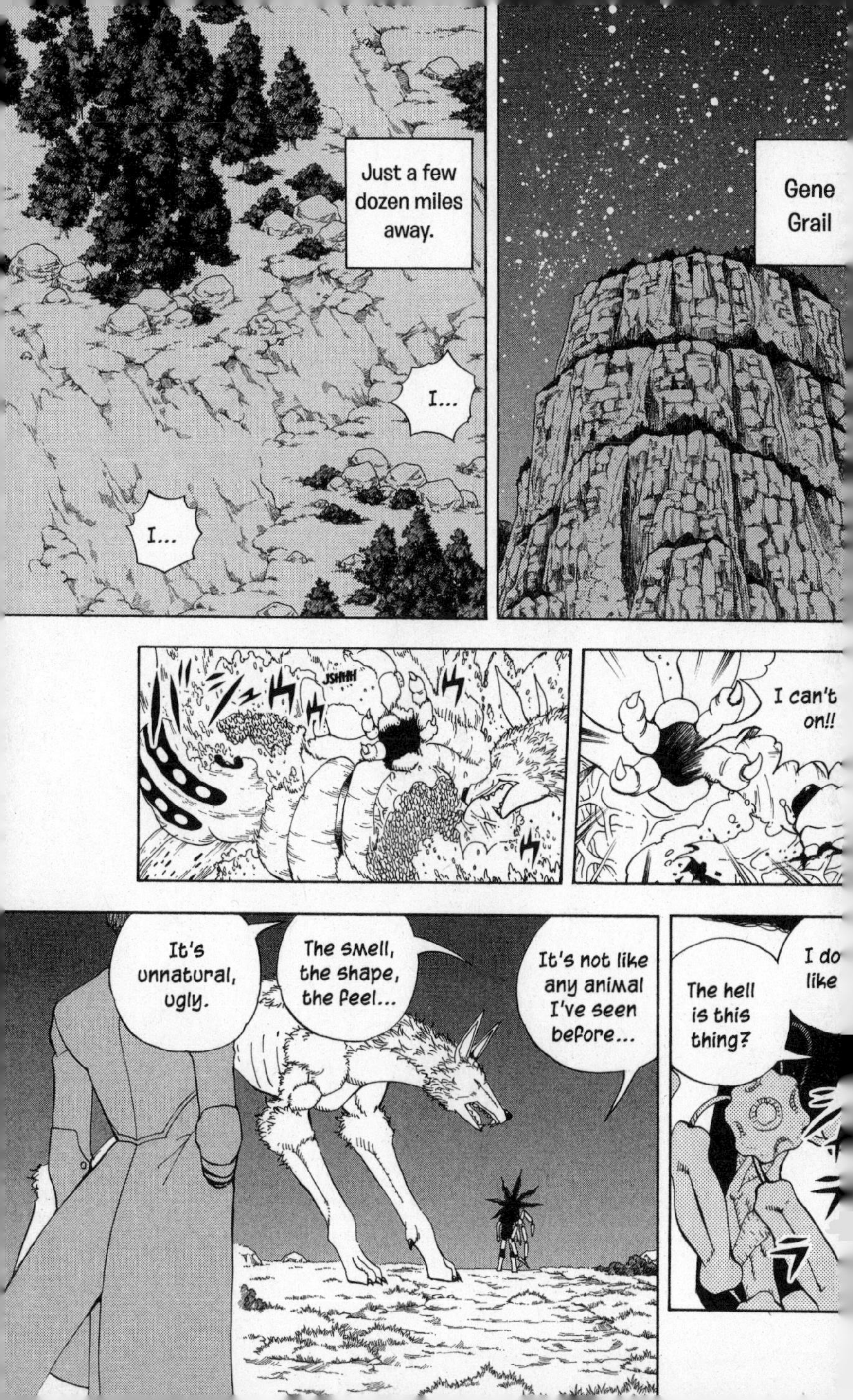
Gene Grail
Just a few dozen miles away.
I...
I...
I can't on!!
JSHHH
I do like
The hell is this thing?
It's not like any animal I've seen before...
The smell, the shape, the feel...
It's unnatural, ugly.

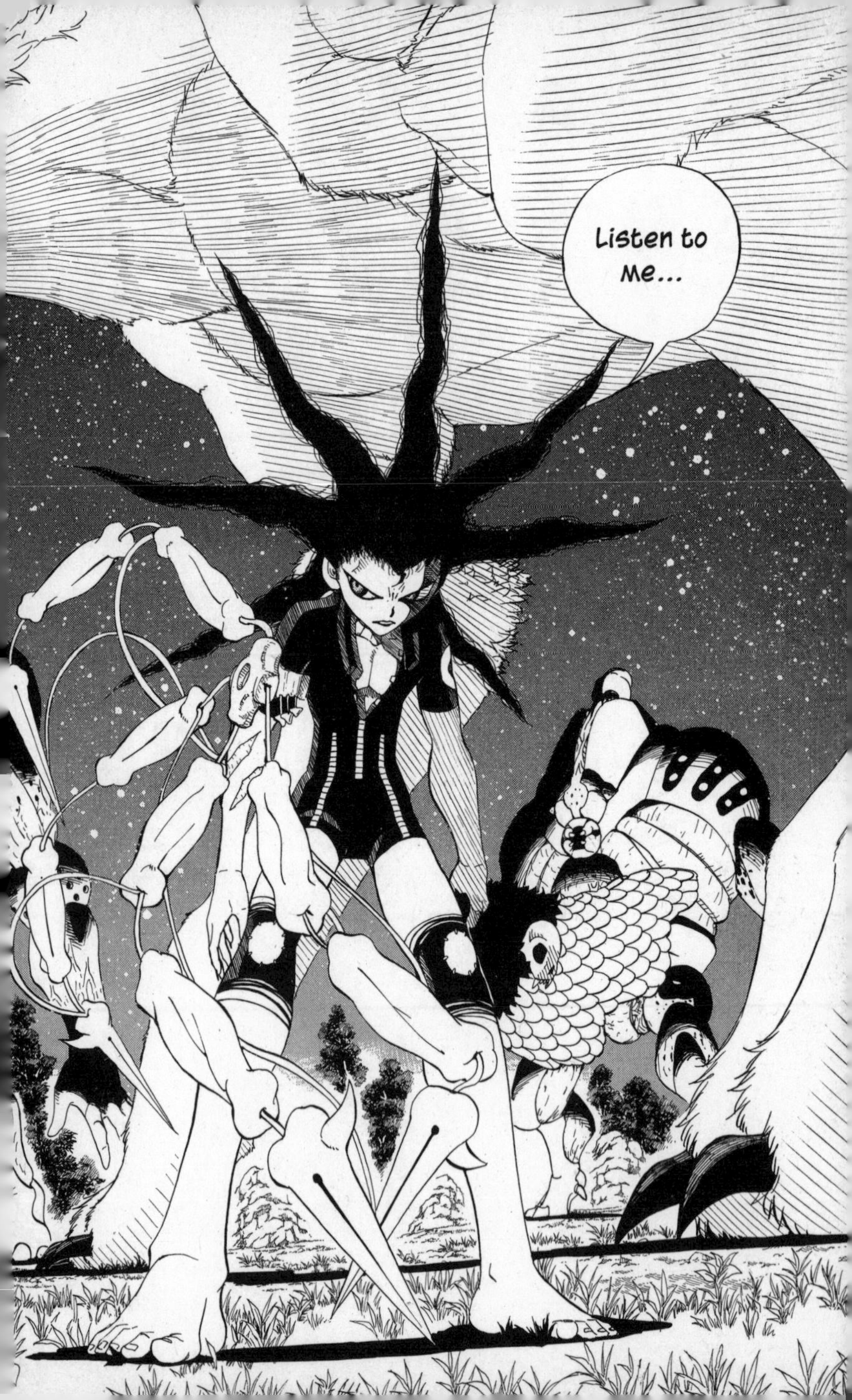
Listen to me...

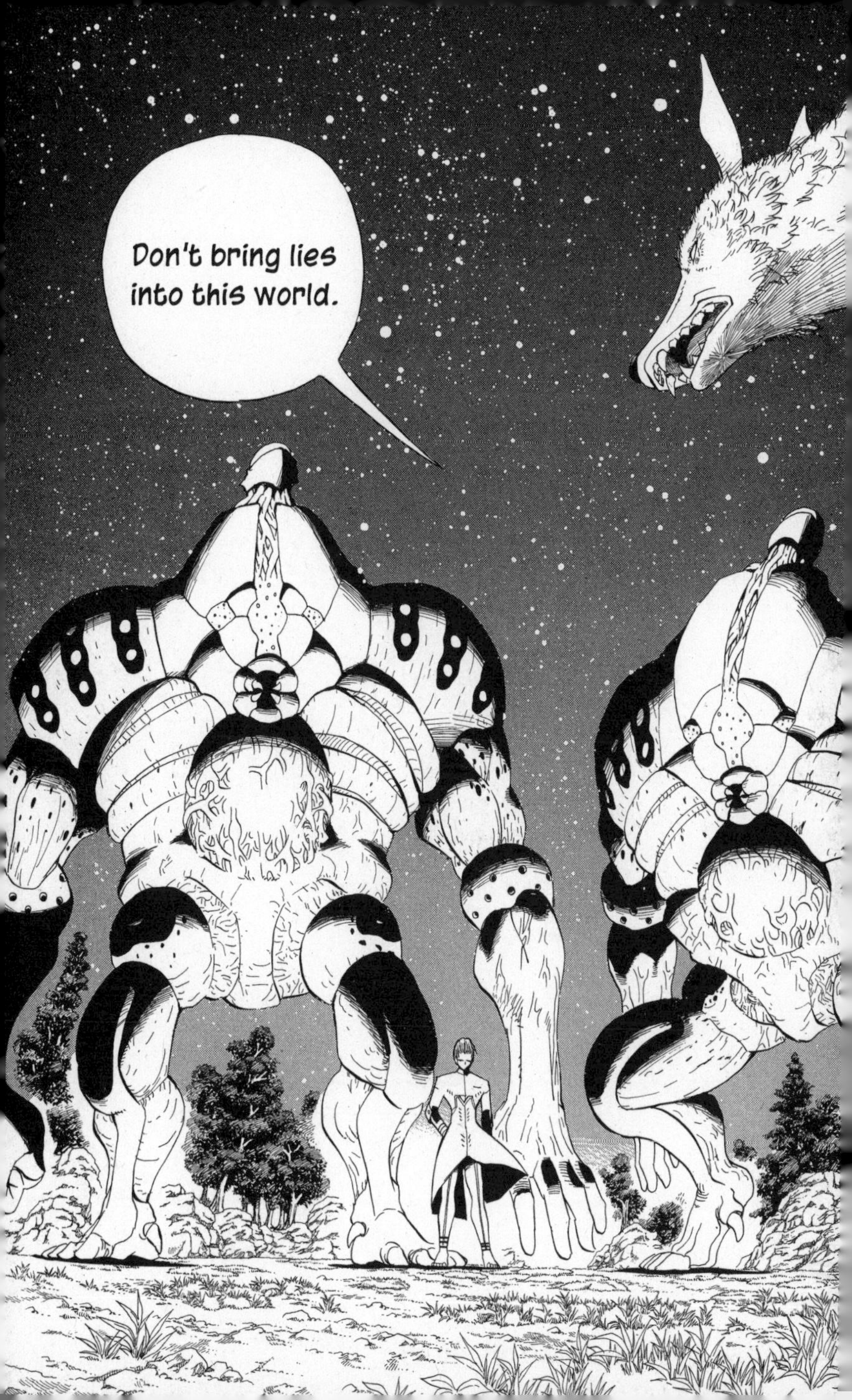
Don't bring lies into this world.

Bonus Page 2

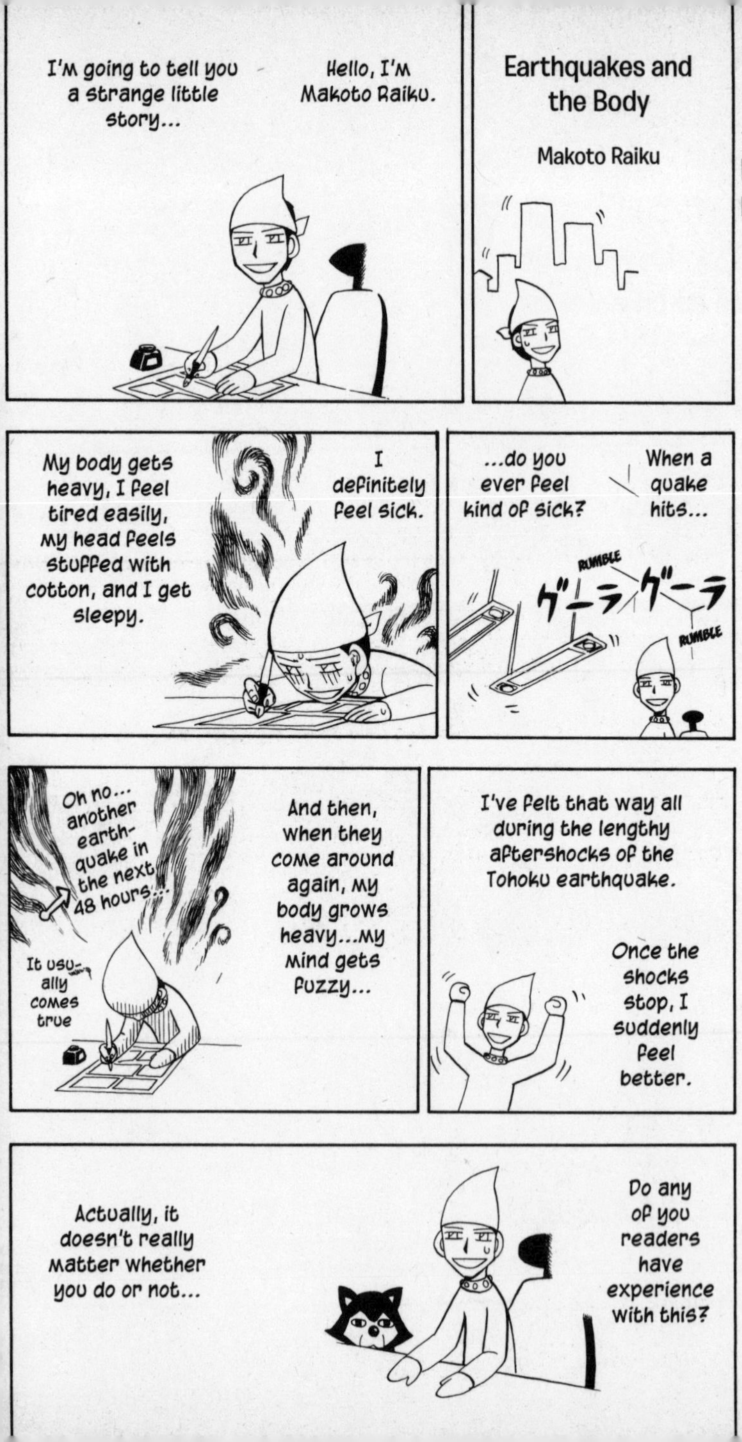
Earthquakes and the Body
Makoto Raiku
Hello, I'm Makoto Raiku.
I'm going to tell you a strange little story...
When a quake hits...
...do you ever feel kind of sick?
RUMBLE
グーラグーラ
RUMBLE
I definitely feel sick.
My body gets heavy, I feel tired easily, my head feels stuffed with cotton, and I get sleepy.
I've felt that way all during the lengthy aftershocks of the Tohoku earthquake.
Once the shocks stop, I suddenly feel better.
And then, when they come around again, my body grows heavy...my mind gets fuzzy...
Oh no... another earthquake in the next 48 hours...
It usually comes true
Do any of you readers have experience with this?
Actually, it doesn't really matter whether you do or not...

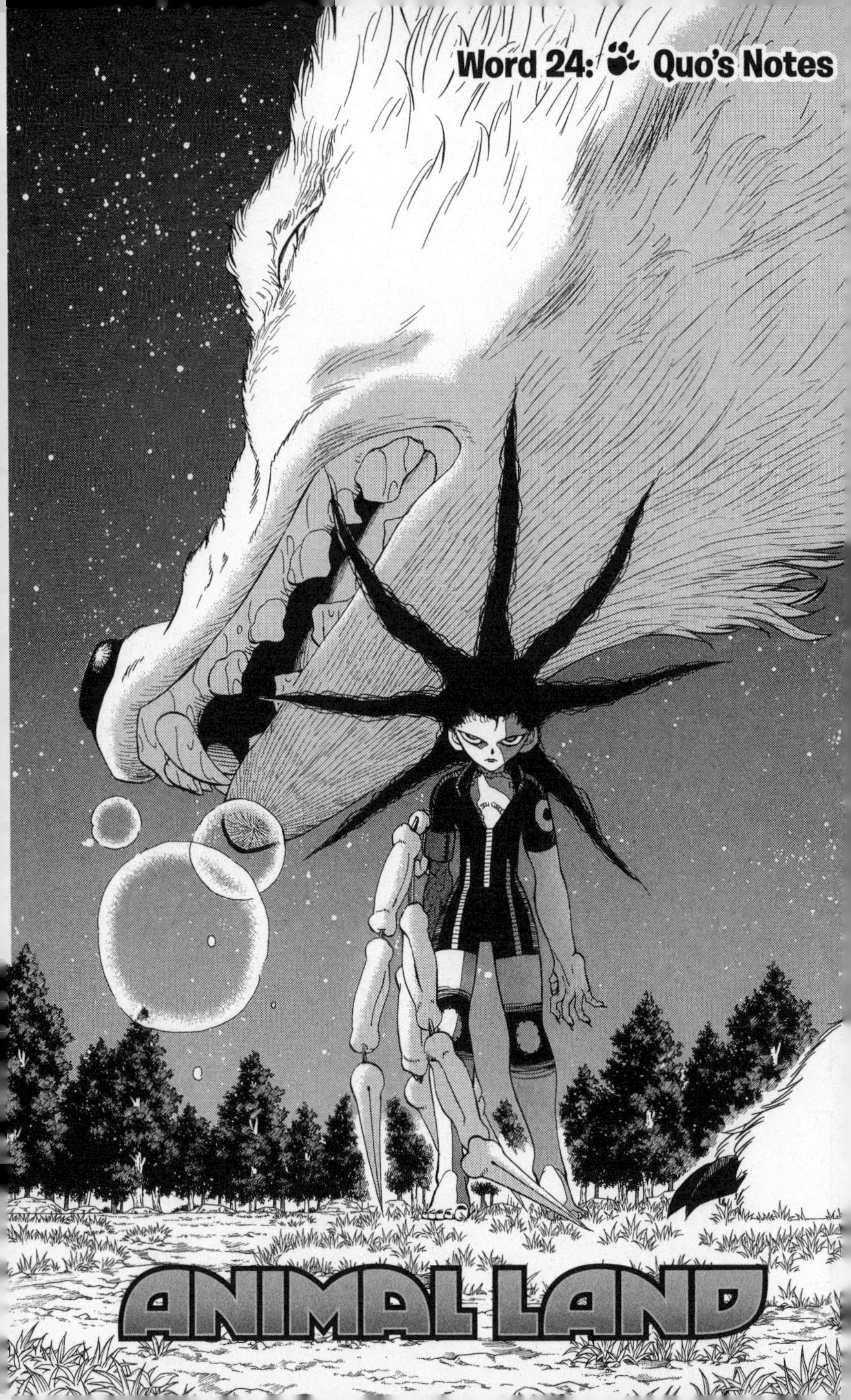
Word 24: Quo's Notes
ANIMAL LAND

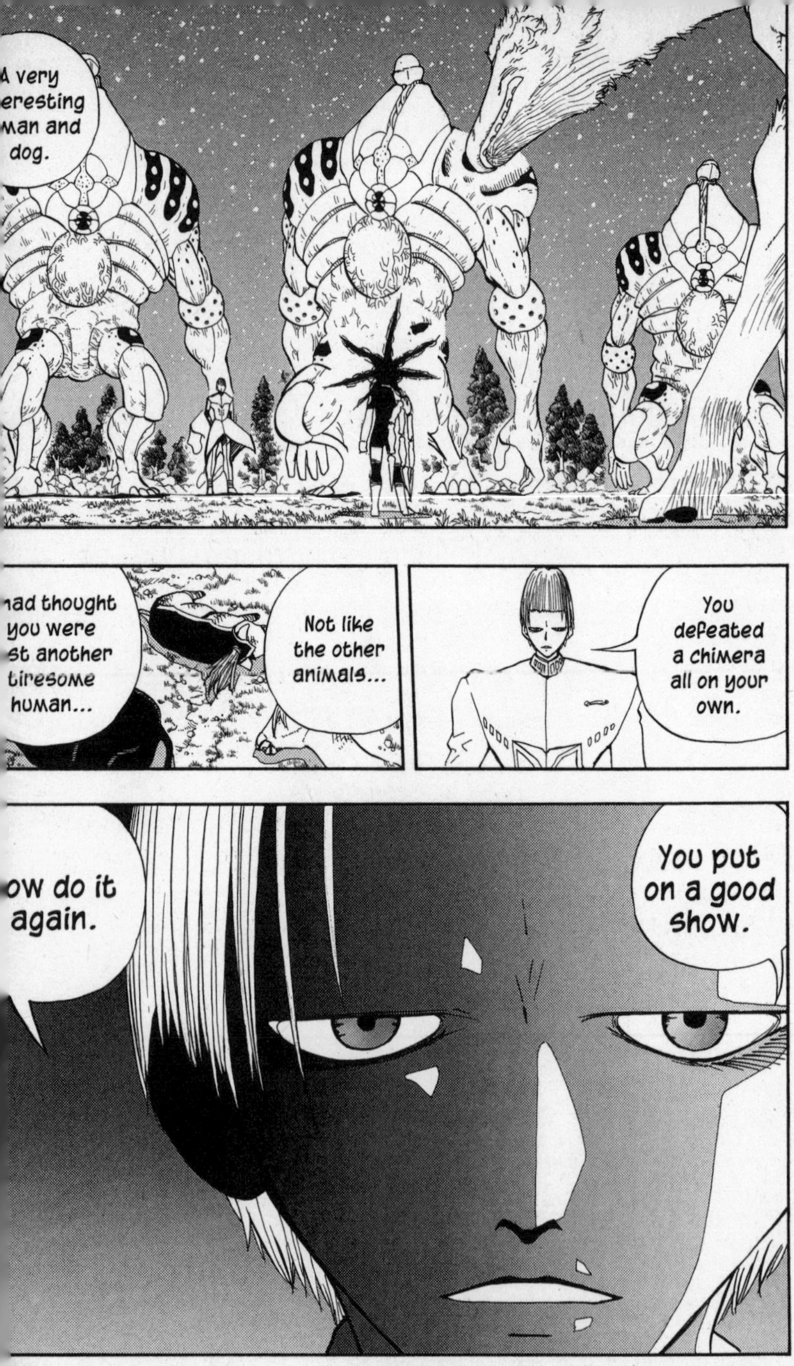

A very eresting man and dog.
You defeated a chimera all on your own.
Not like the other animals...
had thought you were st another tiresome human...
You put on a good show.
ow do it again.

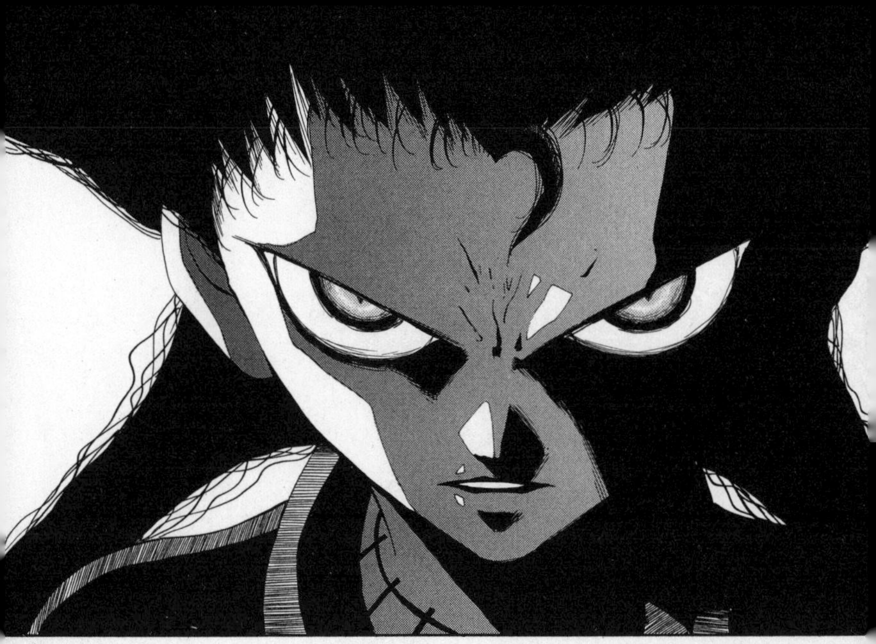
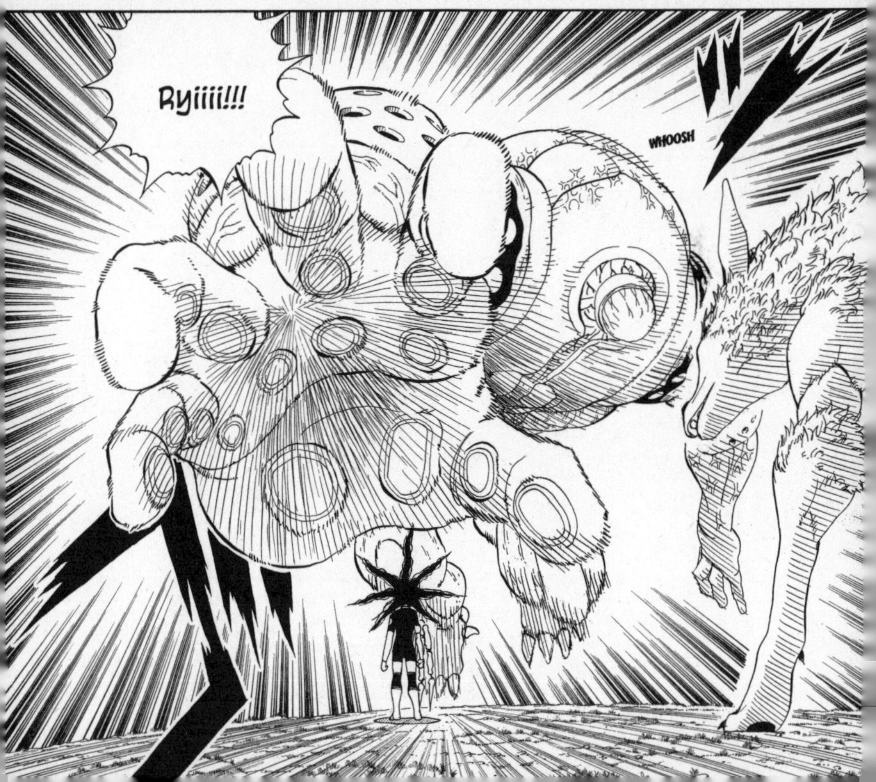
Ryiiii!!!
WHOOSH

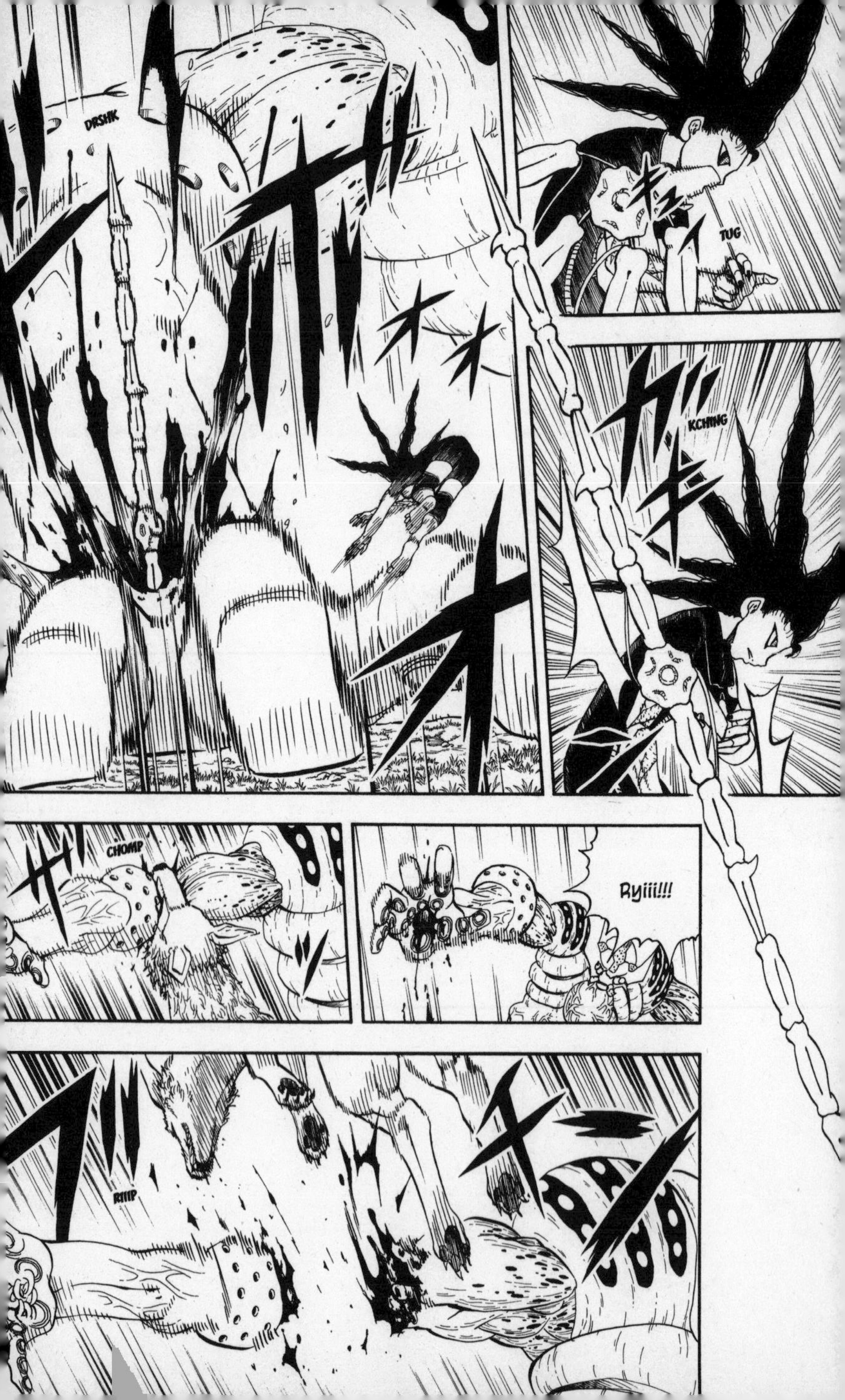
TUG
KCHING
DRSHK
Ryiii!!!
CHOMP
RIIIP

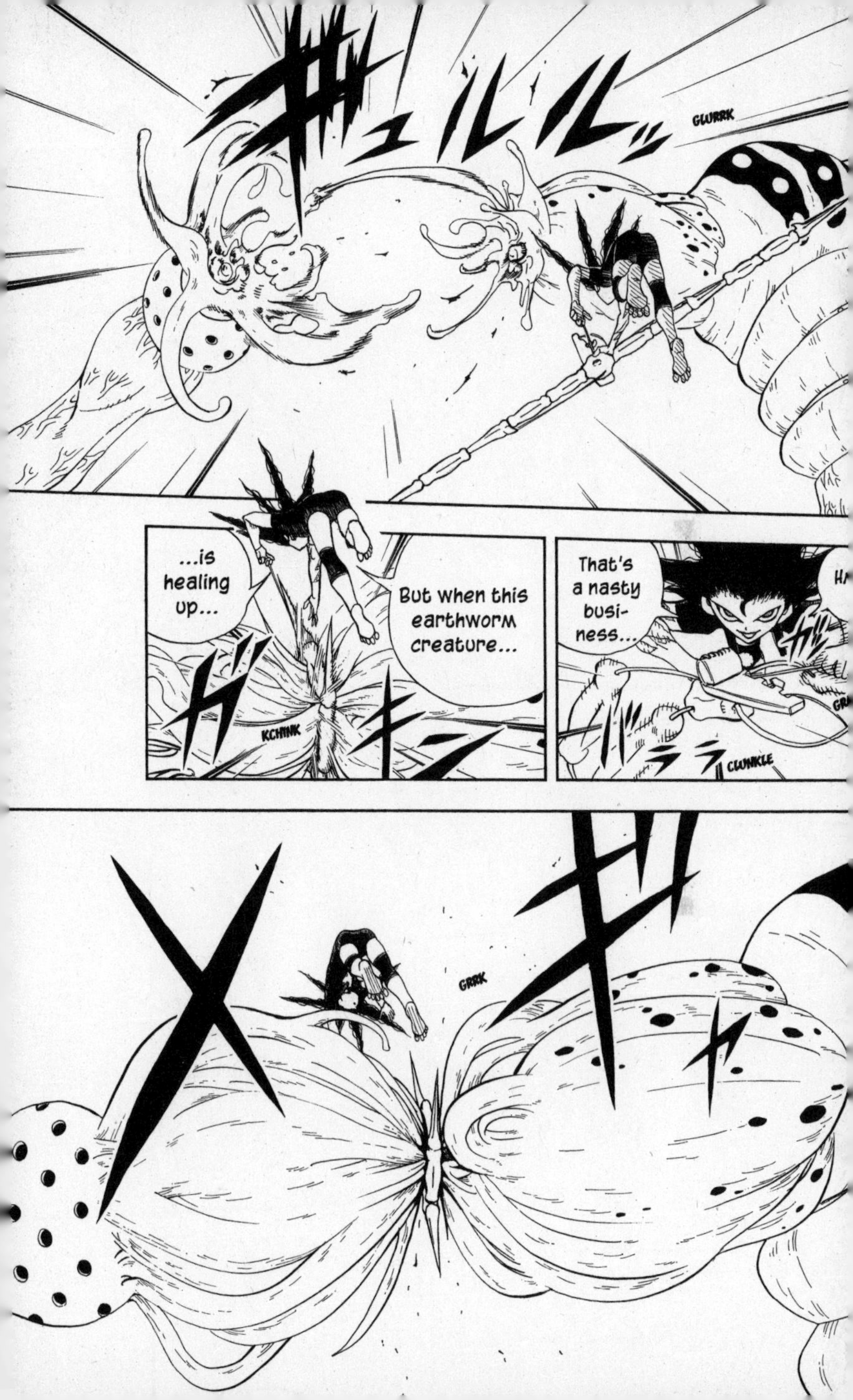
GLURRK
That's a nasty business...
CLUNKLE
But when this earthworm creature...
...is healing up...
KCHINK
GRRK

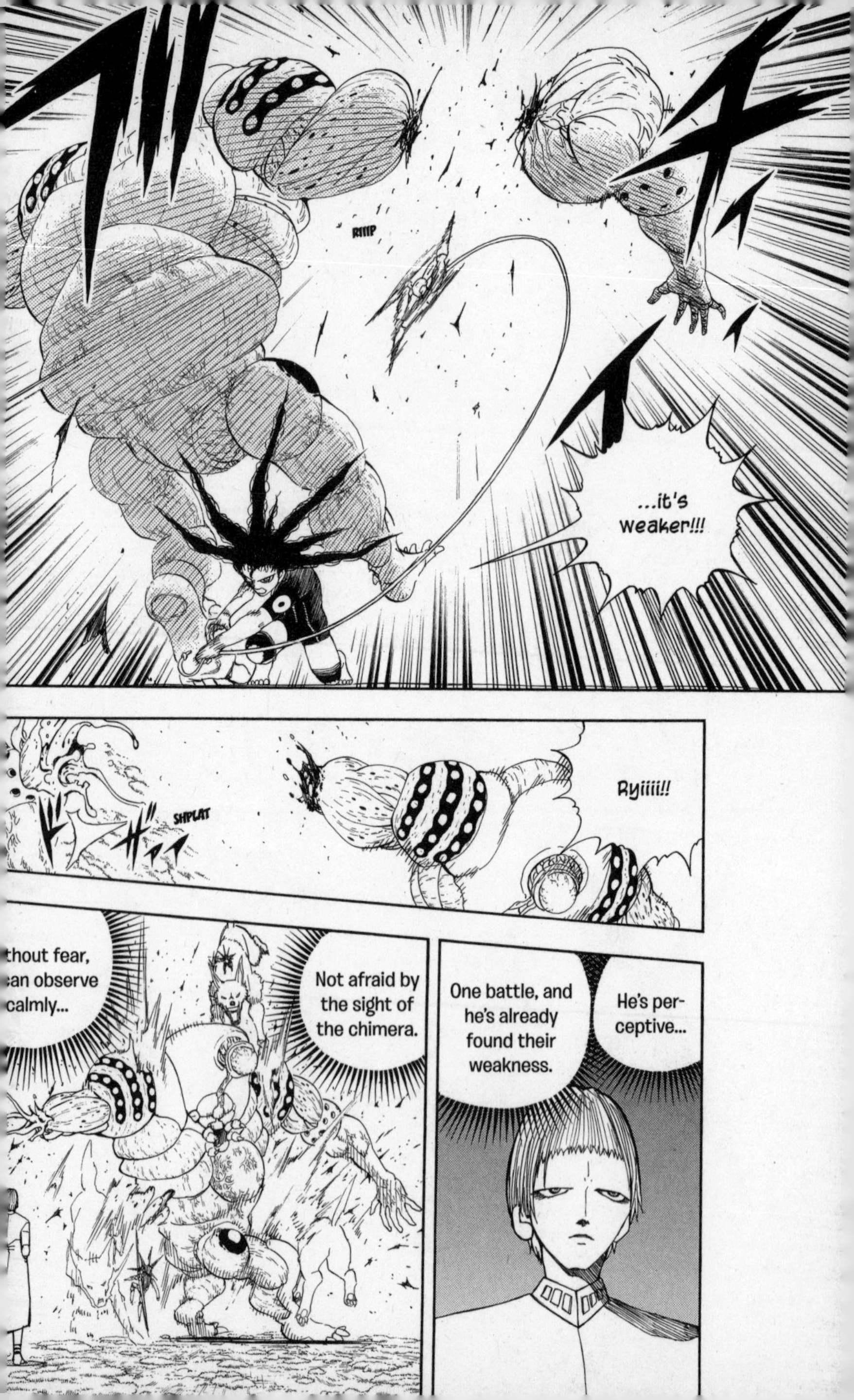
RIIIP
...it's weaker!!!
Ryiiii!!
SHPLAT
He's perceptive...
One battle, and he's already found their weakness.
Not afraid by the sight of the chimera.
thout fear,
an observe
calmly...

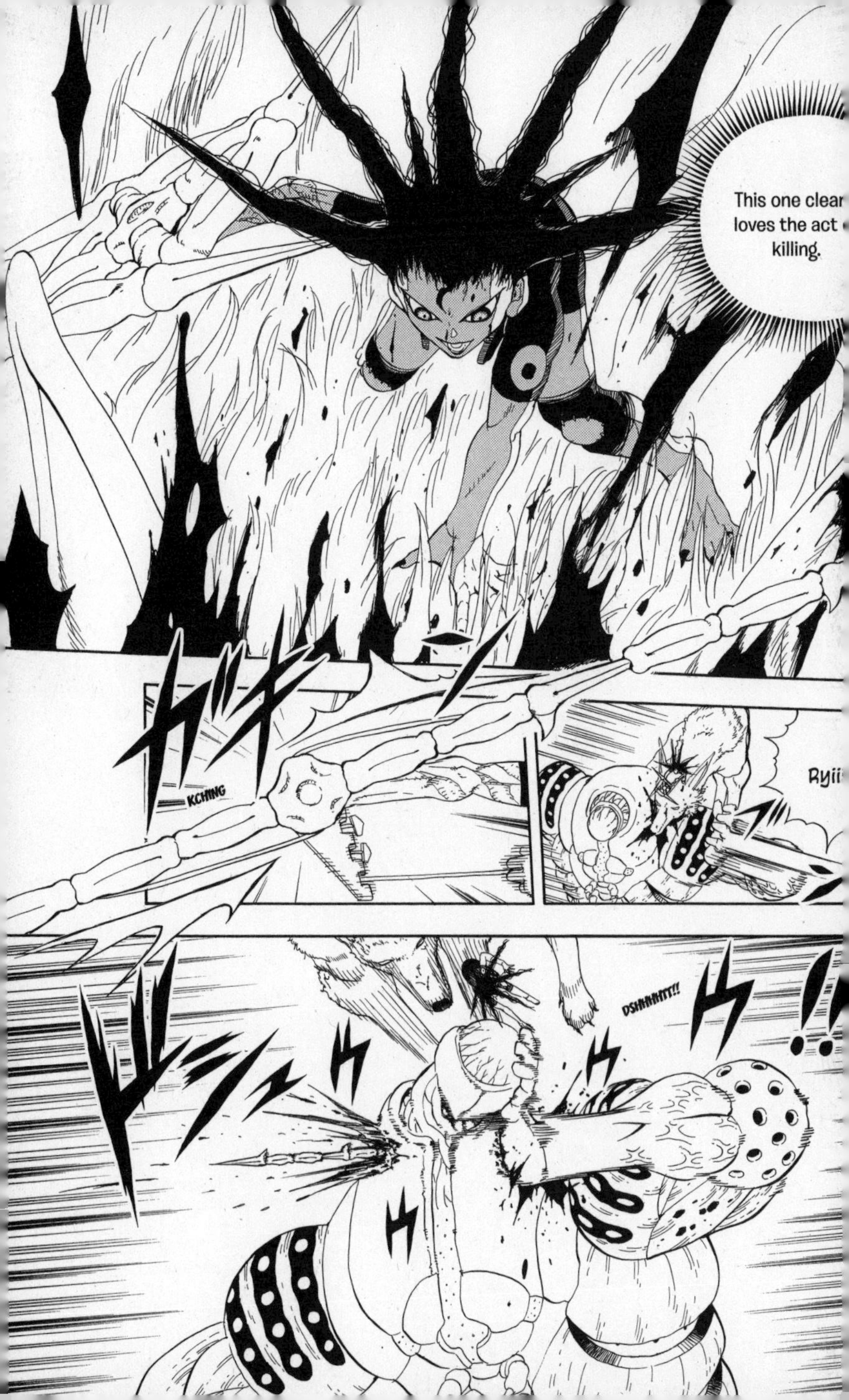
This one clear
loves the act
killing.
Ryii
KCHING
DSHHHHTT!!
!!

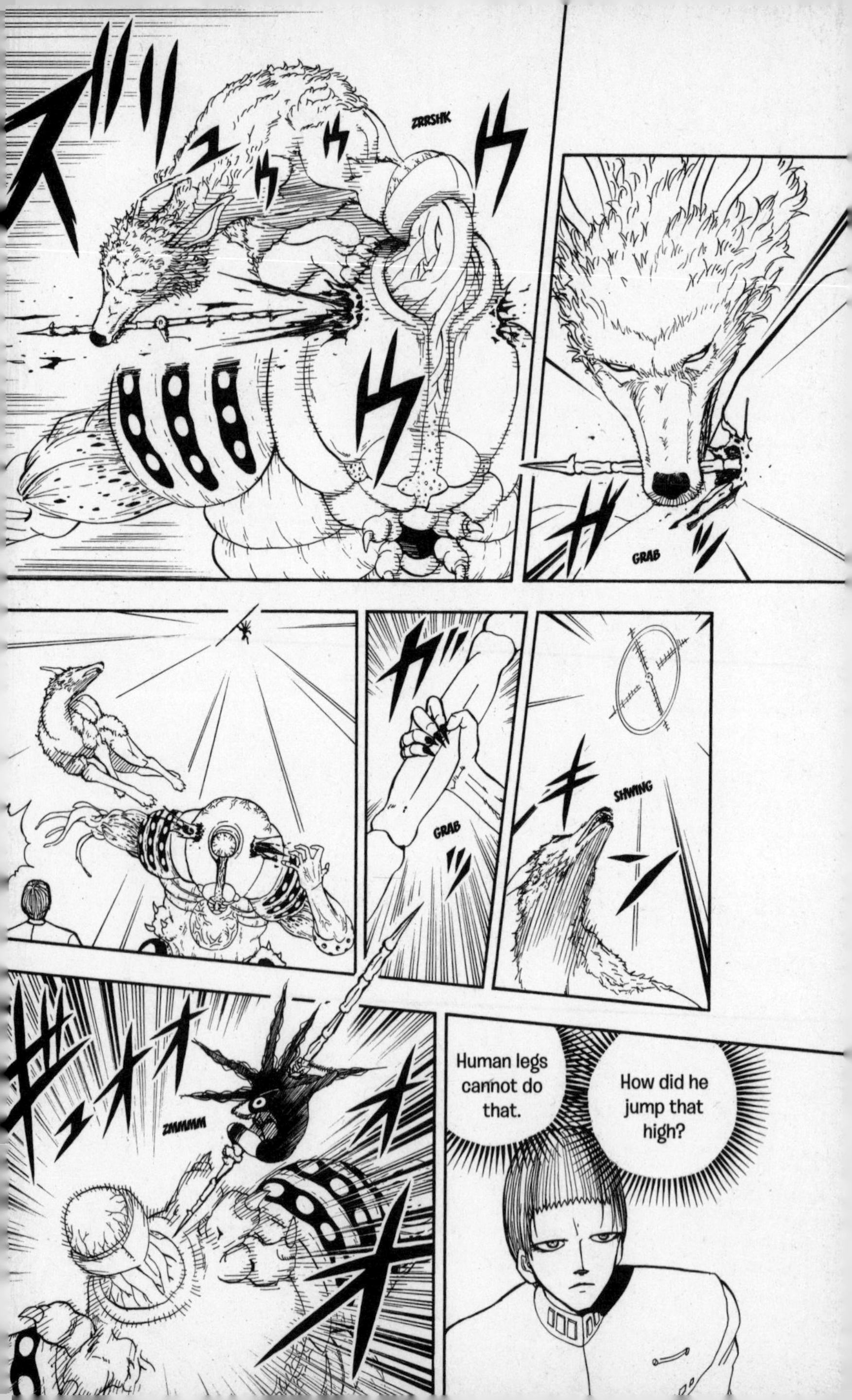
GRAB
ZRRSHK
SHWING
GRAB
How did he jump that high?
Human legs cannot do that.
ZMMMM

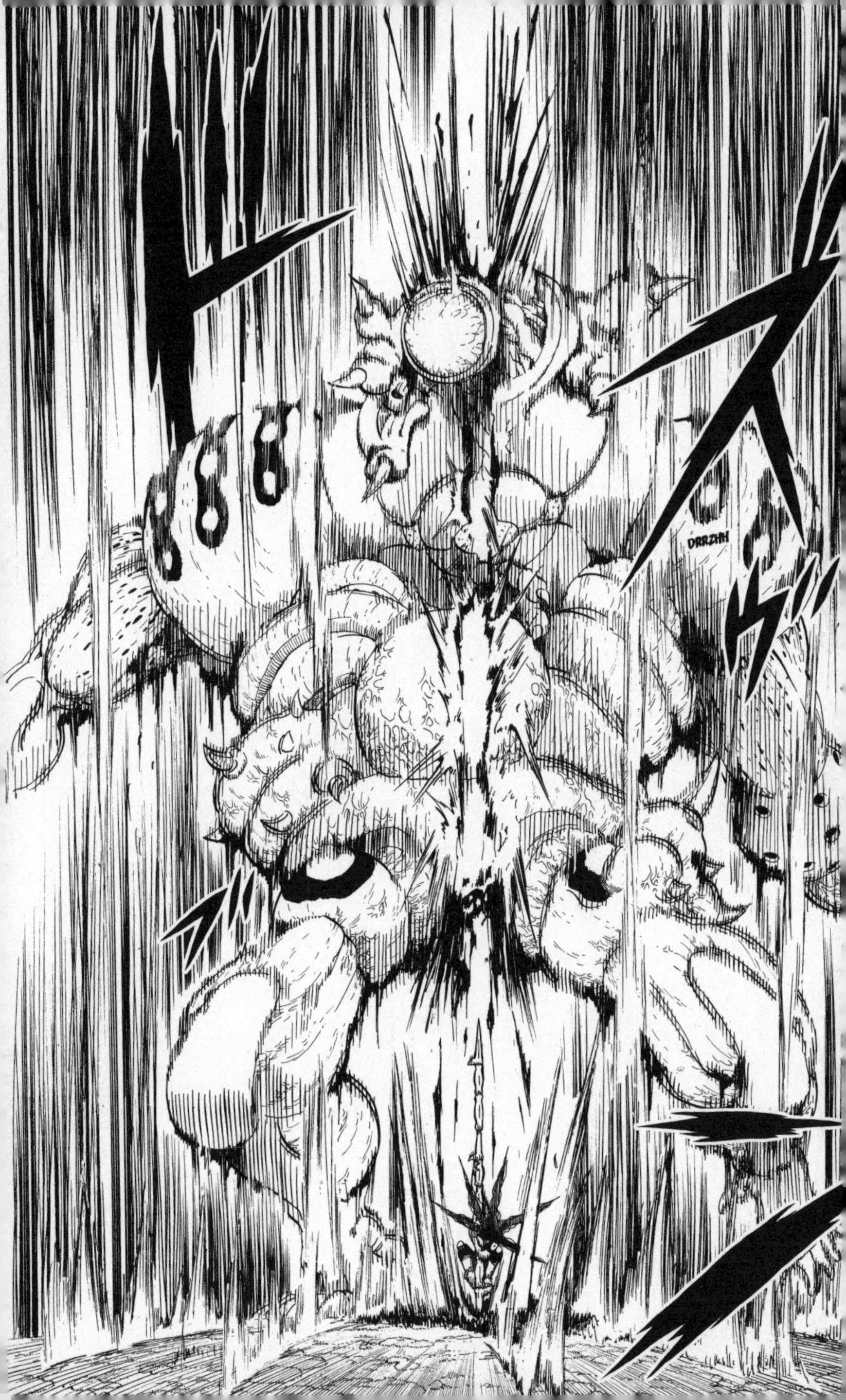
DRRZHH

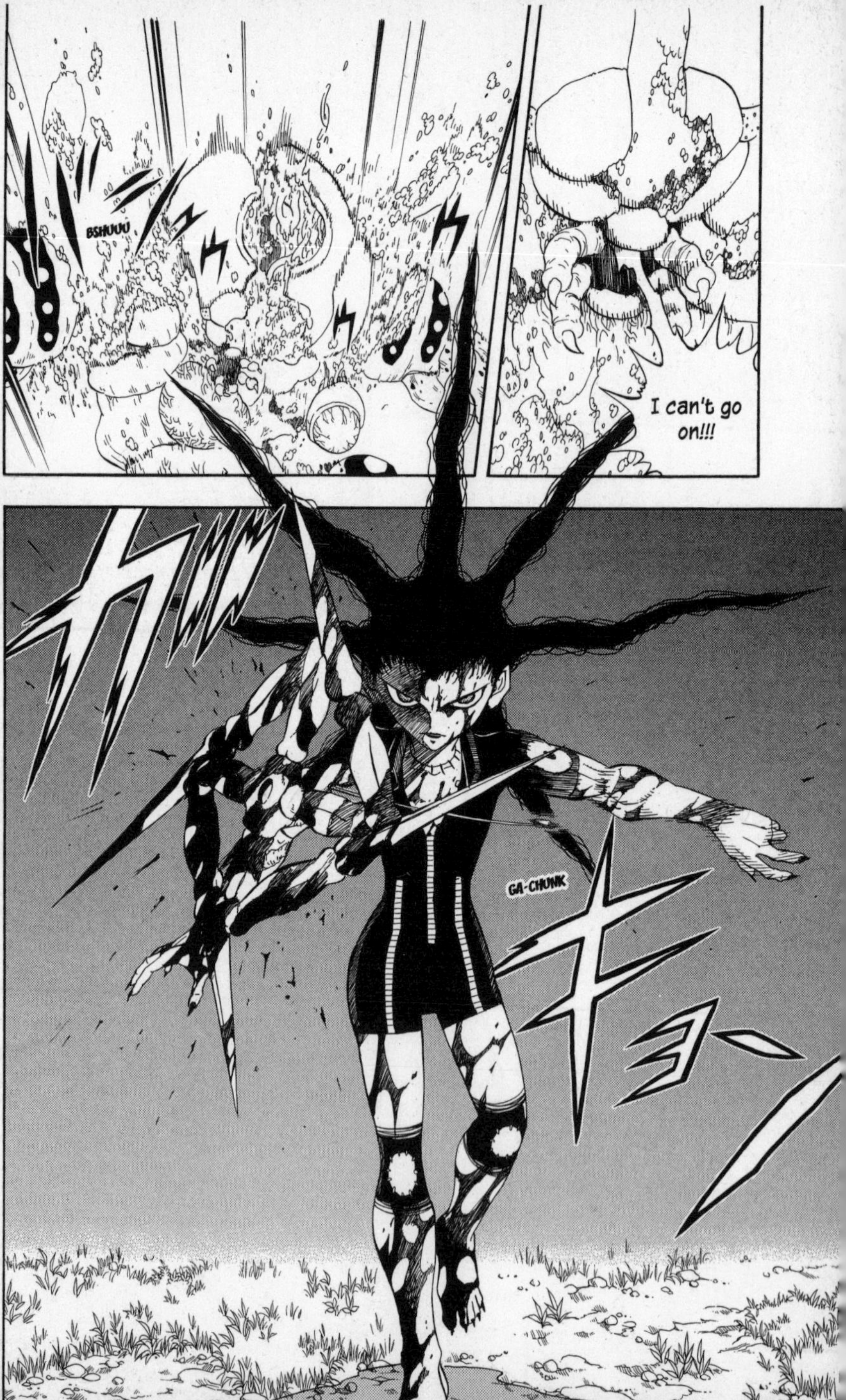
I can't go on!!!
BSHUUU
GA-CHUNK

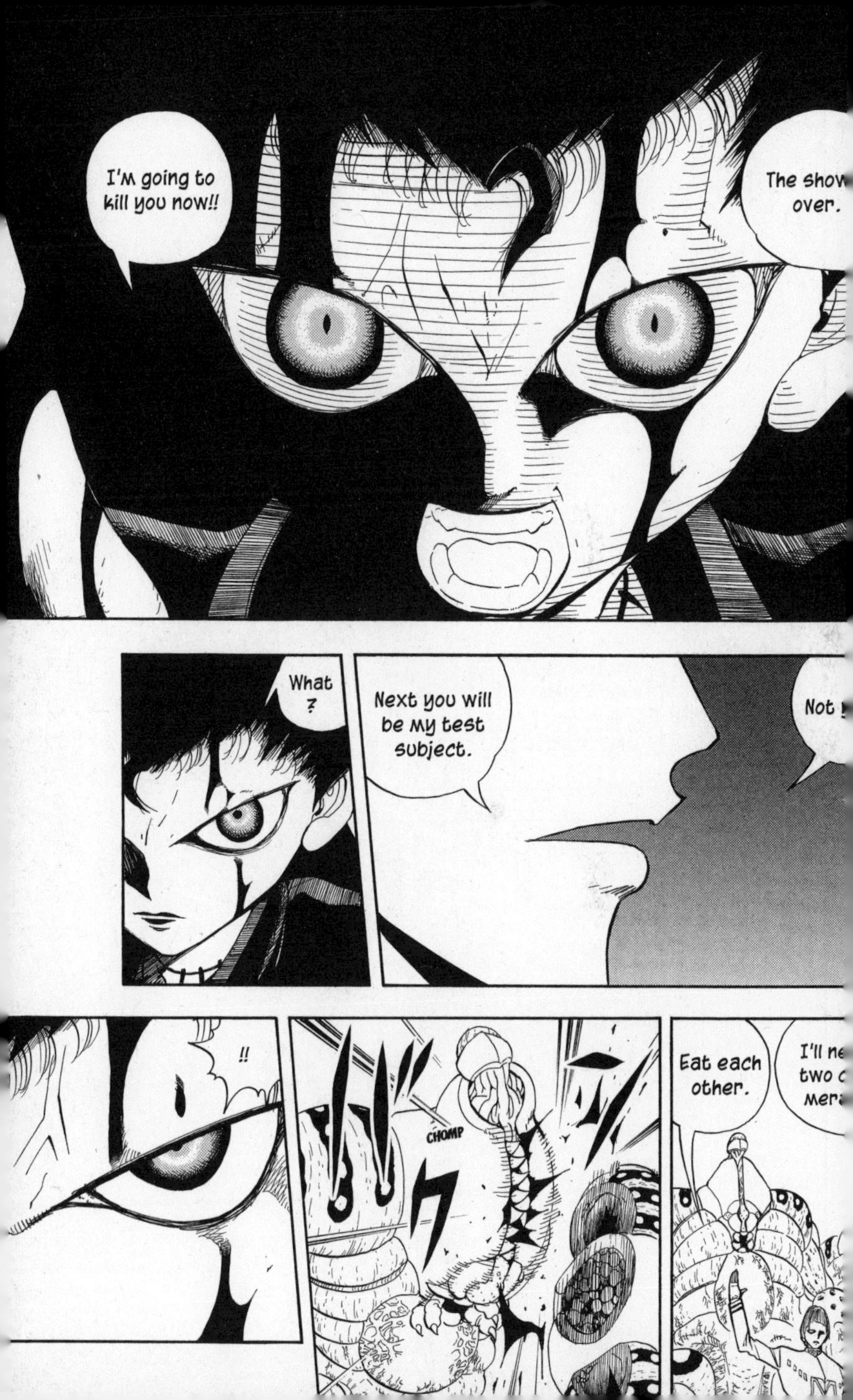
The show over.
I'm going to kill you now!!
Not
Next you will be my test subject.
What?
I'll ne two c mer
Eat each other.
CHOMP
!!

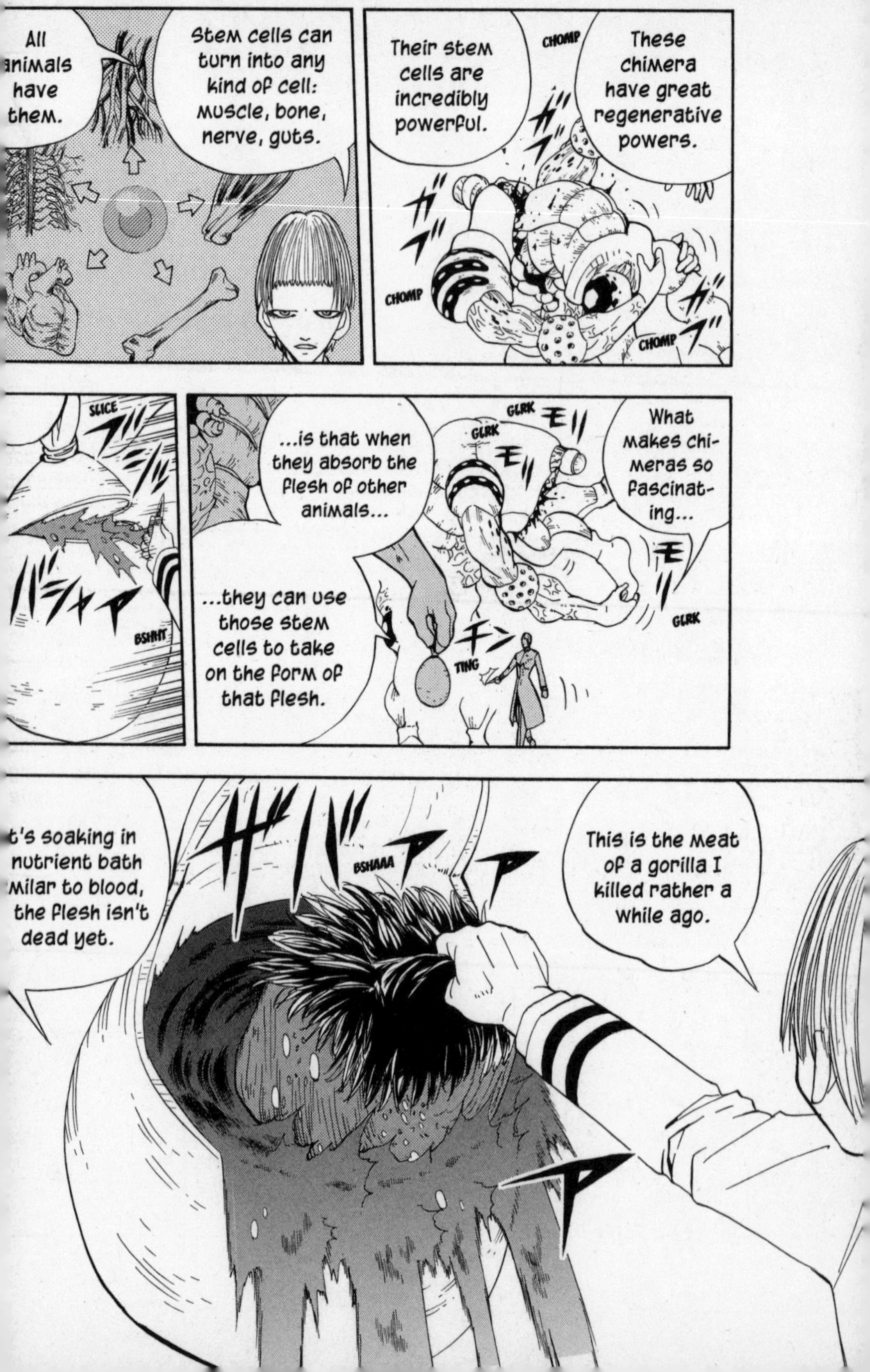
These chimera have great regenerative powers.
CHOMP
Their stem cells are incredibly powerful.
CHOMP
CHOMP
Stem cells can turn into any kind of cell: muscle, bone, nerve, guts.
All animals have them.
What makes chimeras so fascinating...
GLRK
GLRK
...is that when they absorb the flesh of other animals...
GLRK
...they can use those stem cells to take on the form of that flesh.
TING
SLICE
BSHHT
This is the meat of a gorilla I killed rather a while ago.
BSHAAA
t's soaking in nutrient bath milar to blood, the flesh isn't dead yet.

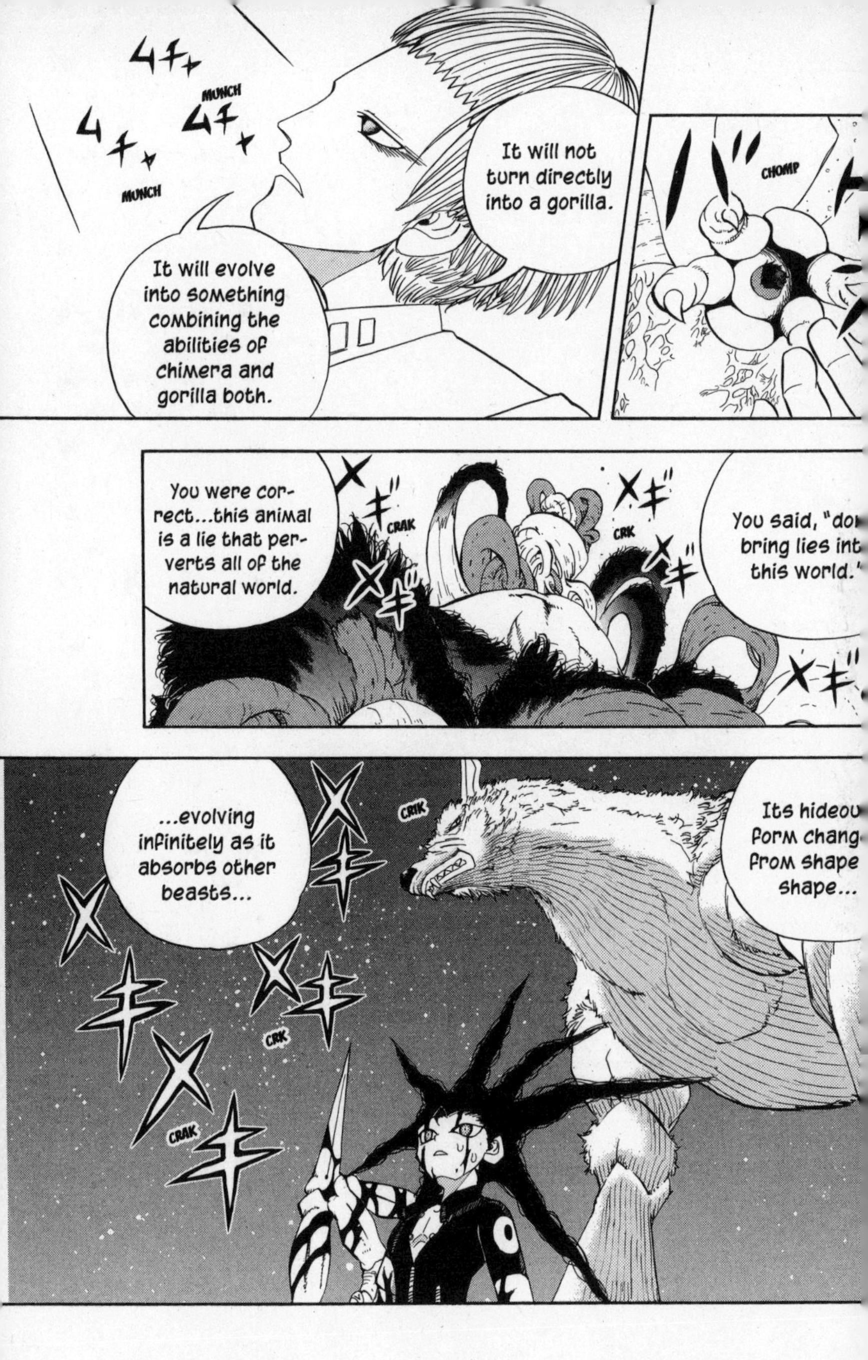
CHOMP
It will not turn directly into a gorilla.
MUNCH
MUNCH
It will evolve into something combining the abilities of chimera and gorilla both.
You said, "do
bring lies int
this world."
CRK
CRAK
You were correct...this animal is a lie that perverts all of the natural world.
Its hideou
form chang
from shape
shape...
CRIK
...evolving infinitely as it absorbs other beasts...
CRK
CRAK

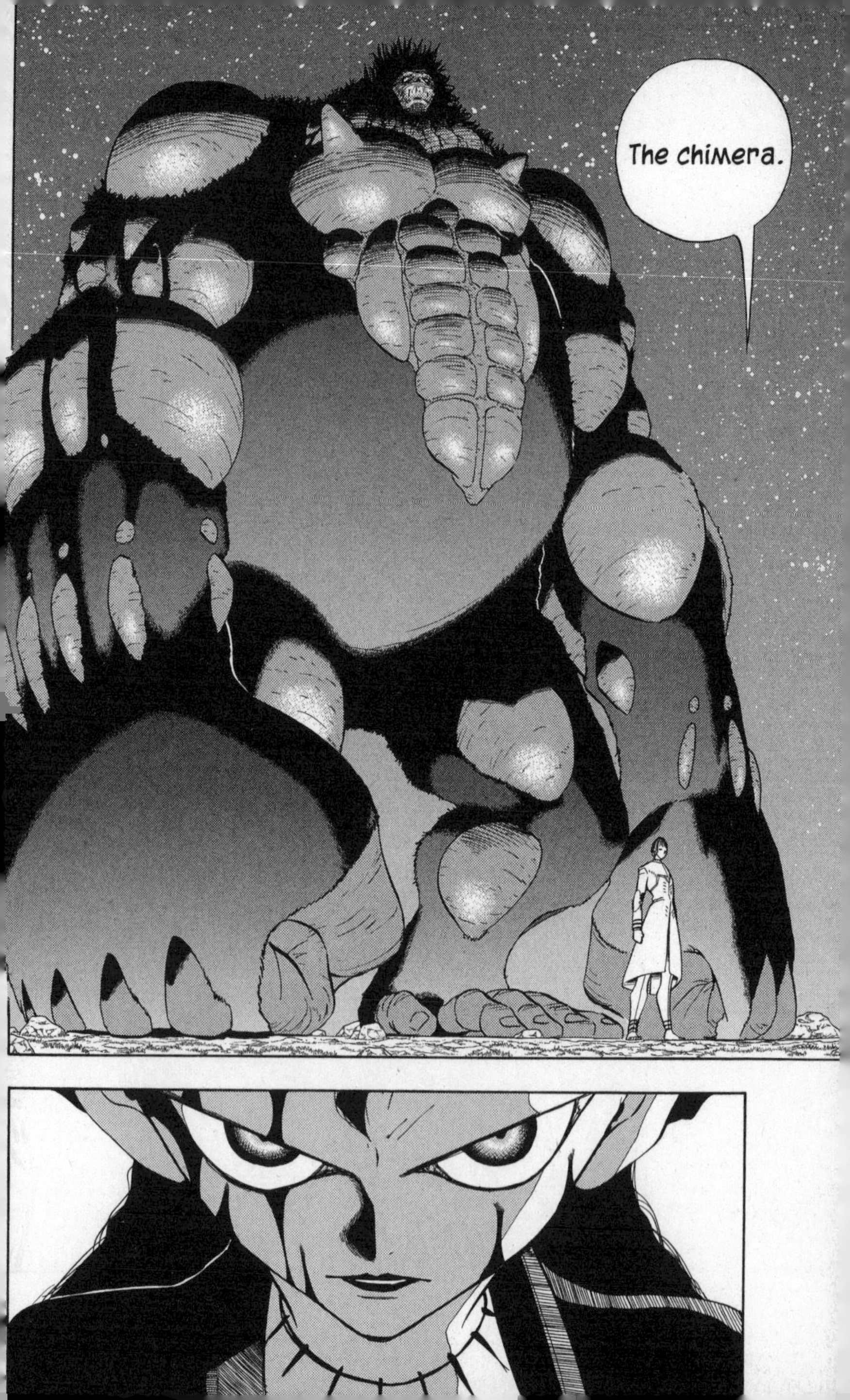
The chimera.

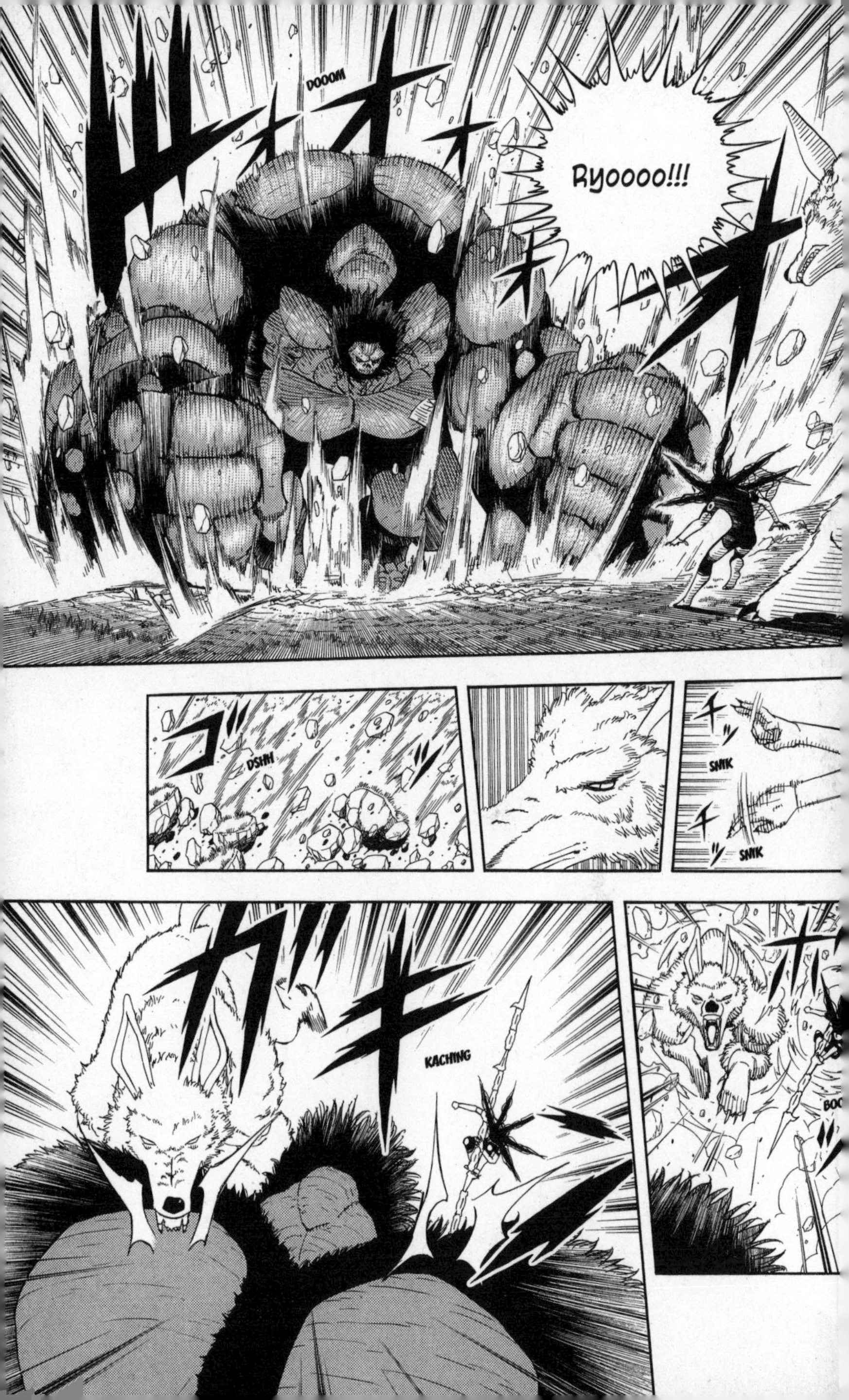
Ryoooo!!!
DOOOM
SNIK
SNIK
DSHH
KACHING

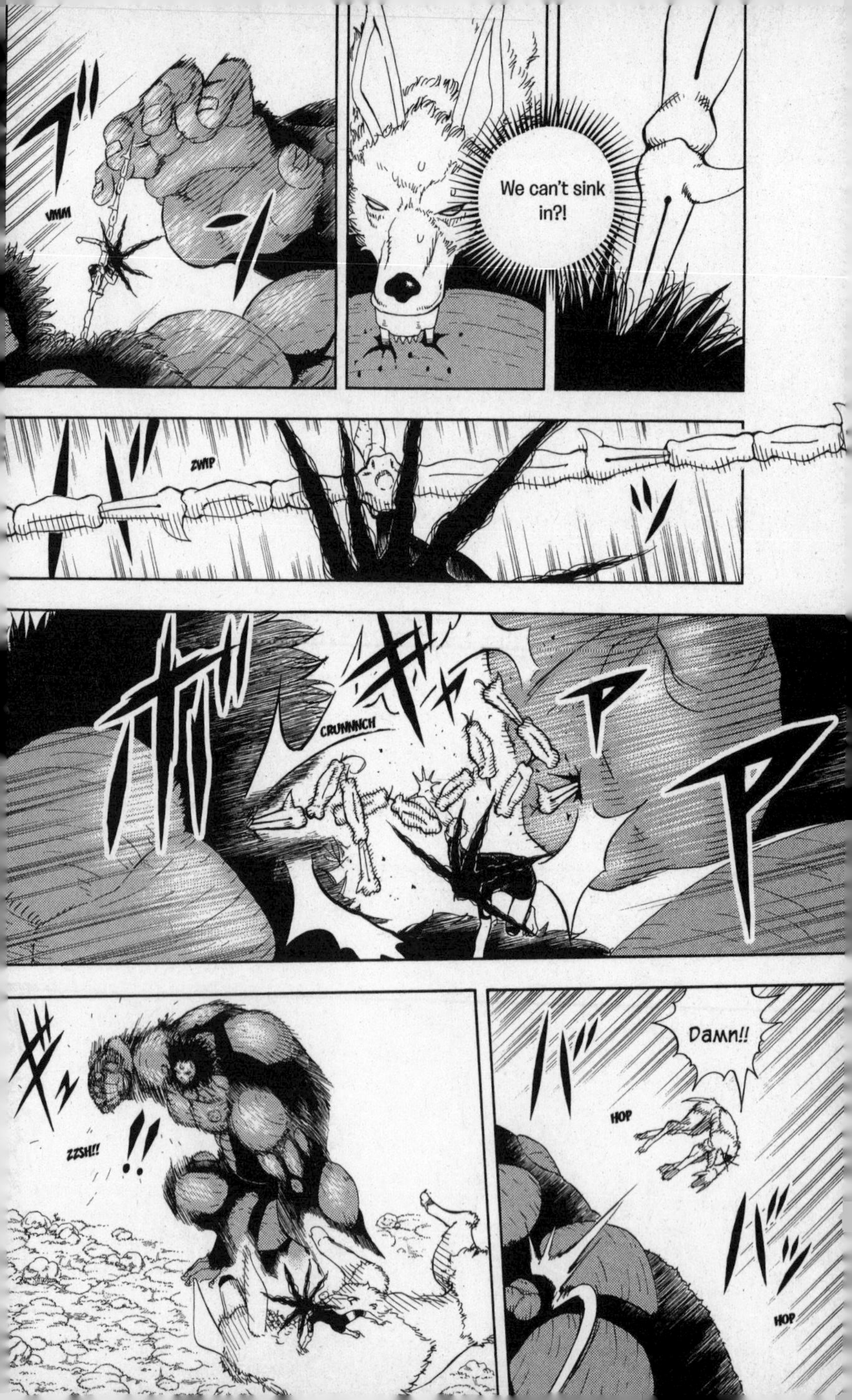
We can't sink in?!
VMM
ZWIP
CRUNNNCH
Damn!!
HOP
HOP
ZZSH!!
!!

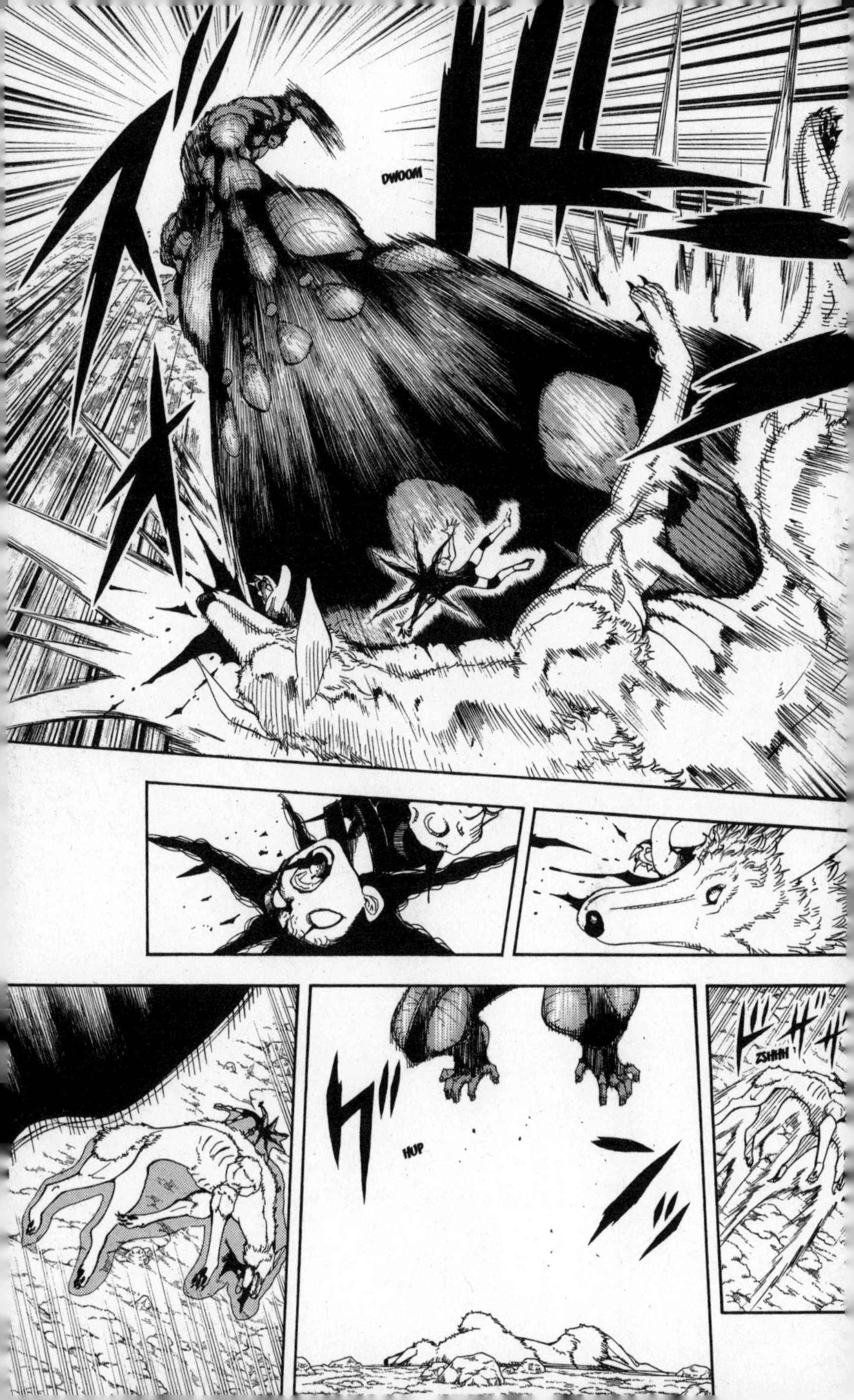
DWOOM
ZSHHH
HUP

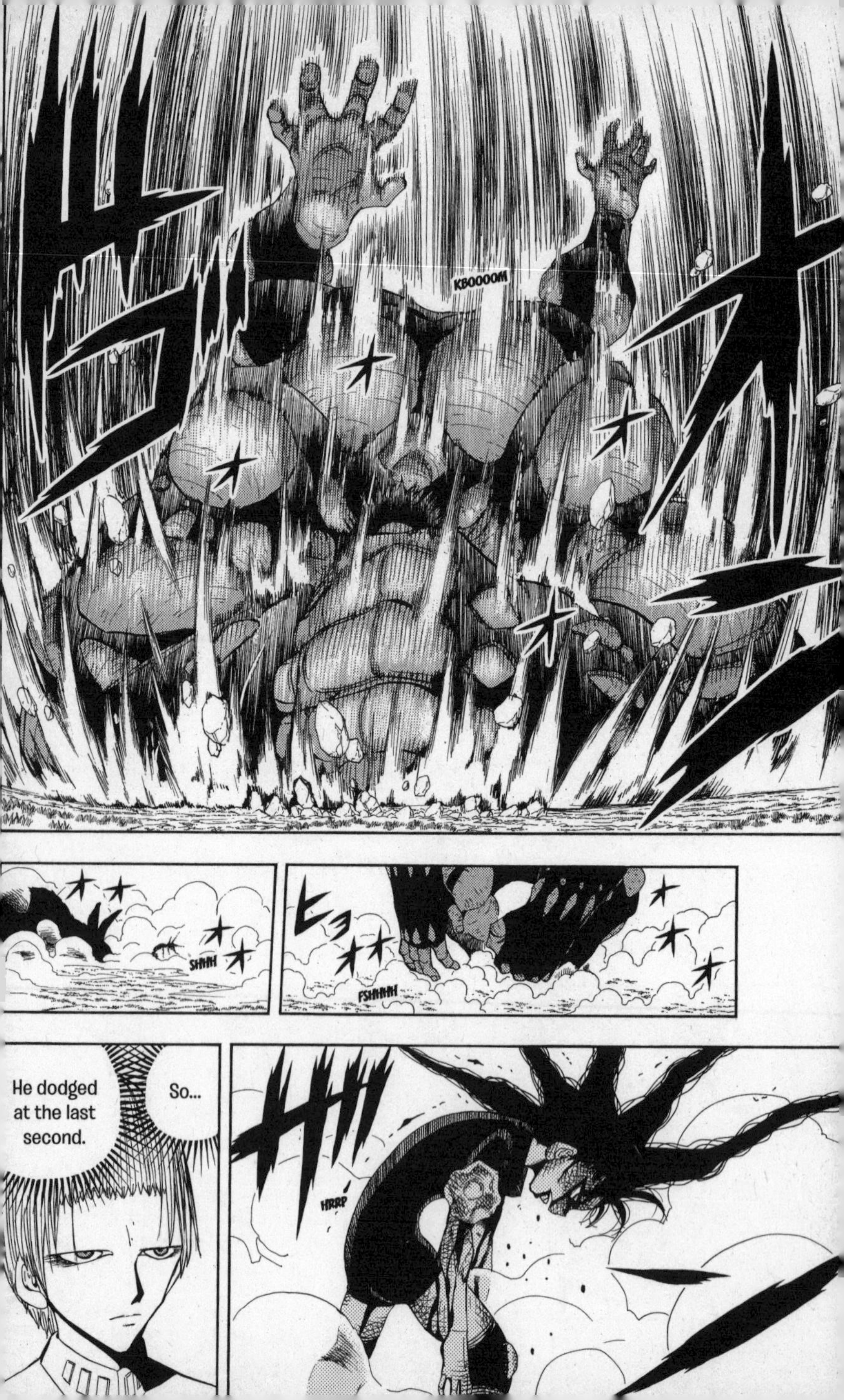
KBOOOOM
FSHHHH
SHHH
HRRP
So...
He dodged at the last second.

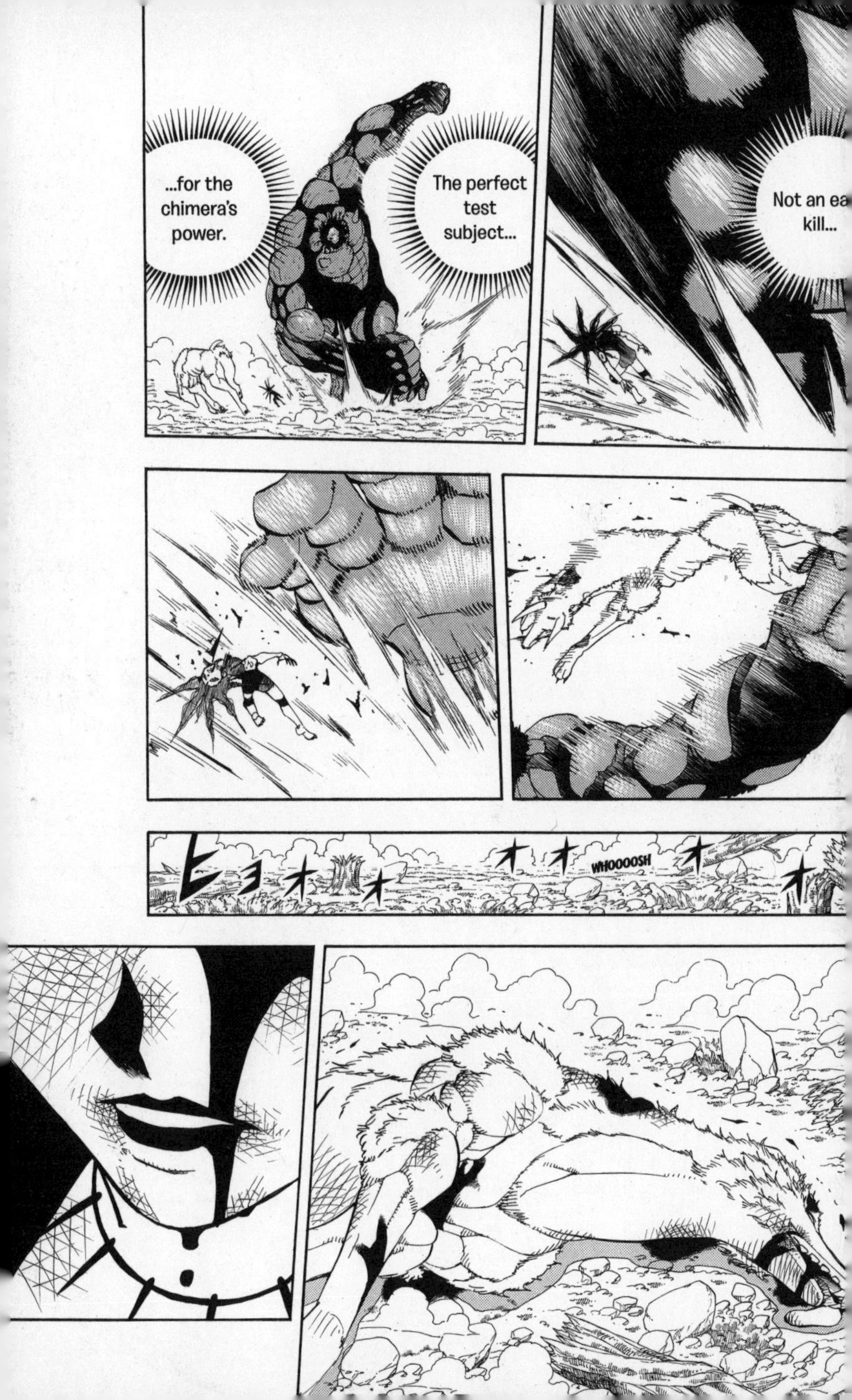
Not an ea
kill...
The perfect test subject...
...for the chimera's power.
WHOOOOSH

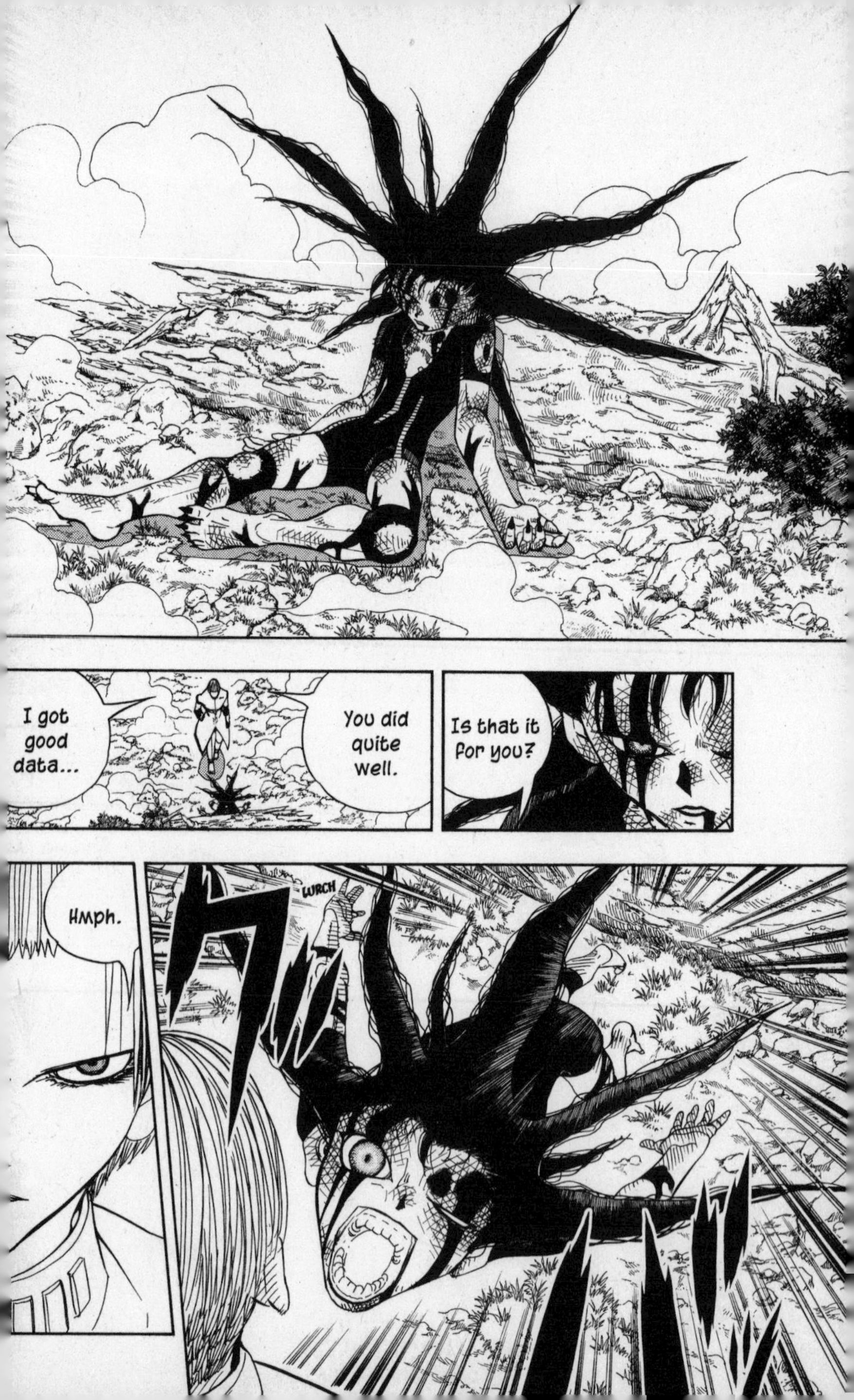
Is that it for you?
You did quite well.
I got good data...
LURCH
Hmph.

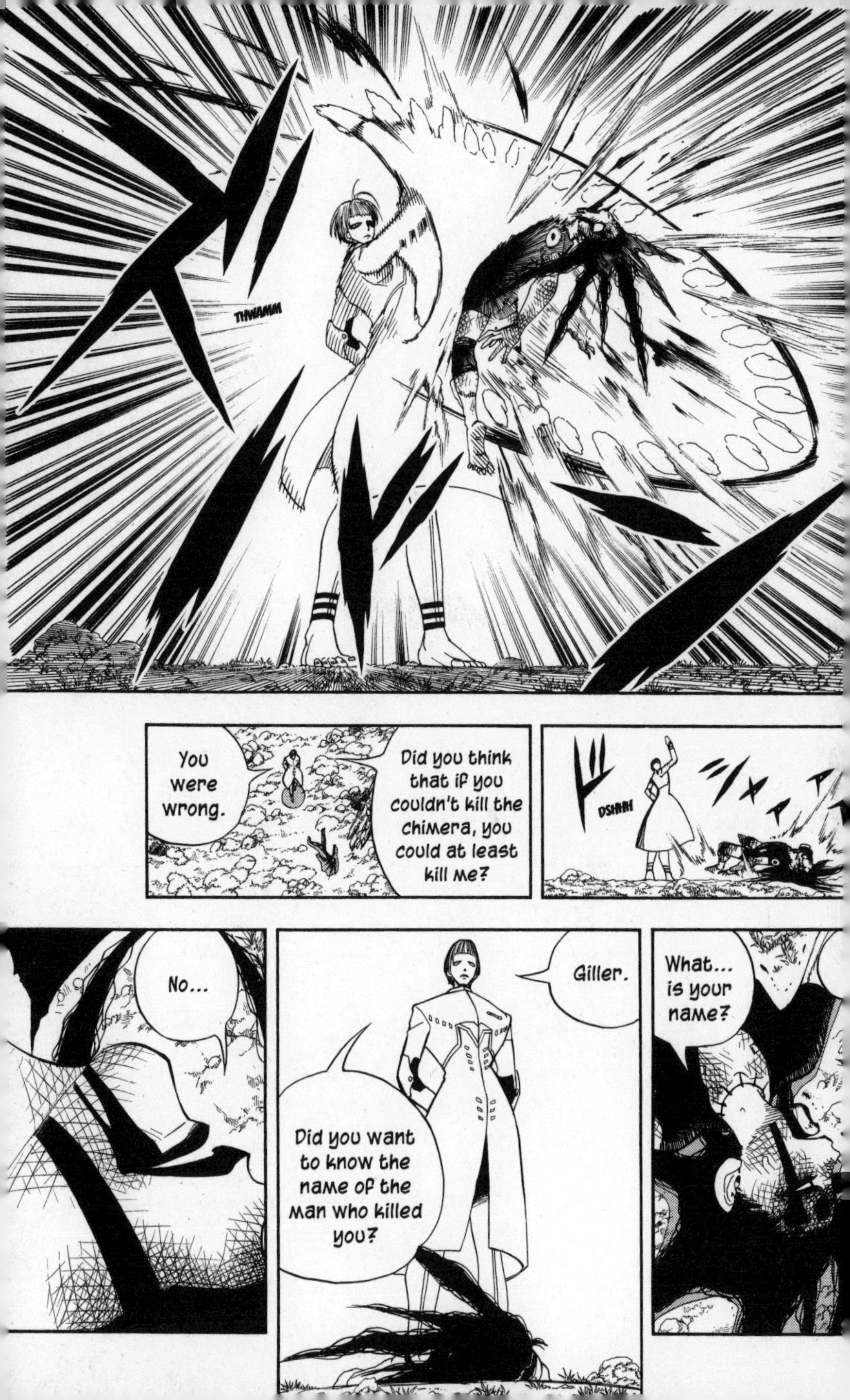
THWAMM
DSHHH
Did you think that if you couldn't kill the chimera, you could at least kill me?
You were wrong.
What... is your name?
Giller.
Did you want to know the name of the man who killed you?
No...

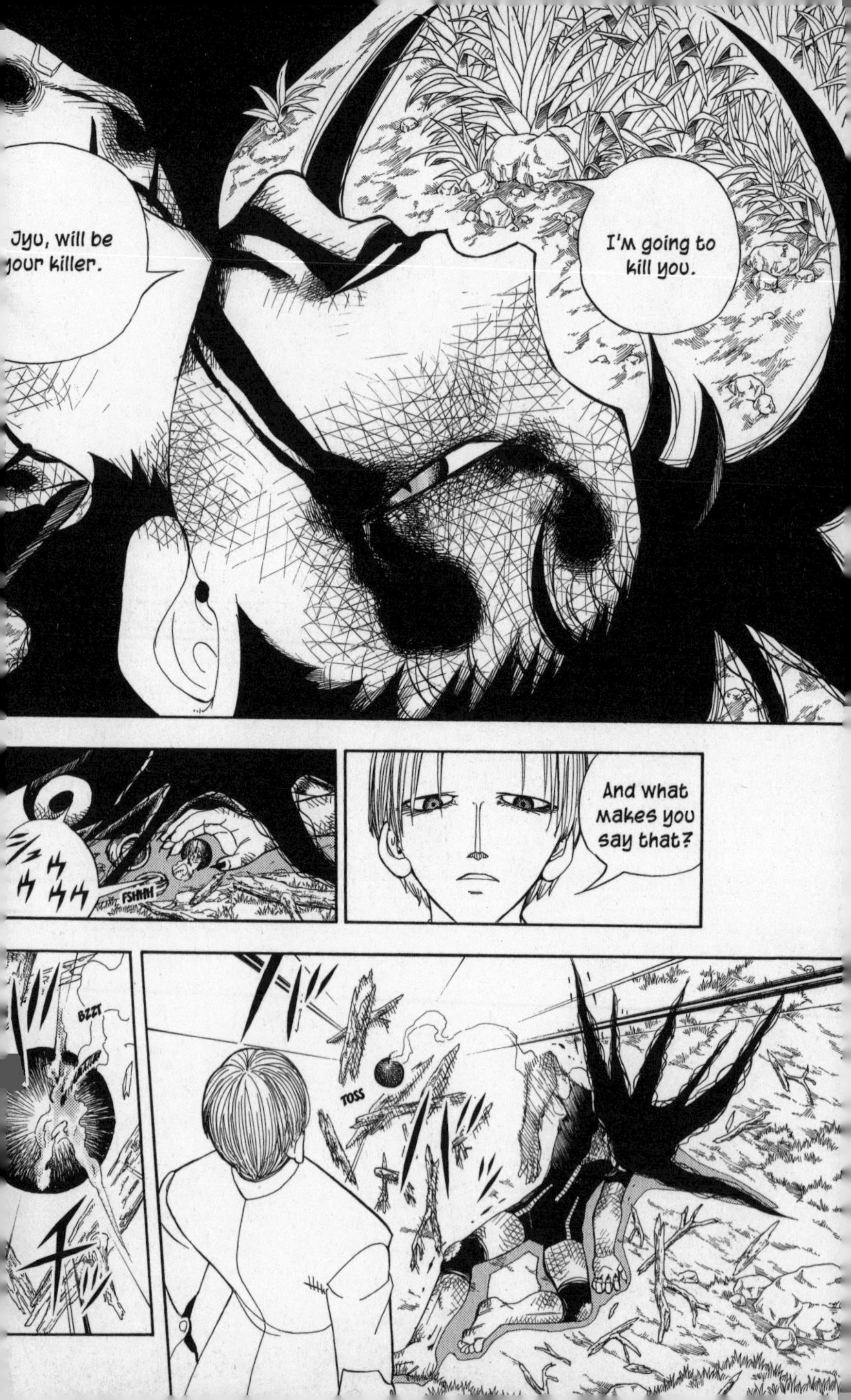
I'm going to kill you.
Jyu, will be your killer.
And what makes you say that?
FSHHH
TOSS
BZZT

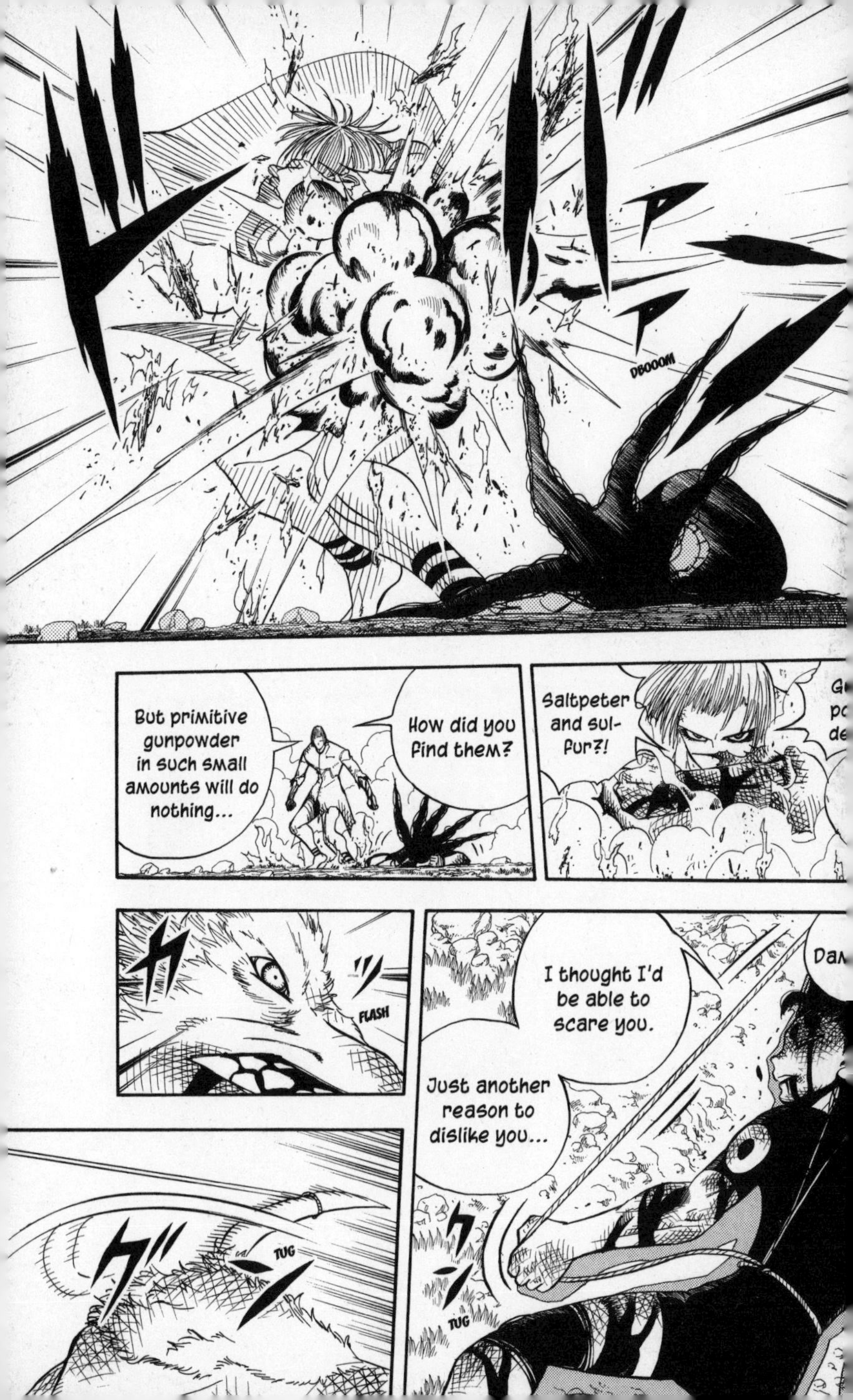
DBOOOM
Saltpeter and sul-fur?!
How did you find them?
But primitive gunpowder in such small amounts will do nothing...
I thought I'd be able to scare you.
Just another reason to dislike you...
TUG
FLASH
TUG

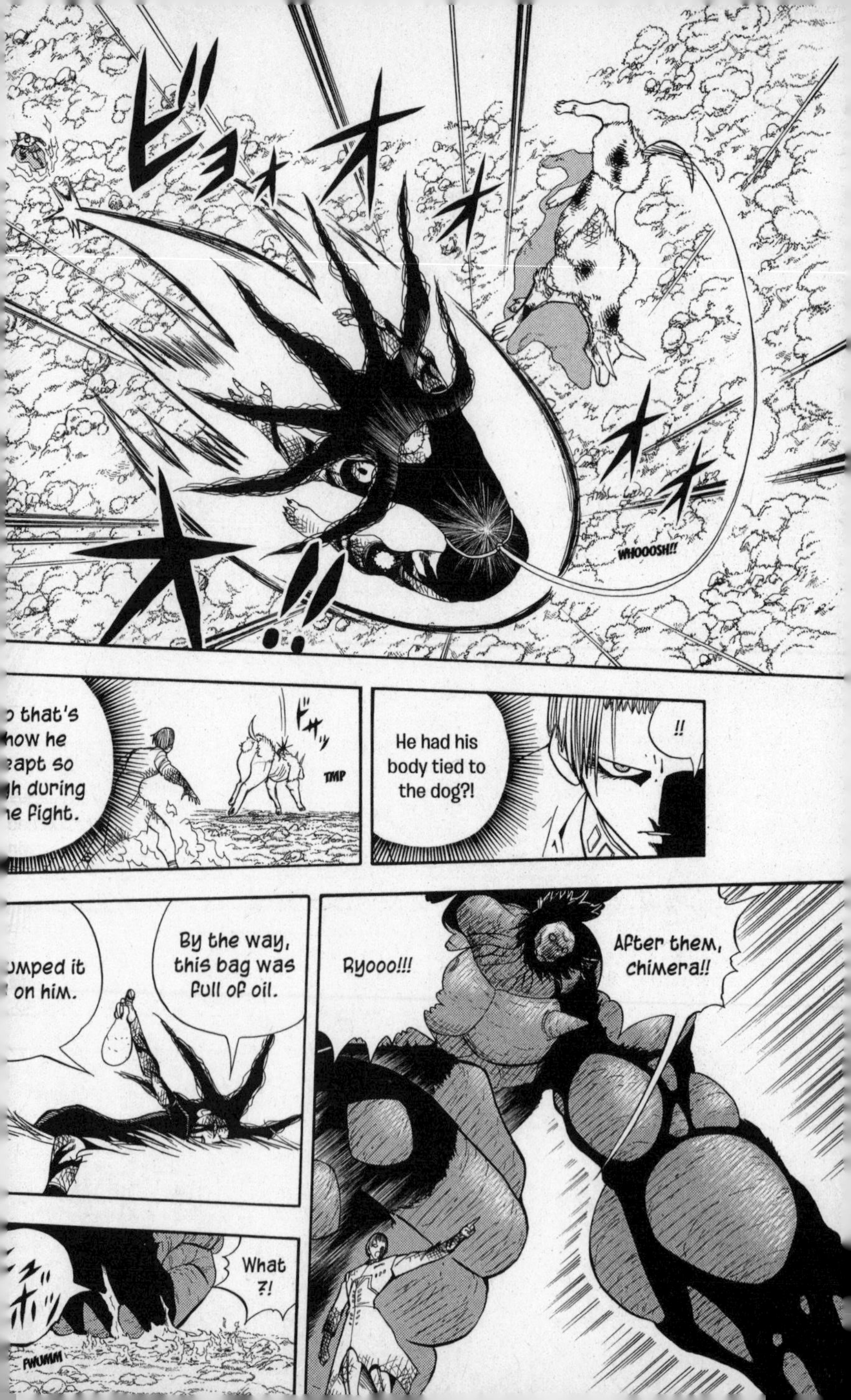
ビョォオオオ
WHOOOSH!!
!!
He had his body tied to the dog?!
ドサッ
TMP
o that's how he eapt so gh during e fight.
After them, chimera!!
Ryooo!!!
By the way, this bag was full of oil.
umped it on him.
What ?!
ボッ
FWUMM

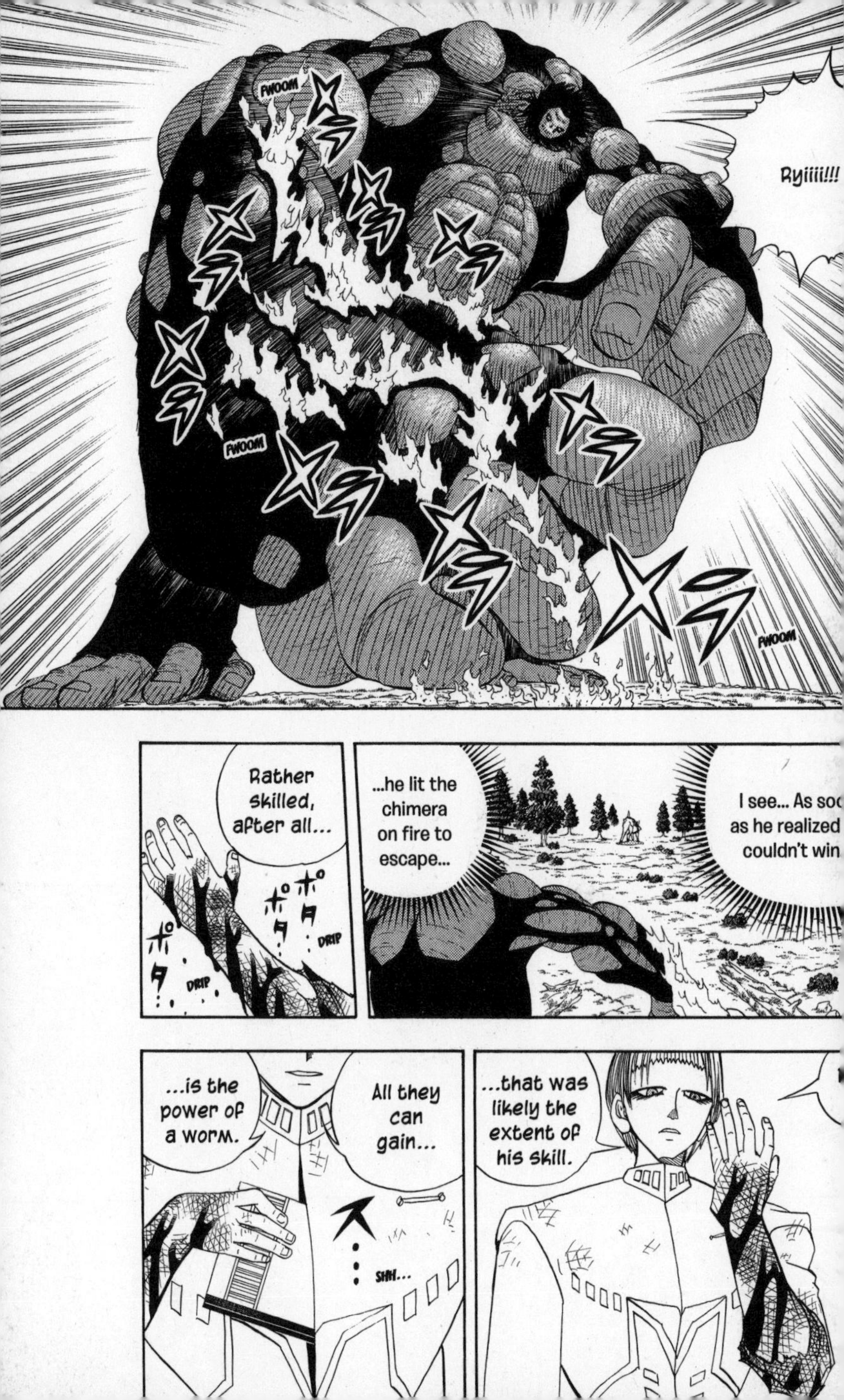

Ryiiii!!!
PWOOM
PWOOM
PWOOM
I see... As soo
as he realized
couldn't win
...he lit the chimera on fire to escape...
Rather skilled, after all...
DRIP
DRIP
...that was likely the extent of his skill.
All they can gain...
...is the power of a worm.
SHH...

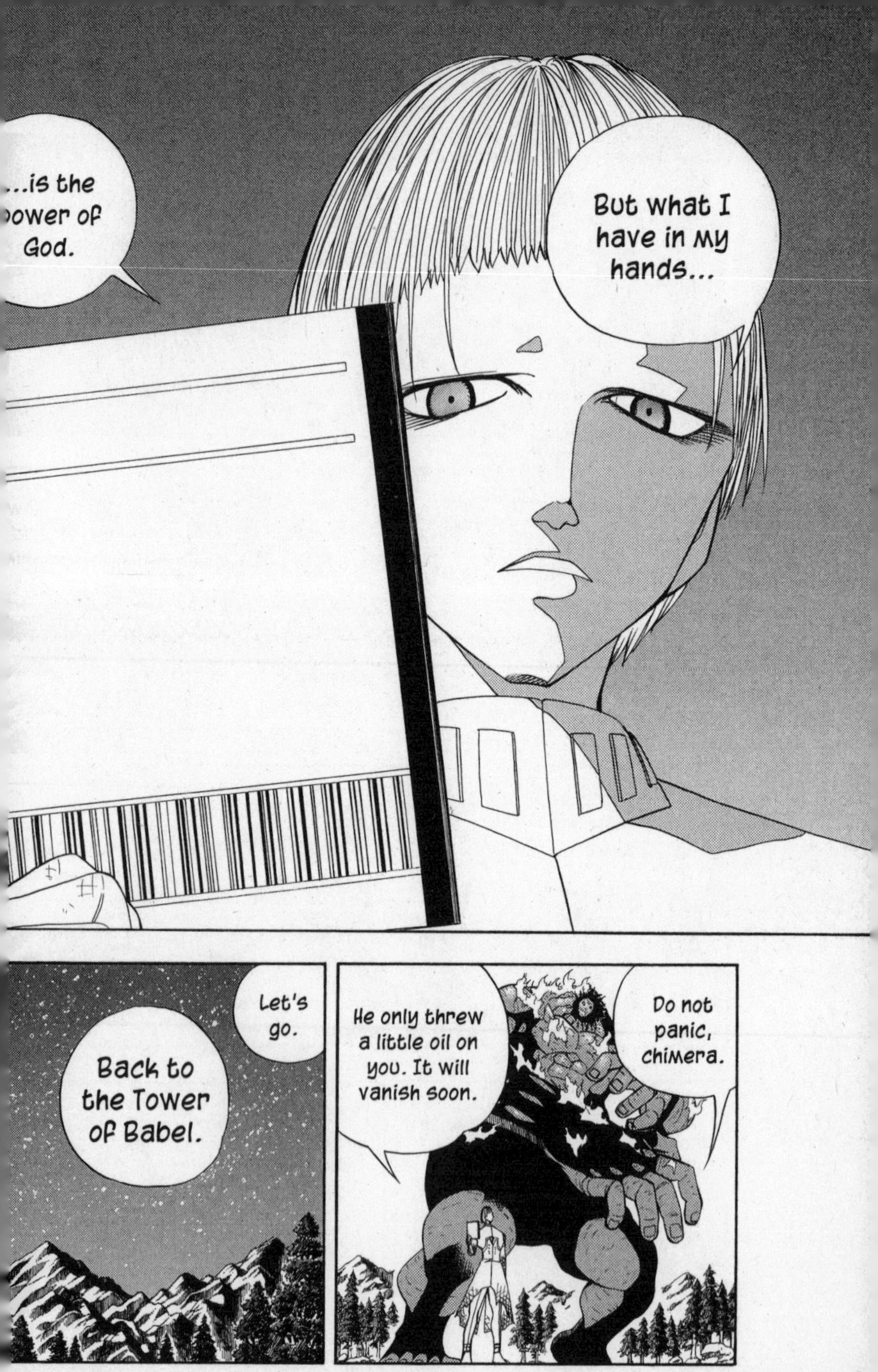
But what I have in my hands...
...is the power of God.
Do not panic, chimera.
He only threw a little oil on you. It will vanish soon.
Let's go.
Back to the Tower of Babel.

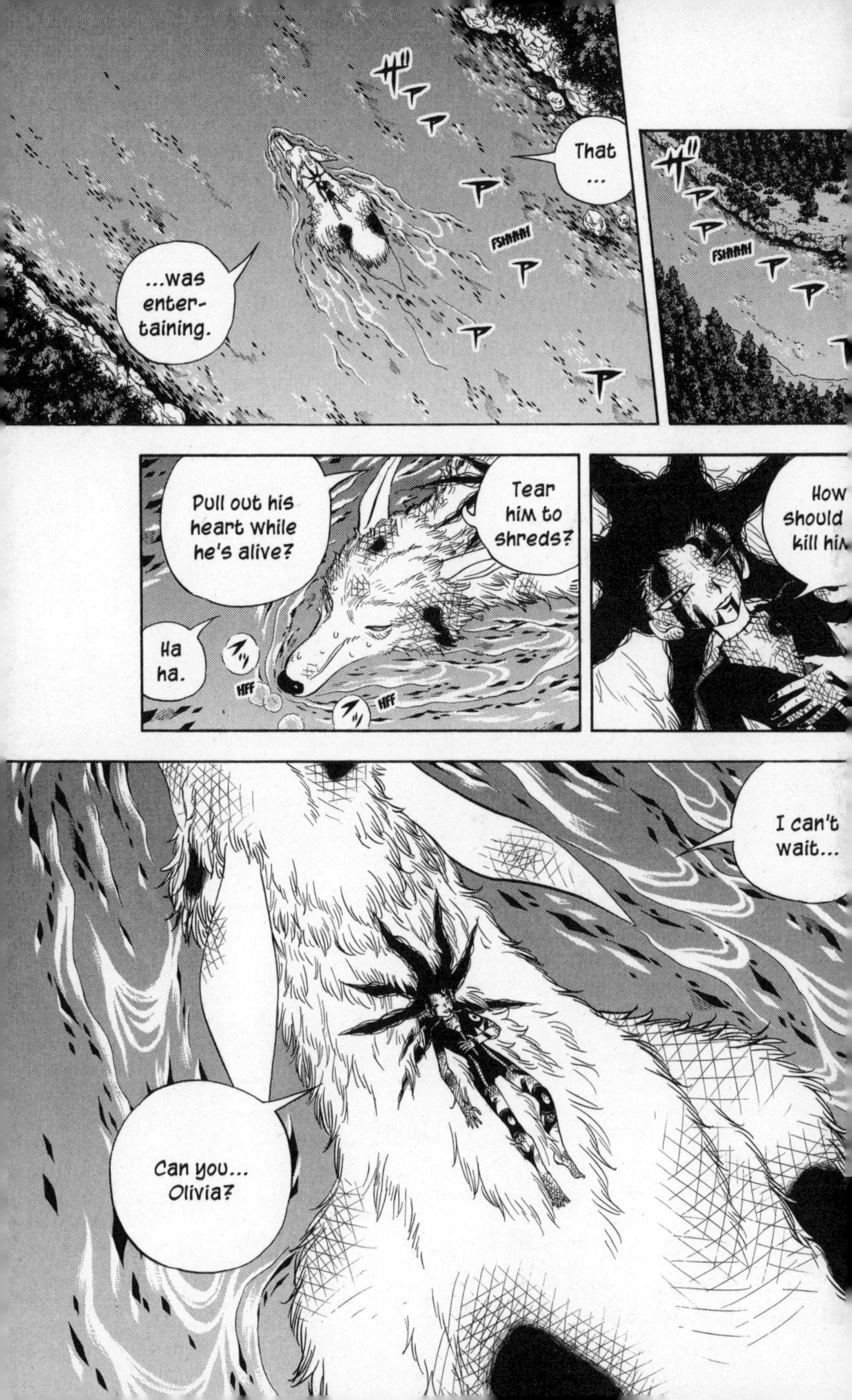
FSHHHH
That ...
...was entertaining.
FSHHHH
How should kill hi
Tear him to shreds?
Pull out his heart while he's alive?
Ha ha.
HFF
HFF
I can't wait...
Can you... Olivia?

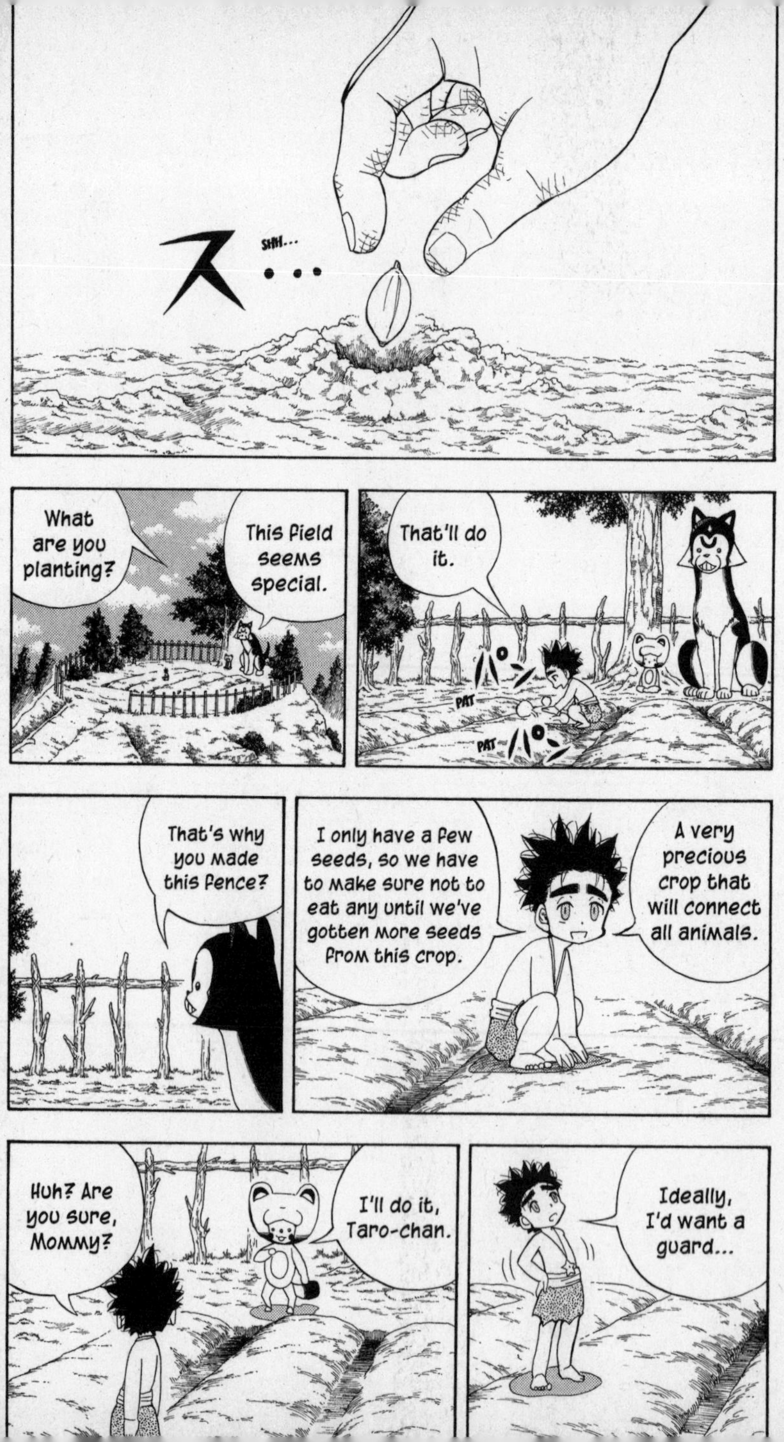
ス
SHH...
...
That'll do it.
PAT
PAT
This field seems special.
What are you planting?
A very precious crop that will connect all animals.
I only have a few seeds, so we have to make sure not to eat any until we've gotten more seeds from this crop.
That's why you made this fence?
Ideally, I'd want a guard...
I'll do it, Taro-chan.
Huh? Are you sure, Mommy?

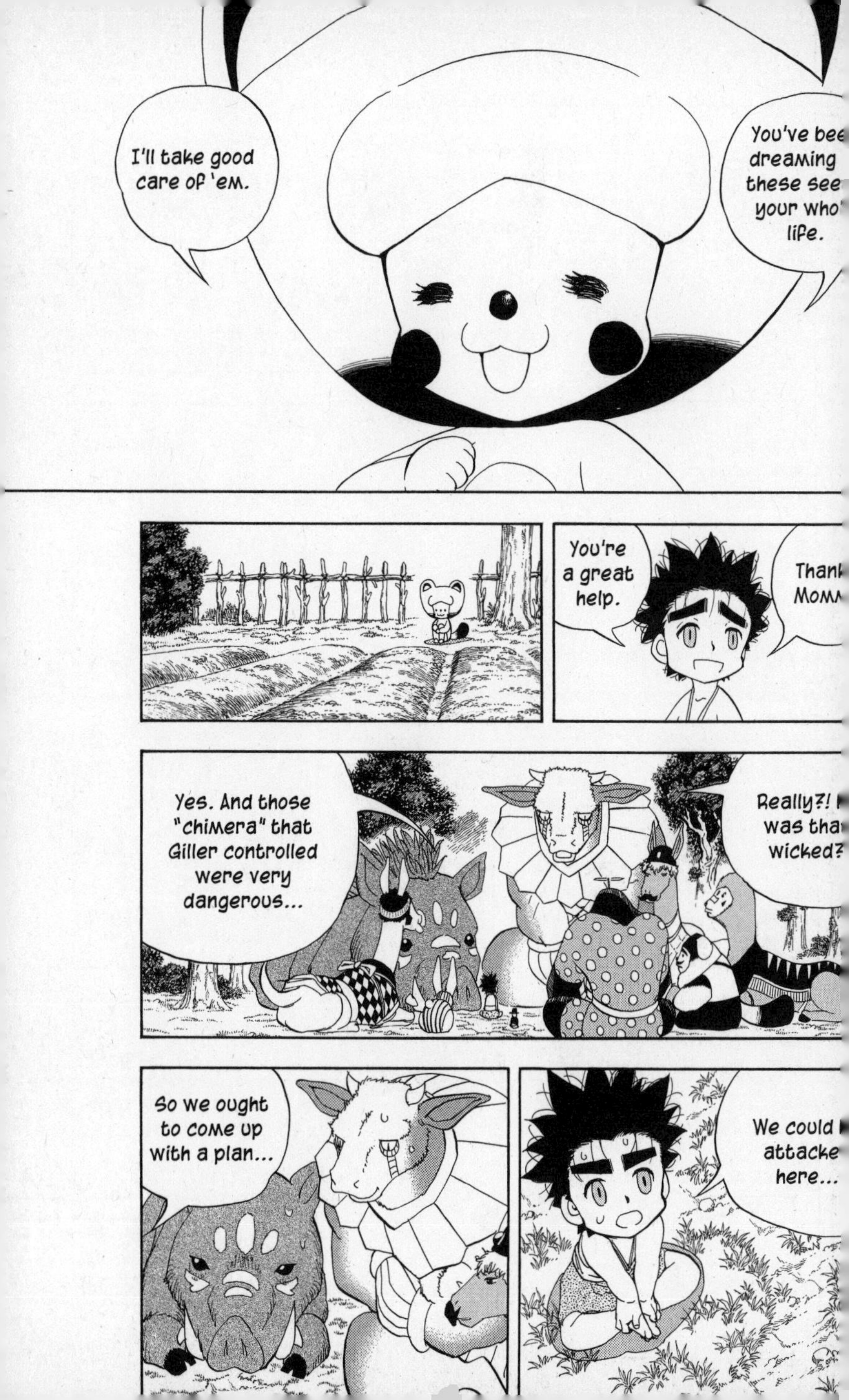
I'll take good care of 'em.
You've bee dreaming these see your who life.
You're a great help.
Than Momm
Yes. And those "chimera" that Giller controlled were very dangerous...
Really?! was tha wicked?
So we ought to come up with a plan...
We could attacke here...

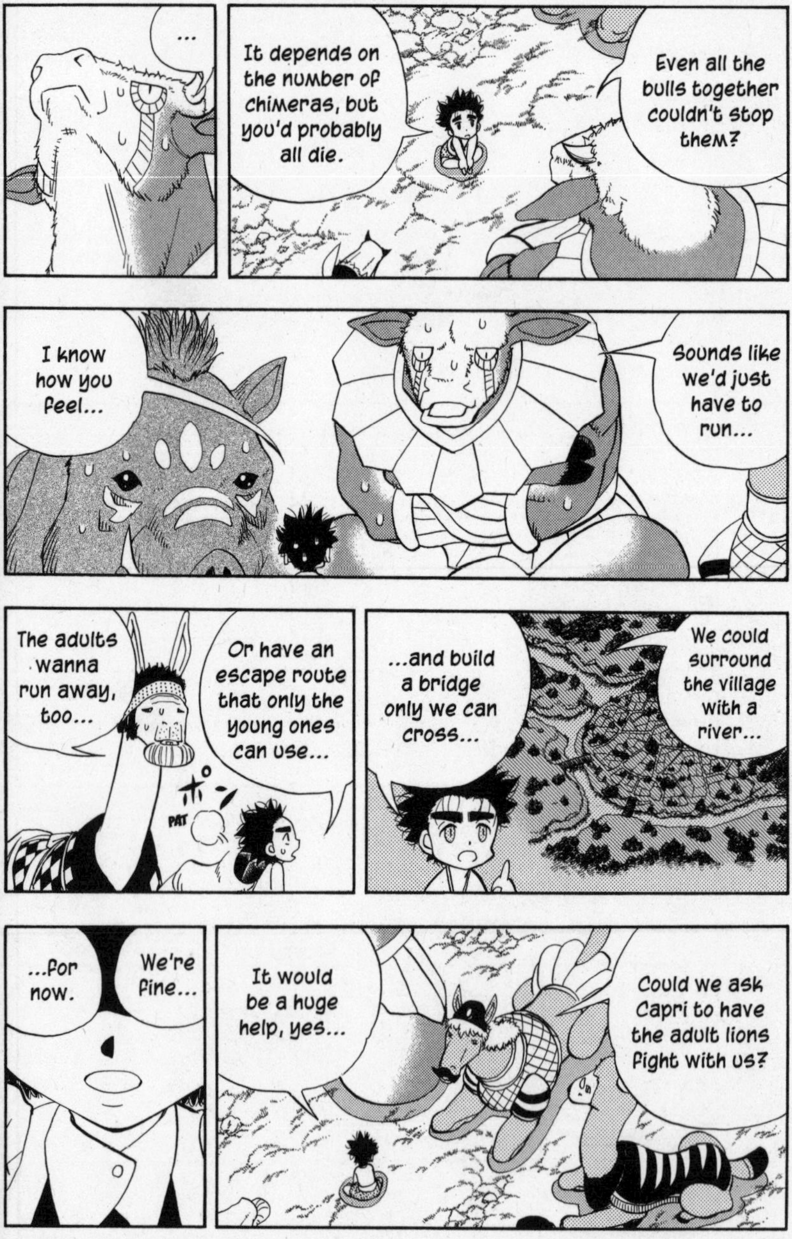
Even all the bulls together couldn't stop them?
It depends on the number of chimeras, but you'd probably all die.
...
Sounds like we'd just have to run...
I know how you feel...
We could surround the village with a river...
...and build a bridge only we can cross...
Or have an escape route that only the young ones can use...
The adults wanna run away, too...
PAT
Could we ask Capri to have the adult lions fight with us?
It would be a huge help, yes...
We're fine...
...for now.

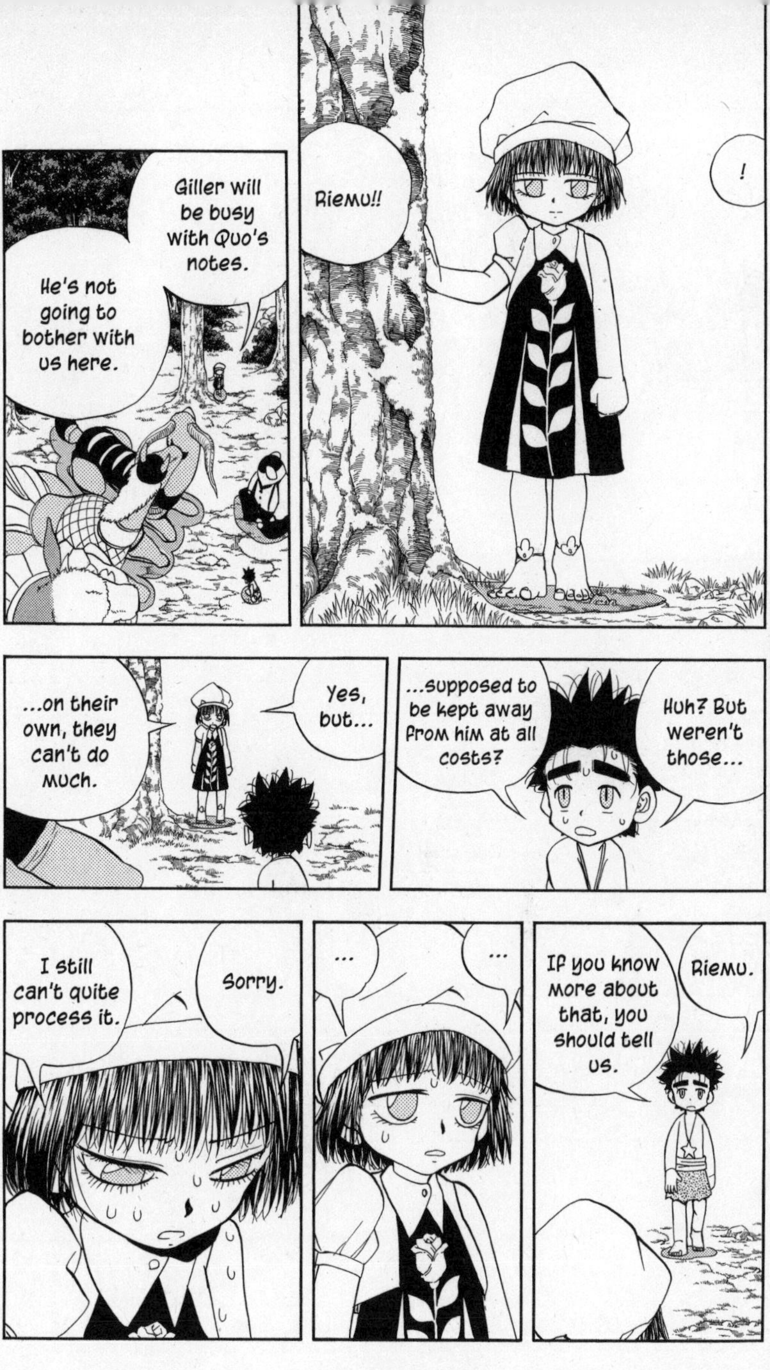
!
Riemu!!
Giller will be busy with Quo's notes.
He's not going to bother with us here.
Huh? But weren't those...
...supposed to be kept away from him at all costs?
Yes, but...
...on their own, they can't do much.
Riemu.
If you know more about that, you should tell us.
...
...
Sorry.
I still can't quite process it.

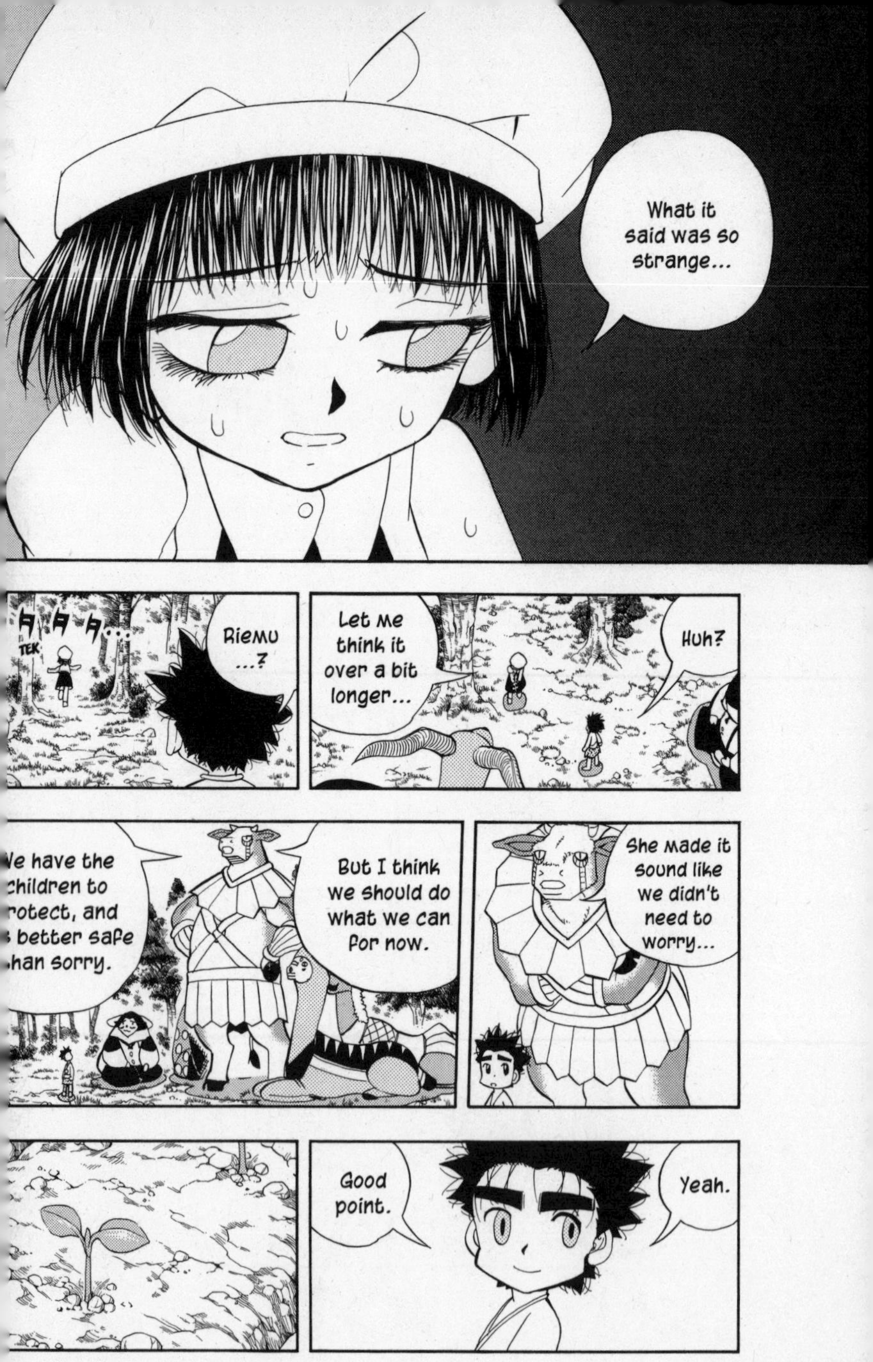
What it said was so strange...
Huh?
Let me think it over a bit longer...
Riemu ...?
TEK
She made it sound like we didn't need to worry...
But I think we should do what we can for now.
e have the children to protect, and better safe han sorry.
Yeah.
Good point.

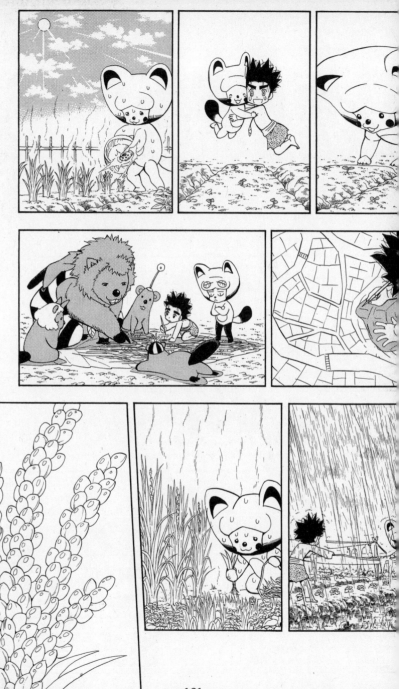

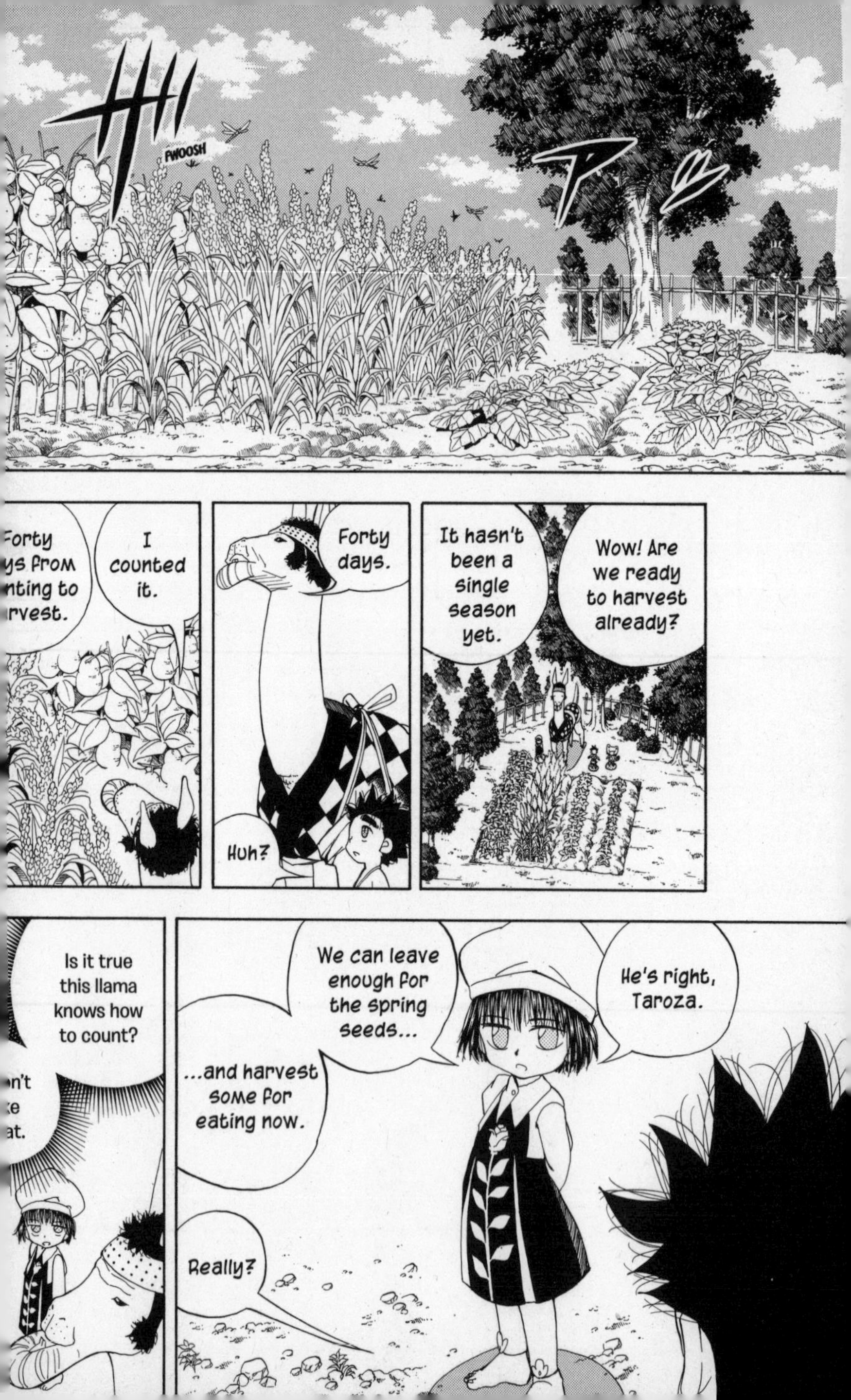
FWOOSH
Wow! Are we ready to harvest already?
It hasn't been a single season yet.
Forty days.
Huh?
I counted it.
Forty ys from nting to rvest.
He's right, Taroza.
We can leave enough for the spring seeds...
...and harvest some for eating now.
Really?
Is it true this llama knows how to count?

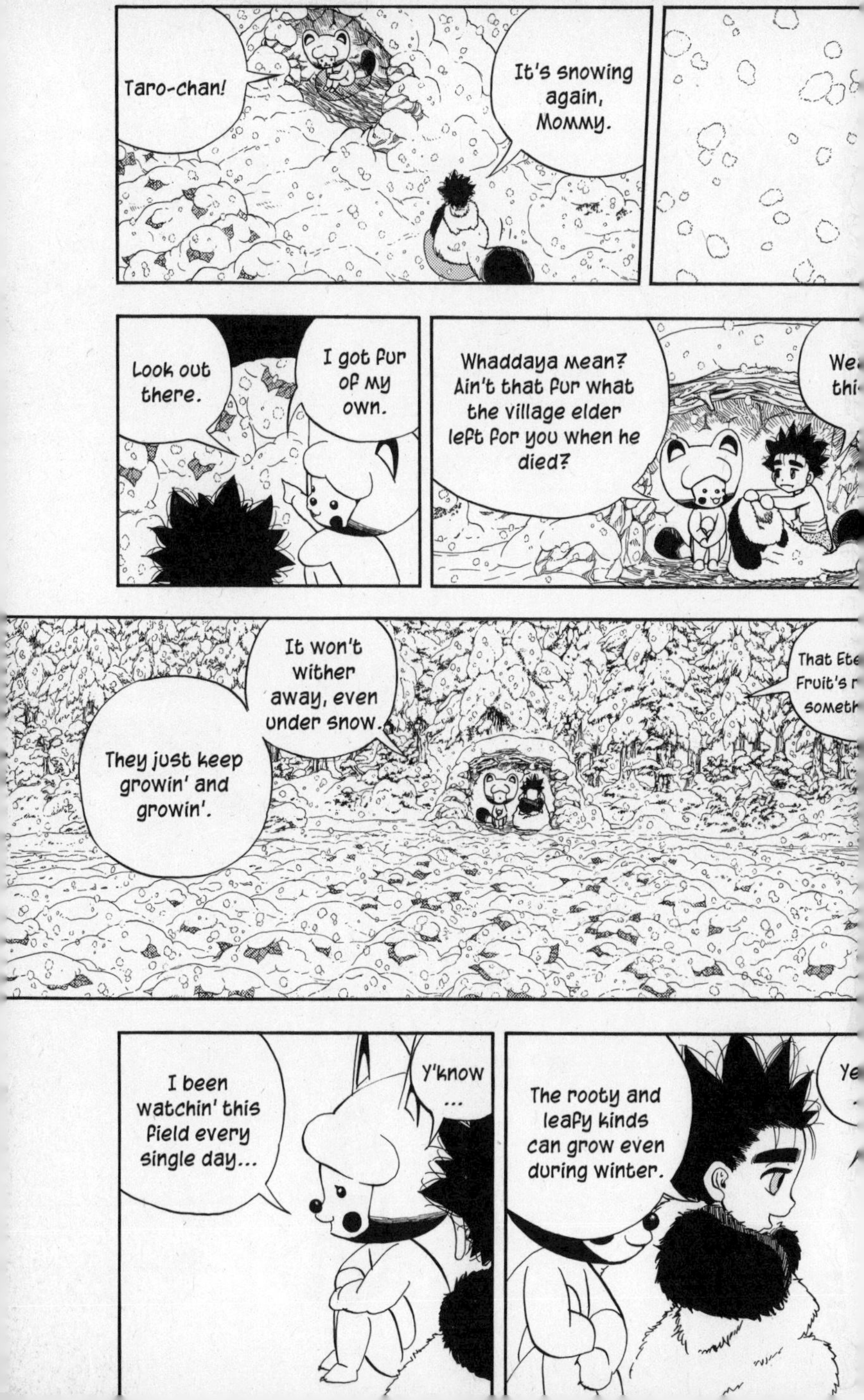
It's snowing again, Mommy.
Taro-chan!
Whaddaya mean? Ain't that fur what the village elder left for you when he died?
I got fur of my own.
Look out there.
It won't wither away, even under snow.
They just keep growin' and growin'.
The rooty and leafy kinds can grow even during winter.
Y'know ...
I been watchin' this field every single day...

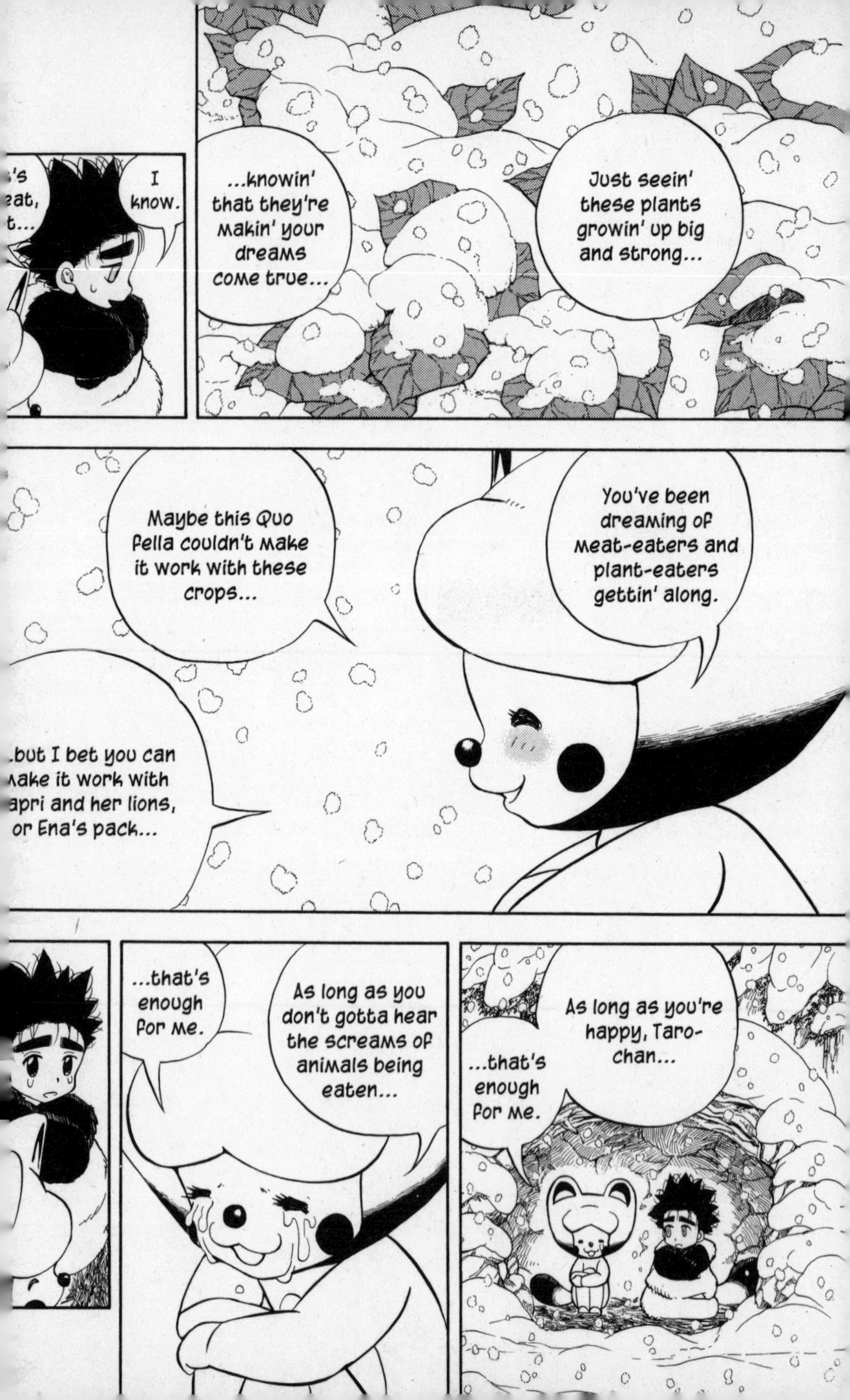
Just seein' these plants growin' up big and strong...
...knowin' that they're makin' your dreams come true...
I know.
You've been dreaming of meat-eaters and plant-eaters gettin' along.
Maybe this Quo fella couldn't make it work with these crops...
.but I bet you can ake it work with apri and her lions, or Ena's pack...
As long as you're happy, Taro-chan...
...that's enough for me.
As long as you don't gotta hear the screams of animals being eaten...
...that's enough for me.

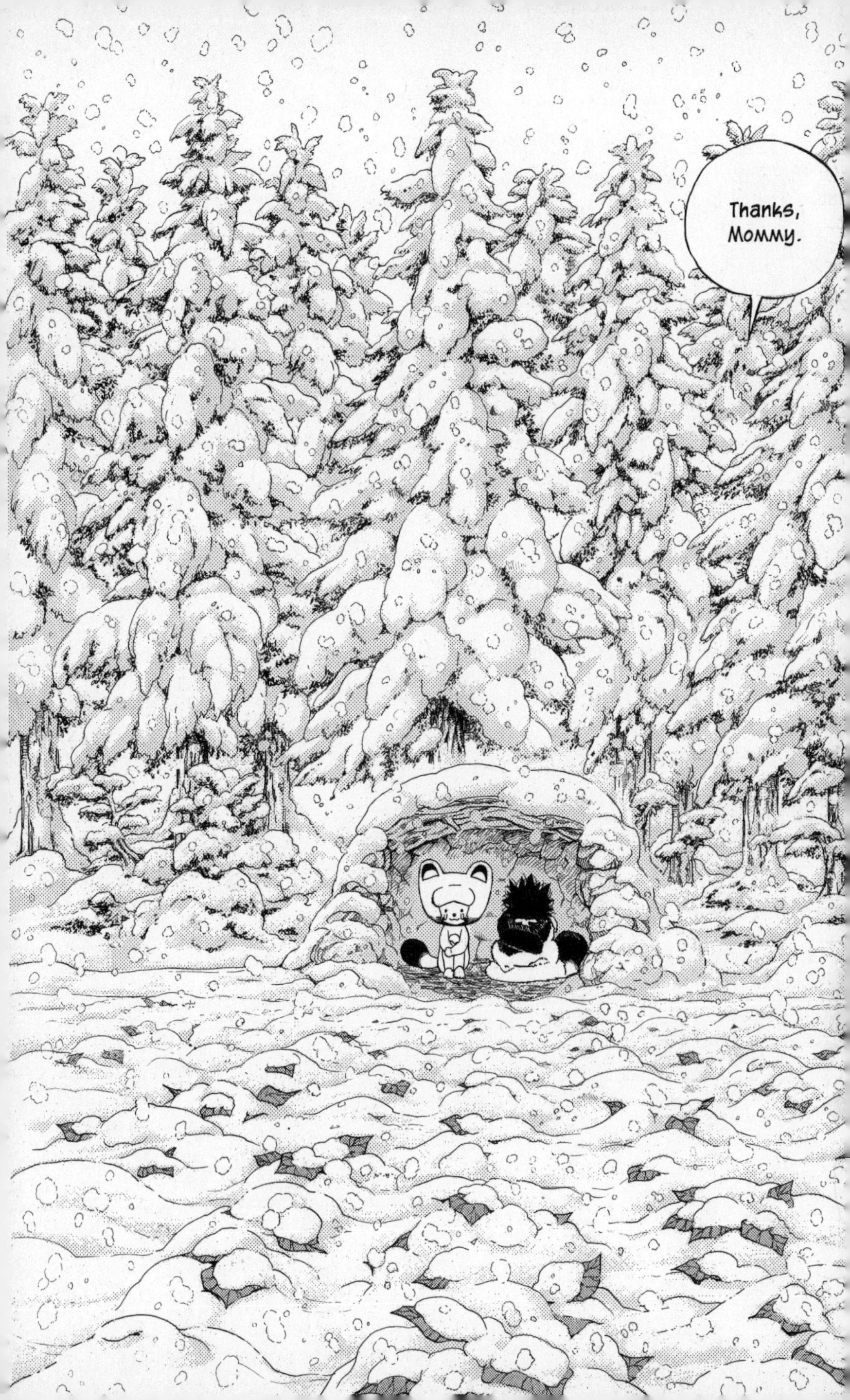
Thanks, Mommy.

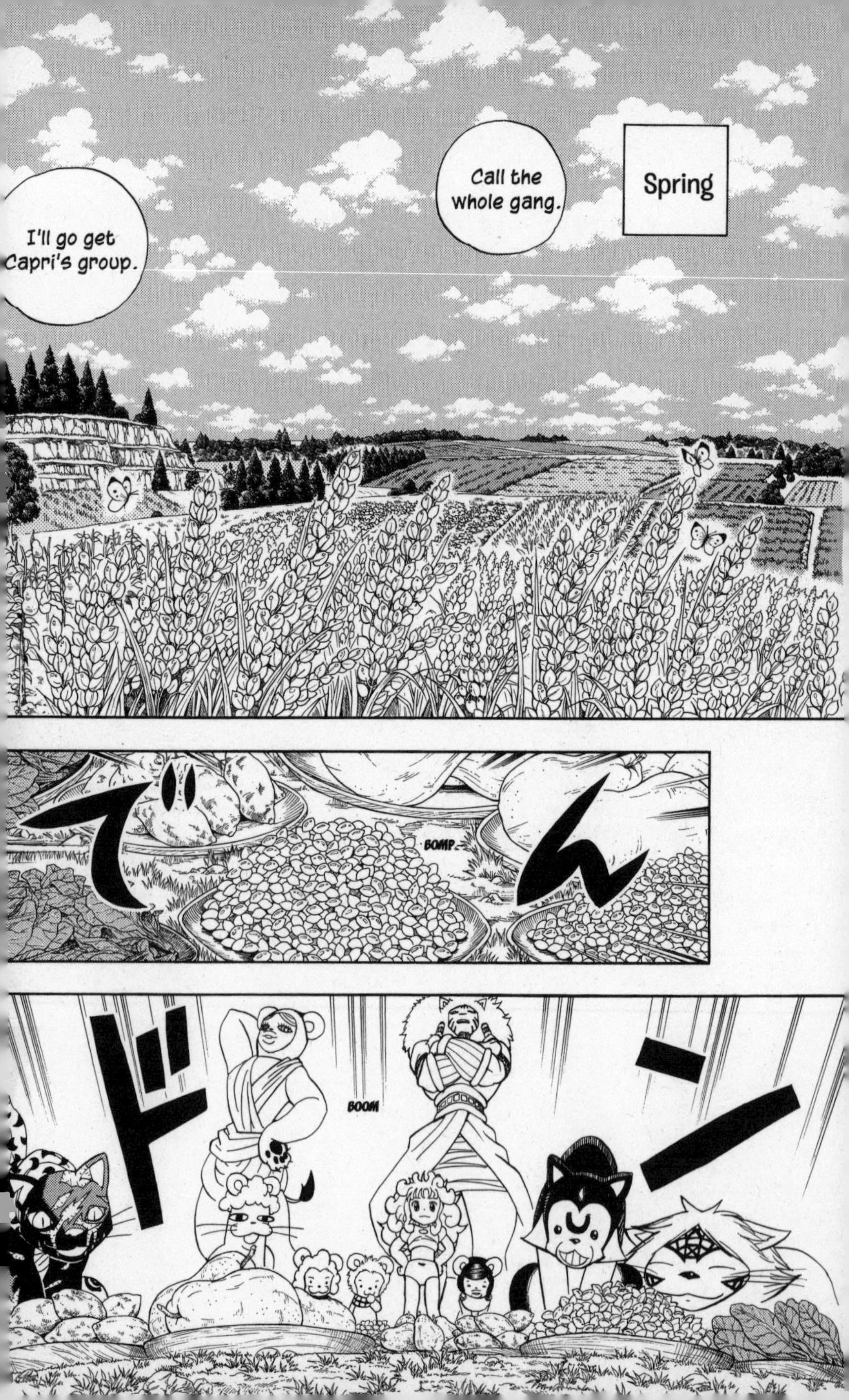
Spring
Call the whole gang.
I'll go get Capri's group.
BOMP
BOOM

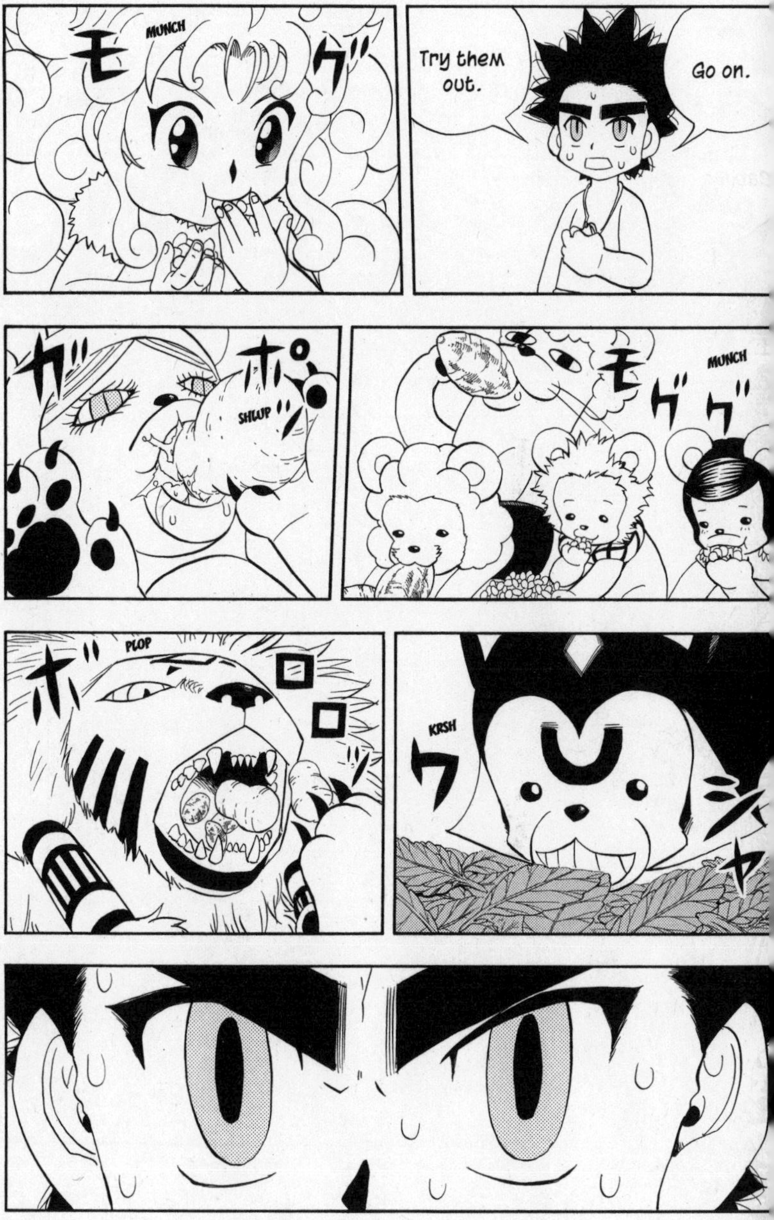

Go on.
Try them out.
MUNCH
MUNCH
SHLUP
KRSH
PLOP

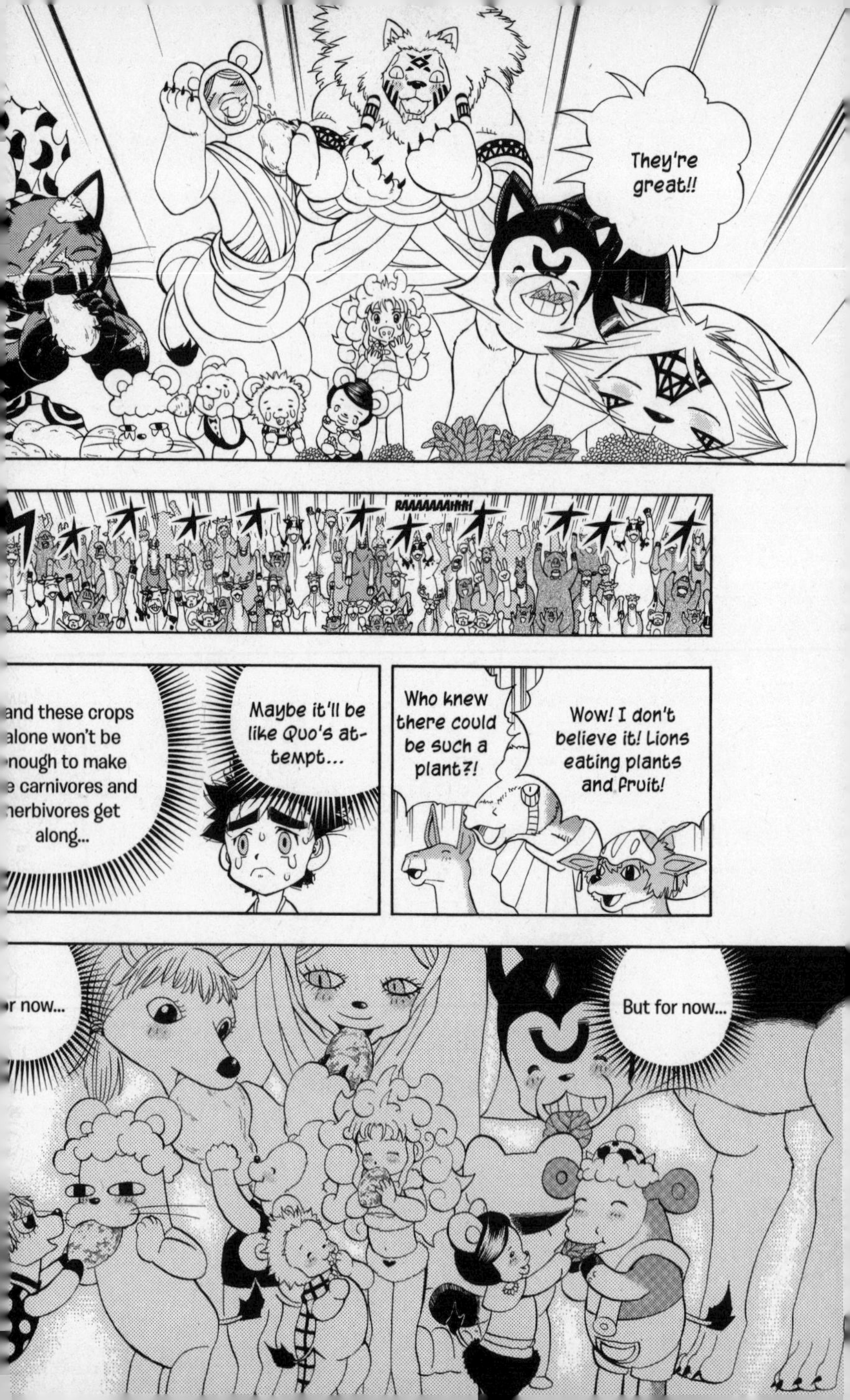

They're great!!
RAAAAAAAHHH
Wow! I don't believe it! Lions eating plants and fruit!
Who knew there could be such a plant?!
Maybe it'll be like Quo's attempt...
and these crops alone won't be nough to make e carnivores and erbivores get along...
But for now...
r now...

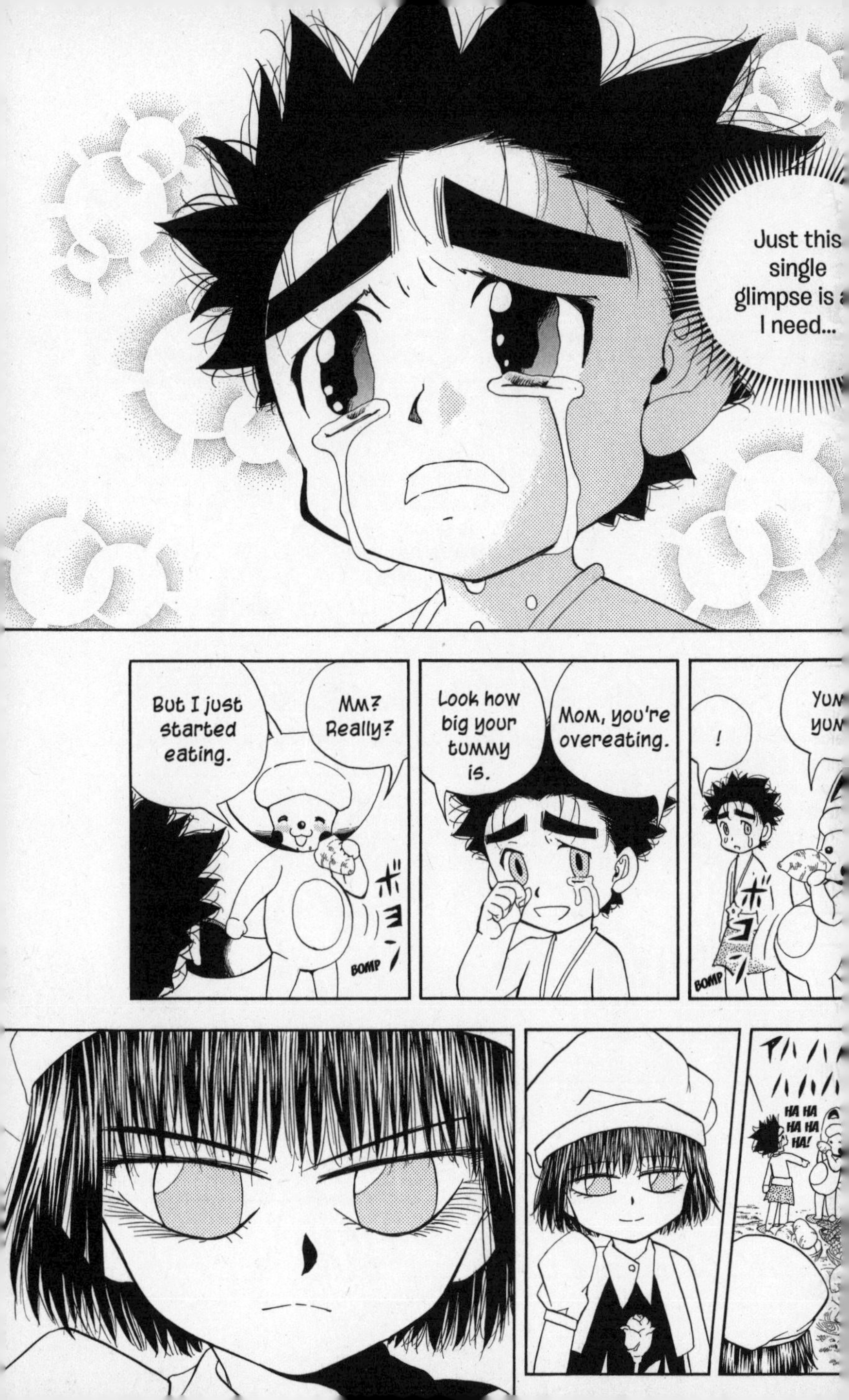
Just this single glimpse is a I need...
!
BOMP
Mom, you're overeating.
Look how big your tummy is.
Mm? Really?
But I just started eating.
BOMP
HA HA HA HA HA!

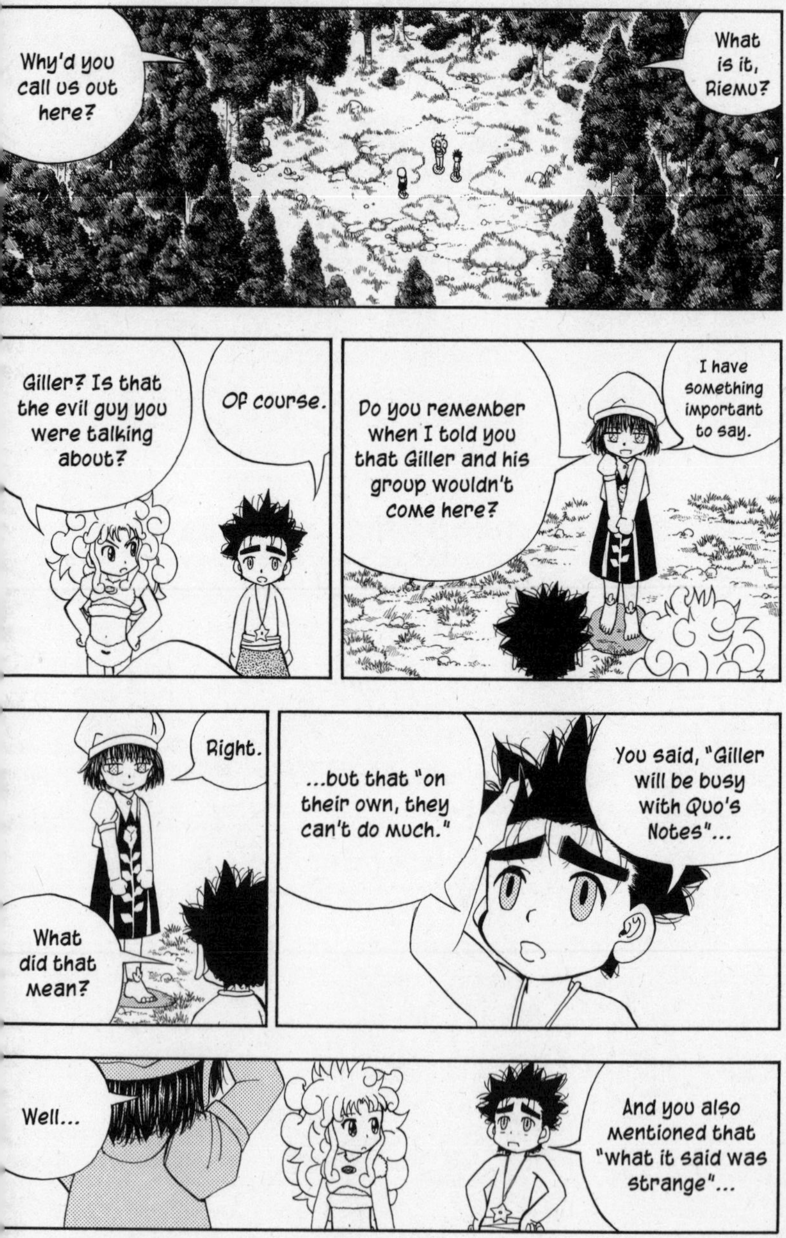
What is it, Riemu?
Why'd you call us out here?
I have something important to say.
Do you remember when I told you that Giller and his group wouldn't come here?
Of course.
Giller? Is that the evil guy you were talking about?
You said, "Giller will be busy with Quo's Notes"...
...but that "on their own, they can't do much."
Right.
What did that mean?
And you also mentioned that "what it said was strange"...
Well...

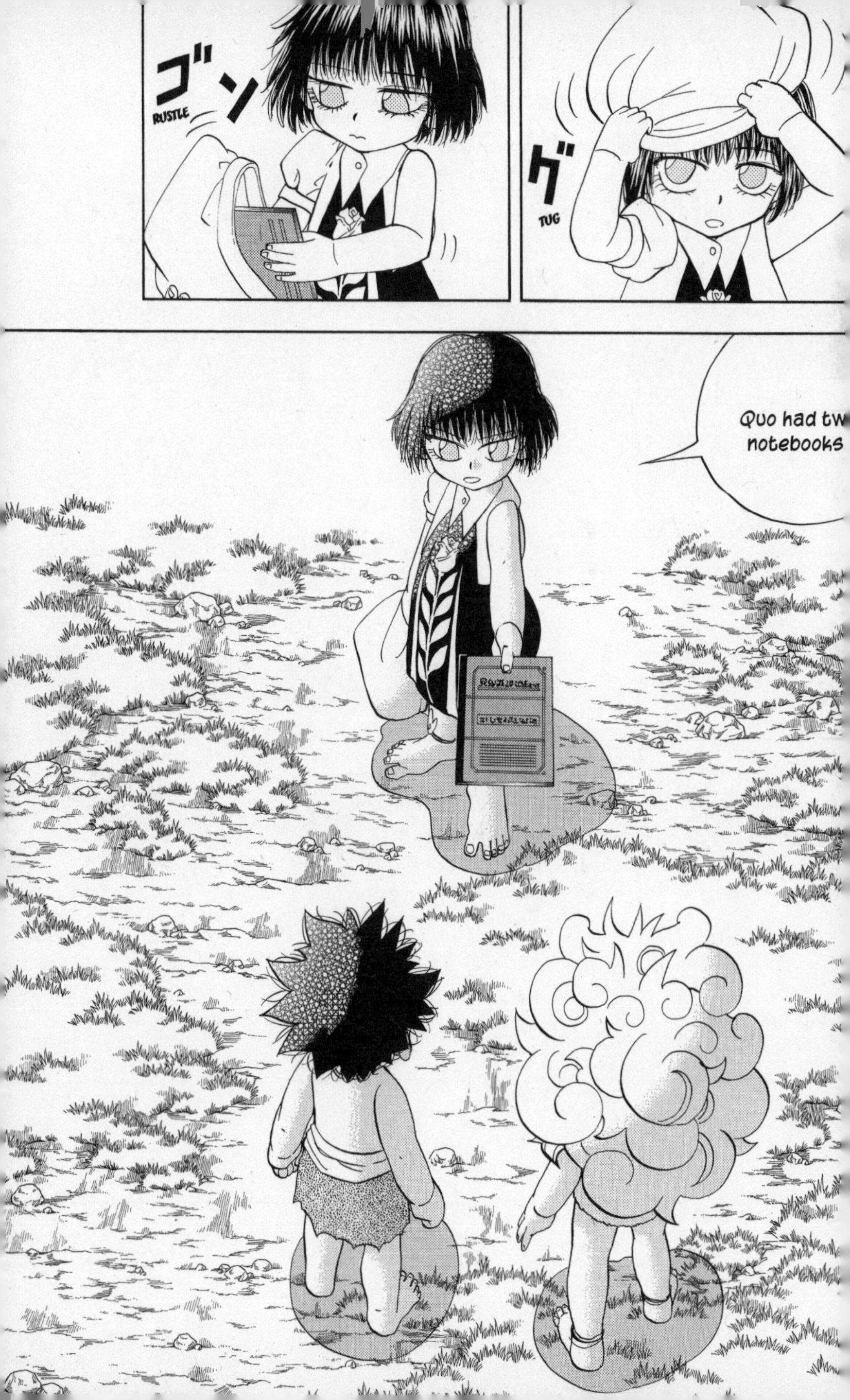

グ
TUG
ゴソ
RUSTLE
Quo had tw
notebooks

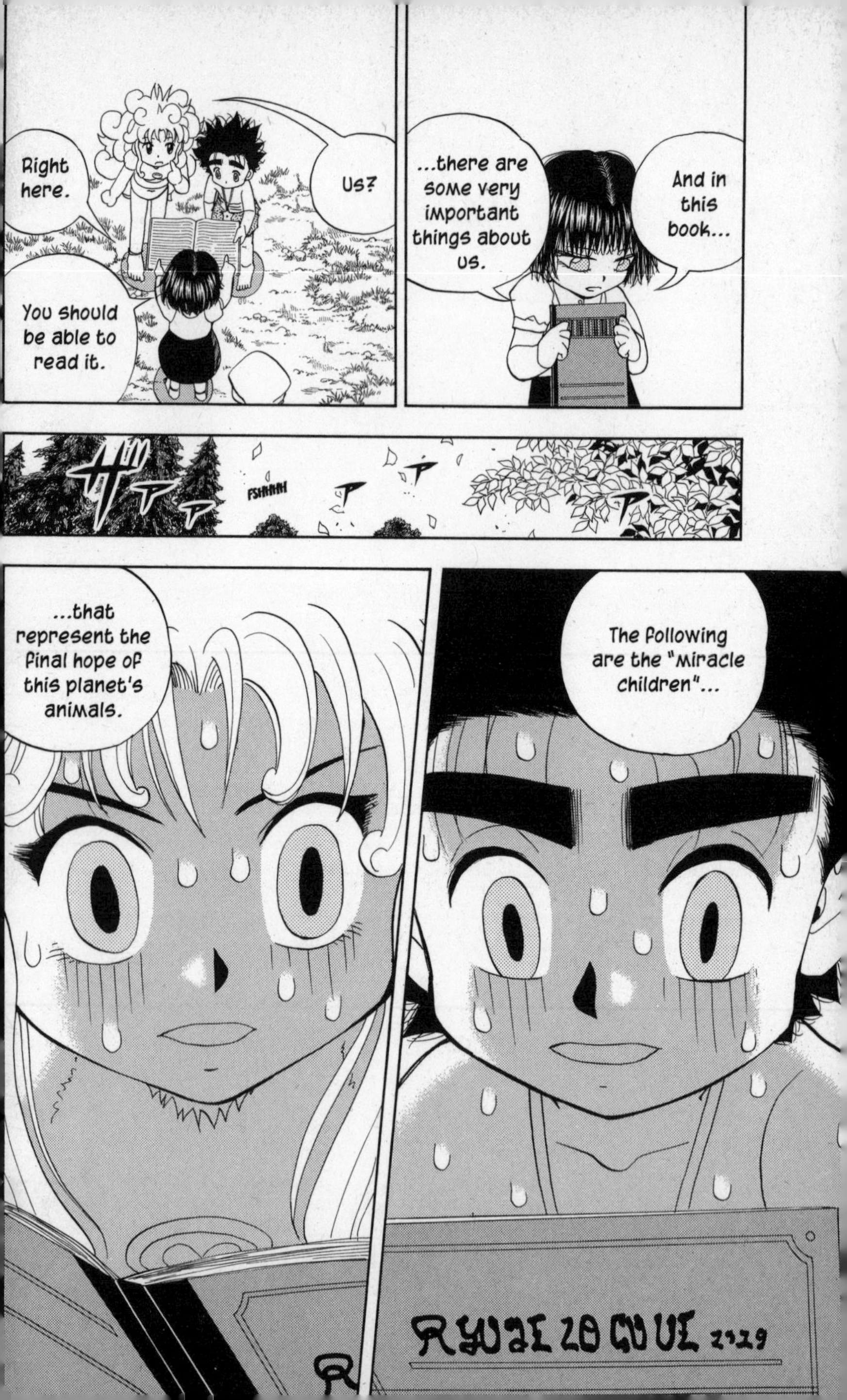
And in this book...
...there are some very important things about us.
Us?
Right here.
You should be able to read it.
FSHHHH
The following are the "miracle children"...
...that represent the final hope of this planet's animals.

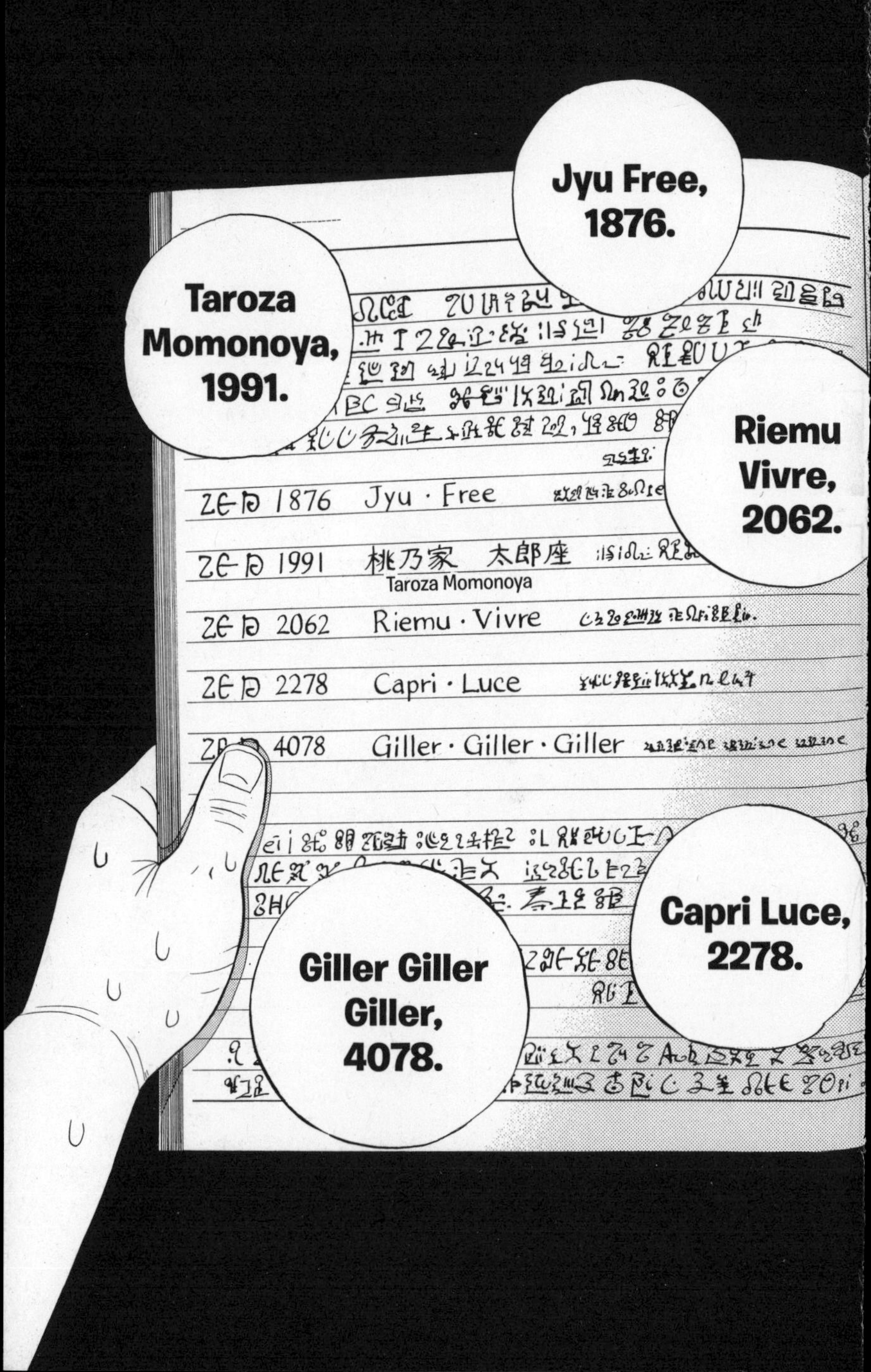
Jyu Free, 1876.
Taroza Momonoya, 1991.
Riemu Vivre, 2062.
Capri Luce, 2278.
Giller Giller Giller, 4078.
1876 Jyu · Free
1991 桃乃家 太郎座
Taroza Momonoya
2062 Riemu · Vivre
2278 Capri · Luce
4078 Giller · Giller · Giller

Bonus Page 3

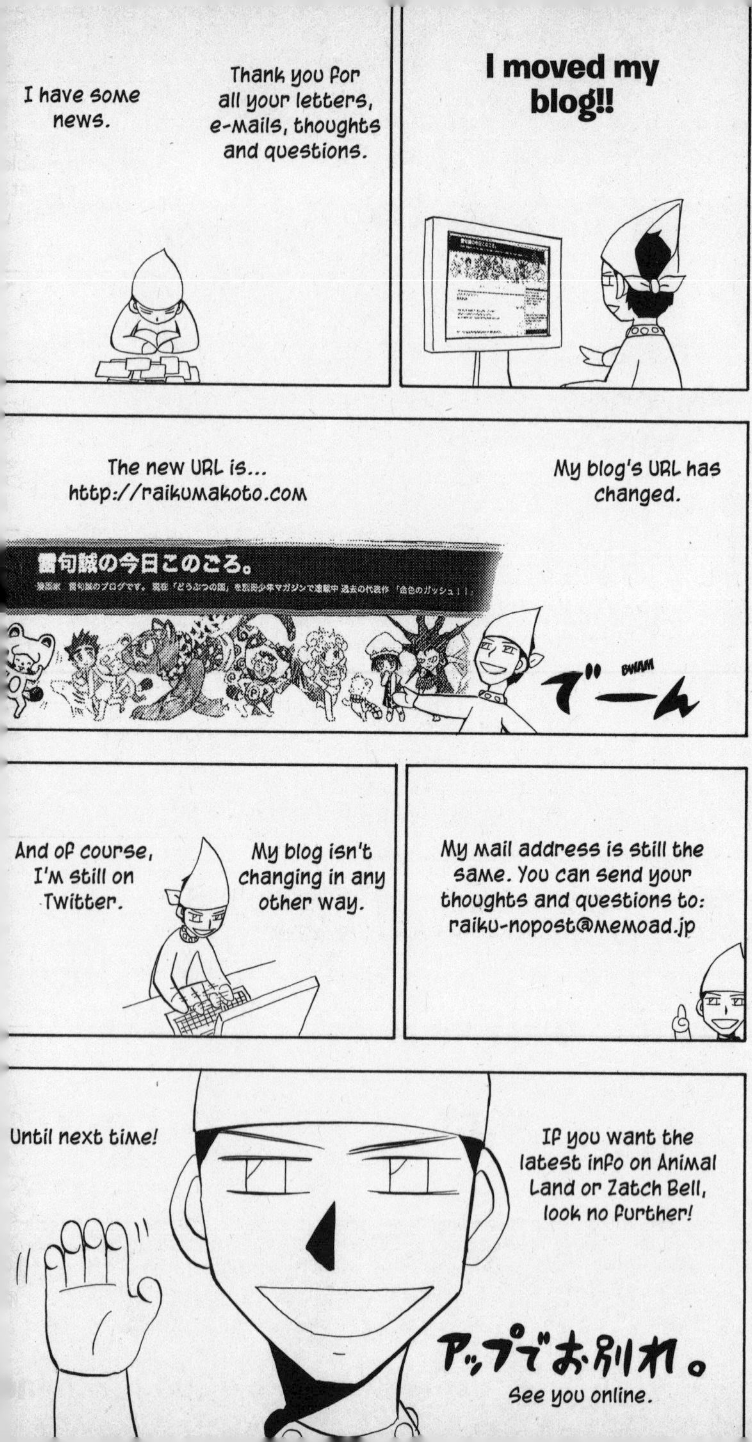
I moved my blog!!
Thank you for all your letters, e-mails, thoughts and questions.
I have some news.
My blog's URL has changed.
The new URL is... http://raikumakoto.com
雷句誠の今日このごろ。
でーん
BWAM
My mail address is still the same. You can send your thoughts and questions to: raiku-nopost@memoad.jp
My blog isn't changing in any other way.
And of course, I'm still on Twitter.
If you want the latest info on Animal Land or Zatch Bell, look no further!
Until next time!
アップでお別れ。
See you online.

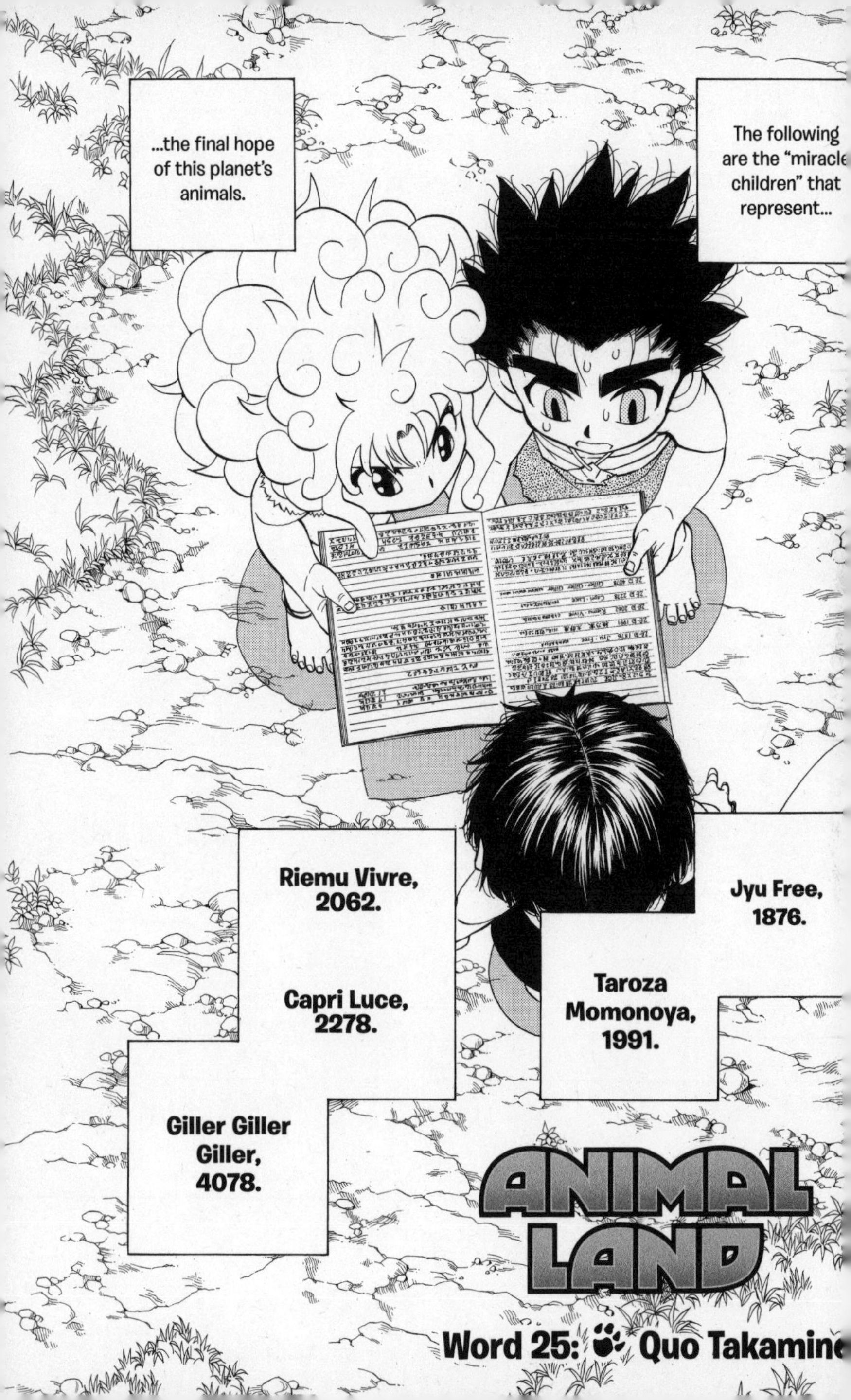
The following are the "miracle children" that represent...
...the final hope of this planet's animals.
Jyu Free, 1876.
Taroza Momonoya, 1991.
Riemu Vivre, 2062.
Capri Luce, 2278.
Giller Giller Giller, 4078.
ANIMAL LAND
Word 25: Quo Takamine

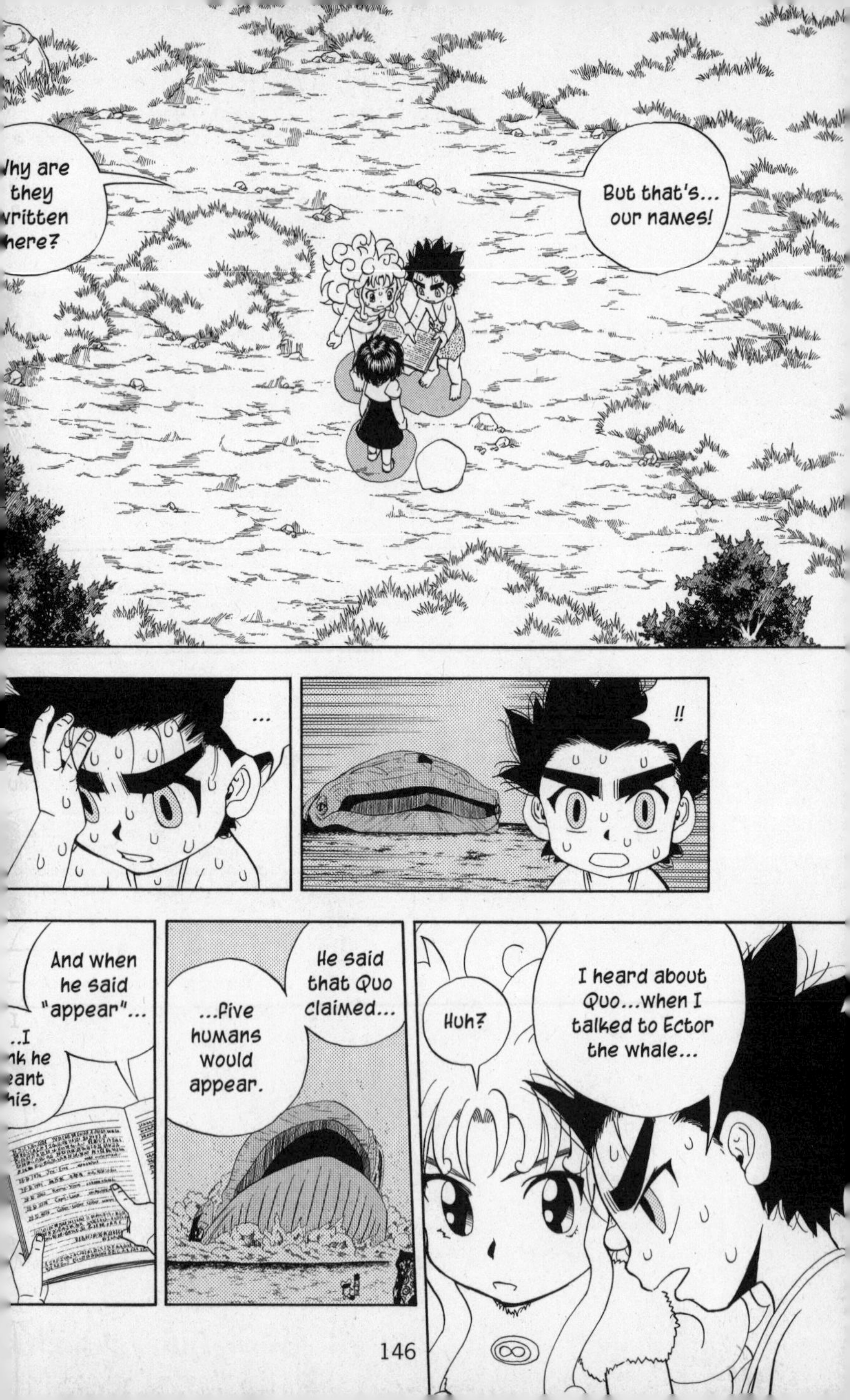

But that's... our names!
hy are they ritten here?
!!
...
I heard about Quo...when I talked to Ector the whale...
Huh?
He said that Quo claimed...
...five humans would appear.
And when he said "appear"...
..I nk he eant his.

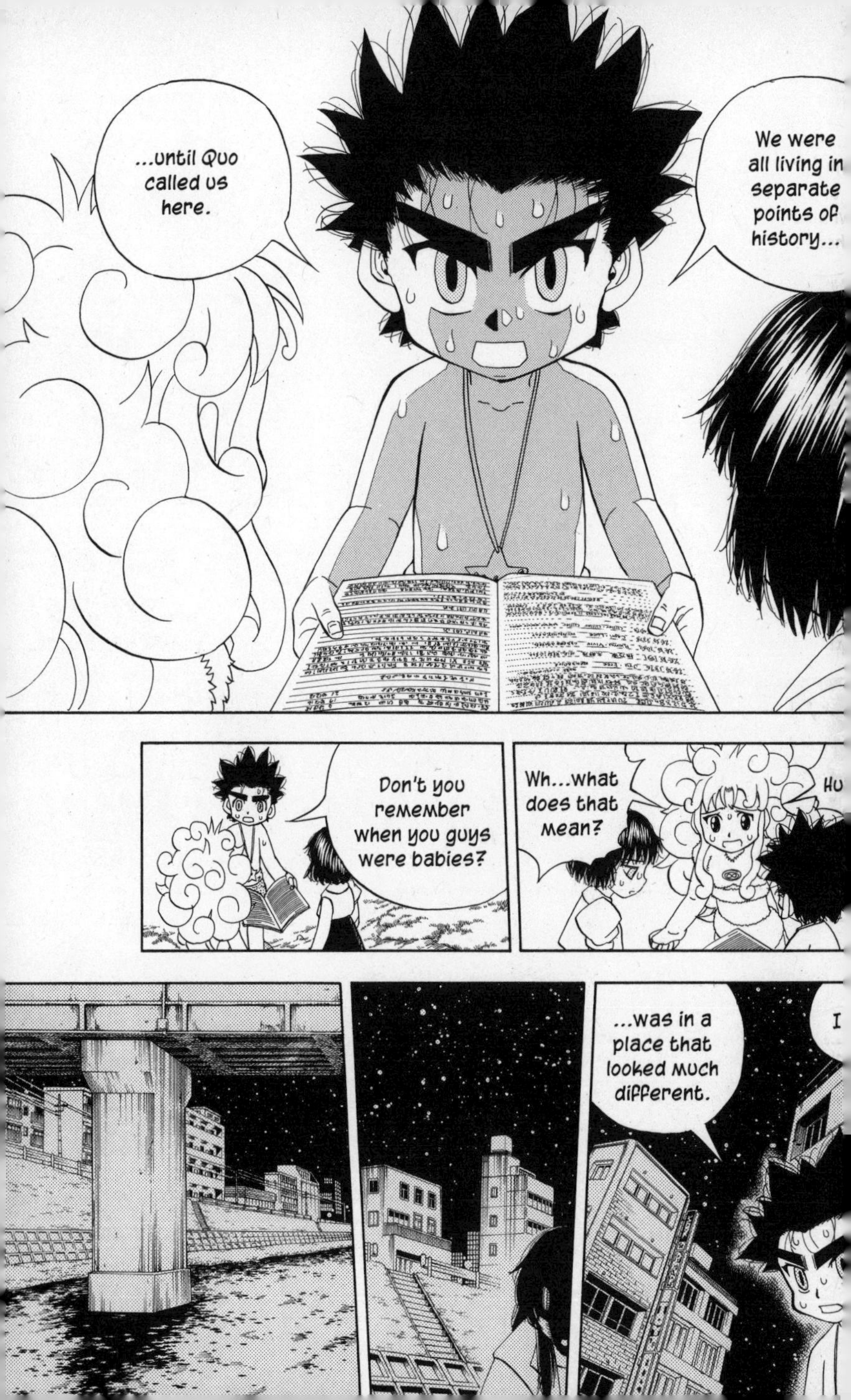
We were all living in separate points of history...
...until Quo called us here.
Hu
Wh...what does that mean?
Don't you remember when you guys were babies?
I
...was in a place that looked much different.

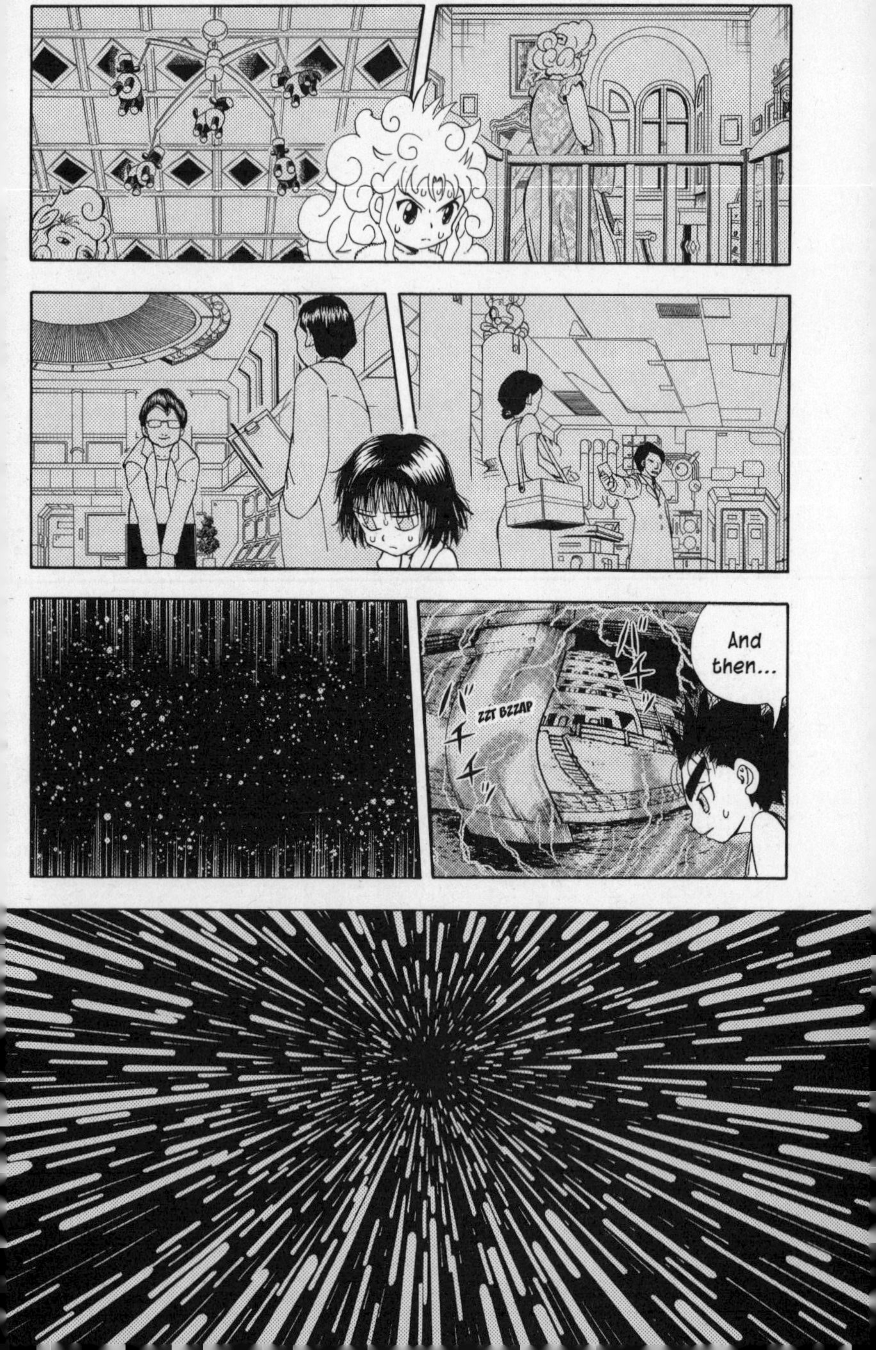
And then...
ZZT BZZAP

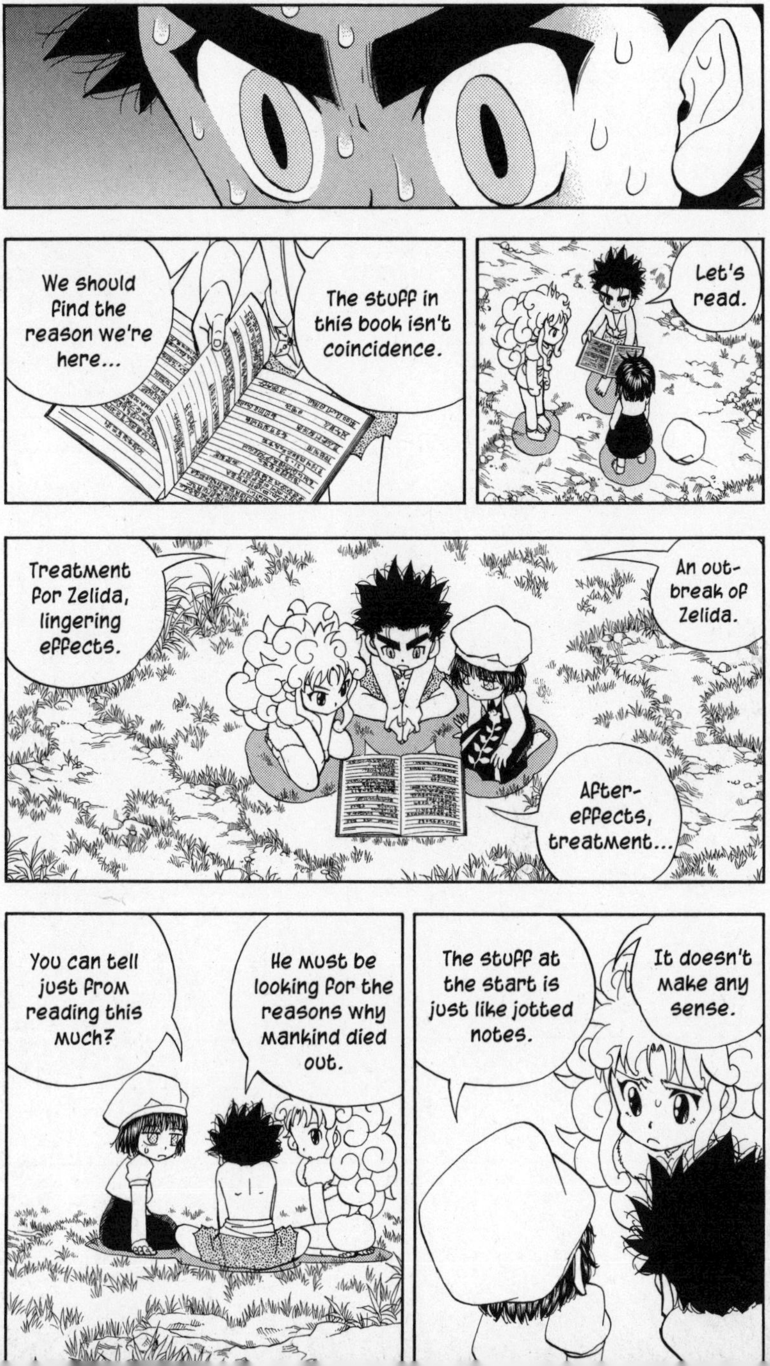
Let's read.
The stuff in this book isn't coincidence.
We should find the reason we're here...
An out-break of Zelida.
Treatment for Zelida, lingering effects.
After-effects, treatment...
It doesn't make any sense.
The stuff at the start is just like jotted notes.
He must be looking for the reasons why mankind died out.
You can tell just from reading this much?

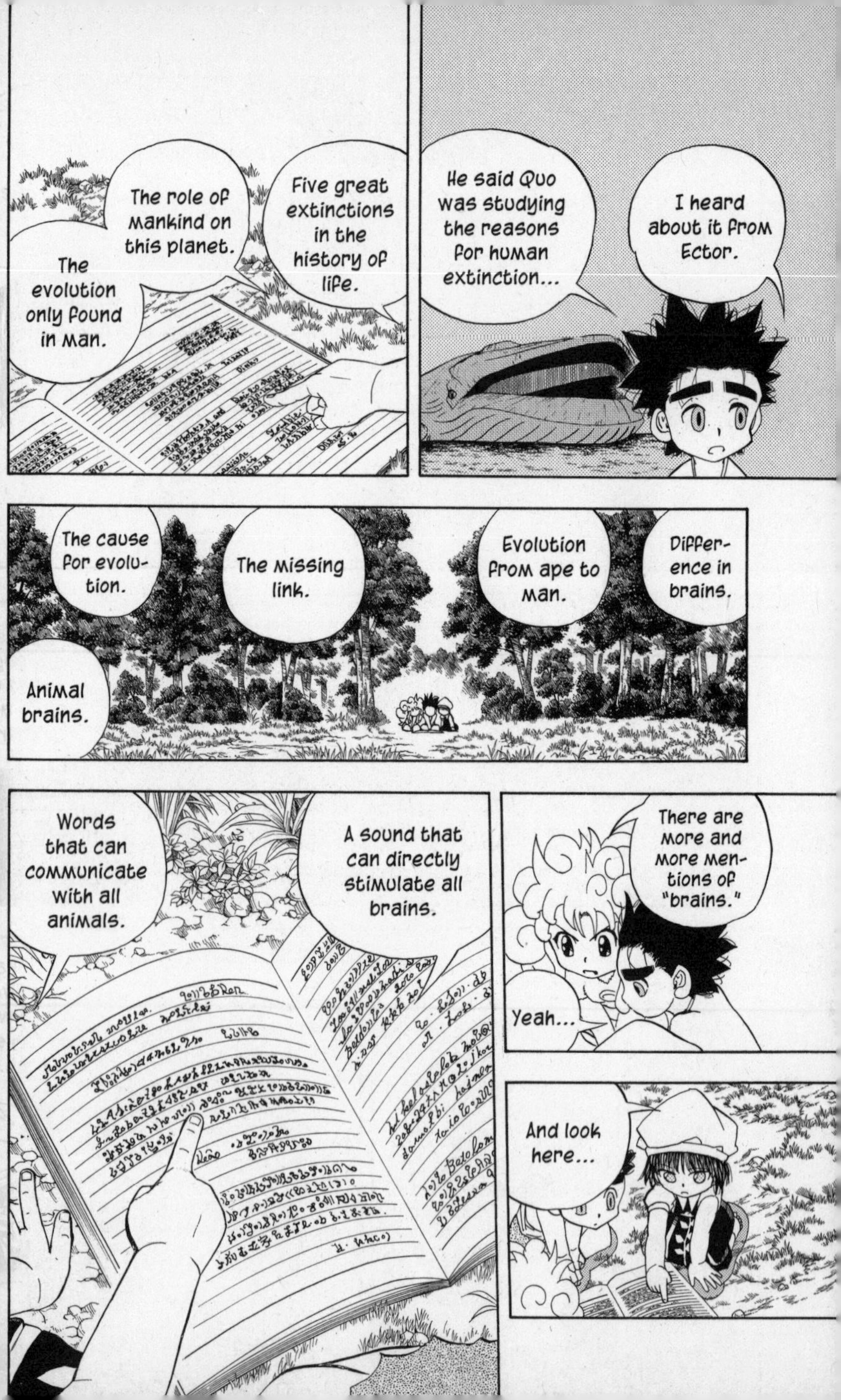
I heard about it from Ector.
He said Quo was studying the reasons for human extinction...
Five great extinctions in the history of life.
The role of Mankind on this planet.
The evolution only found in man.
Differ-ence in brains.
Evolution from ape to man.
The missing link.
The cause for evolu-tion.
Animal brains.
There are more and more men-tions of "brains."
Yeah...
And look here...
A sound that can directly stimulate all brains.
Words that can communicate with all animals.

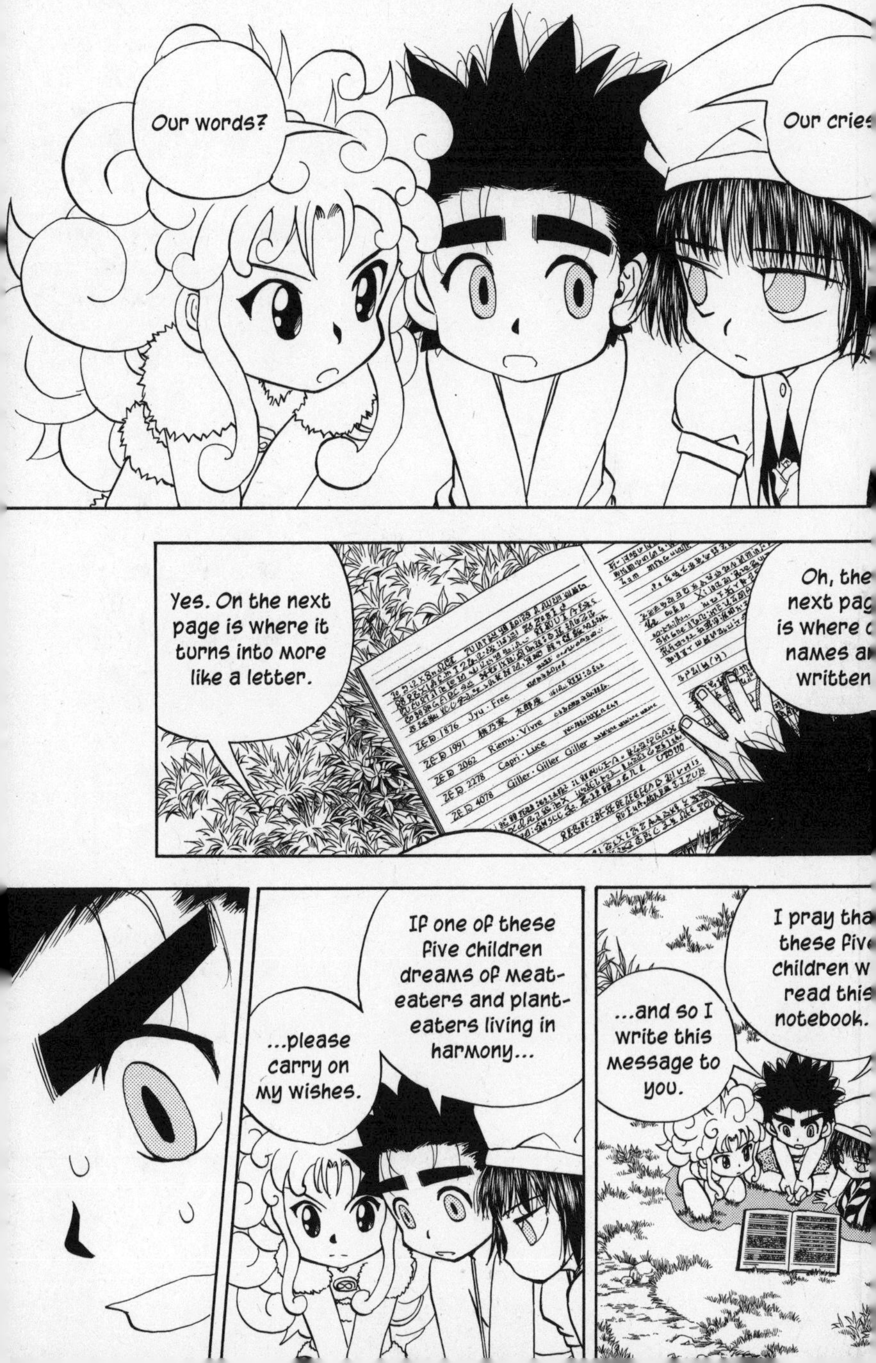
Our cries
Our words?
Oh, the next pag is where c names ar written
Yes. On the next page is where it turns into more like a letter.
I pray tha these five children w read this notebook.
...and so I write this message to you.
If one of these five children dreams of meat-eaters and plant-eaters living in harmony...
...please carry on my wishes.

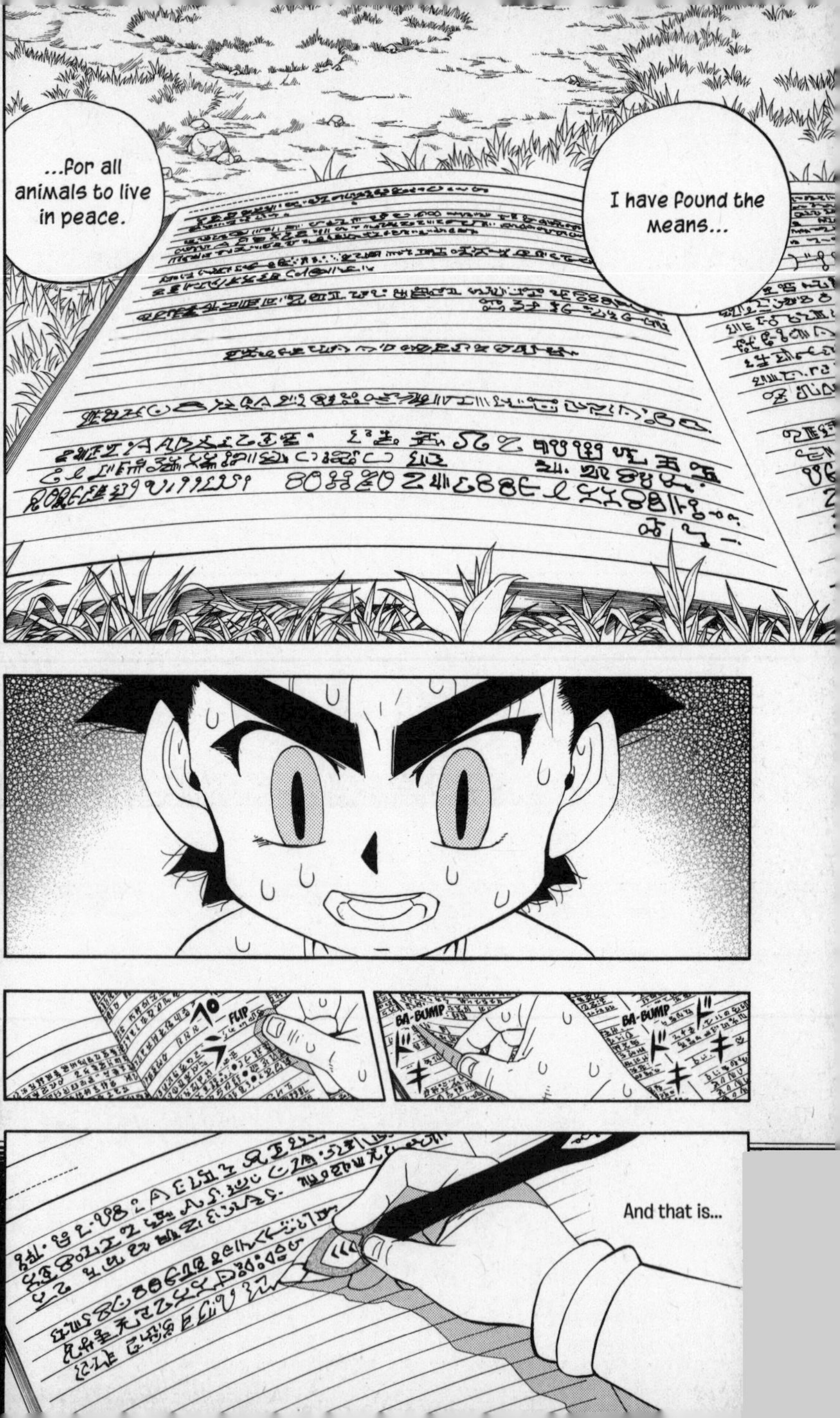
I have found the means...
...for all animals to live in peace.
BA-BUMP
BA-BUMP
FLIP
And that is...

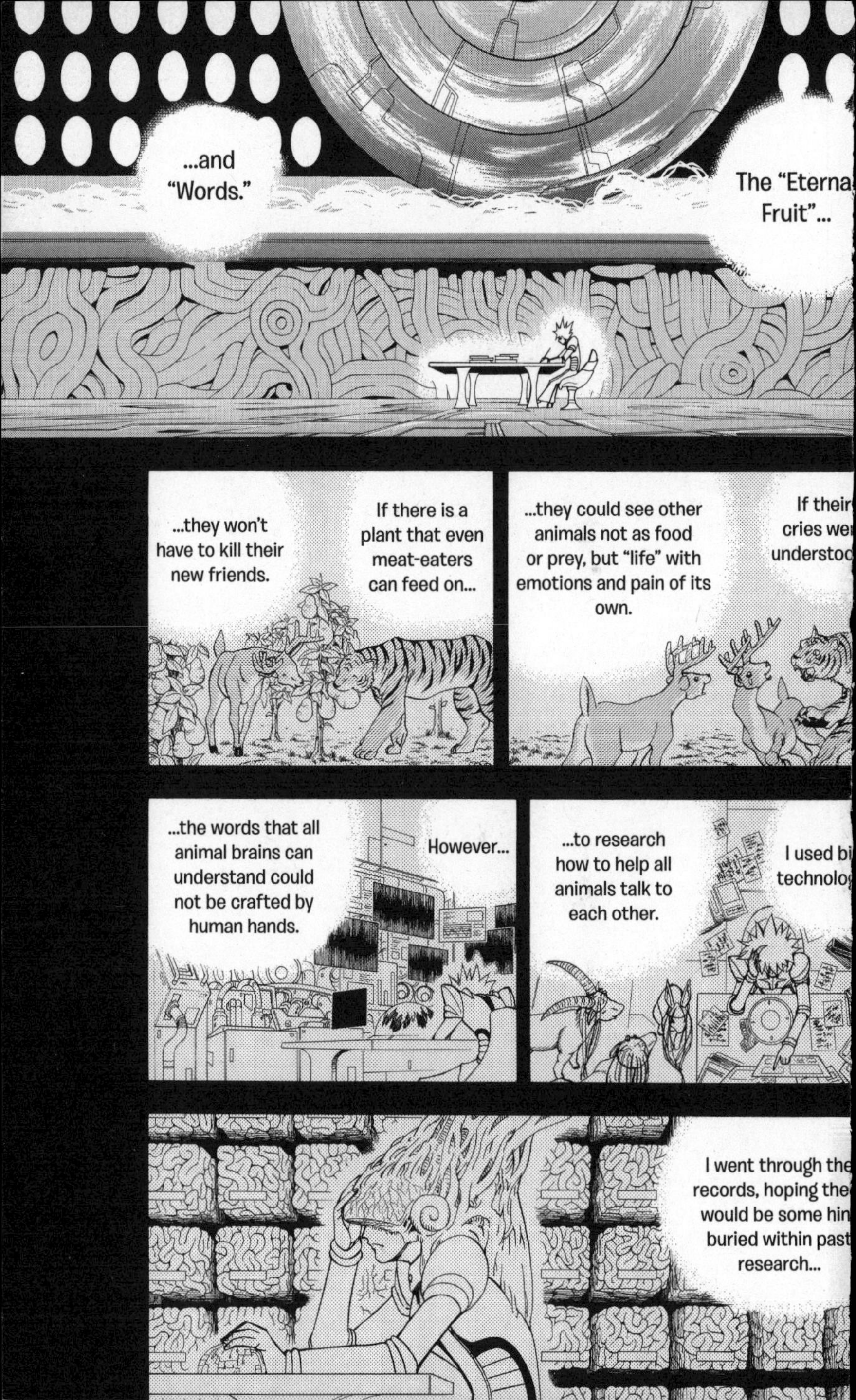
The "Eterna
Fruit"...
...and "Words."
If thei
cries we
understo
...they could see other animals not as food or prey, but "life" with emotions and pain of its own.
If there is a plant that even meat-eaters can feed on...
...they won't have to kill their new friends.
I used bi
technolog
...to research how to help all animals talk to each other.
However...
...the words that all animal brains can understand could not be crafted by human hands.
I went through the
records, hoping the
would be some hin
buried within past
research...

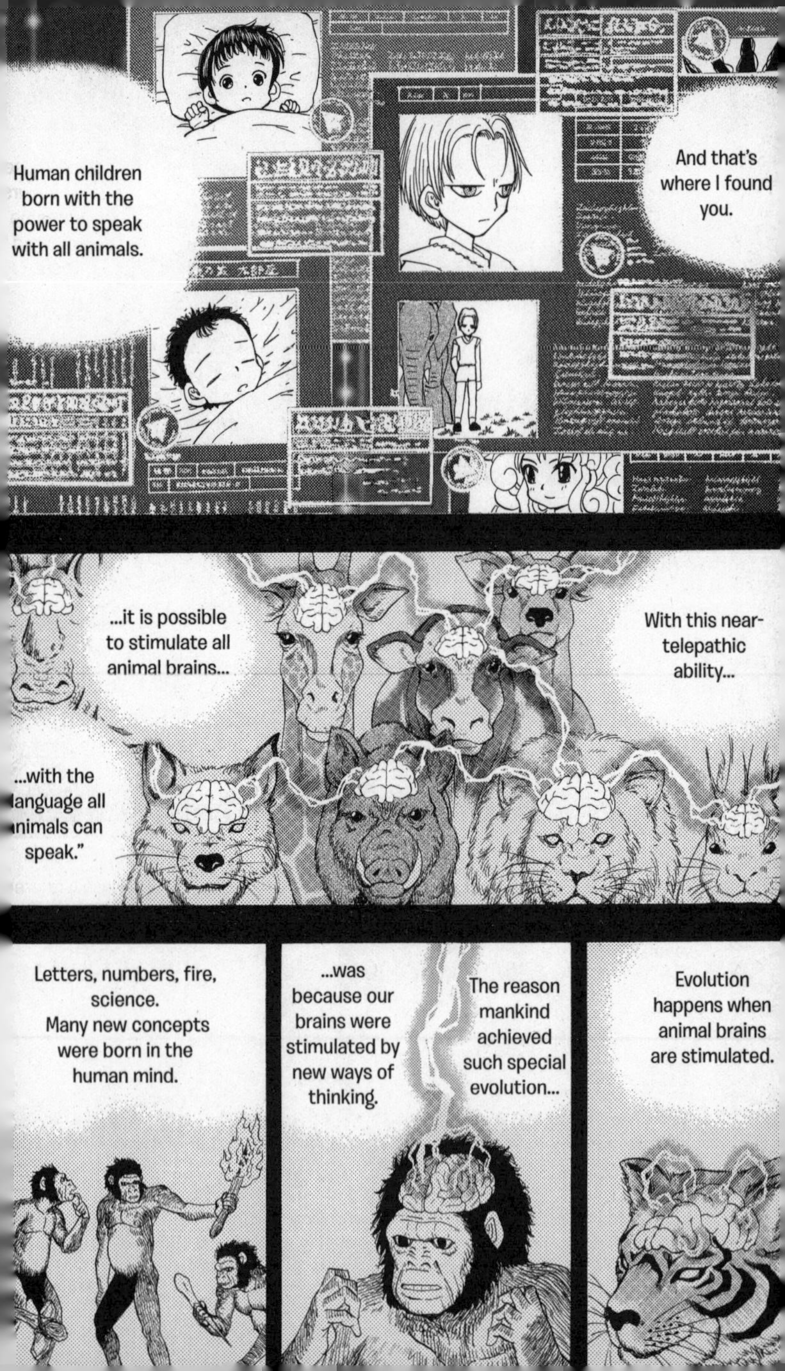
And that's where I found you.
Human children born with the power to speak with all animals.
With this near-telepathic ability...
...it is possible to stimulate all animal brains...
...with the language all nimals can speak.”
Evolution happens when animal brains are stimulated.
The reason mankind achieved such special evolution...
...was because our brains were stimulated by new ways of thinking.
Letters, numbers, fire, science. Many new concepts were born in the human mind.

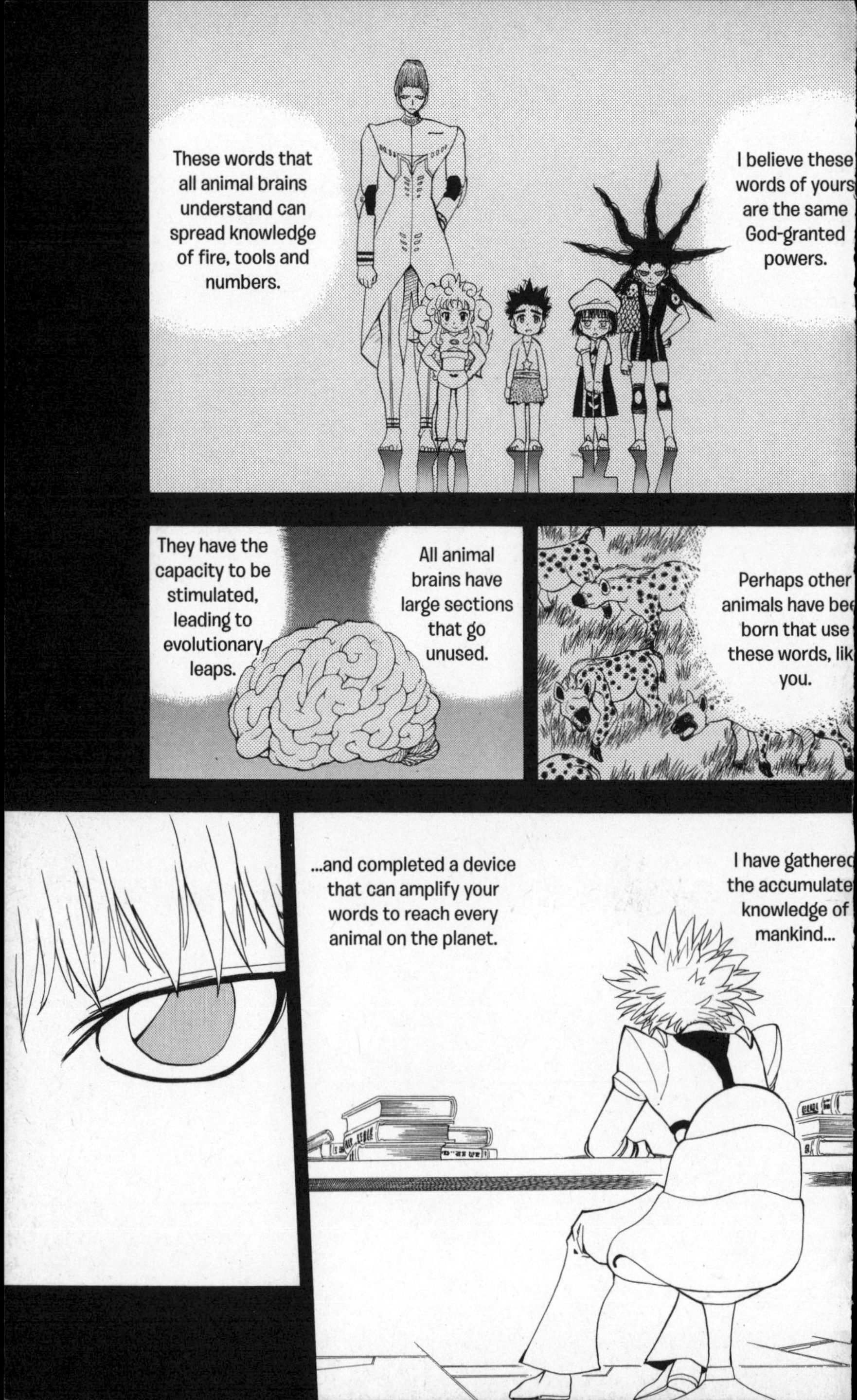
I believe these words of yours are the same God-granted powers.
These words that all animal brains understand can spread knowledge of fire, tools and numbers.
Perhaps other animals have bee born that use these words, lik you.
All animal brains have large sections that go unused.
They have the capacity to be stimulated, leading to evolutionary leaps.
I have gathere the accumulate knowledge of mankind...
...and completed a device that can amplify your words to reach every animal on the planet.

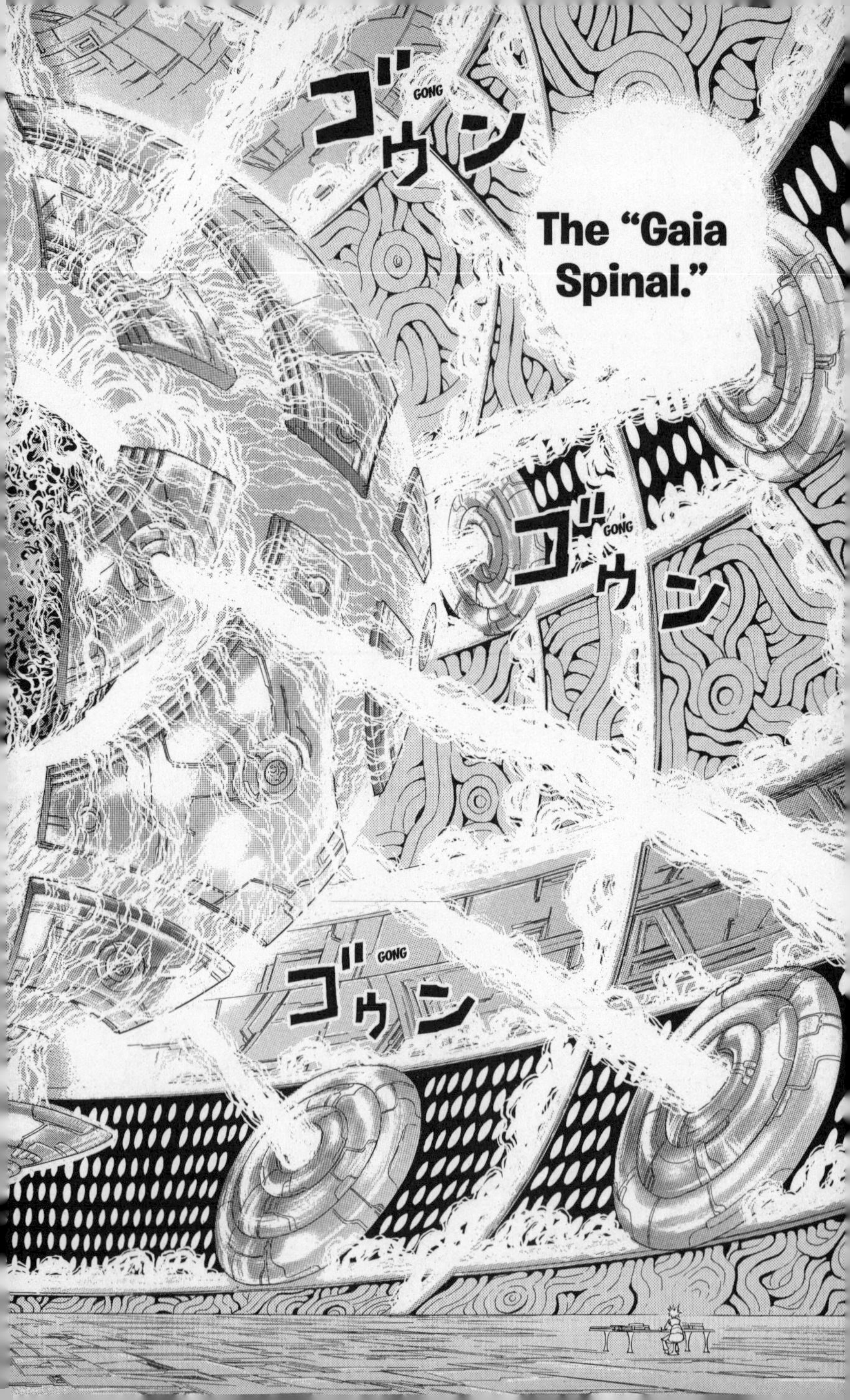
ゴウン
GONG
The "Gaia Spinal."
ゴウン
GONG
ゴウン
GONG

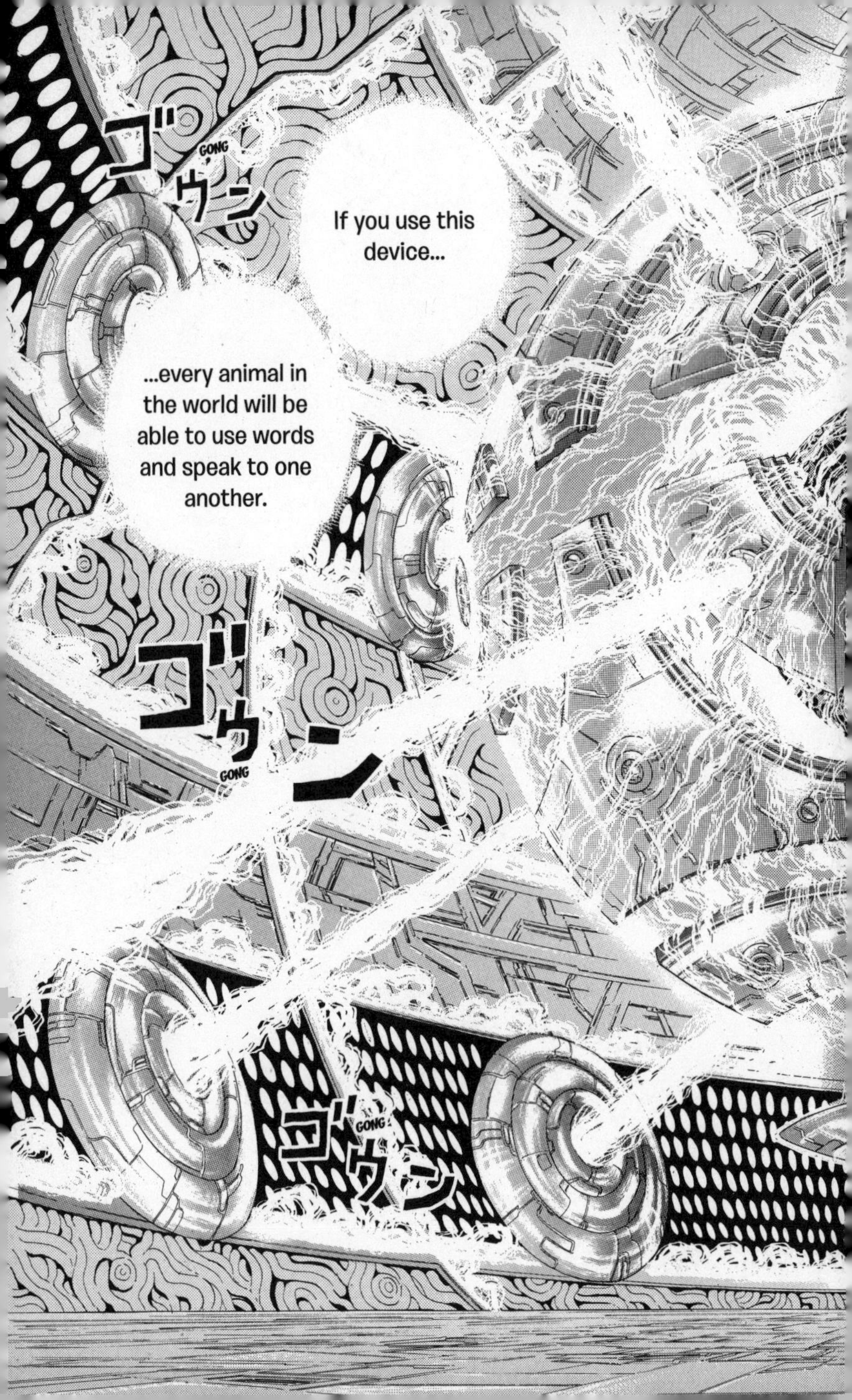

ゴウン
GONG
If you use this device...
...every animal in the world will be able to use words and speak to one another.
ゴウーン
GONG
ゴウン
GONG

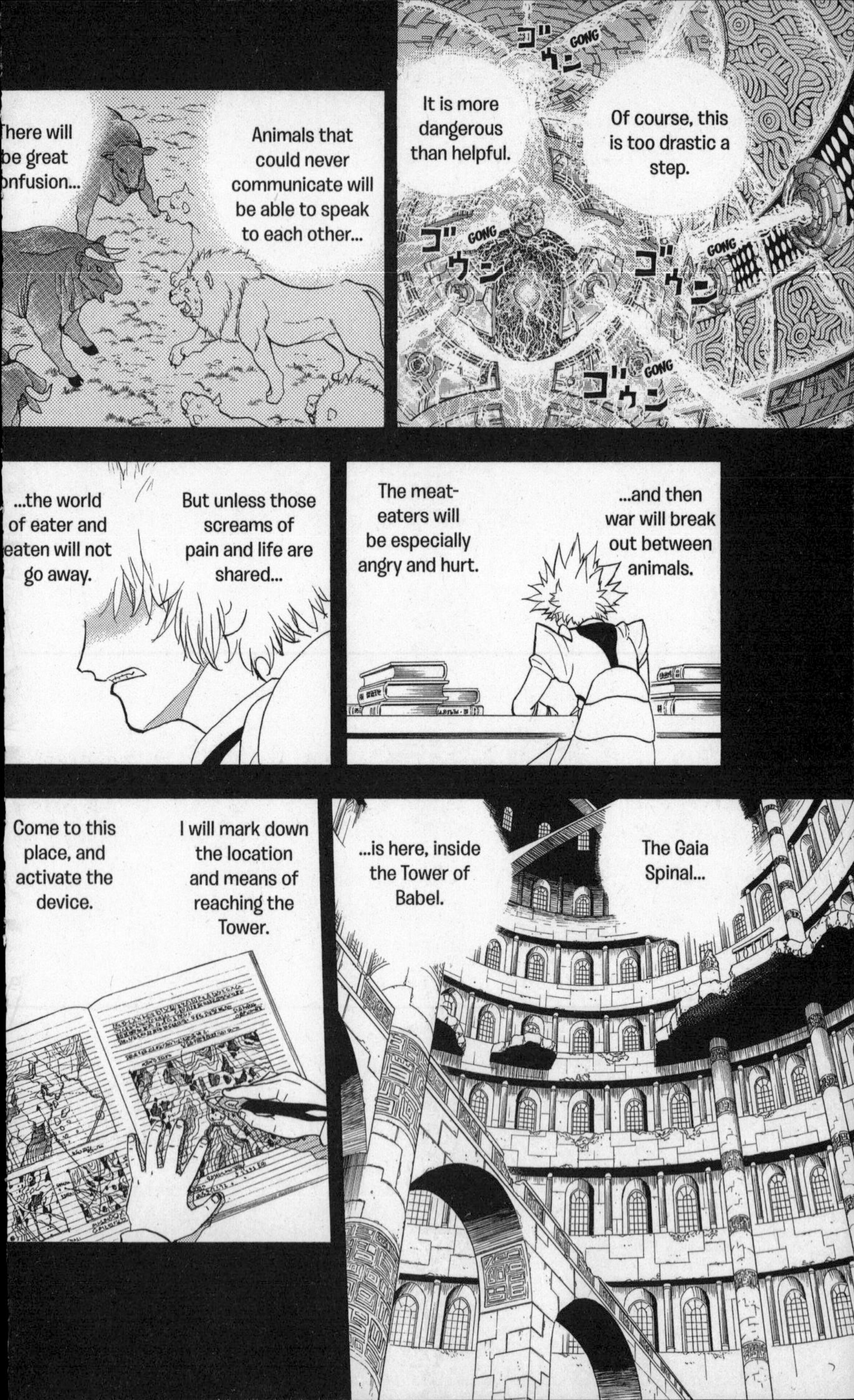

GONG
ゴウン
Of course, this is too drastic a step.
It is more dangerous than helpful.
GONG
ゴウン
GONG
ゴウン
GONG
ゴウン
Animals that could never communicate will be able to speak to each other...
here will be great onfusion...
...and then war will break out between animals.
The meat-eaters will be especially angry and hurt.
But unless those screams of pain and life are shared...
...the world of eater and eaten will not go away.
The Gaia Spinal...
...is here, inside the Tower of Babel.
I will mark down the location and means of reaching the Tower.
Come to this place, and activate the device.

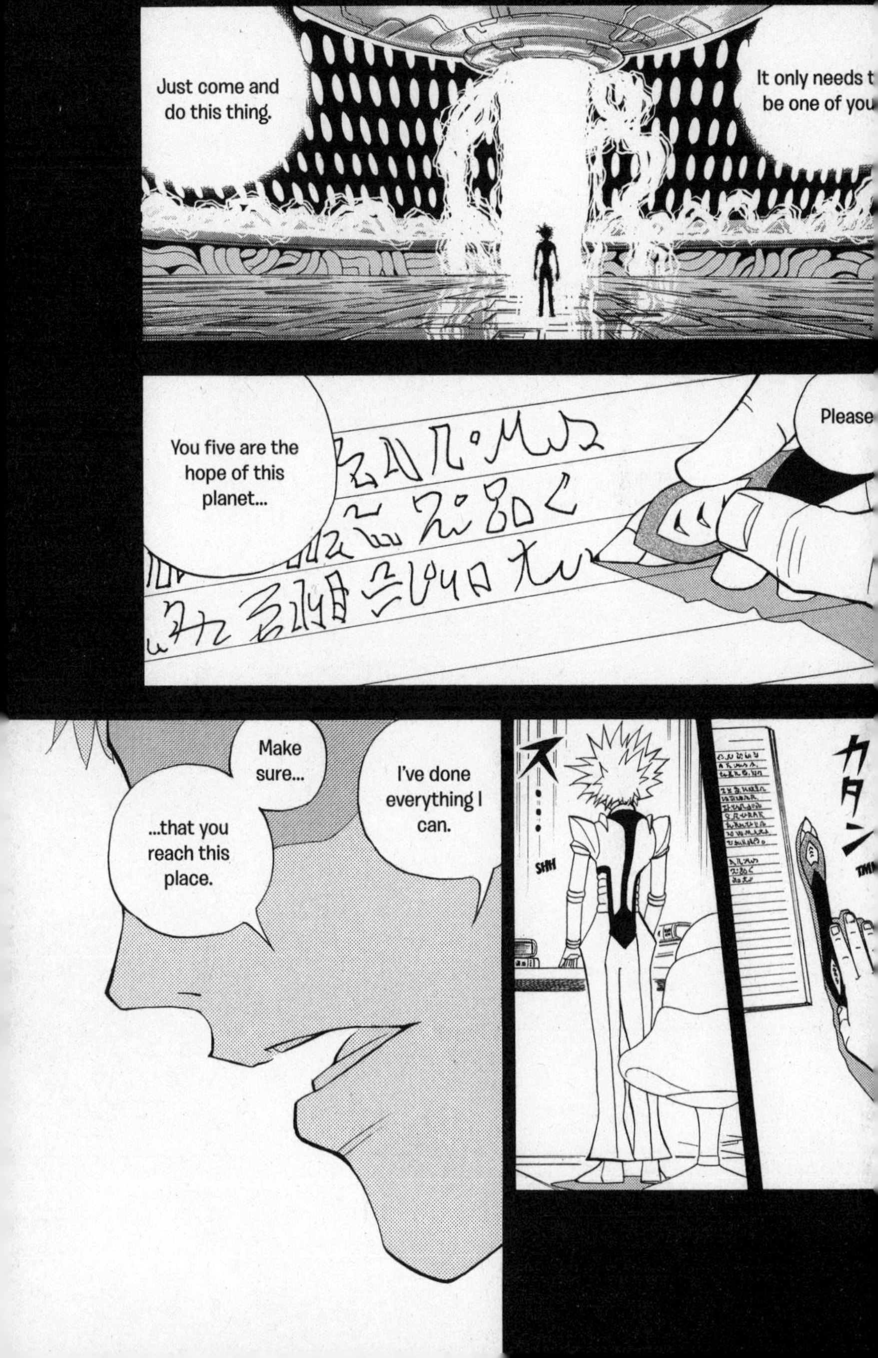
It only needs t
be one of you
Just come and do this thing.
Please
You five are the hope of this planet...
カタン
ス
SHH
I've done everything I can.
Make sure...
...that you reach this place.

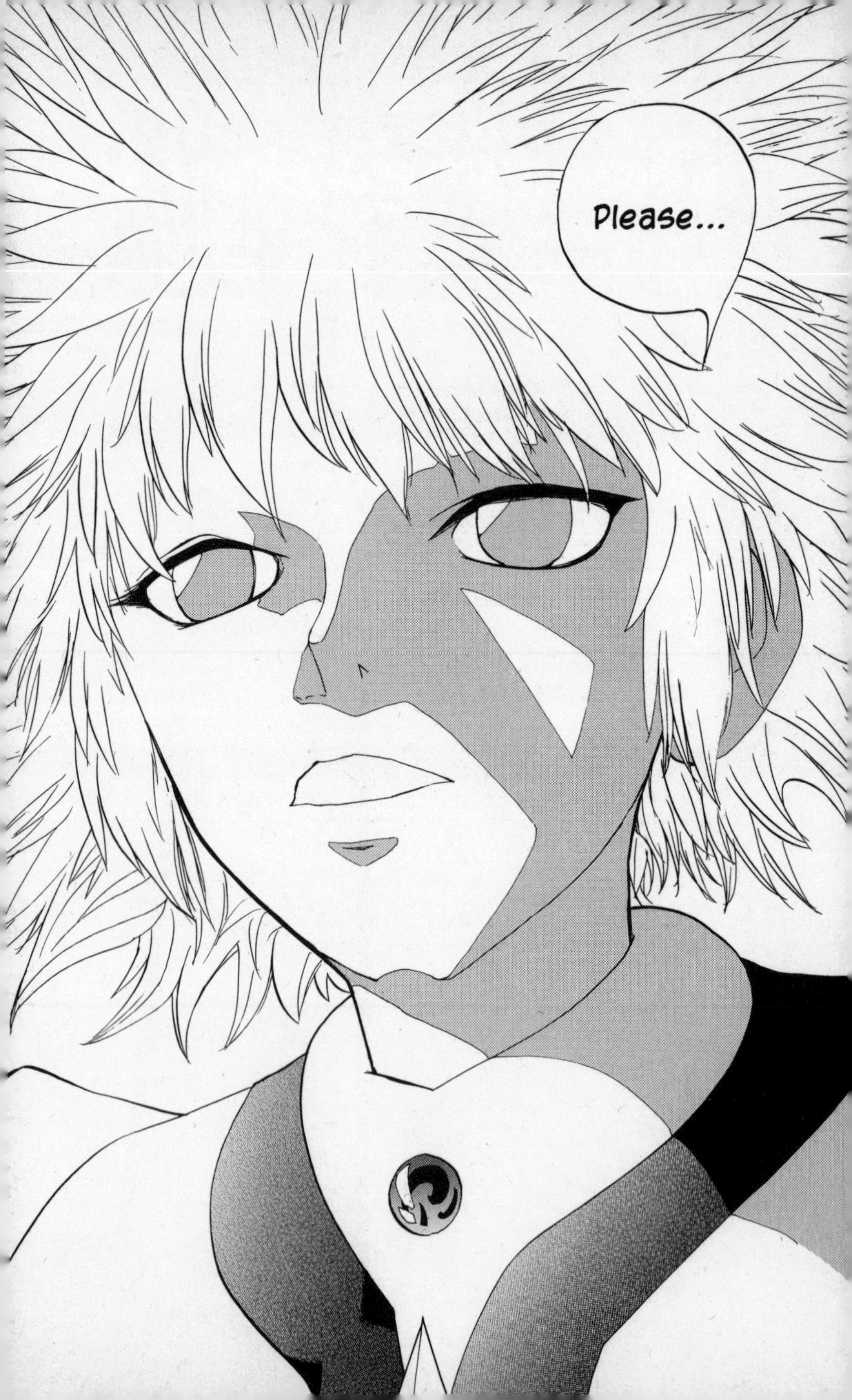
Please...

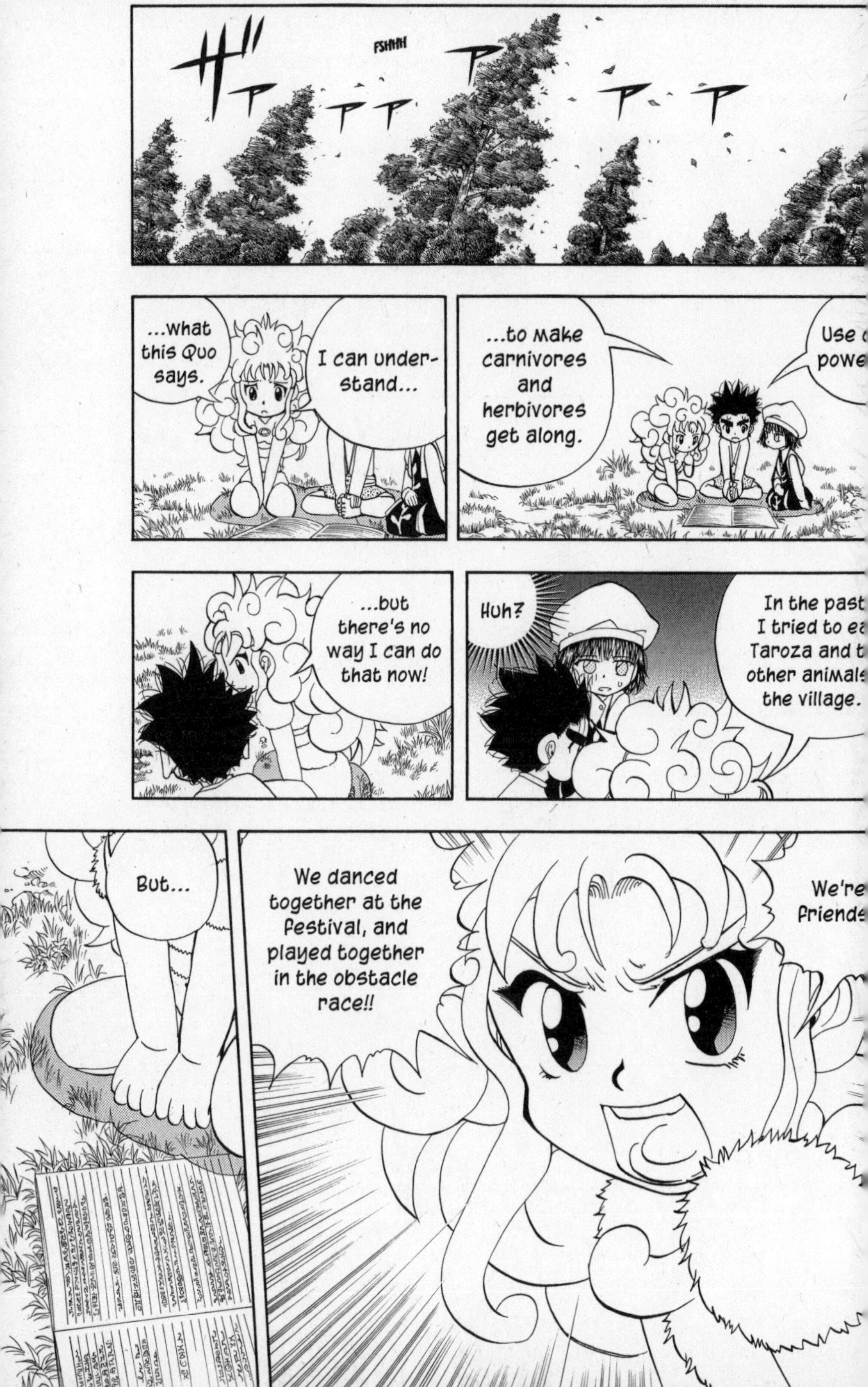
FSHHH
Use
powe
...to make carnivores and herbivores get along.
I can under-stand...
...what this Quo says.
In the past I tried to ea
Taroza and t
other animals
the village.
Huh?
...but there's no way I can do that now!
We're friends
We danced together at the festival, and played together in the obstacle race!!
But...

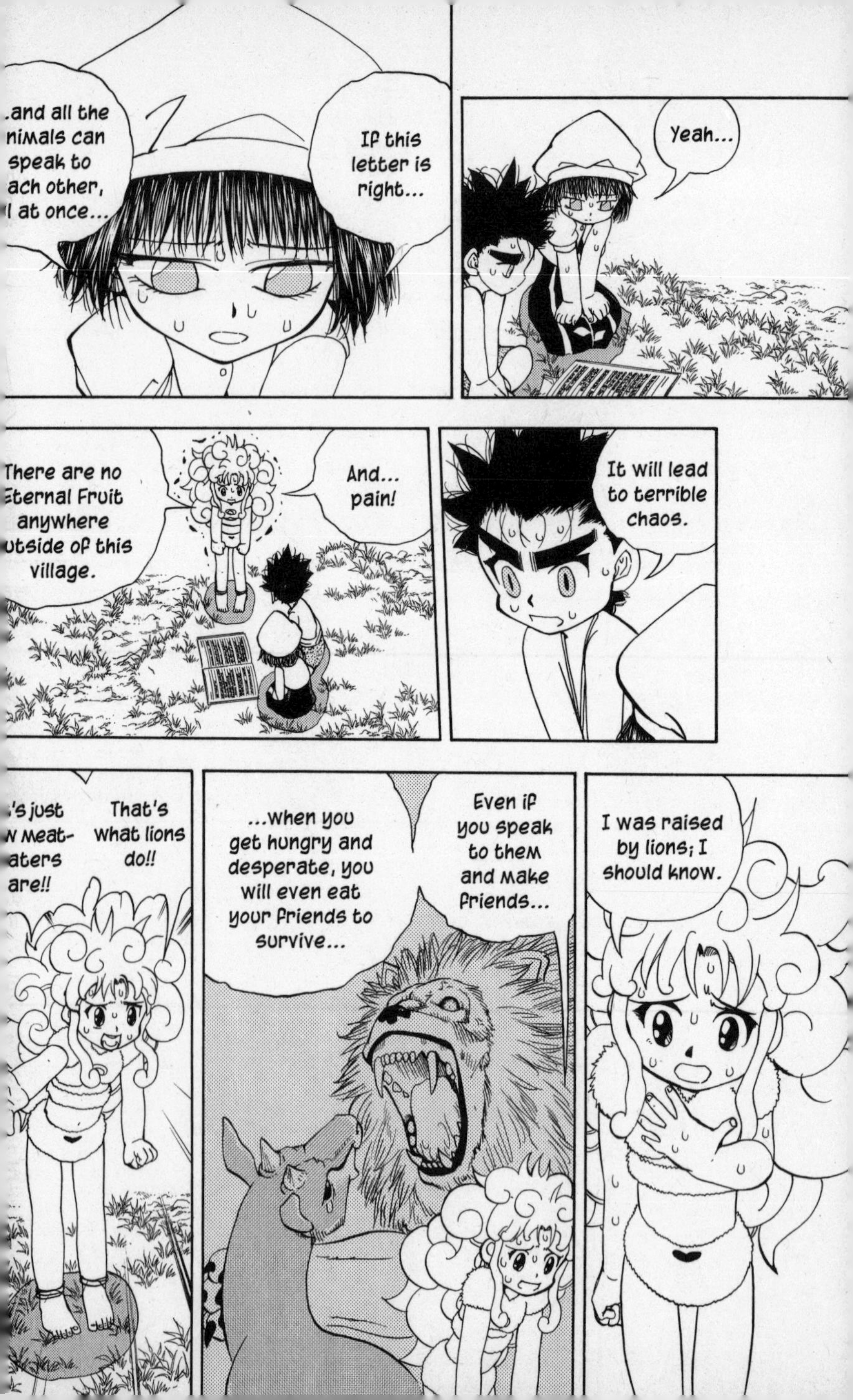
Yeah...
If this letter is right...
.and all the nimals can speak to ach other, l at once...
It will lead to terrible chaos.
And... pain!
There are no Eternal Fruit anywhere utside of this village.
I was raised by lions; I should know.
Even if you speak to them and make friends...
...when you get hungry and desperate, you will even eat your friends to survive...
That's what lions do!!
's just W Meat-aters are!!

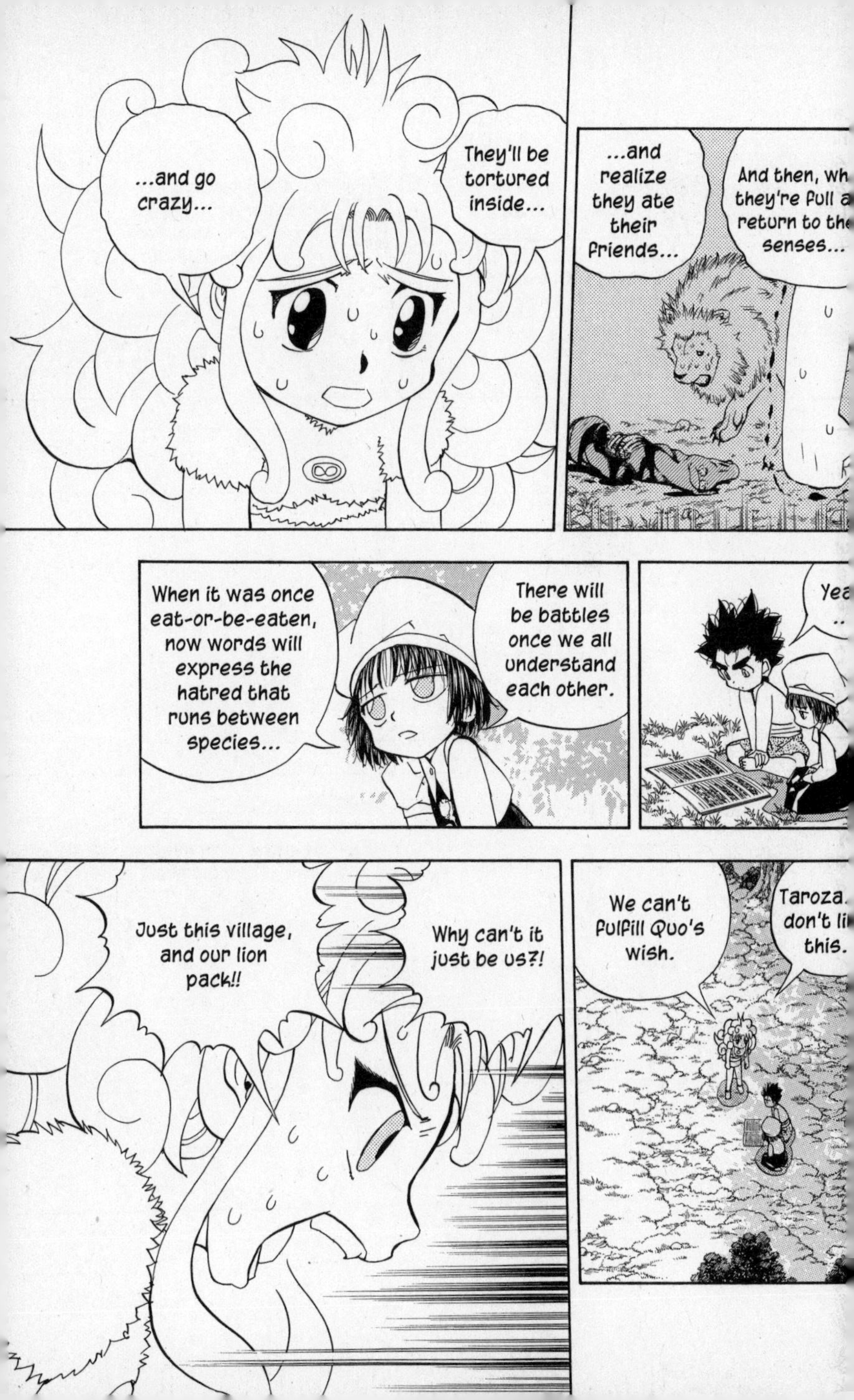

And then, wh they're full a return to the senses...
...and realize they ate their friends...
They'll be tortured inside...
...and go crazy...
Yea
There will be battles once we all understand each other.
When it was once eat-or-be-eaten, now words will express the hatred that runs between species...
Taroza. don't li this.
We can't fulfill Quo's wish.
Why can't it just be us?!
Just this village, and our lion pack!!

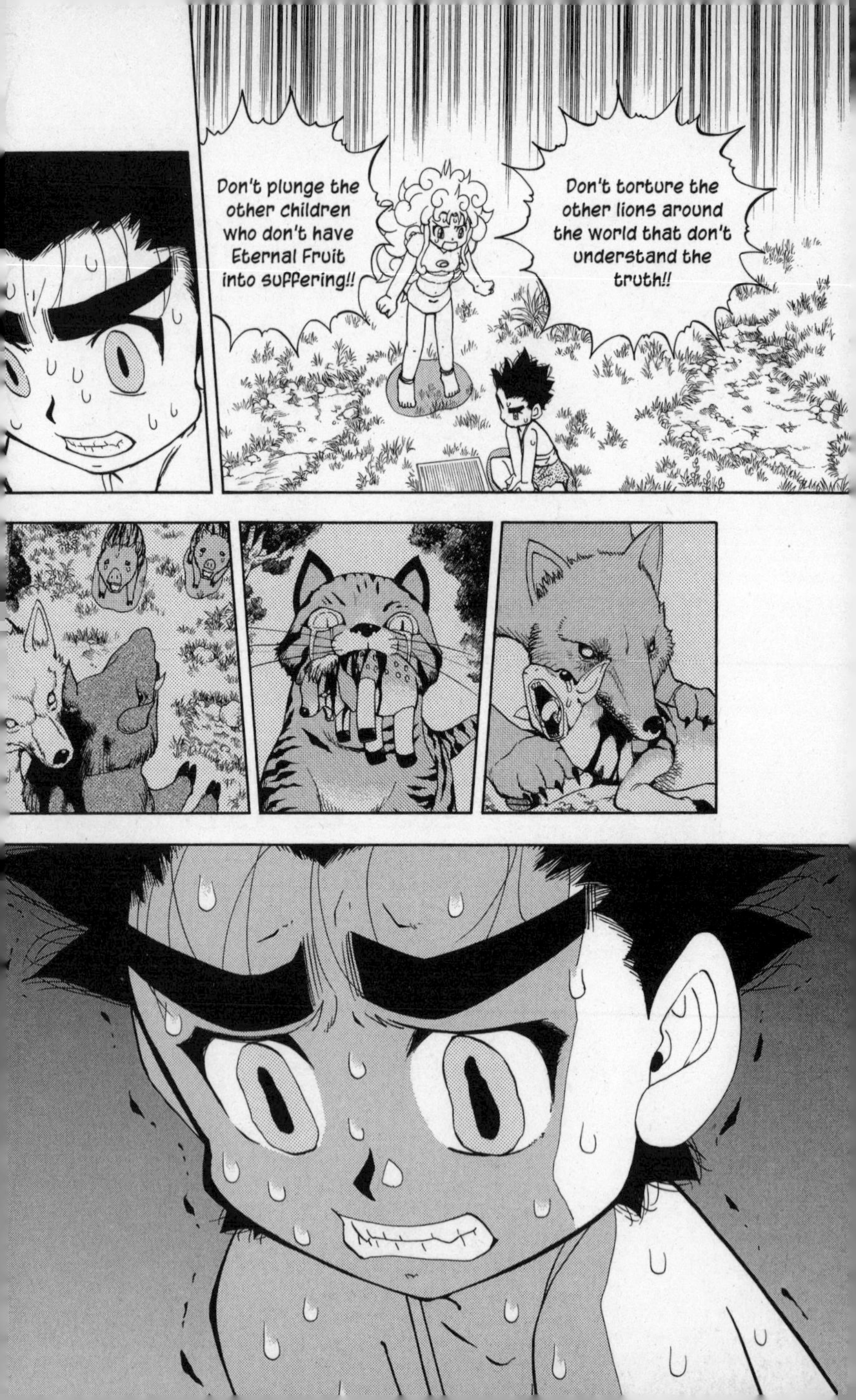
Don't torture the other lions around the world that don't understand the truth!!
Don't plunge the other children who don't have Eternal Fruit into suffering!!

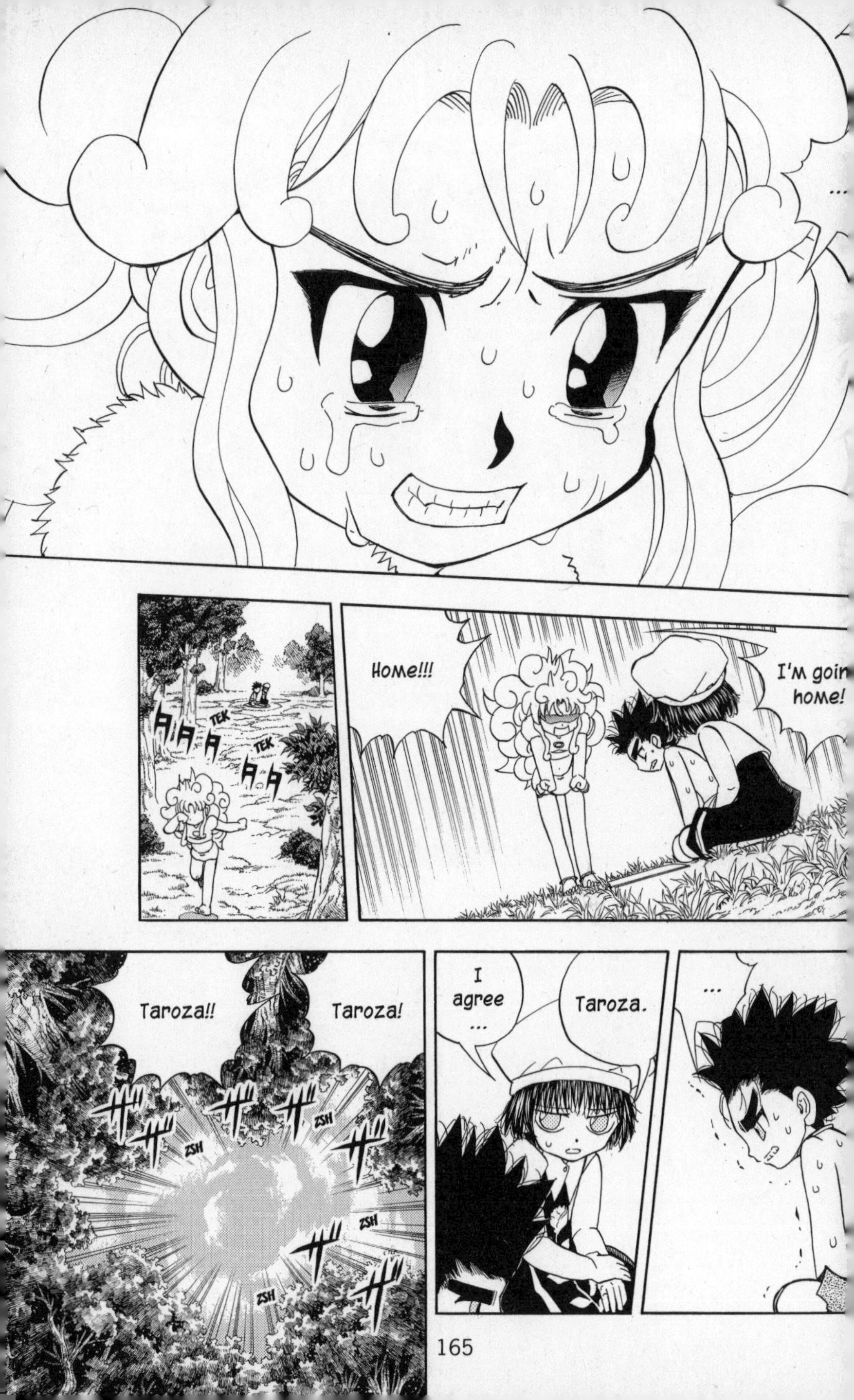
...
I'm goin
home!
Home!!!
TEK
TEK
...
Taroza.
I agree
...
Taroza!
Taroza!!
ZSH
ZSH
ZSH
ZSH

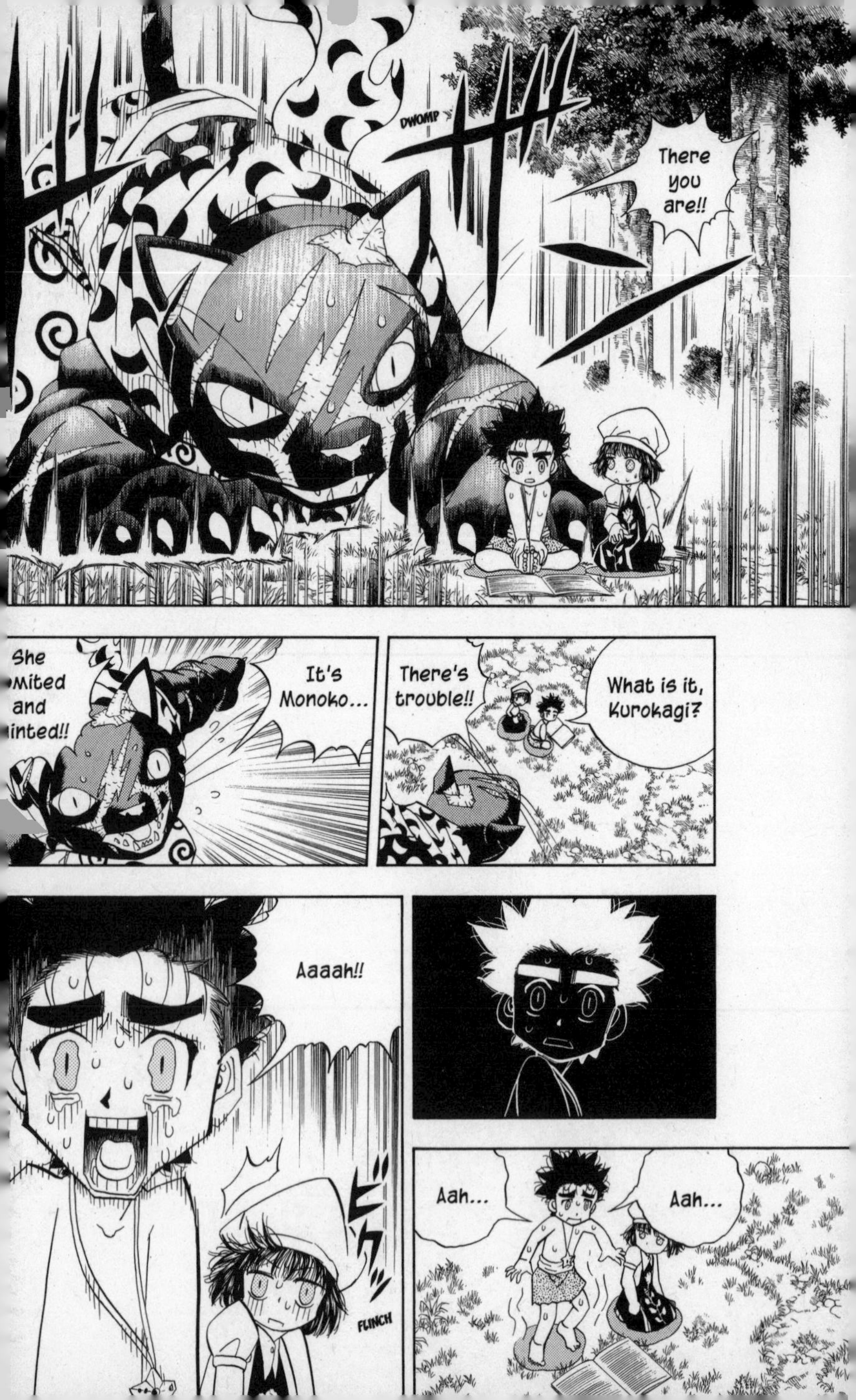
DWOMP
There you are!!
What is it, Kurokagi?
There's trouble!!
It's Monoko...
She mited and inted!!
Aah...
Aah...
Aaaah!!
FLINCH

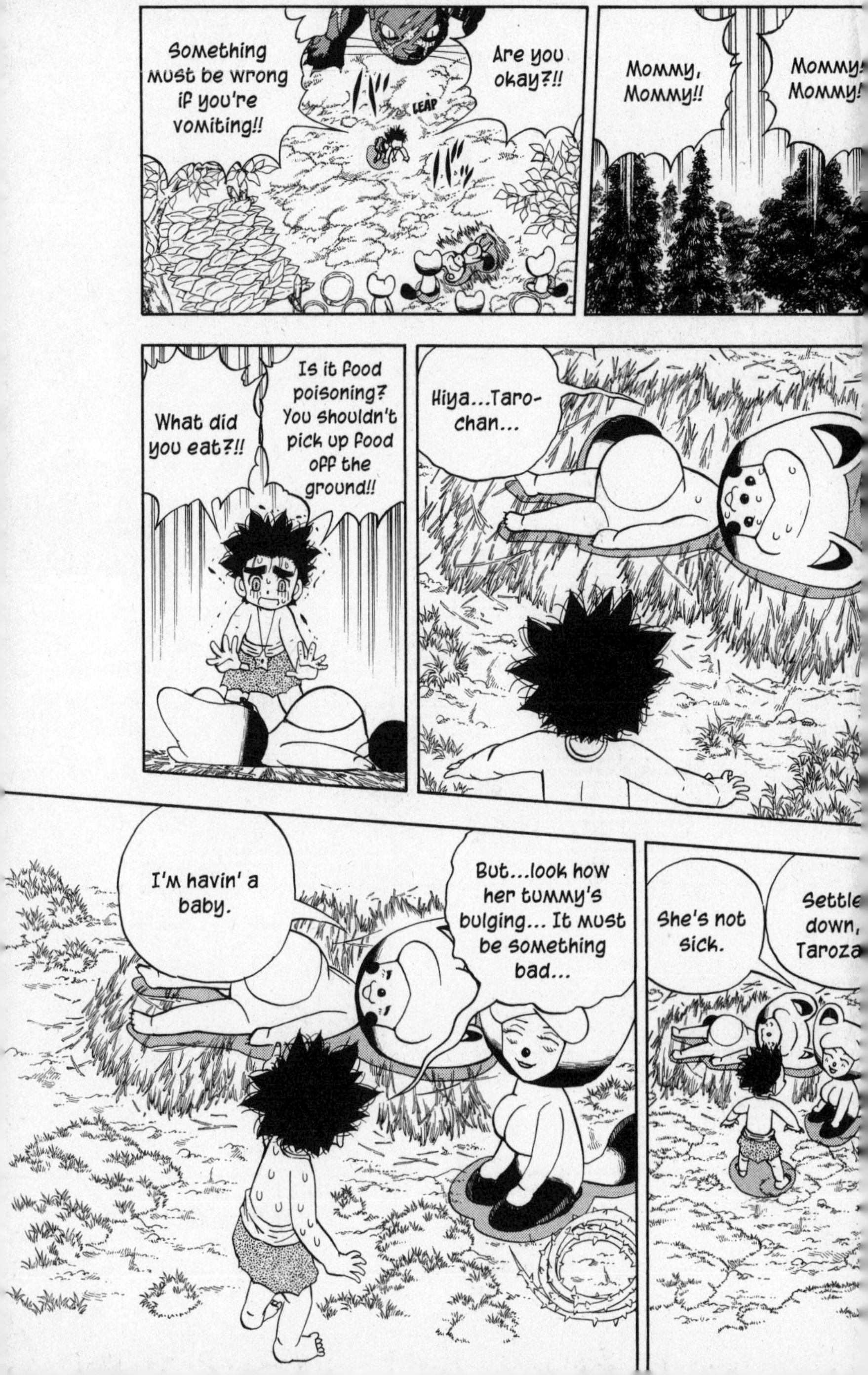
Mommy! Mommy!
Mommy, Mommy!!
Are you okay?!!
LEAP
Something must be wrong if you're vomiting!!
Hiya...Taro-chan...
Is it food poisoning? You shouldn't pick up food off the ground!!
What did you eat?!!
Settle down, Taroza
She's not sick.
But...look how her tummy's bulging... It must be something bad...
I'm havin' a baby.

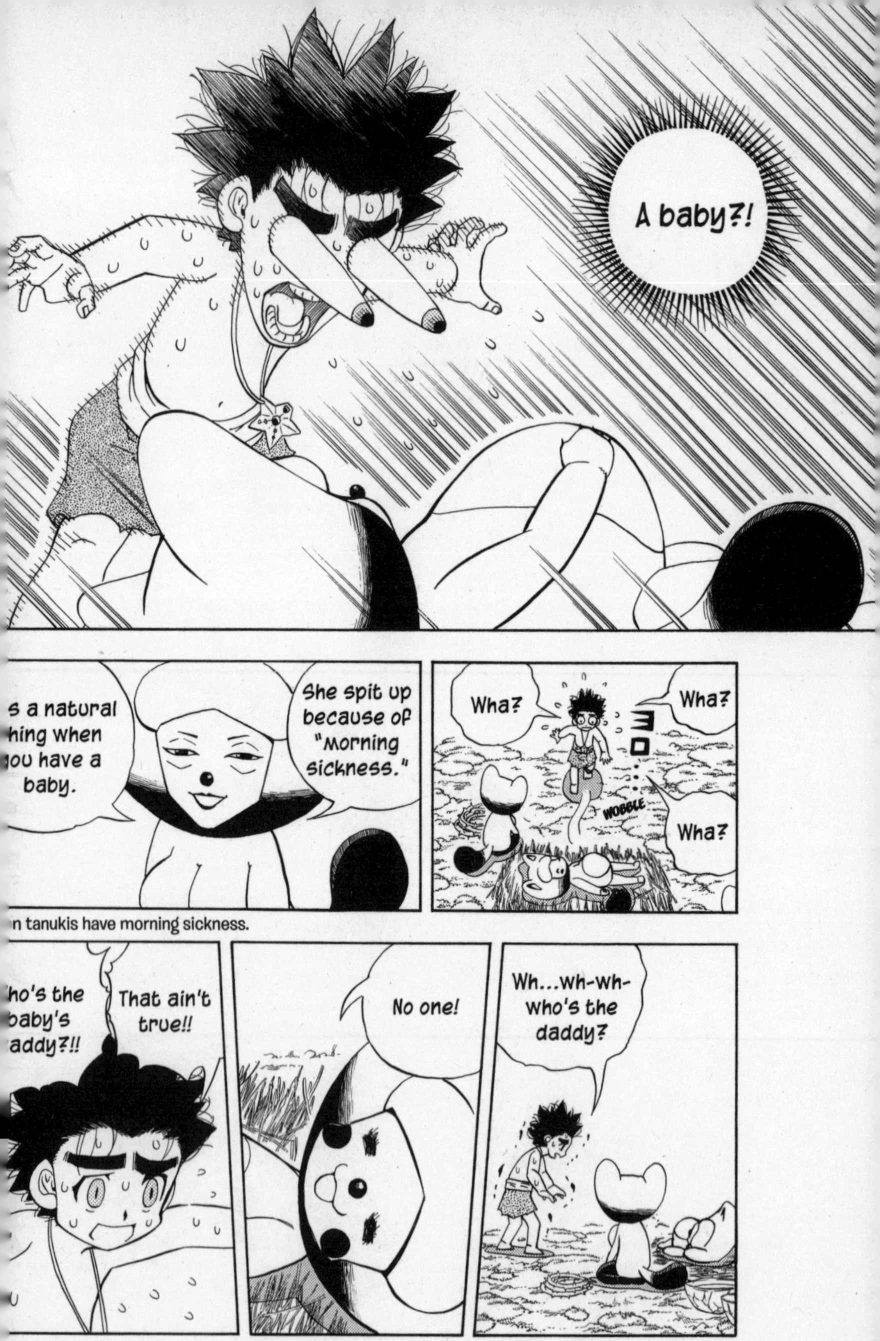
A baby?!
Wha?
Wha?
ヨロ
WOBBLE
Wha?
She spit up because of "morning sickness."
s a natural hing when ou have a baby.
n tanukis have morning sickness.
Wh...wh-wh-who's the daddy?
No one!
That ain't true!!
ho's the baby's addy?!!

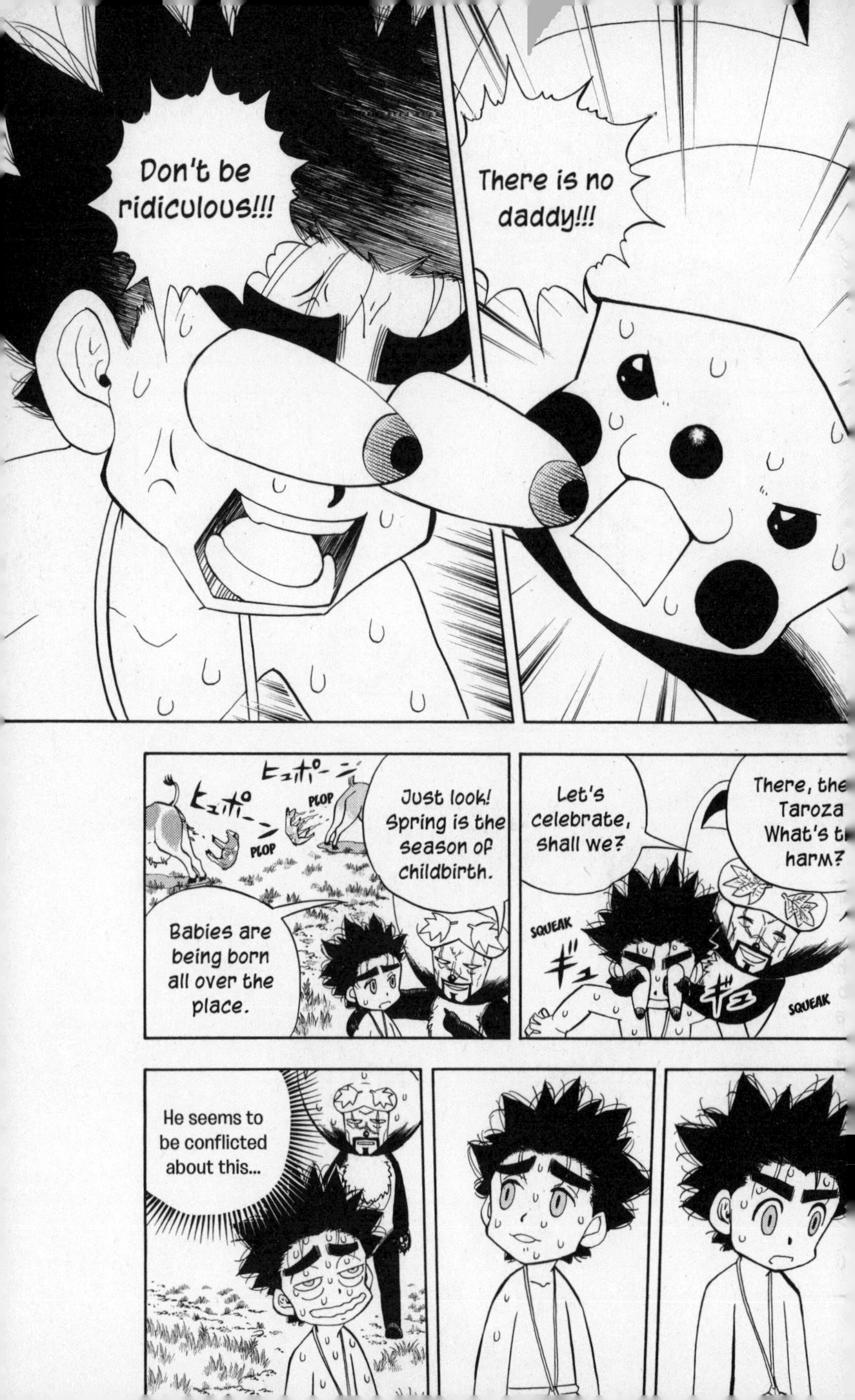
There is no daddy!!!
Don't be ridiculous!!!
There, the Taroza What's t harm?
Let's celebrate, shall we?
SQUEAK
SQUEAK
Just look! Spring is the season of childbirth.
PLOP
PLOP
Babies are being born all over the place.
He seems to be conflicted about this...

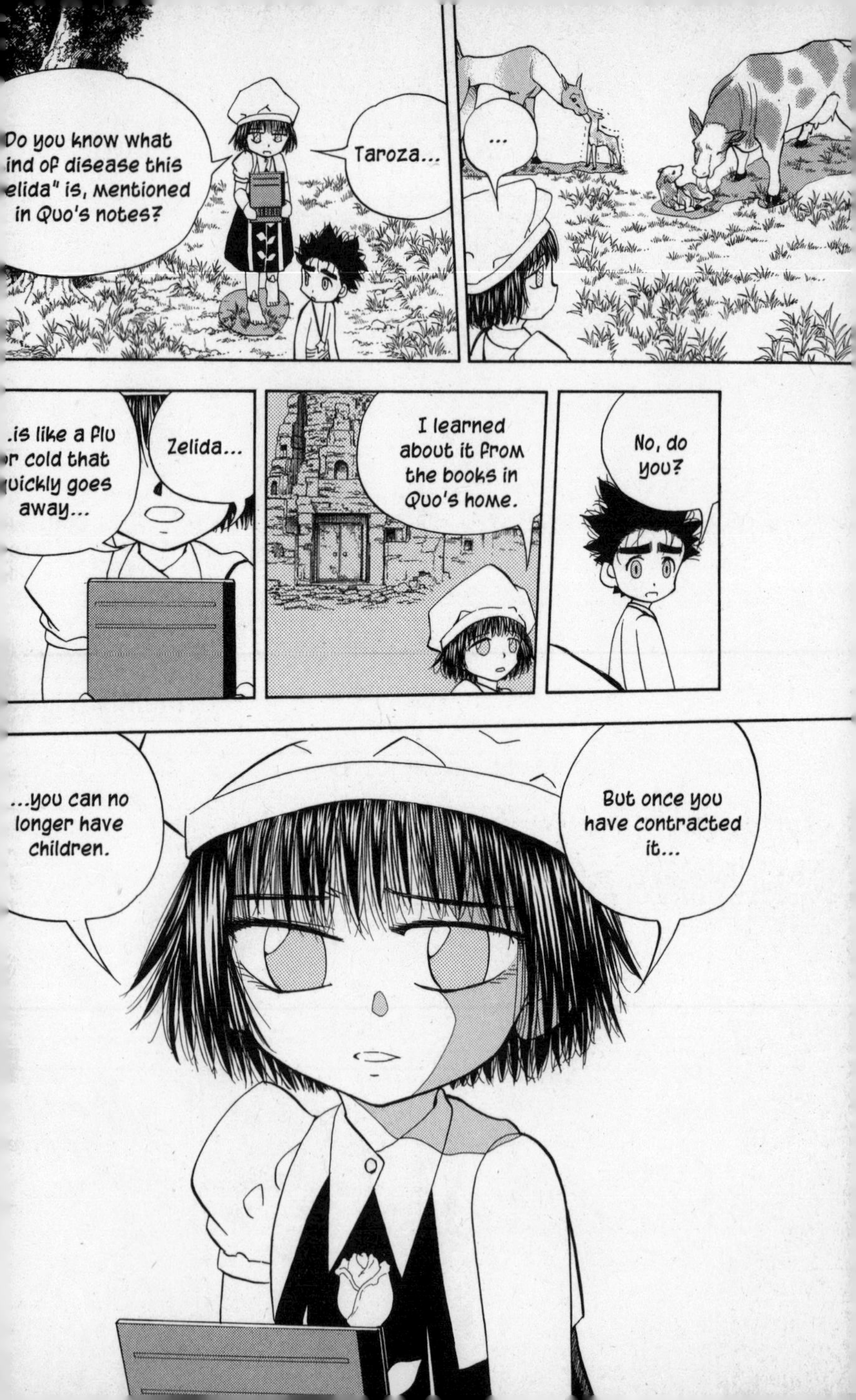
...
Taroza...
Do you know what
ind of disease this
elida" is, mentioned
in Quo's notes?
No, do you?
I learned about it from the books in Quo's home.
Zelida...
.is like a flu
r cold that
uickly goes
away...
But once you have contracted it...
...you can no longer have children.

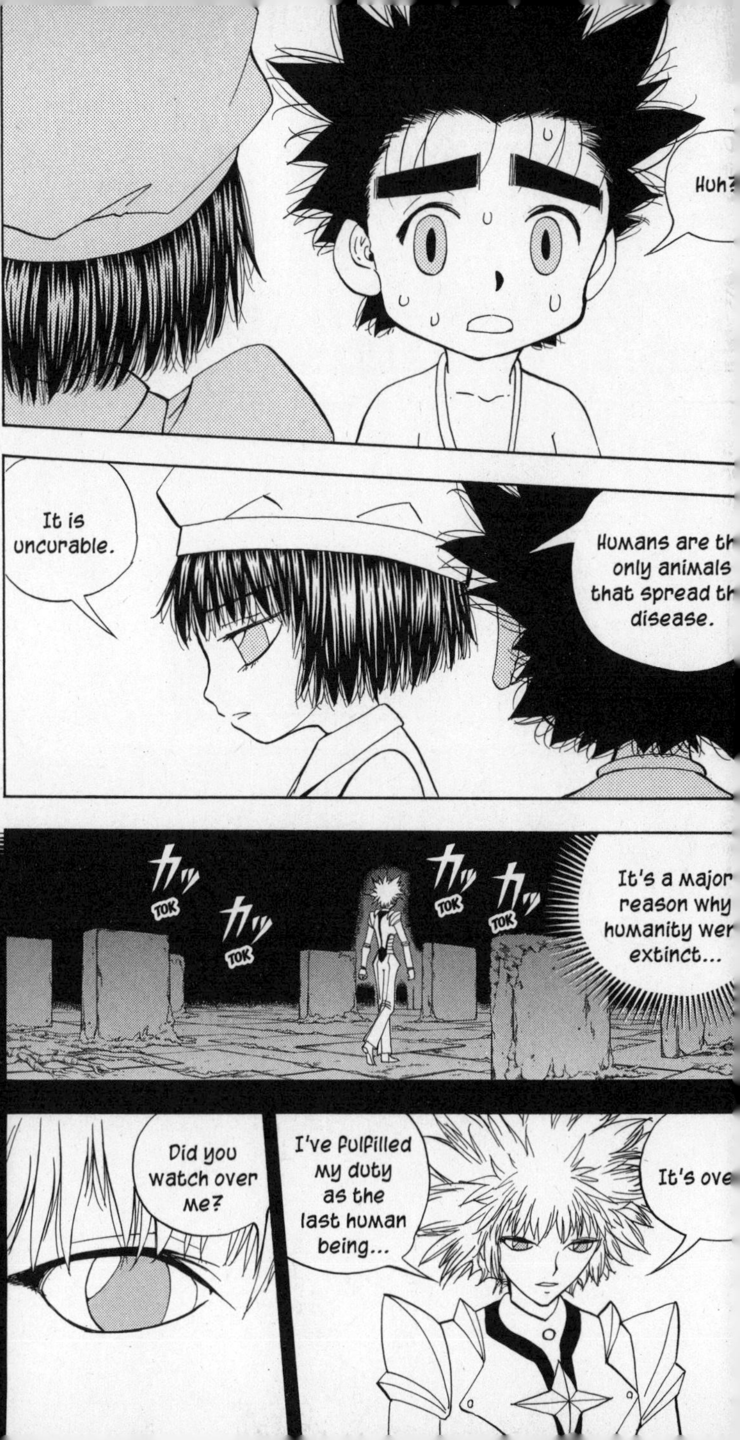
Huh?
Humans are th only animals that spread th disease.
It is uncurable.
It's a major reason why humanity wer extinct...
カッ TOK
カッ TOK
カッ TOK
カッ TOK
It's ove
I've fulfilled my duty as the last human being...
Did you watch over me?

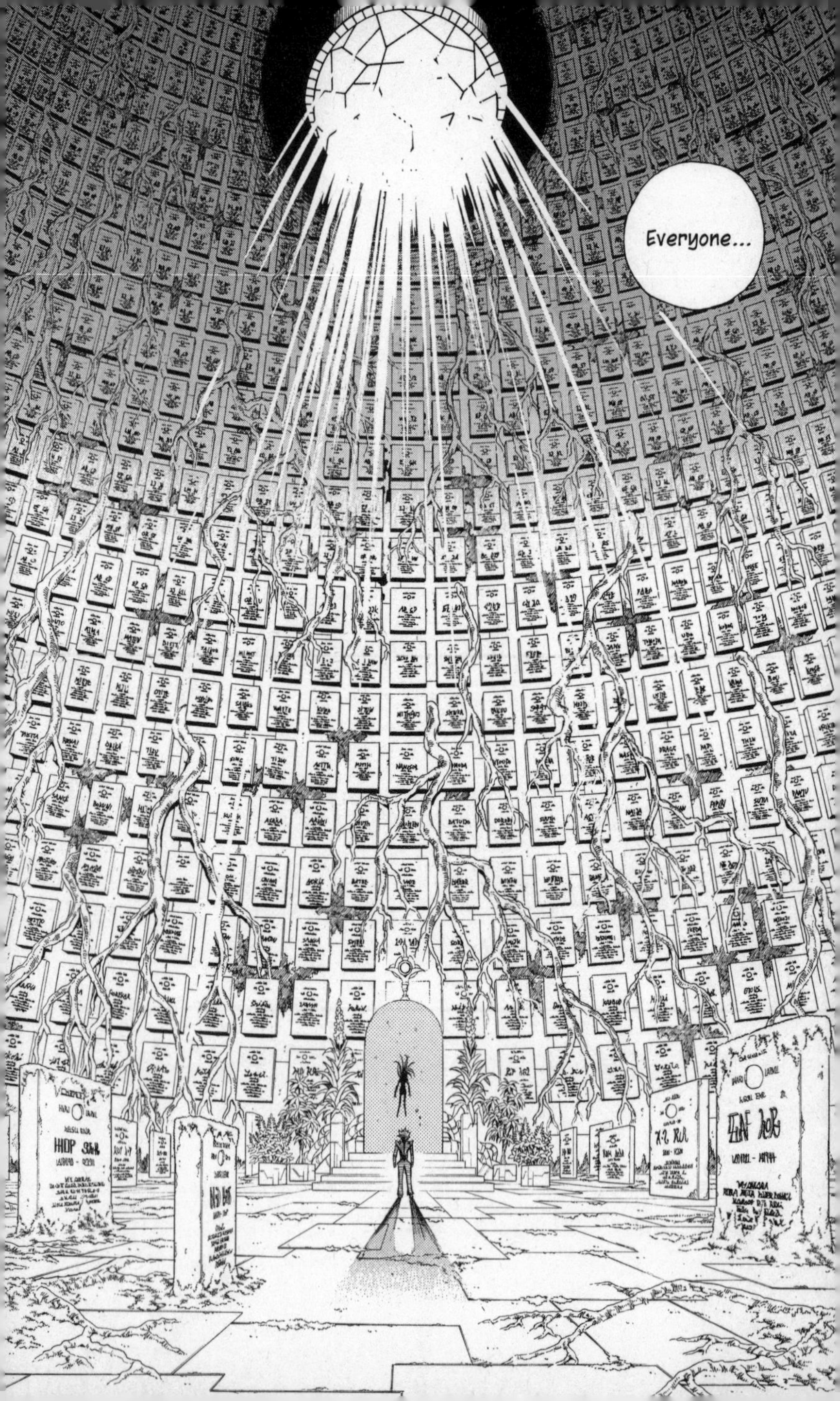
Everyone...

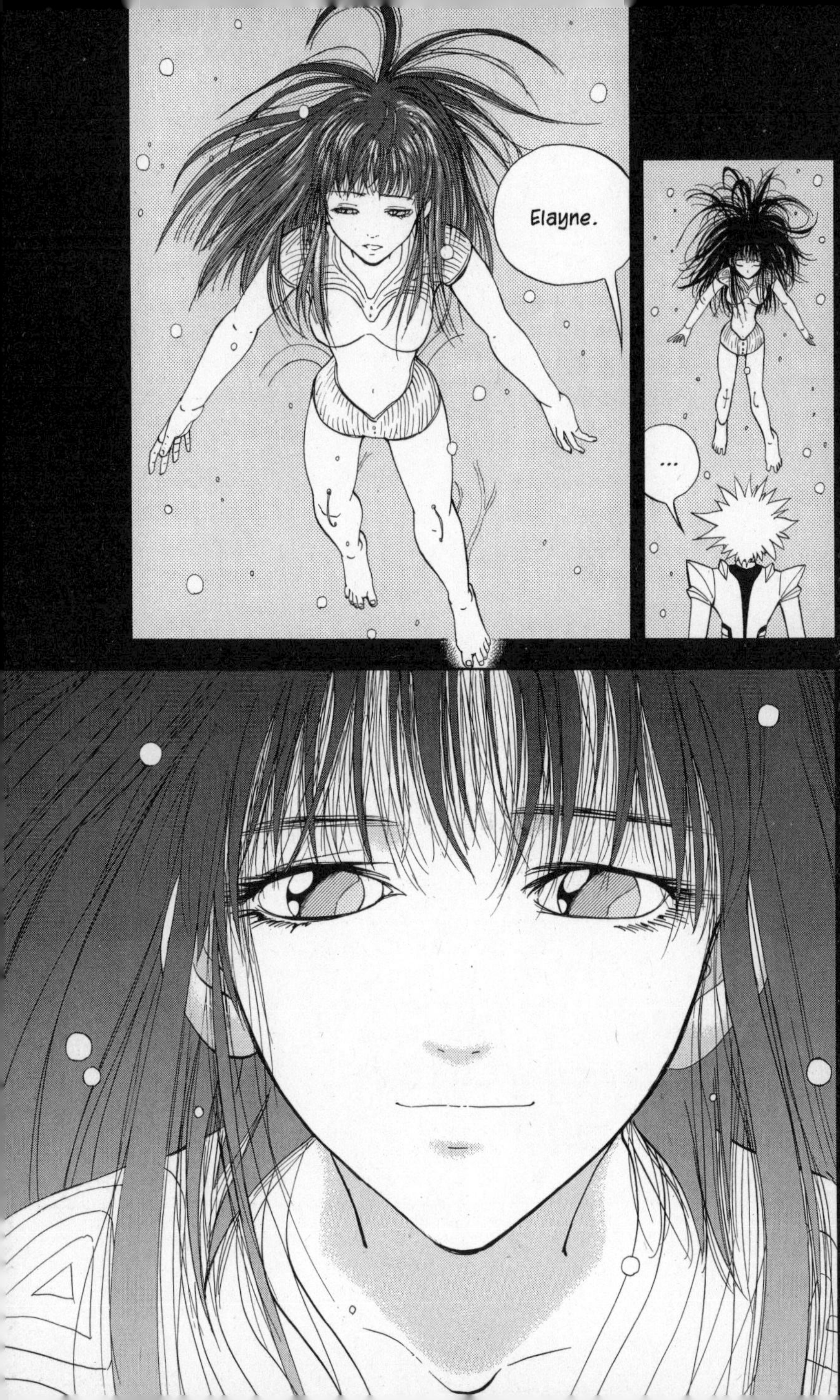
...
Elayne.

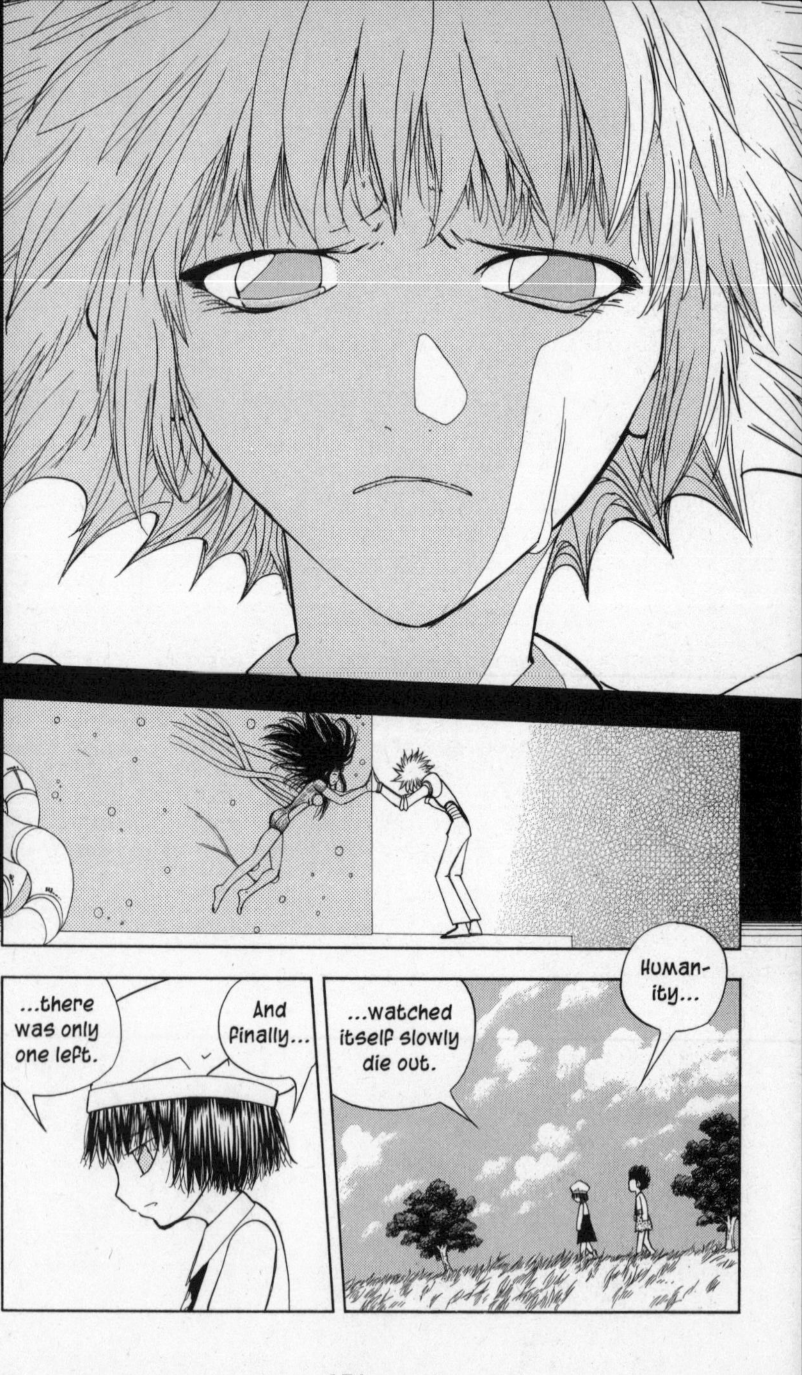
Human-ity...
...watched itself slowly die out.
And finally...
...there was only one left.

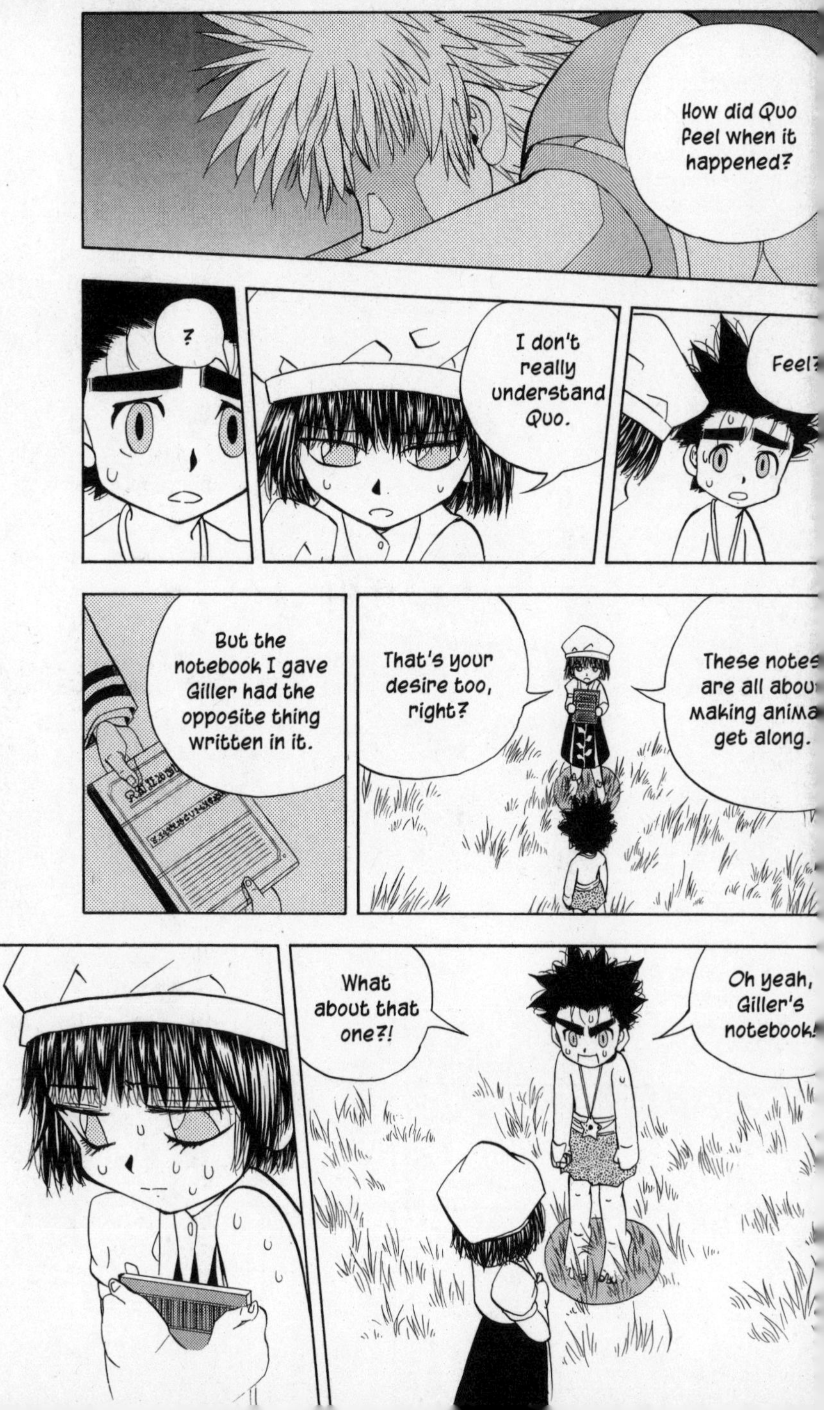
How did Quo feel when it happened?
Feel?
I don't really understand Quo.
?
These notes are all abou making anima get along.
That's your desire too, right?
But the notebook I gave Giller had the opposite thing written in it.
Oh yeah, Giller's notebook!
What about that one?!

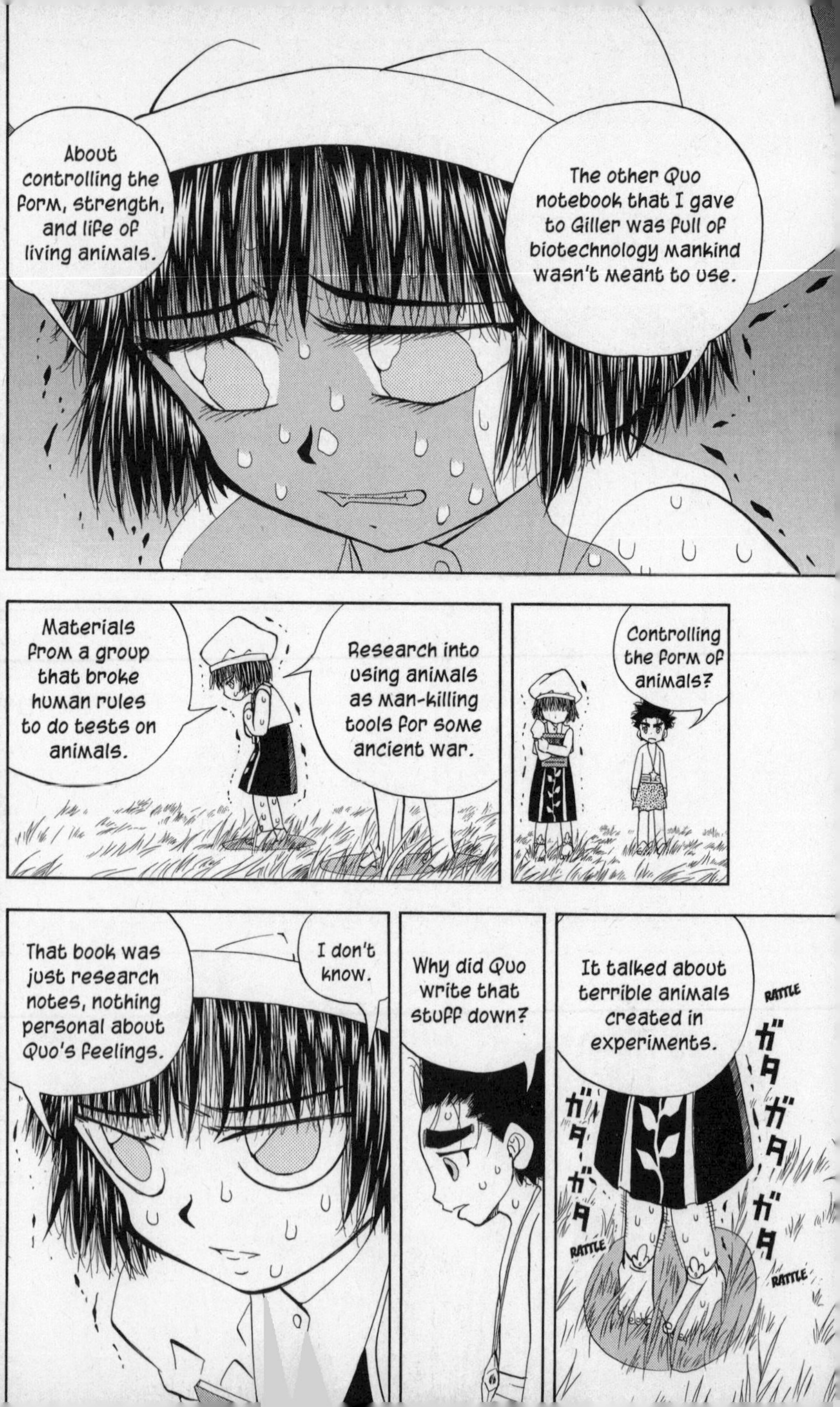
The other Quo notebook that I gave to Giller was full of biotechnology mankind wasn't meant to use.
About controlling the form, strength, and life of living animals.
Controlling the form of animals?
Research into using animals as man-killing tools for some ancient war.
Materials from a group that broke human rules to do tests on animals.
It talked about terrible animals created in experiments.
RATTLE
ガタ ガタ ガタ
ガタ ガタ
RATTLE
RATTLE
Why did Quo write that stuff down?
I don't know.
That book was just research notes, nothing personal about Quo's feelings.

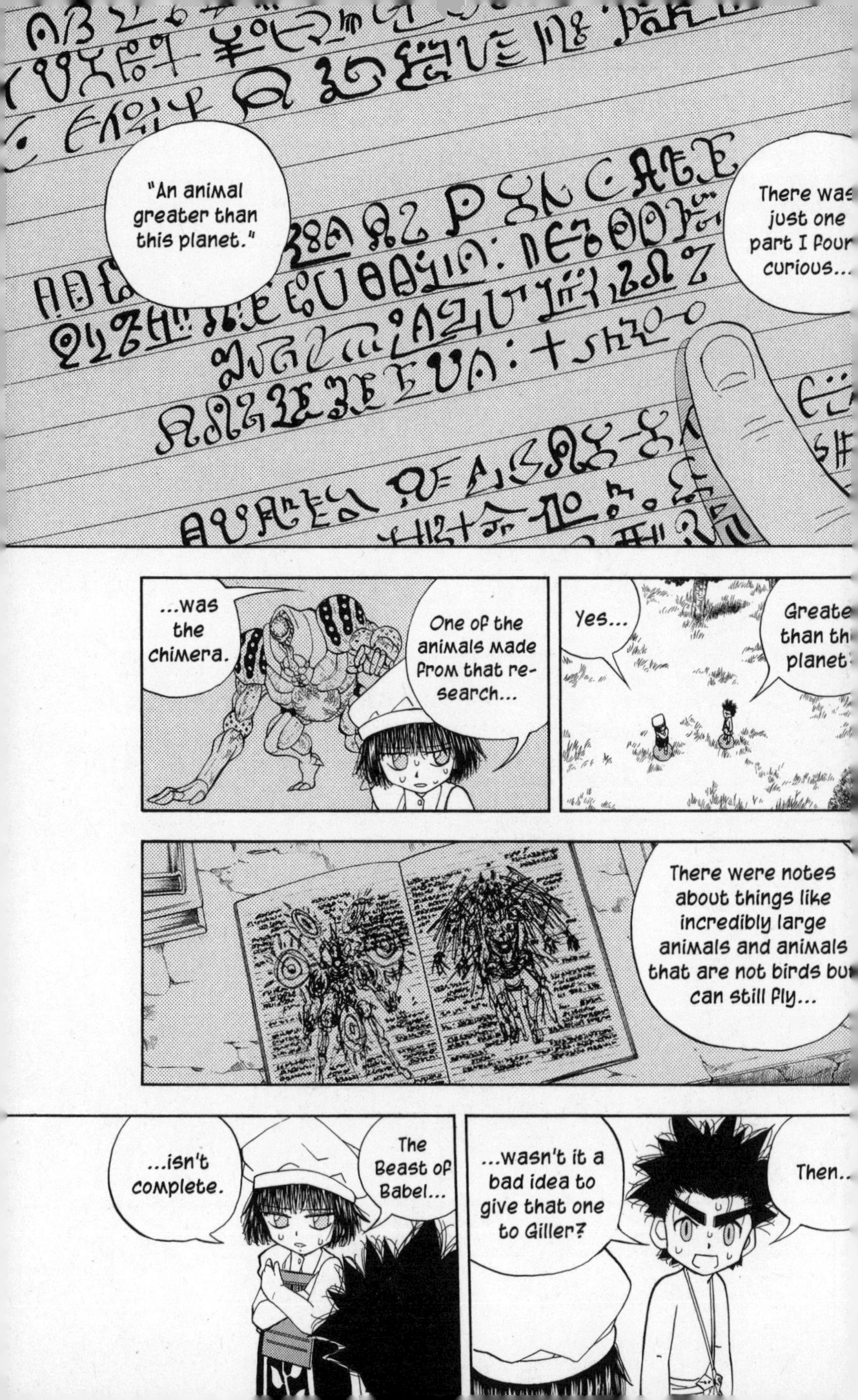
There was just one part I four curious...
"An animal greater than this planet."
Greate than th planet
Yes...
One of the animals made from that re-search...
...was the chimera.
There were notes about things like incredibly large animals and animals that are not birds bu can still fly...
Then...
...wasn't it a bad idea to give that one to Giller?
The Beast of Babel...
...isn't complete.

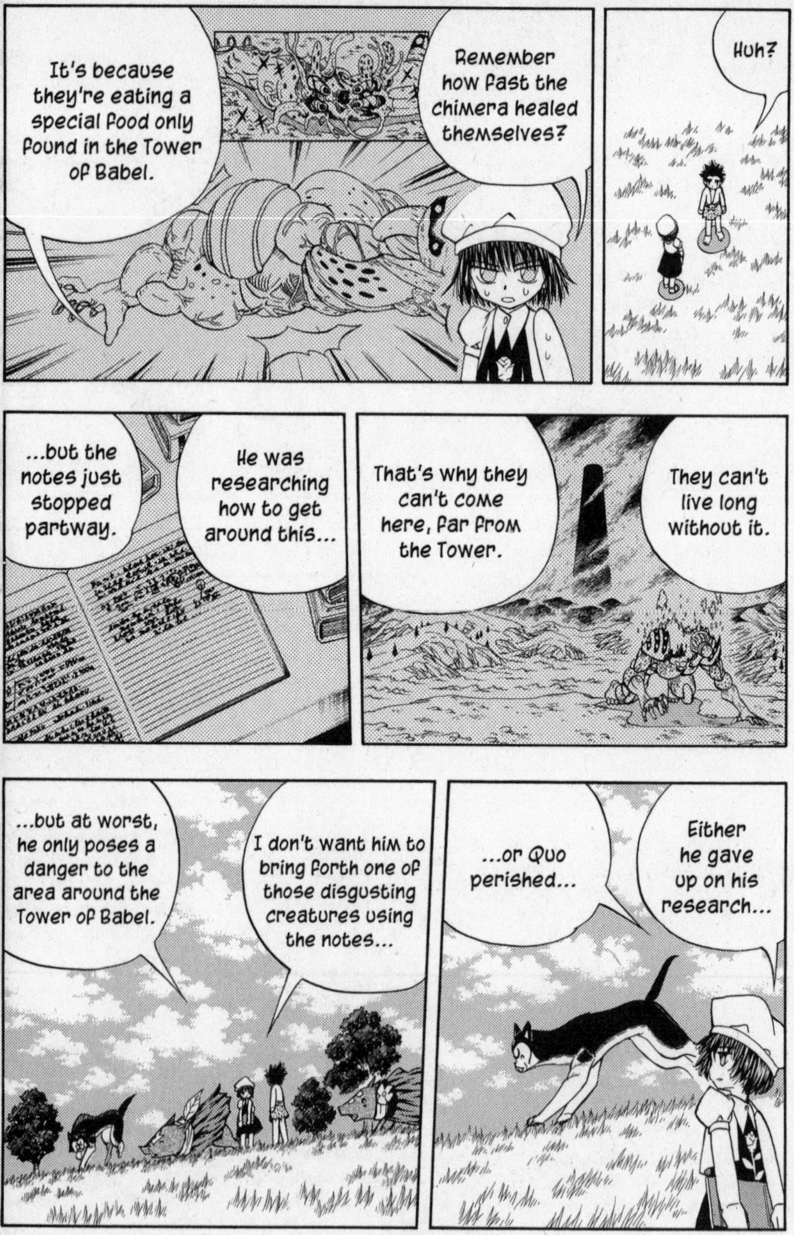
Huh?
Remember how fast the chimera healed themselves?
It's because they're eating a special food only found in the Tower of Babel.
They can't live long without it.
That's why they can't come here, far from the Tower.
He was researching how to get around this...
...but the notes just stopped partway.
Either he gave up on his research...
...or Quo perished...
I don't want him to bring forth one of those disgusting creatures using the notes...
...but at worst, he only poses a danger to the area around the Tower of Babel.

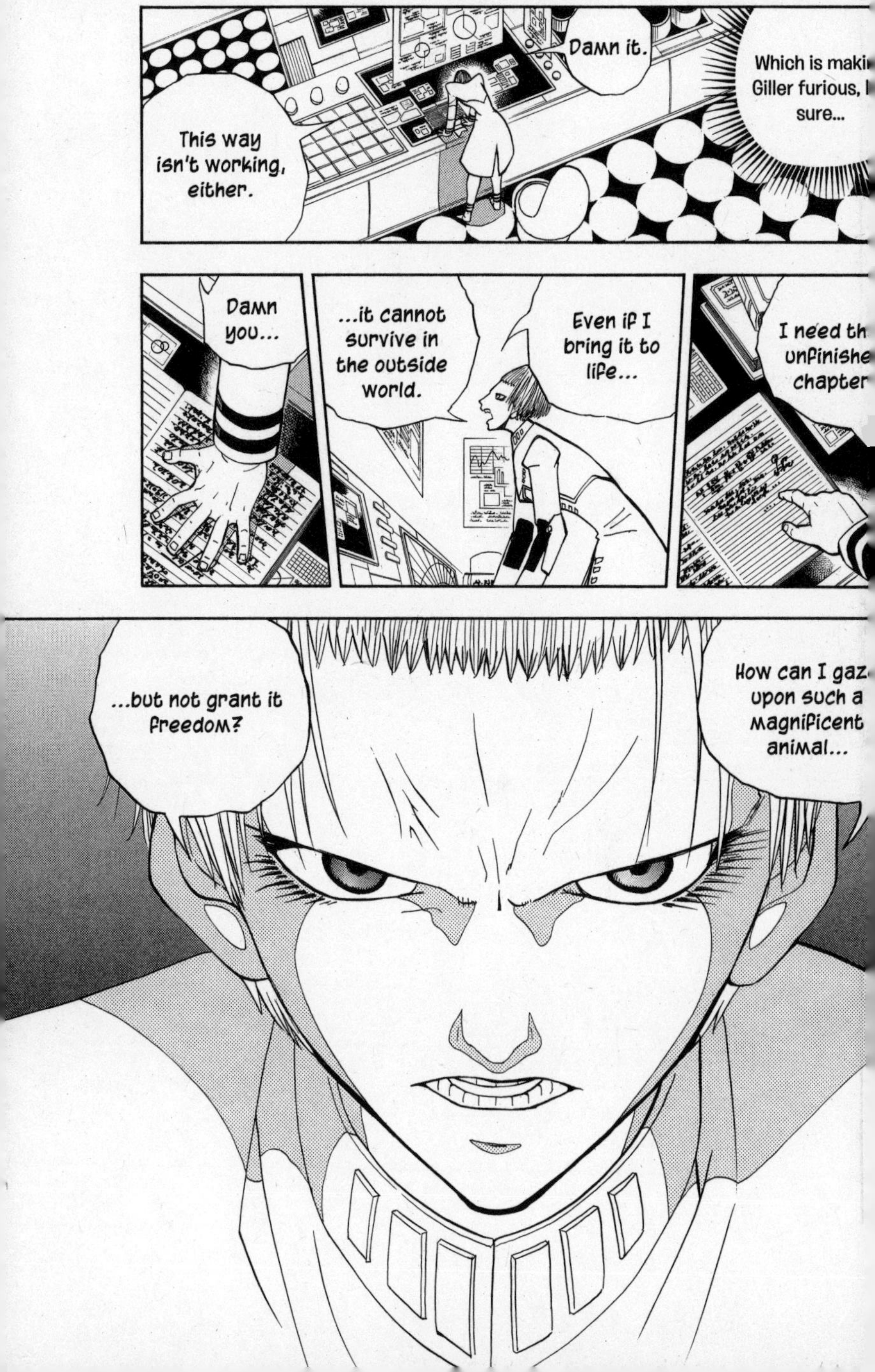
Which is maki Giller furious, I sure...
Damn it.
This way isn't working, either.
I need th unfinishe chapter
Even if I bring it to life...
...it cannot survive in the outside world.
Damn you...
How can I gaz upon such a magnificent animal...
...but not grant it freedom?

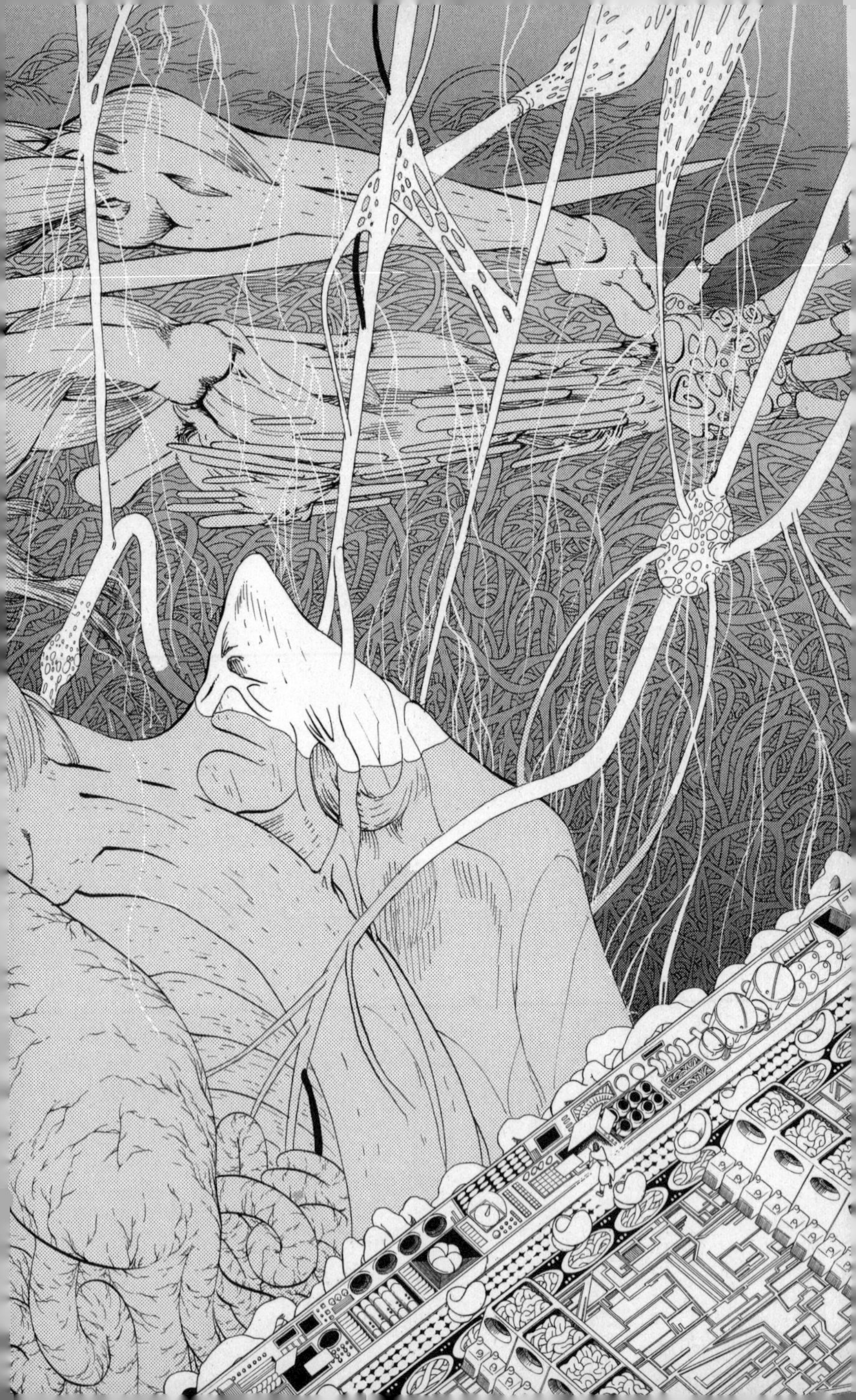

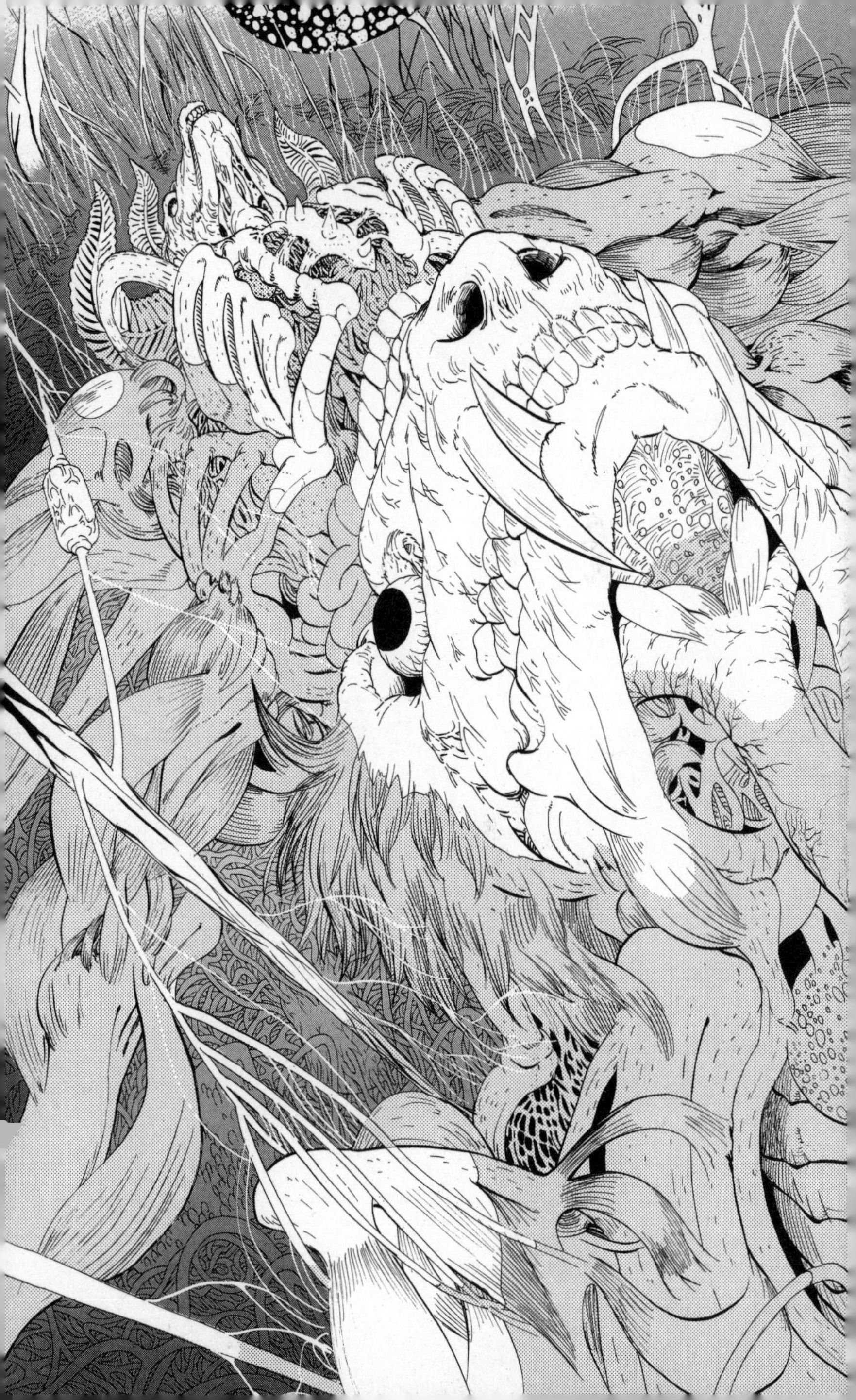

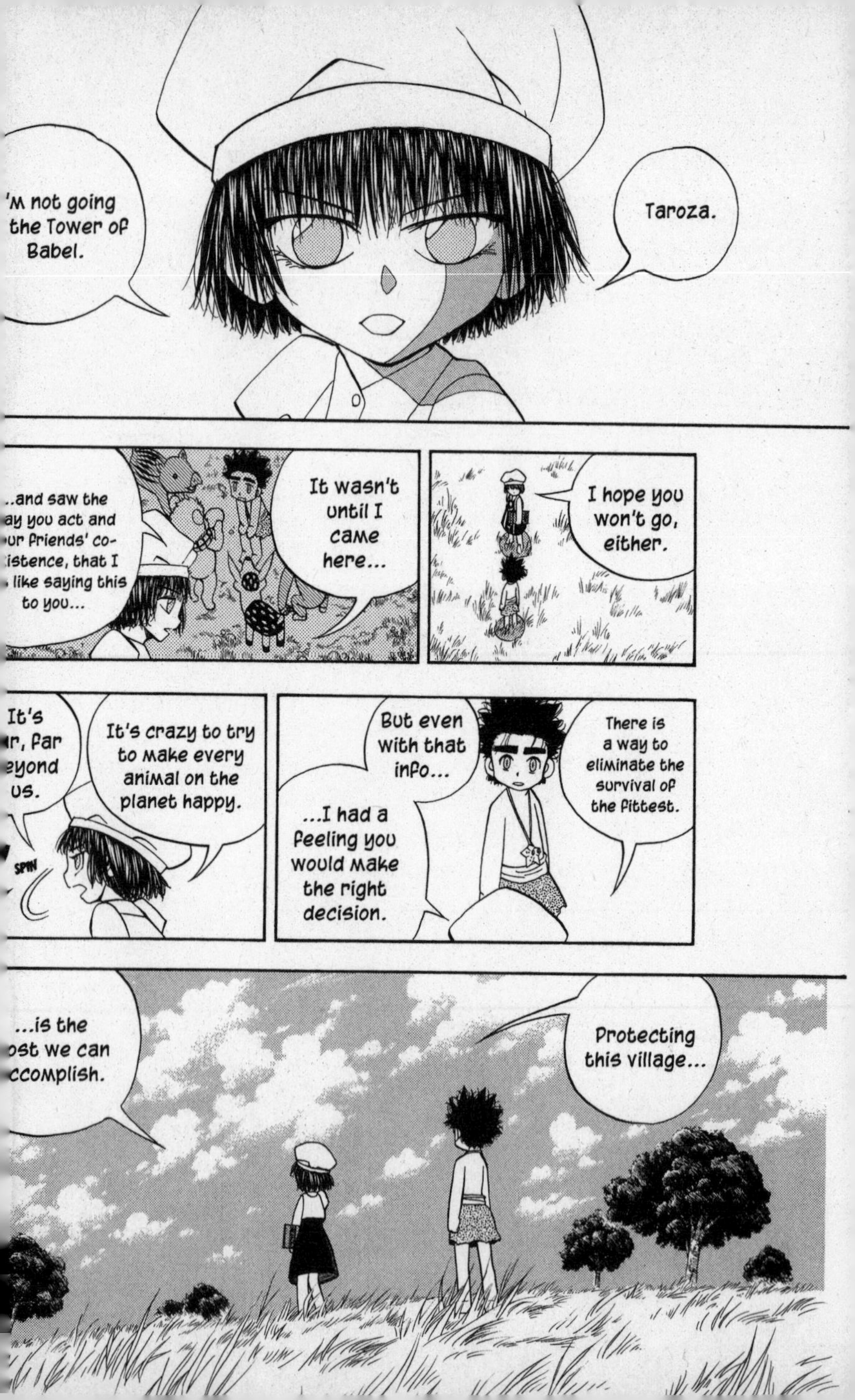
Taroza.
'M not going the Tower of Babel.
I hope you won't go, either.
It wasn't until I came here...
..and saw the ay you act and our friends' co- istence, that I like saying this to you...
There is a way to eliminate the survival of the fittest.
But even with that info...
...I had a feeling you would make the right decision.
It's crazy to try to make every animal on the planet happy.
It's r, far eyond us.
SPIN
Protecting this village...
...is the ost we can ccomplish.

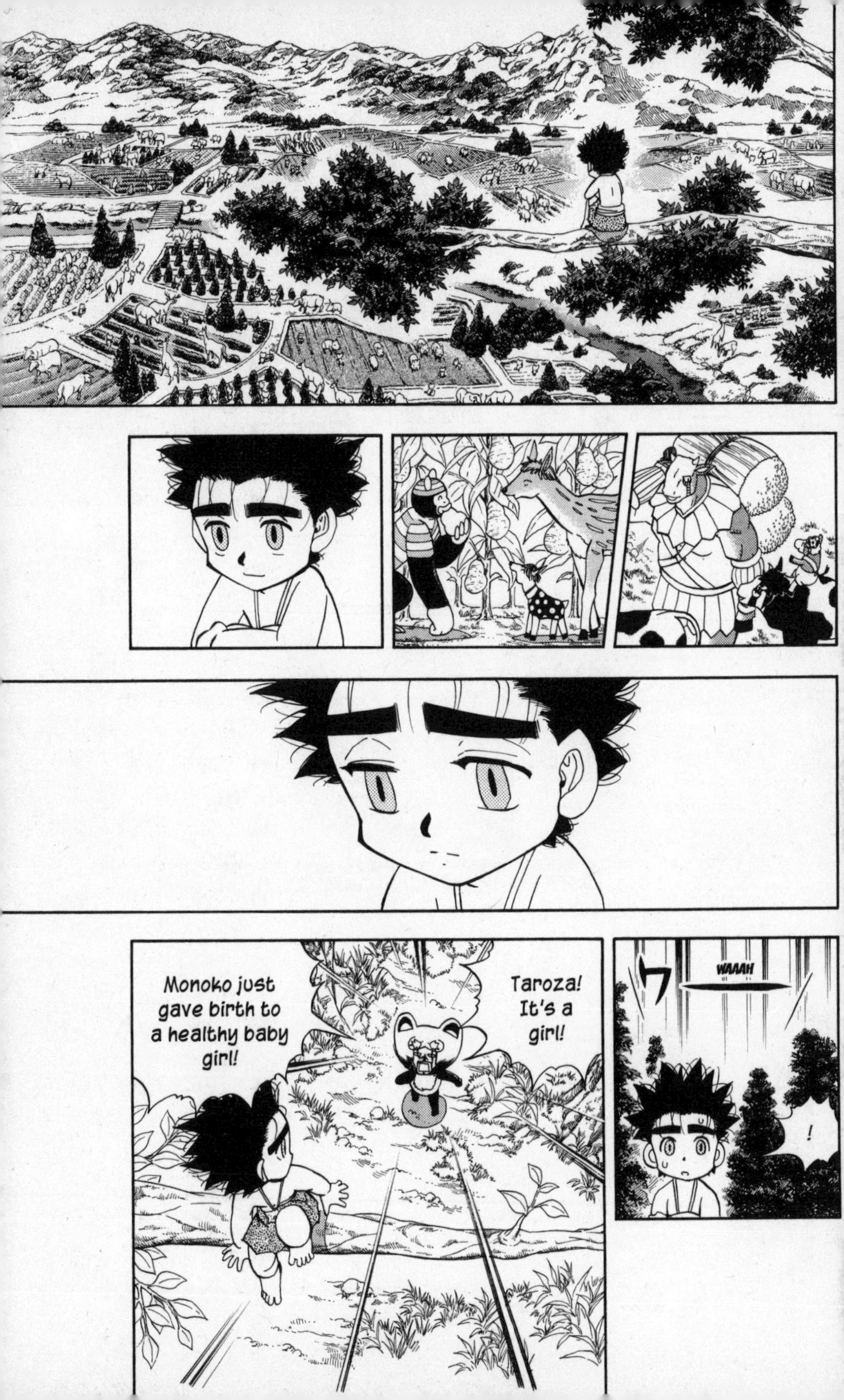
WAAAH
!
Taroza! It's a girl!
Monoko just gave birth to a healthy baby girl!

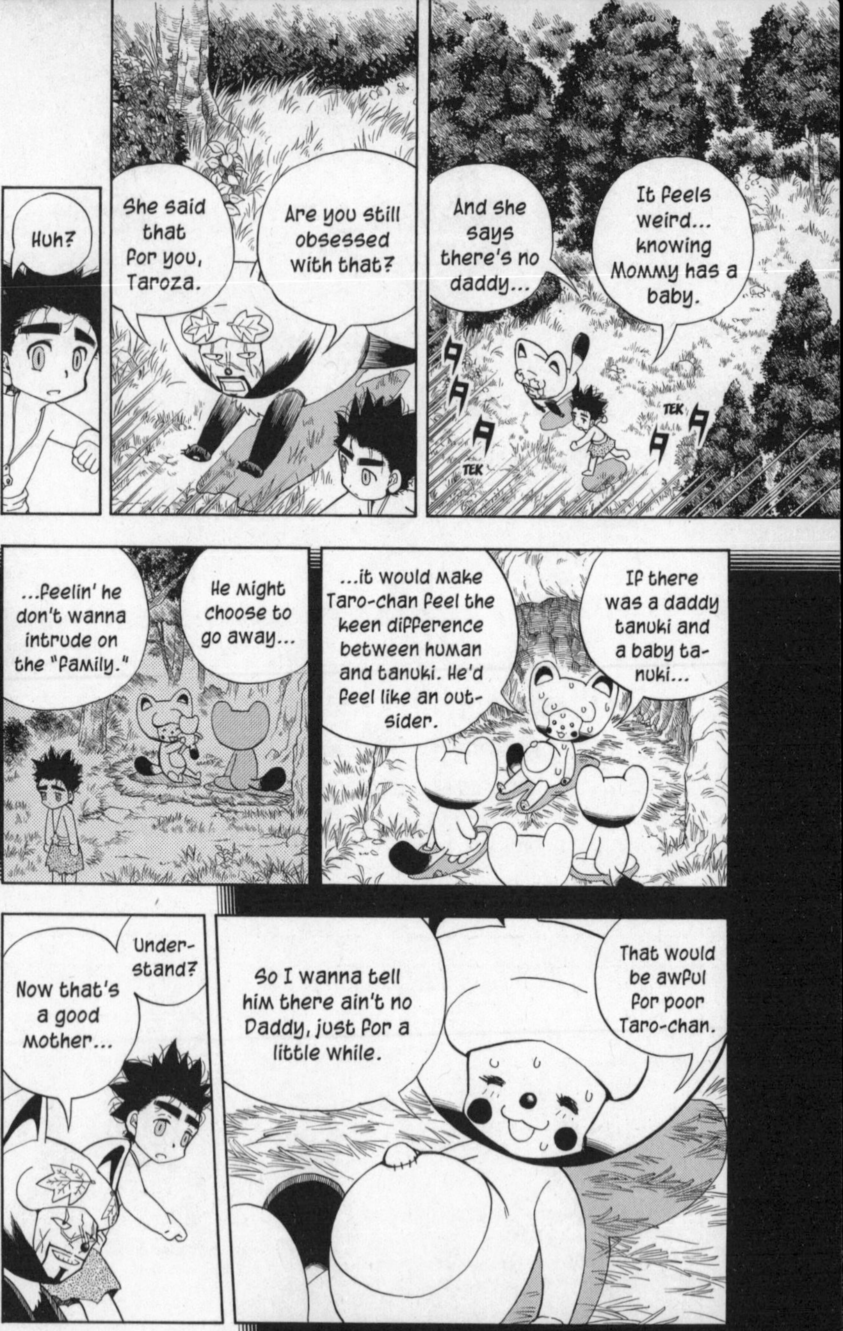
It feels weird... knowing Mommy has a baby.
And she says there's no daddy...
TEK
TEK
Are you still obsessed with that?
She said that for you, Taroza.
Huh?
If there was a daddy tanuki and a baby ta-nuki...
...it would make Taro-chan feel the keen difference between human and tanuki. He'd feel like an out-sider.
He might choose to go away...
...feelin' he don't wanna intrude on the "family."
That would be awful for poor Taro-chan.
So I wanna tell him there ain't no Daddy, just for a little while.
Under-stand?
Now that's a good mother...

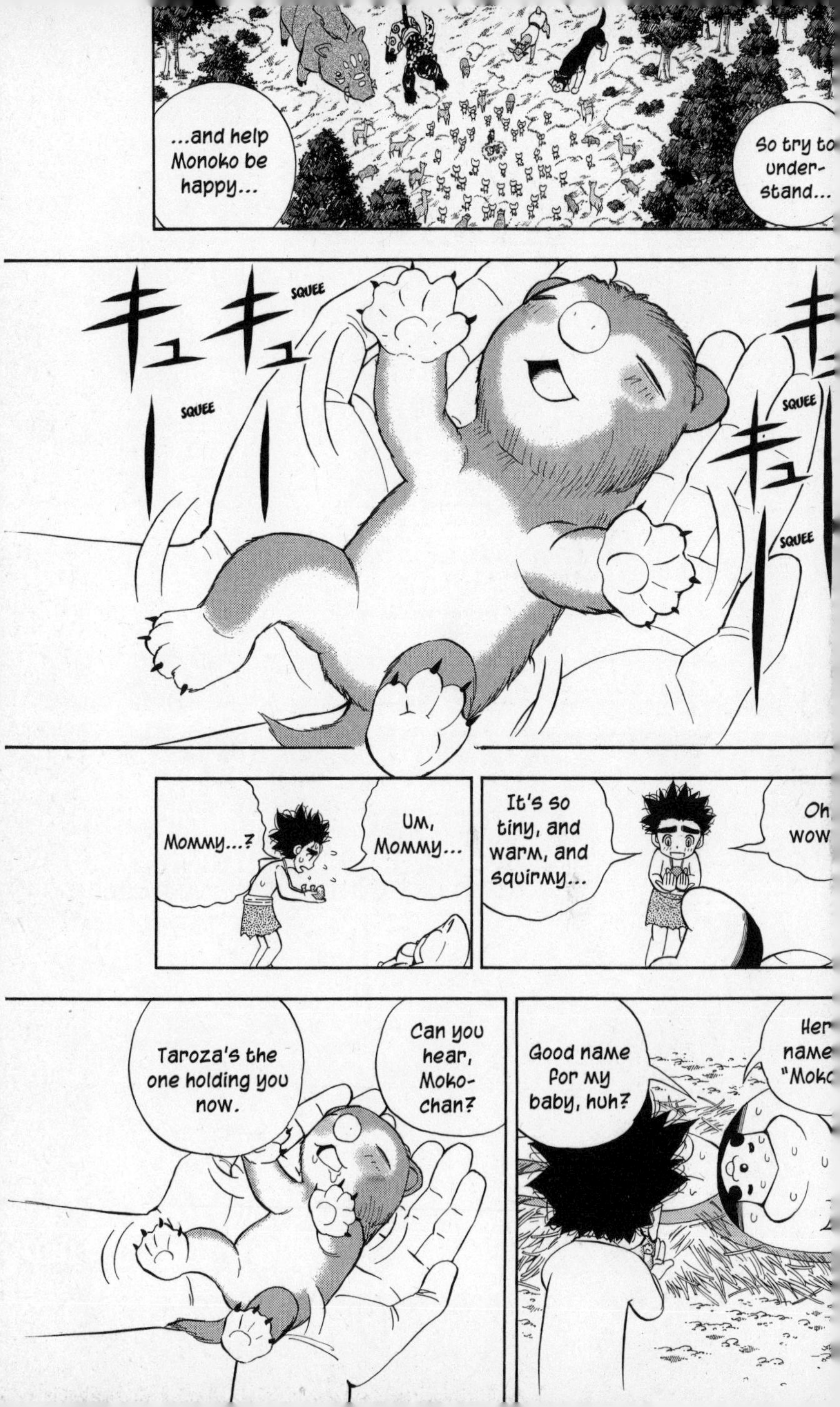
So try to under-stand...
...and help Monoko be happy...
キュー
SQUEE
キュー
SQUEE
キュー
SQUEE
キュー
SQUEE
Oh wow
It's so tiny, and warm, and squirmy...
Um, Mommy...
Mommy...?
Her name "Moko
Good name for my baby, huh?
Can you hear, Moko-chan?
Taroza's the one holding you now.

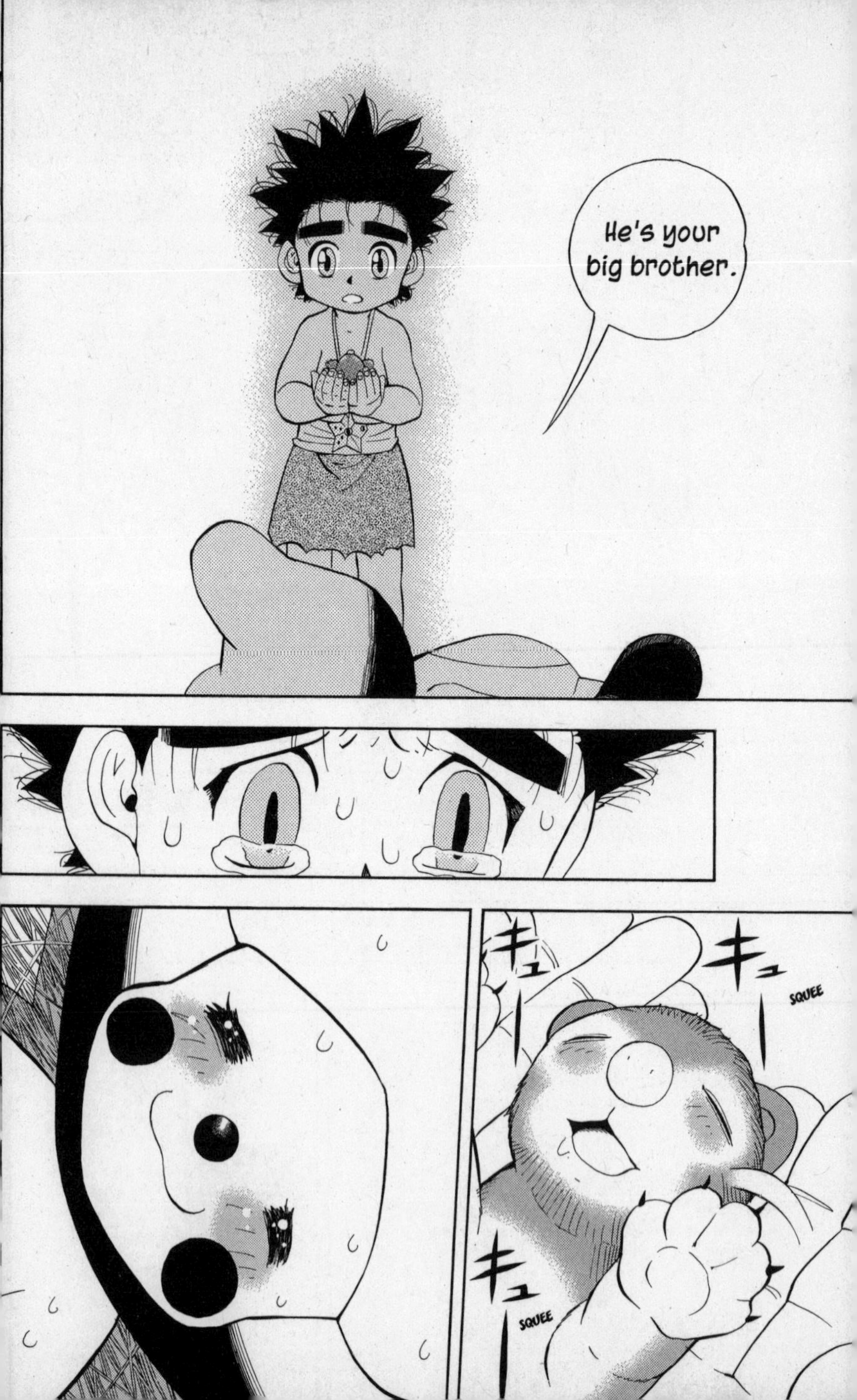
He's your big brother.
キュ
キュ
SQUEE
キュ
SQUEE

Kid Pick!

Title: _____

Author: _____

Picked by: _____

_____

Why I love this book:

_____
_____
_____
_____
_____
_____
_____
_____

Please return this form to
Mrs Heather in Youth Services or email
your review to
gunnell@rockfordpubliclibrary.org

 ROCKFORD PUBLIC LIBRARY

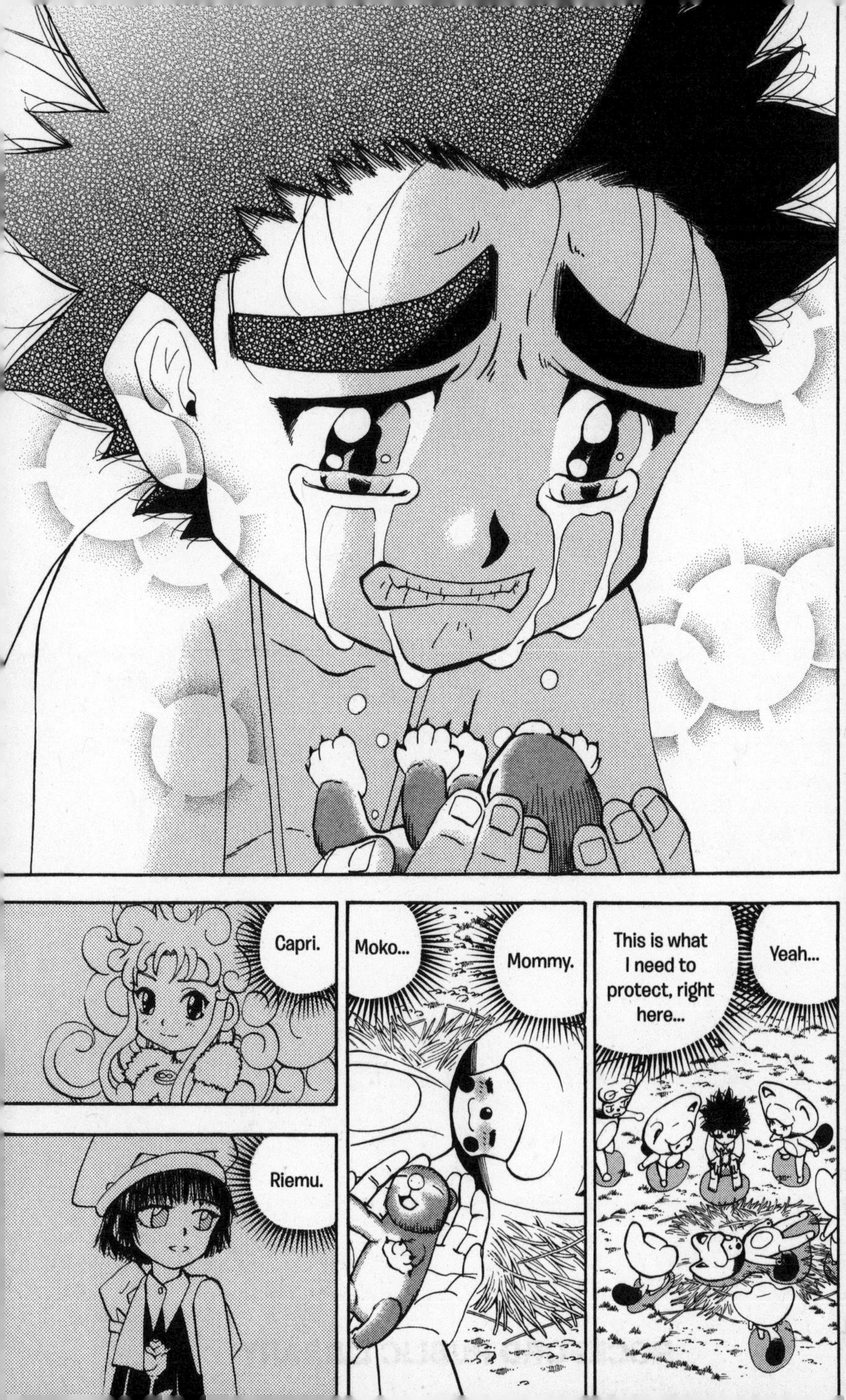
Yeah...
This is what I need to protect, right here...
Mommy.
Moko...
Capri.
Riemu.

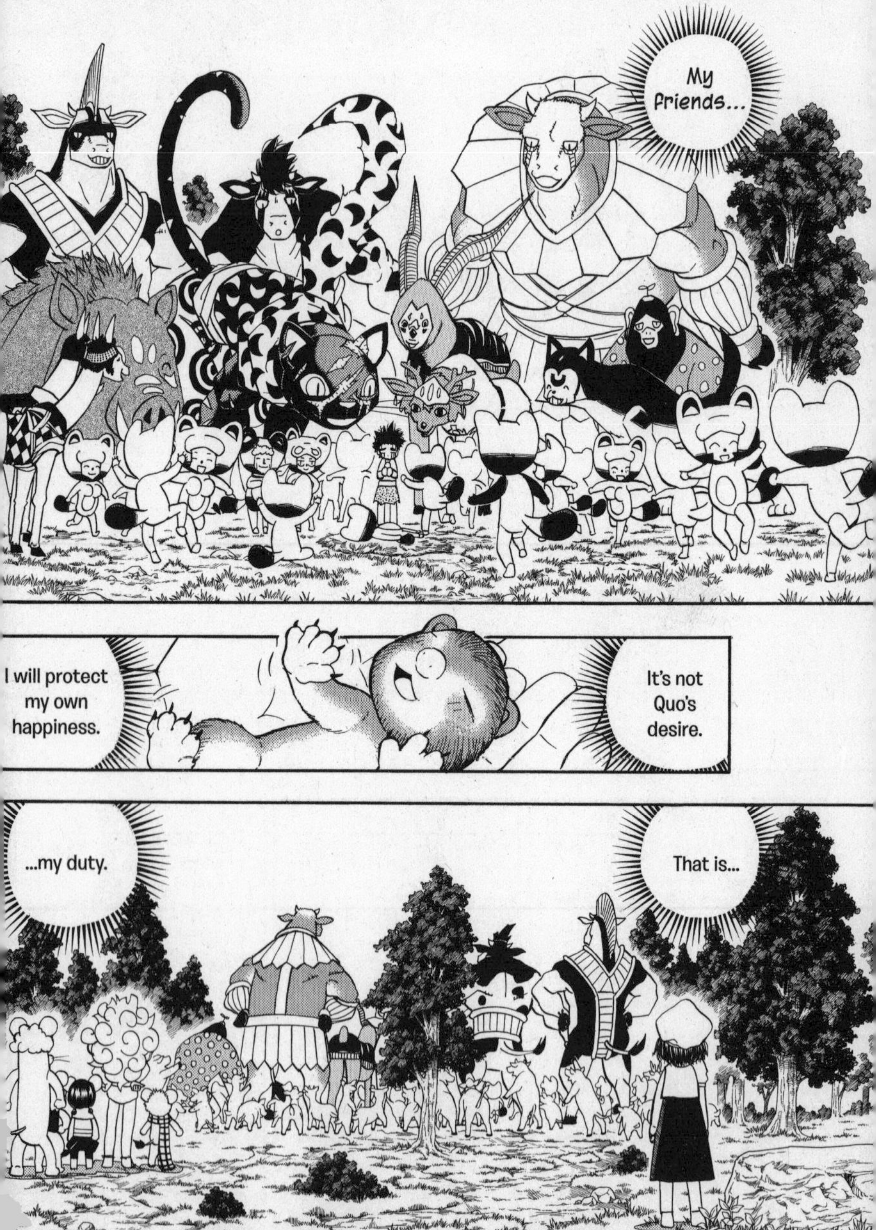
My friends...
It's not Quo's desire.
I will protect my own happiness.
That is...
...my duty.

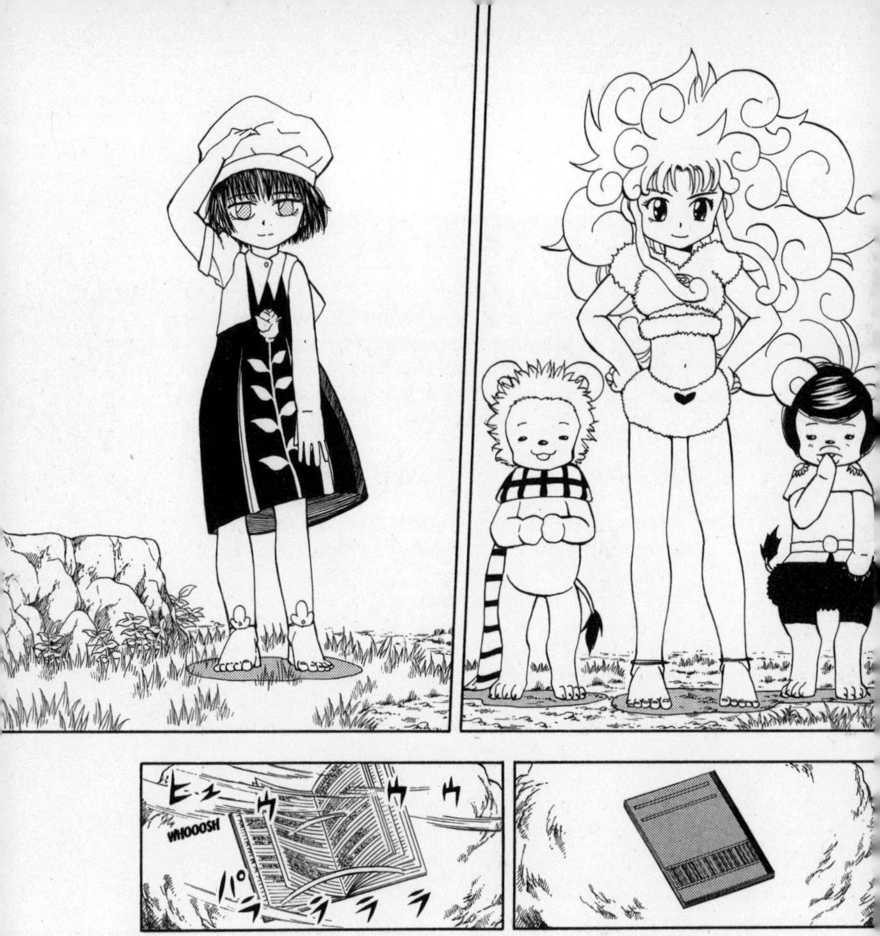
WHOOOSH

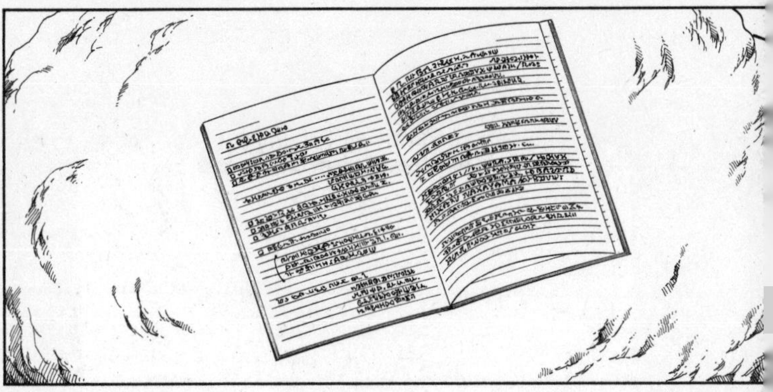

To be continued in Volume 8, Word 26

Animal Land volume 7 is a work of fiction. Names, characters, places, and incidents are the products of the author's imagination or are used fictitiously. Any resemblance to actual events, locales, or persons, living or dead, is entirely coincidental.

A Kodansha Comics Trade Paperback Original.

Published in the United States by Kodansha Comics, an imprint of Kodansha USA Publishing, LLC, New York.

Publication rights for this English edition arranged through Kodansha Ltd., Tokyo.

First published in Japan in 2011 by Kodansha Ltd., Tokyo, as *Doubutsu no Kuni*, volume 7.

ISBN 978-1-61262-249-1

Printed in the United States of America.

www.kodanshacomics.com

9 8 7 6 5 4 3 2 1

Translator: Stephen Paul

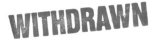